THE ESSENTIAL JEFFERSON

THE AMERICAN HERITAGE SERIES

THE AMERICAN HERITAGE SERIES

THE ESSENTIAL JEFFERSON

Edited, with an Introduction, by
Jean M. Yarbrough

Hackett Publishing Company, Inc.
Indianapolis/Cambridge

06 07 08 09   1 2 3 4 5 6 7

For further information, please address
Hackett Publishing Company, Inc.
P.O. Box 44937
Indianapolis, IN 46244-0937

www.hackettpublishing.com

Cover design by Rick Todhunter and Abigail Coyle
Interior design by Elizabeth Wilson
Composition by Professional Book Compositors
Printed at Edwards Brothers, Inc.

Library of Congress Cataloging-in-Publication Data

Jefferson, Thomas, 1743–1826.
    [Selections. 2006]
    The essential Jefferson / edited, with an introduction, by Jean M. Yarbrough.
        p. cm. — (The American heritage series)
    Includes bibliographical references and index.
    ISBN 0-87220-748-X (cloth) — ISBN 0-87220-747-1 (pbk.)
    1. United States—Politics and government—1775–1783—Sources.
2. United States—Politics and government—1783–1809—Sources.   3. Virginia—
Politics and government—1775–1865—Sources.   I. Yarbrough, Jean M.   II. Title.
III. Series: American heritage series (New York, N.Y.)
    E302.J442 2006
    352.23'809034—dc22

                                                                    2005024725

Contents

PUBLIC PAPERS AND ADDRESSES

EXCERPTS FROM *NOTES ON VIRGINIA* (1782)

CORRESPONDENCE

Acknowledgments

No book is ever simply the work of one person. I have benefited from the able assistance and generous advice of so many people, and it is a great pleasure to thank them for their help. I could not have hoped for a more conscientious research assistant than Jamie Quinn, Bowdoin '06. Jamie read all the selections through the eyes of an intelligent undergraduate, identifying and defining obscure words to make the texts more readable for other students. She also drafted the biographies, and sketched out the time line of Jefferson's life. Tina Lin, Bowdoin '05, helped prepare the bibliography, checked sources, and provided invaluable technical assistance. In response to additional editor's queries, Dustin Brooks, Bowdoin '08, helped with preliminary research. Lynne Atkinson, our indispensable department coordinator, supervised all three assistants. Lynne's energy and initiative guaranteed that every deadline would be met, and every obstacle cheerfully surmounted. The staff at the Bowdoin College Library, especially Leanne Pander, Ginny Hopcroft, Carr Ross, and Carmen Greenlea, helped track down obscure, but necessary, biographical information.

David Morgan, Professor of Romance Languages at Furman University, whom I met at a Liberty Fund Conference on Jefferson at Monticello, graciously volunteered to translate all the foreign phrases Jefferson used in the selections I was compiling. He did so with insight and care.

Barbara Oberg, member of the Princeton University History Department and general editor of *The Papers of Thomas Jefferson*, along with her assistant, Linda Monaco, provided information on a number of fine points. J. Jefferson Looney, editor of *The Papers of Thomas Jefferson: Retirement Series* at the Thomas Jefferson Foundation in Charlottesville, Virginia, answered questions about some of the later letters.

Rick Todhunter, my editor at Hackett, pushed me to expand the number of identifications. This collection is better for it.

Lance Banning, Peter Onuf, and Robert M. S. McDonald all read drafts of the Introduction and helped clarify a number of historical points. In my own field of political theory, James R. Stoner, Jr., of Louisiana State University offered perceptive comments on the Introduction, helped clarify obscure legal references, and lobbied successfully for the inclusion of certain key letters. My husband and colleague, Richard E. Morgan, read numerous drafts of the Introduction, provided historical and legal background, and offered suggestions with unfailing good cheer. I thank my colleagues, students, and friends for their help and encouragement; all errors are mine alone.

Jean M. Yarbrough
Bowdoin College
July 4, 2005

Time Line of the Life of Thomas Jefferson

April 13, 1743	Born to Peter and Jane Randolph Jefferson at Shadwell, in Albemarle County, Virginia.
1757	Peter Jefferson dies.
1760–62	Attends the College of William and Mary.
1762	Studies law in Williamsburg under the direction of George Wythe.
1767	Admitted to the Virginia Bar.
1768	Elected to the Virginia House of Burgesses.
1769	Begins building Monticello according to his own architectural design.
1772	Marries Martha Wayles Skelton; daughter Martha, known as "Patsy," born.
1774	Writes *A Summary View of the Rights of British America.*
	Serves as delegate to First Continental Congress meeting in Philadelphia.
1775	Elected delegate to Second Continental Congress, meeting again in Philadelphia.
	American revolution begins in April with the battles of Lexington and Concord, Massachusetts.
1776	Composes Declaration of Independence, which is adopted by Congress, July 4. Drafts a constitution for Virginia, not adopted.
1777	Returns to Virginia House of Delegates. Drafts Virginia Statute for Religious Freedom. First and only son dies at three weeks.
1778	Drafts Bill for the More General Diffusion of Knowledge.
	Daughter Mary (Maria) born.
1779–81	Governor of Virginia.
1781–82	Begins composing *Notes on the State of Virginia.*
1782	Wife, Martha, dies.
1783	Serves as Virginia delegate in Congress.
1784	Infant daughter Lucy Elizabeth dies. Drafts "Report on Government for Western Territory" to Congress. Appointed

	commissioner and minister to France, where he serves until 1789.
1786	Shays's Rebellion in Massachusetts.
1787	*Notes on the State of Virginia* published in London. Receives copy of the proposed Constitution, which he supports. Writes to Madison urging a Bill of Rights be added.
1789	Named secretary of state by President Washington.
1794	Retires from public life; returns to Monticello.
1796	John Adams elected president; Jefferson elected vice president.
1798	Drafts "Kentucky Resolutions" to protest the Alien and Sedition Acts. Quasi-War with France.
1800–1809	Elected third president of the United States; serves two terms.
1803	Louisiana Purchase; gained as a result of a treaty with France.
	Marbury v. Madison establishes the principle of judicial review.
1804	Lewis and Clark explore and map Louisiana Territory.
	Jefferson reelected president in a landslide. Younger daughter Mary Jefferson Eppes dies.
1807	Signs Embargo Act cutting off American trade with Great Britain.
1808	James Madison elected president.
1809	Jefferson retires for good to Monticello.
1812	John Adams and Jefferson resume their correspondence. War with Great Britain declared.
1814	British burn U.S. Capitol.
1815	Heavily in debt, Jefferson sells personal library to Congress; forms the basis of Library of Congress.
1819	Founds the University of Virginia.
1821	Writes *Autobiography*.
1825	University of Virginia opens.
July 4, 1826	Jefferson dies at Monticello. John Adams dies at Quincy, Massachusetts.

Introduction

Life and Times

Thomas Jefferson was born on April 13, 1743, at Shadwell, in Albemarle County, Virginia, about five miles east of Charlottesville. His father, Peter Jefferson, was a self-educated surveyor, mapmaker, and farmer with wide-ranging interests. His mother, Jane, belonged to the socially prominent Randolph family, which traced its lineage far back in England and Scotland. Of this pedigree, Jefferson observed in his *Autobiography* (1821) "let every one ascribe the faith and merit he chooses."

Jefferson began his schooling at age five, and at age nine entered Latin school, where he picked up the rudiments of Latin and Greek, as well as French. In 1760, the seventeen-year-old Jefferson entered the College of William and Mary in the colonial capital of Williamsburg. While in college, he had the "great good fortune" to study with Dr. William Small, a Scotsman "with an enlarged and liberal mind," who taught natural philosophy, mathematics, and moral philosophy. It was here that Jefferson was first introduced to Scottish moral sense philosophy, which held that human beings are naturally social and, as such, are equipped with a sense of right and wrong, justice and injustice (to Peter Carr, Aug. 10, 1787; to Thomas Law, June 13, 1814). Dr. Small quickly became attached to his young pupil, and introduced him to Francis Fauquier, the Lieutenant Governor of Virginia, and George Wythe, a prominent Virginia lawyer, who invited the young man into their set to discuss politics and make music. It was during this period that Jefferson began to develop his lifelong passion for buying and reading books.

Upon graduation from the College of William and Mary, Jefferson began to study law under the direction of George Wythe, "his faithful and beloved Mentor," (*Autobiography*) and was admitted to the bar in 1767. Two years later, at the age of twenty-six, he was elected to the House of Burgesses, the colonial Virginia legislature. In his first session, he supported a bill giving slaveholders the right to manumit their slaves, but the effort failed. Ordinary legislative business was soon curtailed, however, when the royal governor dissolved the body for its opposition to the British Parliament. In an act of defiance, the House of Burgesses reconstituted itself as a revolutionary assembly, with Jefferson among its leaders.

In response to the deepening crisis with Great Britain, Jefferson drafted "A Summary View of the Rights of British America" (1774), which combined a highly imaginative reading of English history with natural rights philosophy to lay out the proper relationship of the king and Parliament to the colonies. As a good Whig, Jefferson acknowledged that the Glorious Revolution of 1688 shifted sovereignty away from the Crown to Parliament in England, but he denied that the Revolution Settlement gave Parliament any power to tax the colonies. Only the king, acting in concert with the colonial legislatures, could make laws for America. Furthermore, the king was merely the servant of the people, and responsible to them. The rights that the British Americans claimed were not his gift to give, but flowed directly from nature. When, therefore, his ministers encroached on these rights, by dissolving their colonial legislatures, power returned to the people, who might use it as they thought proper. Overall, the tone of the pamphlet was so defiant: "Let those flatter who fear; it is not an American art," and the argument so radical that the assembly refused to adopt it. Indeed, Jefferson himself later confessed in his *Autobiography* that he was never able to persuade anyone of his doctrine that Parliament had no authority over the colonies but his old law instructor, Mr. Wythe. Nevertheless, the assembly was clearly impressed with Jefferson, and elected him a delegate to the Second Continental Congress, which was to meet in Philadelphia the following year.

By the time the Congress convened in May 1775, the shot "heard 'round the world" had already been fired at Lexington, Massachusetts, and the now-famous author of the "Summary View" was tapped to reply to the British. Along with John Dickinson of Pennsylvania, Jefferson helped draft a reply to "Lord North's Conciliatory Proposal," and, in quick succession, the "Declaration of the Causes and Necessity of Taking Up Arms."

Events moved rapidly, and in 1776, Congress appointed a five-man committee, consisting of Benjamin Franklin, John Adams, Roger Sherman, Robert Livingston, and Thomas Jefferson, to draw up an official declaration of independence. Because Jefferson had already displayed what Adams called "a happy talent of composition," (John Adams to Timothy Pickering, Aug. 6, 1822) the committee charged him with producing the first draft. Adams and Franklin suggested several minor revisions, but when Congress took up the declaration, it insisted on several important changes. Most notably, to satisfy South Carolina and Georgia, it deleted the paragraph excoriating the king for failing to abolish the slave trade and for violating the natural rights of the slaves.

Logically, the Declaration enlarged on the argument of the "Summary View." In that earlier pamphlet, Jefferson had already rejected the authority of Parliament to make laws for America. The Declaration of Independence severed the last remaining connection between Americans and Great Britain, the king, whose actions Jefferson here denounced as "a history of unremitting injuries and usurpations." Americans were now an independent "people," free to take their place among the "powers of the earth" and to govern themselves as they saw fit.

Nevertheless, "a decent respect for the opinions of mankind," required the Americans to lay out the causes for their separation. Before proceeding to the catalog of grievances that make up the bulk of the Declaration, Jefferson set forth the principles that he hoped would "be the signal of arousing men" around the world (to Roger C. Weightman, June 24, 1826). Starting from the assertion that all human beings are created equal, in the sense that each is endowed with the same inalienable rights to life, liberty, and the pursuit of happiness, Jefferson concluded that all legitimate government rests on the consent of the governed. He added that whenever government becomes destructive of these ends, the people have the right to alter or abolish it, and to establish a new government that in their view will better secure their safety and happiness. Years later, Jefferson would explain that the object of the Declaration was "not to find out new principles, or new arguments, never before thought of, not merely to say things which had never been said before; but to place before mankind the common sense of the subject in terms so plain and firm as to command their assent. . . ." In short, the principles announced in the Declaration "were intended to be an expression of the American mind"(to Henry Lee, May 8, 1825).

During the summer of 1776, Jefferson was completely absorbed in the excitement of framing new constitutions, and sent his draft constitution to the Virginia legislature for its consideration (to Edmund Pendleton, Aug. 26, 1776). Although not adopted by that body, it did contain two noteworthy provisions: the distribution of fifty acres of public land to every person who did not already possess that amount and a prohibition against all new slavery throughout the state.

In September 1776, Jefferson resigned from Congress to serve once again in the Virginia legislature. With the new constitution already in place, Jefferson turned his attention to legal reform. He played a major role in revising Virginia's colonial laws to weed out their aristocratic features and make them more consistent with the spirit of republicanism, drafting legislation to abolish entail and primogeniture (inheritance laws intended to keep large landholdings intact), liberalize the criminal code, provide for the public education of all free males and females, and, most important, disestablish the Anglican Church and secure religious liberty. To use the power of government to compel religious belief or support for a particular religious denomination violated natural right and fostered corruption in the church ("A Bill for Establishing Religious Freedom," 1777). During his lifetime, all of these measures, except the "Bill for the More General Diffusion of Knowledge," would be enacted (sometimes with revisions) by the Virginia legislature, largely with the assistance of his trusted ally, James Madison.

In 1779, Jefferson was elected Governor of Virginia, just at the moment the British decided to shift their armies to the South. Virginia had neither the troops nor defenses to protect itself from invasion, and when the British struck, the Governor and the legislature were forced to flee the capital (Richmond) for Charlottesville. At the very end of his term, in 1781, the British attempted to capture Jefferson at Monticello, and he and his council beat a hasty retreat. Amidst the terror and confusion, members of the legislature accused Jefferson of personal cowardice, flirted with the idea of installing a dictator, and voted unanimously to investigate his conduct as governor during the crisis. Although Jefferson was fully vindicated, not even a belated unanimous resolution of thanks from the legislature could heal his injured pride. He vowed to retire from public life for good.

In his waning months as wartime governor and in the period immediately following, Jefferson began to compose a series of responses to queries posed by the French official François de Barbé-Marbois. The queries, which circulated among influential politicians in Philadelphia, were intended to provide the French government with information about its new American ally. Jefferson rearranged the questions, so that the first half dealt with natural phenomena, and the second with history, law, and politics. His twenty-three responses were later published in 1785 as *Notes on the State of Virginia*, the only book he ever wrote. In part, Jefferson sought to refute the charge of the great French naturalist, the Comte de Buffon, that animals and aboriginal peoples of the New World were naturally inferior to those of Europe; hence, Jefferson's praise of the Native Americans in Query VI. But the essays, especially in the second half, touch on important aspects of Jefferson's political thought, and highlight the tensions therein. Query XIV reprised Jefferson's plan for the emancipation and expatriation of slaves, yet argued that blacks *as a race* were inferior to whites and could, therefore, never be incorporated into American society. In Query XVIII Jefferson observed that slavery corrupted the moral sensibilities of both master and slave, and asked "can the liberties of a nation be thought secure when we have removed the only firm basis, a conviction in the minds of the people that these liberties are the gift of God? That they are not to be violated but with his wrath?" However, in his defense of religious liberty in Query XVII, Jefferson insisted that religious opinions were not the business of government. "The legitimate powers of government extend to such acts only as are injurious to others. But it does me no injury for my neighbor to say there are twenty gods or no god. It neither picks my pocket, nor breaks my leg." Elsewhere in Query XIV, Jefferson set out his plan for universal education, in which each year "twenty of the best genuisses [sic] will be raked annually from the rubbish" and instructed further at public expense. Finally, Query XIX condemned urban life and manufacturing as dangerous to republican character, and praised the life of the yeoman farmer. Not all occupations were morally equal: "Those who labour in the earth are the chosen people of God, if ever he had a chosen people, whose breasts he has made the peculiar deposit for substantial and genuine virtue." Still, as Query XIX made clear, the cultivation of the earth was a decidedly commercial venture. Jefferson envisioned farmers producing a surplus of raw materials that they would then sell in order to buy imported manufactures not available in America.

Jefferson's thoughts of a quiet retirement at Monticello were shattered by the death of his wife, Martha, in September 1782 from the complications of childbirth. Within a year, he signaled his willingness to return to public life, and was chosen by the Virginia legislature as a delegate to the new Confederation Congress. During his six months' service, Jefferson sat on every important committee and prepared a number of significant state papers, including the *Report on Government for Western Territory*. The report epitomized Jefferson's hopes for America: the territories would be organized on republican principles, and when they reached a certain population, they could petition for admission to the Union on an "equal footing" with the original states. The report also banned slavery after 1800. In his draft, Jefferson proposed names for each of the territories, drawn from Greek and Latin, as well as Native American languages ("Report on Government for Western Territory," Mar. 1, 1784).

Impressed by his service, in May 1784, the Confederation Congress appointed Jefferson, along with John Adams and Benjamin Franklin, to negotiate commercial treaties aimed at opening European ports to American produce. Here, Jefferson experienced firsthand the weaknesses of the Articles of Confederation in promoting American economic interests and defending her vessels against capture by the Barbary pirates. In contrast to the policy pursued by European nations, which preferred to pay tribute to these corsairs, Jefferson recommended decisive action because "weakness provokes insult and injury, while a condition to punish it often prevents it" (to John Jay, Aug. 23, 1785). The following year, Jefferson was named American Minister to the Court of Louis XVI, where he would serve until 1789.

While in Paris, Jefferson cultivated friendships with leading Enlightenment figures, and pursued his interests in science, politics, and the arts. At the same time, he could not help but be struck by the difference between the happiness and virtue of his countrymen and the misery and corruption of the Old World. Observing the morals of the great men and women of Paris, he concluded that conjugal love, and hence, domestic happiness, was unknown there. "Much, very much inferior, this, to the tranquil, permanent felicity with which domestic society in America, blesses most of its inhabitants" (to Charles Bellini, Sept. 30, 1785). He discouraged Americans from studying abroad, worried that the impressionable student would develop a "fondness for European luxury and dissipation, a contempt for the simplicity of his own country," and advised his young ward to remain at study in his own country (to Peter Carr, Aug. 10, 1787). To Madison, he expressed dismay that most of the property of France was concentrated in very few hands, and left uncultivated while so many poor could not find work. "Whenever there are in any country uncultivated lands and unemployed poor, it is clear that the laws of property have been so far extended as to violate natural right." If societies chose to exclude the poor from the land, they had to provide some other means of employment. He ended by warning that it was not too soon for his own country (i.e., Virginia) to begin thinking about how to provide small plots of land to as many as possible. "Small landholders are the most precious part of a state" (to James Madison, Oct. 28, 1785).

Sometime early in 1787, Jefferson received news of Shays's Rebellion, in which angry farmers in western Massachusetts rose up in protest when they could not pay their debts and taxes. At a safe remove, Jefferson made light of the uprising. As early as Query XVII in the *Notes*, he had worried that the revolutionary spirit would slacken once the war ended. Lethargy, in his mind, was the great evil facing republican governments. Shays's Rebellion reassured him that Americans had not yet sunk into a political torpor, and he found it hard to condemn the rebels. Writing to Madison, he calculated that if each of the thirteen states had a rebellion every eleven years, this would add up to one rebellion per state in a century and a half. "No country should be so long without one" (to James Madison, Dec. 20, 1787). To Adams's son-in-law, William S. Smith, Jefferson penned the memorable words: "The tree of liberty must be refreshed from time to time with the blood of patriots and tyrants. It is it's [sic] natural manure" (to William S. Smith, Nov. 13, 1787).

News of Shays's Rebellion had a different effect back home, where leading politicians used the uprising to call for a stronger national government capable of maintaining order and stability. As a delegate to the Constitutional Convention, meeting in Philadelphia during the summer of 1787, Madison played a key role in drafting the new constitution and kept Jefferson apprised of key developments. Although Jefferson, too, had concluded that the Articles of Confederation stood in need of repair, he confided to Adams, who was serving as American Minister to Britain, that he was staggered by the extent of the changes. Still, as he wrote to Madison, he found much to admire, and focused his criticism on two features: the omission of a bill of rights and the failure to limit the number of terms the president could serve (to James Madison, Dec. 20, 1787).

Always the Virginia gentleman, Jefferson, in his letters, made a point of emphasizing areas of agreement with his correspondent. Yet because he wrote to so many people with widely differing views, there frequently arose disputes about what he really thought. Such was the case with the Constitution, prompting one correspondent to ask whether Jefferson was in fact an Antifederalist. Jefferson famously replied that he was neither a Federalist nor an Antifederalist "because I never submitted the whole system of my opinions to the creed of any party of men whatever in religion, in philosophy, in politics, or in anything else where I was capable of thinking for myself. Such an addiction is the last degradation of a free and moral agent. If I could not go to heaven but with a party, I would not go there at all" (to Francis Hopkinson, Mar. 13, 1789). On the whole, however, he admitted that he was closer to the Federalists because he supported the new Constitution, with its flaws, in the expectation that they would soon be corrected through the amendment process.

On the eve of his departure from France, just as the French Revolution was beginning, Jefferson's thoughts took a speculative turn, and he wrote to Madison to ask "whether one generation has the right to bind another." Jefferson concluded that "the earth belongs in usufruct to the living," and that at the end of each generation, which he calculated to be nineteen years, all constitutions, laws, and debts should expire (to James Madison, Sept. 6, 1789). Although this had obvious implications for France, Jefferson made it clear that he was thinking of America, too. The only way that future generations could be as free as the founding generation would be if they could renegotiate the terms of the social compact. On a more practical level, Jefferson thought it might serve as a useful preamble to the law regarding public appropriations, discouraging the present generation from burdening future generations with debt and adding another restraint to the "Dog of war." Madison never warmed to this idea, and Jefferson dropped the subject with him, though he continued to press it with other more sympathetic correspondents (to Samuel Kercheval, July 12, 1816; to Major John Cartwright, June 5, 1824).

Returning to America in November 1789, Jefferson received a letter from President Washington offering him the post of Secretary of State. Almost immediately, he began to clash with Alexander Hamilton, Secretary of the Treasury, over the scope of federal powers. Ironically, the man who only three years earlier had insisted that parties were "the last degradation of a free and moral agent," would rally republican partisans to defeat what he called the aristocratic and monarchical heresies of the Federalists and "Anglo-men."

On the domestic front, Federalists and Republicans divided over how to interpret the Constitution and the scope of federal powers. Jefferson argued for a strict construction of the Constitution, and for a national government of limited powers. He concurred with the Attorney General, Edmund Randolph, that Congress had no power to establish a national bank ("Opinion on the Constitutionality of a National Bank," 1791). Over the next few years, he spoke out against the idea that the public debt was a public blessing, opposed Hamilton's plan to subsidize American manufacturing, and warned against what he considered a corrupt alliance between the paper money men and the legislature. By 1792, Jefferson had become sufficiently alarmed by Hamilton's influence within the Administration to write to the President, not once but twice, warning him in the most dire terms of the dangers Hamilton posed.

Surveying Hamilton's policies, Jefferson detected nothing less than a conspiracy to "undermine and demolish the republic" by consolidating power in the national government and distributing economic favors to corrupt the legislature (to the President of the United States, Sept. 9, 1792).

In foreign affairs, Jefferson remained a staunch Francophile, even after the revolutionaries had executed the king, arguing that America had a moral obligation to honor its treaty, *especially* now that France was a republic. Whereas Hamilton had argued that the 1778 treaty had been concluded with the king and should be suspended until it became clear what kind of government France would establish next, Jefferson countered that the treaty was made with the French nation, not the king, and as such, was still binding ("Opinion on the French Treaties," 1793). Even in the darkest days of the Reign of Terror, Jefferson refused to disavow the revolution because he was convinced that the fates of the two republics were indissolubly linked. To back away from France would undermine the cause of republicanism in America.

These quarrels within the Administration took their toll, and by the end of 1793, Jefferson was determined, once again, to retire for good to his farm, his family, and his books. To Madison, who tried to lure him back into politics, Jefferson protested that "the little spice of ambition" had long since "evaporated" and he no longer cared about fame (to James Madison, Apr. 27, 1795). But Madison persisted, and Jefferson agreed to accept the Republican nomination for President in 1796, though he confessed himself relieved when the Federalist candidate John Adams was elected president, and he vice president.

As the French Revolutionary wars spilled over into American politics, tensions with France increased. French seizures of American ships led Adams unilaterally to abrogate the 1778 Treaty of Alliance with France and to ally America more closely with Britain. The XYZ Affair, in which agents of French Foreign Minister Talleyrand demanded a substantial bribe before entering into negotiations with American emissaries, further inflamed American opinion. By 1798, France and America were involved in an undeclared limited naval war (the Quasi-War) that lasted two years. Against this background, Congress enacted and Adams signed into law the Alien and Sedition Acts in 1798. The Alien Act gave the President the power to expel any alien judged dangerous to the peace and safety of the United States, while the Sedition Act made it a crime to write, print, utter, or publish false or malicious statements about government officials. In Jefferson's view, both acts were unconstitutional. As Republican Party leader, he set out to oppose this Federalist "reign of witches" (to John Taylor, June 4, 1797). Secretly, he drafted the Kentucky Resolutions, which argued that the General Government was created by a compact of each state with its co-states, and as such, was a creature of the states. When the General Government exceeded the scope of its delegated powers, each state had a "natural right" to "nullify" the offending law. Indeed, in such cases where the General Government assumed powers not delegated, nullification was the *only* rightful remedy. In ominous language, Jefferson warned that unless these acts were "arrested at the threshold," they would "necessarily drive these States into revolution and blood," and he called on other states to take action ("Kentucky Resolutions," October 1798).

Despite Jefferson's explicit statement that elections were an inadequate response to so fundamental a breach of the compact, the election of 1800 was fought in large part on this issue, and Jefferson happily accepted the outcome. In arguably the nastiest presidential race in American history, John Adams was defeated, and the Federalist Party would never again win a national election. Yet Adams' defeat did not immediately mean Jefferson's victory. Jefferson and his vice-presidential pick, Aaron Burr, both received the same number of electoral votes, throwing the election into the House of Representatives as mandated in Article II, Section 1 of the Constitution. On the 36th vote, Jefferson was finally elected with the help of his archrival, Alexander Hamilton, who feared Burr's "extreme and irregular ambition," and correctly perceived that Jefferson was not "an enemy of the power of the Executive" (Alexander Hamilton to James A. Bayard, Jan. 16, 1801).

As president, Jefferson sought to strike a conciliatory tone in his inaugural address: in recognizing that "every difference of opinion is not a difference of principle," he seemed to accept that Federalists could also be republican "brethren." With admirable economy, Jefferson proceeded to spell out the "essential principles" around which he hoped to unite the country: "equal and exact justice to all men," regardless of their religious or political beliefs; "peace, commerce, and honest friendship with all nations, entangling alliances with none"; strong support for the state governments "as the surest bulwarks against anti republican tendencies"; the preservation of the General Government in all its "constitutional vigor." Jefferson had special reason to praise elections, which he now considered "a mild and safe corrective of abuses which are lopped by the sword of revolution where peaceable remedies are unprovided." Majority rule, a preference for militias over a standing army in peacetime, the supremacy of civilian over military authority, the primacy of agriculture, with "commerce as its handmaiden," and finally, a pledge to secure those liberties protected by the Bill of Rights summed up the "creed of our political faith." Only one thing more was necessary to complete "the circle of our felicities: a wise and frugal Government, which shall restrain men from injuring one another, shall leave them otherwise free to regulate their own pursuits of industry and improvement, and shall not take from the mouth of labor the bread it has earned" ("First Inaugural Address," Mar. 4, 1801).

In foreign affairs, Jefferson acted forcefully against the Barbary powers that in 1801 declared war on the United States and demanded tribute for not attacking American ships. Heeding his own advice from fifteen years earlier, Jefferson stunned the diplomatic world by sending in the navy and the marines. And with the presidency and Congress now safely in Republican hands, Jefferson purged the army of its Federalist officers and signed the bill establishing the United States Military Academy at West Point. A year later, when feeble Spain announced the retrocession of Louisiana to the powerful French, Jefferson turned on his old ally in an instant, declaring the possessor of New Orleans to be "the natural enemy" of the United States (to the U.S. Minister to France, Robert R. Livingston, Apr. 18, 1802).

In 1803, relations with France took yet another unexpected turn, when Napoleon, after suffering defeat in Santo Domingo, decided to turn his attentions back to Europe and offered to sell the whole of the Louisiana Territory to the United States.

Jefferson did not hesitate. In a stroke, he succeeded in doubling the size of the United States, for the price of about four pennies an acre, thereby helping to fulfill his wish that there would be room enough for small landholders "to the thousandth and thousandth generation" ("First Inaugural Address," Mar. 4, 1801). Still, as a strict constructionist, he was troubled that nowhere in the Constitution was there a specific provision for Congress to create new states out of territory that lay outside the original boundaries of the United States. Rather than interpret the Constitution broadly, Jefferson favored a constitutional amendment. "I had rather ask for an enlargement of power from the nation, where it is found necessary, than to assume it by construction that would make our powers boundless. Our peculiar security is in possession of a written Constitution. Let us not make it a blank paper by construction" (to Wilson Cary Nicholas, Sept. 7, 1803). Yet, when advised that delay might jeopardize the treaty, Jefferson did decide to proceed without an amendment.

Elected to a second term in 1804, Jefferson reviewed the progress his administration had made in restoring the nation to its republican moorings. In four short years, he had eliminated Federalist programs and offices, substantially shrinking the size and expense of the national government; discontinued all internal taxes, including the hated federal excise tax on whiskey; and significantly reduced the national debt. Jefferson looked forward to the day, not very distant, when the government would retire its debt, and distribute the surplus revenue from customs duties to the states, as well as initiate a series of public improvements. His list included not only rivers, canals, and roads, but also arts, manufactures, and education. These projects would, however, require a constitutional amendment, the only legitimate way to enlarge government power. Unlike the Louisiana Purchase, Jefferson would continue to insist upon this amendment until the end of his life.

Having doubled the size of America, Jefferson was compelled to develop a policy for dealing with the Native Americans. He acknowledged that as

Americans expanded westward they would encroach upon the Native American hunting grounds, endangering their traditional way of life. "Humanity" required that the Americans teach them agriculture and the domestic arts, instill in them habits of industry, and prepare them for civilization and eventual citizenship. A prophet of progress, Jefferson dismissed those Native American leaders who, like the Federalists, sought to inculcate "a sanctimonious reverence for the customs of their ancestors" ("Second Inaugural Address," Mar. 4, 1805; to Benjamin Hawkins, Feb. 18, 1803).

By midpoint in his second term, Jefferson could report favorably on the exploration and mapping of the West. Lewis and Clark had successfully returned from their expedition, tracing the mighty Missouri River to its source, and similar explorations of other major waterways were in progress. He could also announce that Congress had passed legislation banning the importation of slaves, and he was prepared to sign it so that it could take effect on January 1, 1808, in accordance with Article I, Section 9 of the Constitution.

Although Jefferson had closed his Sixth Annual Message (in December 1806) by taking note of the dangerous situation in Europe, he recommended only a modest increase in military spending, and this for purely defensive purposes. By the following year, however, as British ships began to impress American sailors into service against France, Jefferson was forced to act. Hoping to avoid an all-out shooting war, the President tried to wage economic warfare by clamping an embargo on trade with Britain, an idea whose seeds could be traced back to his 1793 "Report on the Privileges and Restrictions on the Commerce of the United States in Foreign Countries," while he was Secretary of State. But, lacking a real naval force, the experiment failed dismally. Jefferson succeeded only in antagonizing the commercial Northeast, which defied the law and threatened to secede from the Union. Yet despite the failure of his policy, Jefferson managed to get his trusted Secretary of State, James Madison, elected president in 1808, though only after a promise to repeal the embargo.

Returning to Monticello, Jefferson could at last direct his energies to his family and friends, his books, and his farm. In retirement, he also discovered a new "hobbyhorse," the University of Virginia, which was to be the crowning achievement of his lifetime interest in education. From his mountaintop, he oversaw the university's architectural design and its curriculum, recruiting faculty who would keep alive the "the vestal flame" of republicanism (to James Madison, Feb. 17, 1826). In these years, too, Jefferson would flesh out his proposal that the states divide their counties into wards, so that republican self-government might be brought within the reach of every citizen. Finally, with the help of their mutual friend, Dr. Benjamin Rush, Jefferson and Adams would at last be reconciled and resume their remarkable epistolary friendship. Their correspondence, spanning over fifty years and touching on questions of politics, religion, and philosophy, is unrivaled in American letters.

Jefferson's retirement years were not entirely unclouded. His debts mounted, and he was forced to sell his substantial library to Congress to raise money. Although he professed to have taken leave of politics, and to have given up reading newspapers, he was deeply troubled by the Missouri Compromise of 1820, according to which Maine came into the Union as a free state and Missouri as a slave state. The Missouri Compromise further prohibited slavery in those parts of the Louisiana Territory above the southern border of Missouri. Jefferson shared some of his worries with Adams, but he unburdened himself most memorably to the Maine legislator, John Holmes. Although the question raised by the Missouri Compromise was whether Congress had the power to regulate slavery in the territories (a position Jefferson had earlier embraced in his "Report on Government for Western Territory") he regarded the Missouri Compromise as an unconstitutional exercise of power by Congress. It was the exclusive right of the states to decide whether or not they would permit slavery. On a practical level, Jefferson was convinced that dispersing the slaves over a greater territory would relieve the population pressures on the southern states, thereby facilitating emancipation. As things stood now, the sheer number of slaves concentrated in the south worked against this goal: "we have the wolf by the ears, and we can neither hold him nor safely let him go. Justice is in the one scale and self-preservation in the other" (to John Holmes, Apr. 22, 1820). Another worry in his final years was President John Quincy Adams' support for internal improvements without a constitutional amendment. Although Jefferson warmly congratulated Adams on the election of his son to the presidency in 1824, he understandably did not share with him his opposition to his son's program, and Madison succeeded in persuading Jefferson from making his objections public.

Thomas Jefferson and John Adams both died on July 4, 1826, the fiftieth anniversary of the Declaration of Independence. In accord with Jefferson's instructions, the obelisk marking his grave site in the family cemetery at Monticello records the deeds for which he wished to be remembered: "Author of the Declaration of American Independence, of the statute of Virginia for religious freedom, and father of the University of Virginia." Nothing is said of his having been the third president of the United States.

Political Theory

Thomas Jefferson's great achievement was taking the natural rights philosophy of the Declaration of Independence and wedding it to a distinctive understanding of republicanism. His thought, therefore, cannot be understood in terms of the now familiar Lockean liberal-classical republican dichotomy. According to this paradigm, liberalism appeals to self-interest to get citizens to do their duty, while classical republicanism relies on virtue; liberalism seeks to protect individual rights, while republicanism looks to promote the common good; liberalism understands liberty as essentially private or negative, while republicanism sees liberty as essentially public, and hence, puts a premium on political participation.

Jefferson agreed with Locke that the end of government is the protection of each individual's natural rights, but he grounds his liberalism in a view of human nature that departs from Locke's in three ways, with important consequences for his understanding of politics. First, following the Scottish moral sense philosophers, Jefferson begins with a more amiable view of human nature. Where Locke had argued that morality was grounded in self-interest, Jefferson insisted that self-interest or self-love was "no part of morality." Nature (in other places he referred to a "Benevolent Creator") had made human beings for society, and so, had implanted in them "a love of others, a sense of duty to them, a moral instinct," which told them how to act (to Thomas Law, June 13, 1814). Our interests, soundly calculated, were thus inseparable from our duties ("Second Inaugural Address," Mar. 4, 1805). Thus, Jefferson's understanding of human nature is more philanthropic than the Lockean view.

Second, drawing on the writings of Condorcet and the French Enlightenment, Jefferson believed in progress and was far more optimistic about the future. While not quite prepared to say there were no limits to human perfectibility, he declined to speculate about what they might be. Every field of science held out the hope of new discoveries that would improve and enrich the life of ordinary men and women (to William Green Munford, June 18, 1799). In politics, especially, Jefferson went well beyond Locke in asserting that consent of the governed should ideally result in republican majority rule.

Third, Jefferson saw human nature as more spirited and more political than Locke. As the language in both the "Summary View" and the Declaration of Independence (especially Jefferson's draft) makes clear, the love of liberty is deeply ingrained in human nature. All human beings, if they are not deceived by ignorance and superstition, love liberty. They wish to be free, not only to pursue their private goals, but to govern themselves. Exercising their political liberty gratifies their "manly spirit" in a way that other more private pursuits cannot. Indeed, one of the more striking features of Jefferson's political thought is the extent to which he views spiritedness in distinctively political terms. Where Locke sought to channel this spiritedness into acquisition, Jefferson (even as he complained about his own public service) sought to discover ways of keeping this spirit alive in his fellow citizens. For him, lethargy was "the forerunner of death to the public liberty" (to William S. Smith, Nov. 13, 1787). To nurture this spirit, Jefferson insisted that the republic be brought within reach of every citizen.

But if Jefferson departed from Locke in subtle but important respects, he found almost nothing to admire in the classical republics of Greece and

Rome. The Greek cities, to be sure, were small enough to enable each citizen to participate in the life of the polis, but they had no knowledge of the principle of representation, and so were doomed to remain tiny and weak (to Isaac H. Tiffany, Aug. 26, 1816). Rome, by contrast, was a mighty republic, but all her efforts were organized toward war. Moreover, the virtue these republics fostered in their citizens was harsh and austere. Classical republicanism demanded that citizens sacrifice everything to the common good; it cared little for individual liberty.

Although Jefferson wished to bring the republic within the reach of every citizen, he did not, like the classical republicans, wish to promote civic virtue at the expense of individual liberty. The kind of civic virtue he sought to foster, participation in local government and vigilance in overseeing elected officials, could more easily be reconciled with his commitment to individual rights. Furthermore, he did not believe that civic virtue was the highest or only virtue. His study of philosophy persuaded him that there were other, more important, virtues that flourish in the private realm—in particular, benevolence, friendship, and wisdom—and these were essential to human happiness. The great glory of the modern liberal republicanism he helped to craft was that, unlike classical republicanism, the perfection of the individual was not exclusively or primarily bound up with political participation (to David Rittenhouse, July 19, 1778).

The Political Theory of the Declaration of Independence

As the author of the Declaration of Independence, Jefferson ranks among America's great political poets, second only to Abraham Lincoln. Jefferson begins the Declaration by insisting that there are certain political truths that are unchanging. The first of these is that "all men are created equal." Today these words seem suspect: "all men"? Does that mean blacks, and if so, why did Jefferson hold slaves? If we recall that Jefferson's original draft of the Declaration contained a paragraph denouncing slavery as a violation of natural rights it is clear that Jefferson meant to include blacks. What's more, even though Jefferson himself owned slaves, he recognized that slavery was unjust; the problem was how to *persuade* a majority of his fellow citizens to do what was right and just when this seemed to conflict with their interests. The moral sense may prompt us to do what is right, but, as Jefferson acknowledged, vicious institutions can corrupt that moral sense (Query XVIII, *Notes on Virginia*). Early on, he spoke out forcefully against slavery, both in the "Summary View" and in the Declaration, while drafting a constitution for revolutionary Virginia that emancipated all slaves born after a certain date. Rebuffed in these early efforts, Jefferson gave up the political fight although until the end of his life he continued to explore various plans for emancipation, including one that would have funded the costs of the project with money from the sale of federal lands (to Jared Sparks, Feb. 4, 1824)

At the same time, however, he did not think that blacks and whites could live together in harmony after emancipation. Although Jefferson believed that all religions might flourish in America, he was far less optimistic when it came to race. As he put it in Query XIV of the *Notes*, "deep rooted prejudices entertained by the whites, ten thousand recollections, by the blacks, of the injuries they have sustained; new provocations; the real distinctions nature has made; and many other circumstances will divide us into parties, and produce convulsions which will probably never end but in the extermination of the one or the other race." To these political reasons, Jefferson added others that were physical or aesthetic and moral. Later on, when offered examples of black talent, he backed away from his position in the *Notes*, and expressed the hope that the differences between the races might be explained by the condition of the slaves (to Benjamin Banneker, Aug. 30, 1791). Still, he insisted, whatever their differences from whites, these were "no measure of their rights. Because Sir Isaac Newton was superior to others in understanding, he was not therefore lord of the person or property of others" (to Henri Gregoire, Feb. 25, 1809). Slavery was unjust, and a stain upon the American republic. His solution was emancipation coupled with expatriation. As he saw it, blacks were a separate people, and like the Americans, were entitled to take their place among the nations of the world. There was nothing contradictory in supporting emancipation and then pushing for expatriation, although that was by no means the only solution, and not the one preferred by most emancipated slaves (Frederick Douglass, "The Destiny of Colored Americans").

What about women? Does the phrase "all men" include them? The short answer is yes. Women are indeed equal in the possession of inalienable rights, "among which are life, liberty, and the pursuit of happiness." But Jefferson believed that the pursuit of happiness meant something fundamentally different for the two sexes. For women, happiness was to be found principally in the quiet satisfactions of family and home. As a result, Jefferson saw nothing contradictory in asserting women's natural rights while at the same time denying them equal civil or political rights. In particular, he did not wish to see them hold office or take part in politics. A world in which women concerned themselves with public affairs was a world gone "mad," if not worse. Observing the enthusiasm for politics among French women, Jefferson concluded that American women were far happier because they confined themselves to the "tender and tranquil amusements of domestic life" (to Anne Willing Bingham, May 11, 1788)

How, then, did he expect their inalienable rights to be protected if they were denied equal civil rights? In general, he believed that women's fathers, husbands, sons, and brothers would protect them, because he did not believe that they had different or conflicting interests, and because standing up for one's rights often involved a willingness and ability to fight for them. Nevertheless, when women began to demand equal civil rights, they could successfully invoke Jefferson's own words in the Declaration to remind men that legitimate government must rest on the "consent of the governed" ("Seneca Falls Declaration and Resolves," 1848).

Equality is the first principle of the Declaration of Independence, but its meaning is not immediately clear. Equal in what? Surely not in talent, beauty, strength, wealth, or virtue. Thus, equality is compatible with, and in a free society inevitably produces, a certain degree of inequality. Jefferson did not object to inequality as long as it resulted from the natural, rather than hereditary and artificial, differences among individuals. Indeed, Jefferson himself admitted "the best form of government" was the one that provided "most effectually for a pure selection" of the natural *aristoi* to public office (to John Adams, Oct. 28, 1813). To that end, he made several (unsuccessful) attempts to convince the Virginia legislature to fund the education of the most promising poor students, so that they might be educated along with the wealthy.

Moreover, although Jefferson consistently took the side of the people over the wealthy, praising their disinterestedness and honesty, he was not opposed to wealth as a reward for industry and talent. Thus, he could speak in the same breath of "equality of rights" and "that state of property, equal or unequal, which results to every man from his own industry, or that of his fathers" ("Second Inaugural Address," Mar. 4, 1805). A decade later, Jefferson made the point even more emphatically: "to take from one, because it is thought that his own industry and that of his fathers has acquired too much, in order to spare others, who, or whose fathers have not exercised equal industry and skill, is to violate arbitrarily the first principle of association—the *guarantee* to every one of his industry and fruits acquired by it" ("Prospectus on Political Economy," enclosed to Joseph Milligan, Apr. 6, 1816).

Although Jefferson declined to include property among the inalienable rights enumerated in the Declaration of Independence, his understanding of property was essentially Lockean. As long as private property was rightly used to promote industry and increase productivity, inequalities of property should be protected. Equality, as Jefferson understood it, referred to an equality of rights, which, when exercised, would lead inevitably to an inequality of outcome. At the same time, however, he considered it sound public policy to provide as many as possible with at least a small portion of public land so that they might support themselves (to James Madison, Oct. 28, 1785).

Finally, let us turn to the rights themselves. When we say that certain rights are inalienable, we mean that we can never voluntarily give them up because they are rooted in our permanent and unchanging nature, as it comes to sight through the promptings of the moral sense. All human beings desire to live, but beyond mere life, they want to be free and to be happy. For Jefferson, the right to liberty includes the right of individuals to cultivate the full range of their faculties and sensibilities, subject only to the "Moral law of our nature" ("Opinion on the French Treaties," 1793). It includes those rights connected with self-development, such as the "rights of thinking and publishing our thoughts by speaking and writing," as well as the "right of personal freedom" and freedom of conscience. In addition, it encourages personal enrichment by recognizing the right to immigrate, to trade freely, to choose a vocation, and to labor for a livelihood. But liberty also has a public dimension: we have a "natural right to self-government." This is not merely to ensure that our public officials do not betray our interests; there is something intrinsically valuable in political participation. How to accomplish this in a large republic was something Jefferson thought about all his life.

The pursuit of happiness remains the most elusive of our inalienable rights. What did Jefferson have in mind when he substituted this phrase for Locke's right to property (and later counseled the French to do the same in their "Declaration of the Rights of Man")? Was he merely seeking another way to talk about property or did he mean something more? Certainly, Jefferson believed that the right to acquire, possess, and dispose of one's property was an important element of personal happiness, but it could never be the sum total. Good health and freedom were also important components. Above all, Jefferson insisted, echoing a tradition of moral philosophy that stretched back to the ancient Greeks, happiness depended on virtue. "The order of nature is that individual happiness shall be inseparable from the practice of virtue" (to J. Correa de Serra, Apr. 19, 1814).

If Jefferson believed that virtues lay at the core of happiness, which virtues were they? Were they the stern classical republican virtues of self-command and love of country? The Christian virtues of faith, hope, and charity? Or the more amiable virtues recommended by the Scottish moral sense philosophers? After careful consideration, Jefferson settled on an amalgam of the Christian and Scottish virtues: happiness consisted in the exercise of the social virtues, and especially benevolence, or doing good for others (to Thomas Law, June 13, 1814). In short, we do well by doing good.

Although the moral implications of this understanding of happiness are profound, the political implications are minimal. As the Declaration makes clear, government is obliged only to protect the *pursuit* of happiness. It cannot, as a general rule, compel us to do good to others, even if it is part of what would make us truly happy. For Jefferson the tasks of a liberal republic are few: government should restrain individuals from encroaching on the equal rights of others, compel them to contribute to the necessities of society, and require them to submit their disputes to an impartial judge. "When the laws have declared and enforced all this, they have fulfilled their functions" (to

Francis W. Gilmer, June 7, 1816). It was not the purpose of government to enforce the full range of our moral obligations. Thus, although the right to pursue happiness entails certain duties to others, which places it on a different footing from those rights that are grounded in the selfish passions, it does not fundamentally alter the limited role of government. The political theory of the Declaration presupposes a vision of human happiness, linked to the exercise of the moral and social virtues, but it leaves individuals free to pursue happiness as they see fit.

Republicanism

The Declaration of Independence announces what the *ends* of government are, but it says nothing about the *form* of government that will secure these ends. This question is left for the people to determine, subject only to the requirement that government rest on the "consent of the governed." Although republican government is not the only form of government to which a people may consent, it was certainly the only form of government that Americans would accept. But what precisely is a republic? At a minimum, Americans understood that establishing a republic would mean abolishing monarchy. Beyond that, however, opinion was divided. Was republicanism consistent with aristocracy (as in Rome) or did it require democracy? And, if democracy, did it need a complex set of institutions that would successively filter and refine the public views? Or was a simple government, concentrating power in a legislature that more closely resembled the people, better? Running through all these questions about political architecture, or the design of the government, was another question: did republicanism require more virtue in its citizens than other forms of government and, if so, how to promote it?

Jefferson's draft constitution for Virginia in 1776 suggests that early on he understood the question largely in institutional terms: republican government meant a greatly weakened executive, appointed by the legislature for a one-year term, and stripped of both the veto and all monarchical prerogatives. In the lower house, Jefferson favored equal representation, with a broad suffrage. At the same time, he remained suspicious of the people's capacity for wise decisions, and recommended that the lower house of the legislature, rather than the people, select the members of the Senate, who would hold office for a term of nine years, and then be permanently ineligible for reelection to that body. On the subject of penal laws, Jefferson dismissed as "fantastical" the idea that "virtue and the public good" might by themselves be sufficient to preserve the social order. Republicanism did not repeal human nature; there would still be a need for laws to punish wrongdoers (to Edmund Pendleton, Aug. 26, 1776).

Jefferson's comments in his *Notes on Virginia* (1782) on the constitution drawn up by the Virginia legislature in 1776 shed further light on his understanding of republicanism. The constitution, he observed in Query XIII, "was formed when we were new and unexperienced in the science of government." Specifically, Jefferson objected that, contrary to his draft constitution, far too many of the men who fought and paid taxes were barred from voting and that those who did have the right to vote were represented unequally. Republicanism must rest on a broad democratic foundation. He further objected that both houses were elected by the same group of electors, producing an undesirable homogeneity between the two bodies. "The purpose of establishing different houses of legislation is to introduce the influence of different interests or different principles."

Experience also caused Jefferson to rethink some of his own earlier proposals. Whereas in 1776, he sought to strip the executive of much of his powers, as governor of the state during wartime, he now saw that concentrating all power in the legislature did not make the government more republican. On the contrary, "the concentrating these in the same hands is precisely the definition of despotic government" (Query XIII). And finally, Jefferson came to see that the act of constituting a government could not be entrusted to the legislature, because that would give the Constitution no more authority than an ordinary act of legislation, capable of being altered by future legislatures. Only an extraordinary convention, acting directly on behalf of the people, could endow the Constitution with a higher authority.

Constituting a republic in Virginia was one thing; it was quite another to establish one for the United States. Following Montesquieu, opponents of the Constitution proposed by the Philadelphia Convention of 1787 were persuaded that republican government could only exist in a small area. If the republic grew too large, citizens would forget about the common good and devote themselves to their own private ends, while their representatives pursued their own selfish interests out of the public eye. Although Jefferson was sometimes thought to sympathize with the views of the Antifederalists, he never doubted the possibility of a large republic. Indeed, he was far more optimistic about the possibilities of expansion in the West than even the most dedicated Federalists. Speaking to the issue in his second Inaugural Address soon after the Louisiana Purchase, Jefferson acknowledged that there were some who feared that the enlargement of the United States might threaten its union. But, Jefferson asked, "Who can limit the extent to which the federative principle may operate effectively?" Echoing the argument of Madison in favor of the large republic in *Federalist* 10, Jefferson then added "The larger our association, the less it will be shaken by local passions. . . ." ("Second Inaugural Address," Mar. 4, 1805).

What doubts Jefferson did harbor about the American republic centered on the Federalists' interpretation of the powers given to the national government. Having asserted early on that he was not a friend of energetic government (except for those powers enumerated in the Constitution), he surveyed the decade of Federalist dominance under Washington and then Adams, and spoke out against the "monarchizing" tendencies of the executive branch and the Senate. After Adams appointed John Marshall as chief justice of the Supreme Court, Jefferson would never again wish that the court shared a veto power with the executive, or possessed one of its own (to James Madison, Mar. 15, 1789). Reining in the courts, and making them responsive to popular opinion, would become a crucial part of his mature understanding of republicanism (to Judge Spencer Roane, Sept. 6, 1819).

When, in 1776, Jefferson expressed doubts about the capacity of the people for wise action, he hoped that experience might prove him wrong and to his mind, it did. Reflecting on these experiences in his retirement, Jefferson now conceded that at the time of the Revolution Americans were too much in thrall to European political thinkers for their understanding of republicanism. Back then, "we imagined everything was republican which was not monarchy. We had not yet penetrated to the mother principle that 'governments are republican only in proportion as they embody the will of the people, and execute it.'" This was further proof that progress was possible, and that it was a mistake to look back on the founding generation with "sanctimonious reverence" (to Samuel Kercheval, July 12, 1816).

To another correspondent, Jefferson acknowledged that although the term *republic* was admittedly vague, he thought it meant "purely and simply . . . government by its citizens in mass, acting directly and personally, according to the rules established by the majority. . ." (to John Taylor, May 28, 1816). Jefferson conceded that this definition, if strictly applied, would limit a republic to the size of a New England township, and so, was unworkable. By means of representation (a principle, he wrote to Isaac H. Tiffany, that rendered the political science of Aristotle obsolete), republicanism could be made to work over a wider area, provided that the representatives served for short terms and were directly accountable to the people in proportion to their numbers. Using this standard, he now judged the lower house of the Virginia legislature the most republican, the Senate and executive less so, and the judiciary the least because it is an appointment for life. For forty years the citizens of Virginia had stumbled along with their first flawed republican constitution and it was past time to revise it to reflect the lessons of experience. Jefferson proposed seven amendments (to Samuel Kercheval, July 12, 1816).

Yet Jefferson's understanding of republicanism was not simply institutional. More than any other Founder, Jefferson believed that republican government also depended on preserving a certain kind of spirit in the people. Indeed, analyzing the Virginia Constitution in 1816, Jefferson asked, "Where is our republicanism to be found?" His answer was "not in our constitution certainly, but merely in the spirit of our people" (to Samuel Kercheval, July 12, 1816). Preserving this spirit was the major work of the republican statesman.

Jefferson himself took several stabs at the problem, not all of them successful. His early defense of periodic armed rebellions may be seen as one flawed attempt to keep alive the spirit of republicanism, as was his suggestion that all laws and constitutions be remade every generation. In both these proposals, Jefferson seemed to be using the Founding (i.e., the overthrow of British rule and the round of constitution-making in the states) as a model for how to preserve the spirit of the revolution once the Founding was complete. Yet he also suggested several positive ways by which civic spirit might be cultivated.

As early as 1778, in the preamble to his "Bill for the More General Diffusion of Knowledge," Jefferson observed that "the most effectual means" of warding off "degeneracy" in even the best government was "to illuminate, as far as it practicable, the minds of the people." The tasks of universal education were distinctly political: first, to instruct citizens in "their rights, interests and duties as men and citizens," and second, to cull from each of these local school districts, or wards, the most virtuous and talented boys to be educated further at public expense. In return, these natural *aristoi* were expected to use their knowledge to improve the lives of their fellow citizens, either through public service or scientific research ("Report of the Commissioners for the University of Virginia," Aug. 4, 1818).

To these ends, the elementary school curriculum Jefferson devised was heavily weighted in favor of history, especially the histories of Greece, Rome, England, and America. If the boys and girls of Virginia would study the ways in which other nations, and especially republican nations, had risen to greatness, and by what errors and vices they had declined, they would be better able to preserve their own republican institutions.

At the same time, Jefferson's educational plan was decidedly secular: he did not believe that religion, especially orthodox Christianity, with its impenetrable doctrines and miraculous teachings, had any place in the schools. In Query XIV of the *Notes*, Jefferson explicitly ruled out "the Bible and Testament," on the grounds that at that early age the judgments of children were "not sufficiently matured for religious inquiries." Instead of religious doctrine, children were to be taught the virtues of independence, industry, and self-reliance, and to learn that their "greatest happiness" depended largely on their own character and actions.

In addition to education, Jefferson looked to local self-government organized in what he called wards to foster the civic spirit so crucial to his understanding of republicanism. Although Jefferson first mentioned the wards as a way of organizing local school districts, he later realized their greater potential. "Begin them for a single purpose, they will soon show for what others they are the best instruments" (to Joseph C. Cabell, Feb. 2, 1816). In a series of letters written after he had retired from public office, Jefferson envisaged a variety of tasks that citizens might usefully manage themselves: caring for the local poor, maintaining roads, supervising the police, overseeing elections, selecting jurors, administering justice in small matters, organizing the militia, and of course, superintending the education of their children. Accordingly, Jefferson proposed that the Virginia Constitution be amended to create a system of wards—similar to the New England townships—out of the larger and less responsible county divisions. "Each ward would thus be a small republic within itself, and each man in the State would thus become an acting member of the common government, transacting in person a great portion of its rights and duties, subordinate indeed, yet important, and entirely within his competence"(to Major John Cartwright, June 5, 1824).

The wards were Jefferson's most original contribution to the modern theory of liberal republicanism. Instead of consolidating political power or attempting to forge a general will, Jefferson went in the opposite direction, "dividing and subdividing" political power, while multiplying the number of interests and views that would be heard. The wards offered a way to bring the large republic within reach of every citizen and so keep alive the civic spirit so vital to its preservation. "Where every man is a sharer in the direction of his ward-republic, or of some higher ones, and feels that he is a participator in the Government of affairs, not merely at an election one day in the year, but everyday; where there shall not be a man in the State who will not be a member of some one of its councils, great or small, he will let the heart be torn out of his body sooner than his power wrested from him by a Caesar or a Bonaparte"(to Joseph C. Cabell, Feb. 2, 1816).

The Jeffersonian Legacy

The great historian Merrill Peterson once observed that, alone among the Founders, Thomas Jefferson acted as a mirror in which subsequent generations of Americans found reflected their most urgent concerns. In the crisis over slavery that led to the Civil War, Abraham Lincoln helped create the Republican Party to fight against the party of Jefferson, but even as he did, he insisted that he had "never had a feeling politically that did not spring from the sentiments embodied in the Declaration of Independence" ("Address in Independence Hall," Feb. 22, 1861). In debate after debate with Stephen Douglas, Lincoln argued that slaves too were endowed with the rights to life, liberty, and the pursuit of happiness, and that no man could justly rule over another without his consent. These principles, which he had learned from Jefferson, were "the definitions and axioms of a free society" (to H. L. Pierce and others, Apr. 6, 1859).

In the midst of the Depression, Franklin Delano Roosevelt cast Jefferson as the voice of the people against the "economic royalists," and erected a monument in his name to honor his "hostility to every form of tyranny over the mind of man." Two generations later, John F. Kennedy revered him for the cool, rational, scientific qualities Kennedy wished to project to the country as it developed the technology to face down the Soviet Union and send Americans to the moon. Hosting a group of American Nobel Prize Laureates in the 1960s, President Kennedy famously remarked that there was more intelligence in that room than at any other time in the history of the White House, with the possible exception of evenings when Thomas Jefferson dined alone.

Still, the legacy of Jefferson has not always been so positive. In the run-up to the Civil War, John C. Calhoun used the Kentucky Resolutions to argue in favor of states' sovereignty, nullification, and slavery. After the Civil War an entire generation of progressive reformers dismissed Jefferson's political philosophy of individual rights and limited government as obsolete. Acceding to the Presidency in 1901, one hundred years after Jefferson's election, Theodore Roosevelt charged that Jefferson's program of limited national power promoted selfish individualism and fostered national weakness. For Roosevelt, Jefferson's failings boiled down to a question of character: Roosevelt judged him a "scholarly, timid, and shifty doctrinaire" (*Gouverneur Morris*, 1888).

For different reasons, character continues to be an issue in our current assessment of Jefferson. As America struggles with its history of slavery and racism, we wonder how Jefferson could have penned the majestic phrases of the Declaration of Independence, yet continued to hold slaves. Or why, after his early and unsuccessful efforts to abolish slavery in Virginia, he seemed to give up on the problem, and let others take the lead. Turning from slavery to race, we ask how the man who spoke so eloquently of individual rights could in his only book speak so disparagingly of an entire race. More recently, as DNA evidence has confirmed that someone in the male Jefferson line fathered one or more children by Jefferson's slave Sally Hemings, Jefferson's reputation has been further tarnished. But this cannot be the last word on the achievement of Thomas Jefferson. Whatever his failings as a man, Jefferson offered to Americans and to the world a particular vision of how free people might govern themselves. It is altogether fitting that each generation should revisit that legacy and make Jefferson's political thought new again.

Select Bibliography

Appleby, Joyce Oldham. *Capitalism and a New Social Order: The Republican Vision of the 1790s*. New York: New York University Press, 1984.

———. *Liberalism and Republicanism in the Historical Imagination*. Cambridge, MA: Harvard University Press, 1992.

Banning, Lance. *Jefferson and Madison: Three Conversations*. Madison, WI: Madison House, 1995.

Bernstein, R. B. *Thomas Jefferson*. New York: Oxford University Press, 2003.

Boorstin, Daniel. *The Lost World of Thomas Jefferson*. Chicago: University of Chicago Press, 1981.

Burstein, Andrew. *The Inner Jefferson: Portrait of a Grieving Optimist*. Charlottesville: University Press of Virginia, 1995.

Cappon, Lester J., ed. *The Adams-Jefferson Letters: The Complete Correspondence Between Thomas Jefferson and Abigail and John Adams*. Chapel Hill: University of North Carolina Press, 1988.

Ellis, Joseph. *American Sphinx: The Character of Thomas Jefferson*. New York: Alfred A. Knopf, Inc., 1997.

Jayne, Allen. *Jefferson's Declaration of Independence: Origins, Philosophy and Theology*. Lexington: University Press of Kentucky, 1998.

Ketcham, Ralph. *Presidents Above Party: The First American Presidency, 1789–1829*. Chapel Hill: University of North Carolina Press, 1984.

Koch, Adrienne. *Jefferson and Madison: The Great Collaboration*. New York: Alfred A. Knopf, Inc., 1950.

———. *The Philosophy of Thomas Jefferson*. Chicago: Quadrangle Books, 1964.

Lehmann, Karl. *Thomas Jefferson: American Humanist*. New York: Macmillan, 1947.

Lerner, Ralph. *The Thinking Revolutionary: Principle and Practice in the New Republic*. Ithaca, NY: Cornell University Press, 1979.

Levy, Leonard. *Jefferson and Civil Liberties: The Darker Side*. Cambridge, MA: Belknap Press of Harvard University Press, 1963.

Malone, Dumas. *Jefferson in his Time*. 6 vols. Boston: Little, Brown, 1948–81.

Matthews, Richard. *The Radical Politics of Thomas Jefferson*. Lawrence: University Press of Kansas, 1984.

Mayer, David N. *The Constitutional Thought of Thomas Jefferson*. Charlottesville: University Press of Virginia, 1994.

McCoy, Drew. *The Elusive Republic: Political Economy in Jeffersonian America*. Chapel Hill: University of North Carolina Press, 1980.

McDonald, Robert M. S. *Thomas Jefferson's Military Academy: Founding West Point.* Charlottesville: University Press of Virginia, 2004.

McDowell, Gary L., and Sharon L. Noble. *Reason and Republicanism: Thomas Jefferson's Legacy of Liberty.* Lanham, MD: Rowman and Littlefield, 1997.

Miller, John Chester. *The Wolf by the Ears: Thomas Jefferson and Slavery.* New York: Free Press, 1977.

Onuf, Peter S., ed. *Jeffersonian Legacies.* Charlottesville: University Press of Virginia, 1993.

———. ed. *Jefferson's Empire: The Language of American Nationhood.* Charlottesville: University Press of Virginia, 2000.

Pangle, Lorraine Smith, and Thomas L. Pangle. *The Learning of Liberty: The Educational Ideas of the American Founders.* Lawrence: University Press of Kansas, 1993.

Peterson, Merrill. *Adams and Jefferson: A Revolutionary Dialogue.* Athens: University of Georgia Press, 1976.

———. *The Jeffersonian Image in the American Mind.* New York: Oxford University Press, 1960.

———. *Thomas Jefferson and the New Nation.* New York: Oxford University Press, 1970.

Sheldon, Garret Ward. *The Political Philosophy of Thomas Jefferson.* Baltimore, MD: Johns Hopkins University Press, 1991.

Smith, James Morton, ed. *The Republic of Letters: The Correspondence between Thomas Jefferson and James Madison, 1776–1826.* 3 vols. New York: W. W. Norton and Company, 1995.

Yarbrough, Jean M. *American Virtues: Thomas Jefferson on the Character of a Free People.* Lawrence: University Press of Kansas, 1998.

Zuckert, Michael. *The Natural Rights Republic: Studies in the Foundation of the American Political Tradition.* Notre Dame: University of Notre Dame Press, 1996.

Public Papers and Addresses

A SUMMARY VIEW OF THE RIGHTS OF BRITISH AMERICA[1]

(1774)

Resolved, that it be an instruction to the said deputies,[2] when assembled in general congress with the deputies from the other states of British America, to propose to the said congress that an humble and dutiful address be presented to his majesty,[3] begging leave to lay before him, as chief magistrate of the British empire, the united complaints of his majesty's subjects in America; complaints which are excited by many unwarrantable encroachments and usurpations, attempted to be made by the legislature of one part of the empire, upon those rights which God and the laws have given equally and independently to all. To represent to his majesty that these his states have often individually made humble application to his imperial throne to obtain, through its intervention, some redress of their injured rights, to none of which was ever even an answer condescended; humbly to hope that this their joint address, penned in the language of truth, and divested of those expressions of servility which would persuade his majesty that we are asking favours, and not rights, shall obtain from his majesty a more respectful acceptance. And this his majesty will think we have reason to expect when he reflects that he is no more than the chief officer of the people, appointed by the laws, and circumscribed with definite powers, to assist in working the great machine of government, erected for their use, and consequently subject to their superintendance. And in order that these our rights, as well as the invasions of them, may be laid more fully before his majesty, to take a view of them from the origin and first settlement of these countries.

To remind him that our ancestors, before their emigration to America, were the free inhabitants of the British dominions in Europe, and possessed a right which nature has given to all men, of departing from the country in

---

1. See Introduction, pp. xiii–xiv.

2. The Virginia delegates to the First Continental Congress in Philadelphia: Peyton Randolph (1721–75), Richard Henry Lee (1732–94), George Washington (1732–99), Patrick Henry (1736–99), Richard Bland (1710–76), Benjamin Harrison (1726–91), and Edmund Pendleton (1721–1803).

3. George III, King of Great Britain and Ireland (reigned 1760–1820).

which chance, not choice, has placed them, of going in quest of new habitations, and of there establishing new societies, under such laws and regulations as to them shall seem most likely to promote public happiness. That their Saxon ancestors had, under this universal law, in like manner left their native wilds and woods in the north of Europe, had possessed themselves of the island of Britain, then less charged with inhabitants, and had established there that system of laws which has so long been the glory and protection of that country. Nor was ever any claim of superiority or dependence asserted over them by that mother country from which they had migrated; and were such a claim made, it is believed that his majesty's subjects in Great Britain have too firm a feeling of the rights derived to them from their ancestors, to bow down the sovereignty of their state before such visionary pretensions. And it is thought that no circumstance has occurred to distinguish materially the British from the Saxon[4] emigration. America was conquered, and her settlements made, and firmly established, at the expence of individuals, and not of the British public. Their own blood was spilt in acquiring lands for their settlement, their own fortunes expended in making that settlement effectual; for themselves they fought, for themselves they conquered, and for themselves alone they have right to hold. Not a shilling was ever issued from the public treasures of his majesty, or his ancestors, for their assistance, till of very late times, after the colonies had become established on a firm and permanent footing. That then, indeed, having become valuable to Great Britain for her commercial purposes, his parliament was pleased to lend them assistance against an enemy, who would fain[5] have drawn to herself the benefits of their commerce, to the great aggrandizement of herself, and danger of Great Britain. Such assistance, and in such circumstances, they had often before given to Portugal, and other allied states, with whom they carry on a commercial intercourse; yet these states never supposed, that by calling in her aid, they thereby submitted themselves to her sovereignty. Had such terms been proposed, they would have rejected them with disdain, and trusted for better to the moderation of their enemies, or to a vigorous exertion of their own force. We do not, however, mean to under-rate those aids, which to us were doubtless valuable, on whatever principles granted; but we would shew that they cannot give a title to that authority which the British parliament would arrogate over us, and that they may amply be repaid by our giving to the inhabitants of Great Britain such exclusive privileges in trade as may be advan-

---

4. One of the north European tribes, along with the Angles and the Jutes, that invaded Britain in the fifth and sixth centuries and came to be known as the Anglo-Saxons. The Normans defeated the Anglo-Saxons in 1066. Jefferson especially admired this period in British history, crediting it with developing institutions of self-government.
5. Happily or gladly.

tageous to them, and at the same time not too restrictive to ourselves. That settlements having been thus effected in the wilds of America, the emigrants thought proper to adopt that system of laws under which they had hitherto lived in the mother country, and to continue their union with her by submitting themselves to the same common sovereign, who was thereby made the central link connecting the several parts of the empire thus newly multiplied.

But that not long were they permitted, however far they thought themselves removed from the hand of oppression, to hold undisturbed the rights thus acquired, at the hazard of their lives, and loss of their fortunes. A family of princes[6] was then on the British throne, whose treasonable crimes against their people brought on them afterwards the exertion of those sacred and sovereign rights of punishment reserved in the hands of the people for cases of extreme necessity, and judged by the constitution unsafe to be delegated to any other judicature. While every day brought forth some new and unjustifiable exertion of power over their subjects on that side of the water, it was not to be expected that those here, much less able at that time to oppose the designs of despotism, should be exempted from injury.

Accordingly that country, which had been acquired by the lives, the labours, and the fortunes, of individual adventurers, was by these princes, at several times, parted out and distributed among the favourites and followers* of their fortunes, and, by an assumed right of the crown alone, were erected into distinct and independent governments; a measure which it is believed his majesty's prudence and understanding would prevent him from imitating at this day, as no exercise of such a power, of dividing and dismembering a country, has ever occurred in his majesty's realm of England, though now of very

*1632 Maryland was granted to lord Baltimore, 14. c. 2. Pennsylvania to Penn, and the province of Carolina was in the year 1663 granted by letters patent of majesty, king Charles II. in the 15th year of his reign, in propriety, unto the right honourable Edward earl of Clarendon, George duke of Albemarle, William earl of Craven, John lord Berkeley, Anthony lord Ashley, sir George Carteret, sir John Coletone, knight and baronet, and sir William Berkeley, knight; by which letters patent the laws of England were to be in force in Carolina: But the lords proprietors had power, *with the consent of the inhabitants*, to make bye-laws for the better government of the said province; so that no money could be received, or law made, without the consent of the inhabitants, or their representatives.

6. The Stuart Monarchs. In 1649, at the height of the English Civil War (1642–49), Charles I was publicly tried on charges of being "tyrant, traitor and murderer; and a public and implacable enemy to the Commonwealth of England" and executed. Having dissolved the monarchy, the British Council of State, led by Lord Protector Oliver Cromwell (1599–1658), took control of the nation. When Charles II restored the monarchy in 1660, he tried—and executed—those who had conspired against his father.

antient standing; nor could it be justified or acquiesced under there, or in any other part of his majesty's empire.

That the exercise of a free trade with all parts of the world, possessed by the American colonists, as of natural right, and which no law of their own had taken away or abridged, was next the object of unjust encroachment. Some of the colonies having thought proper to continue the administration of their government in the name and under the authority of his majesty king Charles the first, whom, notwithstanding his late deposition by the commonwealth of England, they continued in the sovereignty of their state; the parliament for the commonwealth took the same in high offence, and assumed upon themselves the power of prohibiting their trade with all other parts of the world, except the island of Great Britain. This arbitrary act, however, they soon recalled, and by solemn treaty, entered into on the 12th day of March, 1651, between the said commonwealth by their commissioners, and the colony of Virginia by their House of Burgesses,[7] it was expressly stipulated, by the 8th article of the said treaty, that they should have "free trade as the people of England do enjoy to all places and with all nations, according to the laws of that commonwealth." But that, upon the restoration of his majesty king Charles the second, their rights of free commerce fell once more a victim to arbitrary power; and by several acts* of his[8] reign, as well as of some of his successors, the trade of the colonies was laid under such restrictions, as shew what hopes they might form from the justice of a British parliament, were its uncontrouled power admitted over these states. History has informed us that bodies of men, as well as individuals, are susceptible of the spirit of tyranny. A view of these acts of parliament for regulation, as it has been affectedly called, of the American trade, if all other evidence were removed out of the case, would undeniably evince the truth of this observation. Besides the duties they impose on our articles of export and import, they prohibit our going to any markets northward of Cape Finesterre, in the kingdom of Spain, for the sale of commodities which Great Britain will not take from us, and for the purchase of others, with which she cannot supply us, and that for no other than the arbitrary purposes of purchasing for themselves, by a sacrifice of our rights and interests, certain privileges in their commerce with an allied state, who in confidence that their exclusive trade with America will be continued, while the principles and power of the British parliament be the same, have indulged

*12. c. 2. c. 18. 15. c. 2. II. 25. c. 2. c. 7. 7. 8. W. M. c. 22. II. W. 3. 4. Anne. 6. G. 2. c. 13.

---

7. Lower house of the Virginia colonial legislature.
8. Charles II, oldest surviving son of Charles I. See note 6, above.

themselves in every exorbitance which their avarice could dictate, or our necessities extort; have raised their commodities, called for in America, to the double and treble of what they sold for before such exclusive privileges were given them, and of what better commodities of the same kind would cost us elsewhere, and at the same time give us much less for what we carry thither than might be had at more convenient ports. That these acts prohibit us from carrying in quest of other purchasers the surplus of our tobaccoes remaining after the consumption of Great Britain is supplied; so that we must leave them with the British merchant for whatever he will please to allow us, to be by him reshipped to foreign markets, where he will reap the benefits of making sale of them for full value. That to heighten still the idea of parliamentary justice, and to shew with what moderation they are like to exercise power, where themselves are to feel no part of its weight, we take leave to mention to his majesty certain other acts of British parliament, by which they would prohibit us from manufacturing for our own use the articles we raise on our own lands with our own labour. By an act[*] passed in the 5th Year of the reign of his late majesty king George the second, an American subject is forbidden to make a hat for himself of the fur which he has taken perhaps on his own soil; an instance of despotism to which no parrallel can be produced in the most arbitrary ages of British history. By one other act,[†] passed in the 23d year of the same reign, the iron which we make we are forbidden to manufacture, and heavy as that article is, and necessary in every branch of husbandry, besides commission and insurance, we are to pay freight for it to Great Britain, and freight for it back again, for the purpose of supporting not men, but machines, in the island of Great Britain. In the same spirit of equal and impartial legislation is to be viewed the act of parliament,[‡] passed in the 5th year of the same reign, by which American lands are made subject to the demands of British creditors, while their own lands were still continued unanswerable for their debts; from which one of these conclusions must necessarily follow, either that justice is not the same in America as in Britain, or else that the British parliament pay less regard to it here than there. But that we do not point out to his majesty the injustice of these acts, with intent to rest on that principle the cause of their nullity; but to shew that experience confirms the propriety of those political principles which exempt us from the jurisdiction of the British parliament. The true ground on which we declare these acts void is, that the British parliament has no right to exercise authority over us.

[*]5. G. 2.
[†]23. G. 2. c. 29.
[‡]5. G. 270.

That these exercises of usurped power have not been confined to instances alone, in which themselves were interested, but they have also intermeddled with the regulation of the internal affairs of the colonies. The act of the 9th of Anne for establishing a post office in America seems to have had little connection with British convenience, except that of accommodating his majesty's ministers and favourites with the sale of a lucrative and easy office.

That thus have we hastened through the reigns which preceded his majesty's, during which the violations of our right were less alarming, because repeated at more distant intervals than that rapid and bold succession of injuries which is likely to distinguish the present from all other periods of American story. Scarcely have our minds been able to emerge from the astonishment into which one stroke of parliamentary thunder has involved us, before another more heavy, and more alarming, is fallen on us. Single acts of tyranny may be ascribed to the accidental opinion of a day; but a series of oppressions, begun at a distinguished period, and pursued unalterably through every change of ministers, too plainly prove a deliberate and systematical plan of reducing us to slavery.

That the act[*] passed in the 4th year of his majesty's reign, intitled "An act for granting certain duties in the British colonies and plantations in America, &c."

One other act,[†] passed in the 5th year of his reign, intitled "An act for granting and applying certain stamp duties and other duties in the British colonies and plantations in America, &c."

One other act,[‡] passed in the 6th year of his reign, intituled "An act for the better securing the dependency of his majesty's dominions in America upon the crown and parliament of Great Britain;" and one other act,[§] passed in the 7th year of his reign, intituled "An act for granting duties on paper, tea, &c." form that connected chain of parliamentary usurpation, which has already been the subject of frequent applications to his majesty, and the houses of lords and commons of Great Britain; and no answers having yet been condescended to any of these, we shall not trouble his majesty with a repetition of the matters they contained.

But that one other act,[**] passed in the same 7th year of the reign, having been a peculiar attempt, must ever require peculiar mention; it is intituled "An act for suspending the legislature of New York." One free and independent legislature hereby takes upon itself to suspend the powers of another, free

---

[*]4. G. 3. c. 15.

[†]G. 3. c. 12.

[‡]6. G. 3. c. 12.

[§]7. G. 3.

[**]7. G. 3. c. 59.

and independent as itself; thus exhibiting a phœnomenon unknown in nature, the creator and creature of its own power. Not only the principles of common sense, but the common feelings of human nature, must be surrendered up before his majesty's subjects here can be persuaded to believe that they hold their political existence at the will of a British parliament. Shall these governments be dissolved, their property annihilated, and their people reduced to a state of nature, at the imperious breath of a body of men, whom they never saw, in whom they never confided, and over whom they have no powers of punishment or removal, let their crimes against the American public be ever so great? Can any one reason be assigned why 160,000 electors in the island of Great Britain should give law to four millions in the states of America, every individual of whom is equal to every individual of them, in virtue, in understanding, and in bodily strength? Were this to be admitted, instead of being a free people, as we have hitherto supposed, and mean to continue ourselves, we should suddenly be found the slaves, not of one, but of 160,000 tyrants, distinguished too from all others by this singular circumstance, that they are removed from the reach of fear, the only restraining motive which may hold the hand of a tyrant.

That by "an act* to discontinue in such manner and for such time as are therein mentioned the landing and discharging, lading or shipping, of goods, wares, and merchandize, at the town and within the harbour of Boston, in the province of Massachusetts Bay, in North America," which was passed at the last session of British parliament; a large and populous town, whose trade was their sole subsistence, was deprived of that trade, and involved in utter ruin. Let us for a while suppose the question of right suspended, in order to examine this act on principles of justice: An act of parliament had been passed imposing duties on teas, to be paid in America, against which act the Americans had protested as inauthoritative. The East India company, who till that time had never sent a pound of tea to America on their own account, step forth on that occasion the assertors of parliamentary right, and send hither many ship loads of that obnoxious commodity. The masters of their several vessels, however, on their arrival in America, wisely attended to admonition, and returned with their cargoes. In the province of New England alone the remonstrances of the people were disregarded, and a compliance, after being many days waited for, was flatly refused. Whether in this the master of the vessel was governed by his obstinacy, or his instructions, let those who know, say. There are extraordinary situations which require extraordinary interposition. An exasperated people, who feel that they possess power, are not easily restrained within limits strictly regular. A number of them assembled in the town of

*14. G. 3.

Boston, threw the tea into the ocean, and dispersed without doing any other act of violence.[9] If in this they did wrong, they were known and were amenable to the laws of the land, against which it could not be objected that they had ever, in any instance, been obstructed or diverted from their regular course in favour of popular offenders. They should therefore not have been distrusted on this occasion. But that ill fated colony had formerly been bold in their enmities against the house of Stuart,[10] and were now devoted to ruin by that unseen hand which governs the momentous affairs of this great empire. On the partial representations of a few worthless ministerial dependents, whose constant office it has been to keep that government embroiled, and who, by their treacheries, hope to obtain the dignity of the British knighthood, without calling for a party accused, without asking a proof, without attempting a distinction between the guilty and the innocent, the whole of that antient and wealthy town is in a moment reduced from opulence to beggary. Men who had spent their lives in extending the British commerce, who had invested in that place the wealth their honest endeavours had merited, found themselves and their families thrown at once on the world for subsistence by its charities. Not the hundredth part of the inhabitants of that town had been concerned in the act complained of; many of them were in Great Britain and in other parts beyond sea; yet all were involved in one indiscriminate ruin, by a new executive power, unheard of till then, that of a British parliament. A property, of the value of many millions of money, was sacrificed to revenge, not repay, the loss of a few thousands. This is administering justice with a heavy hand indeed! and when is this tempest to be arrested in its course? Two wharfs are to be opened again when his majesty shall think proper. The residue which lined the extensive shores of the bay of Boston are forever interdicted[11] the exercise of commerce. This little exception seems to have been thrown in for no other purpose than that of setting a precedent for investing his majesty with legislative powers. If the pulse of his people shall beat calmly under this experiment, another and another will be tried, till the measure of despotism be filled up. It would be an insult on common sense to pretend that this exception was made in order to restore its commerce to that great town. The trade which cannot be received at two wharfs alone must of necessity be transferred to some other place; to which it will soon be followed

---

9. A reference to the Boston Tea Party on December 16, 1773, in which Massachusetts patriots, protesting the tax on tea imposed by Parliament, boarded several British merchant ships and dumped cargoes of tea into Boston Harbor.

10. The House of Stuart reigned over England and Scotland from 1603–49 and from 1660–1714. See note 6, above.

11. Prohibited.

by that of the two wharfs. Considered in this light, it would be an insolent and cruel mockery at the annihilation of the town of Boston.

By the act[*] for the suppression of riots and tumults in the town of Boston, passed also in the last session of parliament, a murder committed there is, if the governor pleases, to be tried in the court of King's Bench, in the island of Great Britain, by a jury of Middlesex. The witnesses, too, on receipt of such a sum as the governor shall think it reasonable for them to expend, are to enter into recognizance to appear at the trial. This is, in other words, taxing them to the amount of their recognizance,[12] and that amount may be whatever a governor pleases; for who does his majesty think can be prevailed on to cross the Atlantic for the sole purpose of bearing evidence to a fact? His expences are to be borne, indeed, as they shall be estimated by a governor; but who are to feed the wife and children whom he leaves behind, and who have had no other subsistence but his daily labour? Those epidemical disorders, too, so terrible in a foreign climate, is the cure of them to be estimated among the articles of expence, and their danger to be warded off by the almighty power of parliament? And the wretched criminal, if he happen to have offended on the American side, stripped of his privilege of trial by peers of his vicinage, removed from the place where alone full evidence could be obtained, without money, without counsel, without friends, without exculpatory proof, is tried before judges predetermined to condemn. The cowards who would suffer a countryman to be torn from the bowels of their society, in order to be thus offered a sacrifice to parliamentary tyranny, would merit that everlasting infamy now fixed on the authors of the act! A clause[†] for a similar purpose had been introduced into an act, passed in the 12th year of his majesty's reign, intitled "An act for the better securing and preserving his majesty's dockyards, magazines, ships, ammunition, and stores;" against which, as meriting the same censures, the several colonies have already protested.

That these are the acts of power, assumed by a body of men, foreign to our constitutions, and unacknowledged by our laws, against which we do, on behalf of the inhabitants of British America, enter this our solemn and determined protest; and we do earnestly entreat his majesty, as yet the only mediatory power between the several states of the British empire, to recommend to his parliament of Great Britain the total revocation of these acts,

[*]14. G. 3.
[†]12. G. 3. c. 24.

---

12. A court order to perform a particular act or a pre-established monetary fine that can be levied if the act is not performed as ordered.

which, however nugatory[13] they be, may yet prove the cause of further discontents and jealousies among us.

That we next proceed to consider the conduct of his majesty, as holding the executive powers of the laws of these states, and mark out his deviations from the line of duty: By the constitution of Great Britain, as well as of the several American states, his majesty possesses the power of refusing to pass into a law any bill which has already passed the other two branches of legislature. His majesty, however, and his ancestors, conscious of the impropriety of opposing their single opinion to the united wisdom of two houses of parliament, while their proceedings were unbiassed by interested principles, for several ages past have modestly declined the exercise of this power in that part of his empire called Great Britain. But by change of circumstances, other principles than those of justice simply have obtained an influence on their determinations; the addition of new states to the British empire has produced an addition of new, and sometimes opposite interests. It is now, therefore, the great office of his majesty, to resume the exercise of his negative power, and to prevent the passage of laws by any one legislature of the empire, which might bear injuriously on the rights and interests of another. Yet this will not excuse the wanton exercise of this power which we have seen his majesty practise on the laws of the American legislatures. For the most trifling reasons, and sometimes for no conceivable reason at all, his majesty has rejected laws of the most salutary tendency. The abolition of domestic slavery is the great object of desire in those colonies, where it was unhappily introduced in their infant state. But previous to the enfranchisement of the slaves we have, it is necessary to exclude all further importations from Africa; yet our repeated attempts to effect this by prohibitions, and by imposing duties which might amount to a prohibition, have been hitherto defeated by his majesty's negative: Thus preferring the immediate advantages of a few African corsairs[14] to the lasting interests of the American states, and to the rights of human nature, deeply wounded by this infamous practice. Nay, the single interposition of an interested individual against a law was scarcely ever known to fail of success, though in the opposite scale were placed the interests of a whole country. That this is so shameful an abuse of a power trusted with his majesty for other purposes, as if not reformed, would call for some legal restrictions.

With equal inattention to the necessities of his people here has his majesty permitted our laws to lie neglected in England for years, neither confirming them by his assent, nor annulling them by his negative; so that such of them as have no suspending clause we hold on the most precarious of all tenures,

---

13. Trifling, without value.

14. Barbary pirates who engaged in the slave trade (see Introduction, pp. xvii, xxi–xxii).

his majesty's will, and such of them as suspend themselves till his majesty's assent be obtained, we have feared, might be called into existence at some future and distant period, when time, and change of circumstances, shall have rendered them destructive to his people here. And to render this grievance still more oppressive, his majesty by his instructions has laid his governors under such restrictions that they can pass no law of any moment unless it have such suspending clause; so that, however immediate may be the call for legislative interposition, the law cannot be executed till it has twice crossed the atlantic, by which time the evil may have spent its whole force.

But in what terms, reconcileable to majesty, and at the same time to truth, shall we speak of a late instruction to his majesty's governor of the colony of Virginia,[15] by which he is forbidden to assent to any law for the division of a county, unless the new county will consent to have no representative in assembly? That colony has as yet fixed no boundary to the westward. Their western counties, therefore, are of indefinite extent; some of them are actually seated many hundred miles from their eastern limits. Is it possible, then, that his majesty can have bestowed a single thought on the situation of those people, who, in order to obtain justice for injuries, however great or small, must, by the laws of that colony, attend their county court, at such a distance, with all their witnesses, monthly, till their litigation be determined? Or does his majesty seriously wish, and publish it to the world, that his subjects should give up the glorious right of representation, with all the benefits derived from that, and submit themselves the absolute slaves of his sovereign will? Or is it rather meant to confine the legislative body to their present numbers, that they may be the cheaper bargain whenever they shall become worth a purchase.

One of the articles of impeachment against Tresilian,[16] and the other judges of Westminister Hall, in the reign of Richard the second, for which they suffered death, as traitors to their country, was, that they had advised the king that he might dissolve his parliament at any time; and succeeding kings have adopted the opinion of these unjust judges. Since the establishment, however, of the British constitution, at the glorious revolution, on its free and antient principles, neither his majesty, nor his ancestors, have exercised such a power of dissolution in the island of Great Britain; and when his majesty was petitioned, by the united voice of his people there, to dissolve the present parliament, who had become obnoxious to them, his ministers were heard to declare, in open parliament, that his majesty possessed no such power by the constitution. But how different their language and his practice here! To

---

15. John Murray, Fourth Earl of Dunmore (1732–1809); governor of Virginia from 1771–76.

16. English chief justice executed in 1388 for misadvising the king.

declare, as their duty required, the known rights of their country, to oppose
the usurpations of every foreign judicature, to disregard the imperious mandates of a minister or governor, have been the avowed causes of dissolving
houses of representatives in America. But if such powers be really vested in his
majesty, can he suppose they are there placed to awe the members from such
purposes as these? When the representative body have lost the confidence of
their constituents, when they have notoriously made sale of their most valuable rights, when they have assumed to themselves powers which the people
never put into their hands, then indeed their continuing in office becomes
dangerous to the state, and calls for an exercise of the power of dissolution.
Such being the causes for which the representative body should, and should
not, be dissolved, will it not appear strange to an unbiassed observer, that that
of Great Britain was not dissolved, while those of the colonies have repeatedly
incurred that sentence?

But your majesty, or your governors, have carried this power beyond every
limit known, or provided for, by the laws: After dissolving one house of representatives, they have refused to call another, so that, for a great length of time,
the legislature provided by the laws has been out of existence.[17] From the nature of things, every society must at all times possess within itself the sovereign
powers of legislation. The feelings of human nature revolt against the supposition of a state so situated as that it may not in any emergency provide against
dangers which perhaps threaten immediate ruin. While those bodies are in
existence to whom the people have delegated the powers of legislation, they
alone possess and may exercise those powers; but when they are dissolved by
the lopping off one or more of their branches, the power reverts to the people,
who may exercise it to unlimited extent, either assembling together in person,
sending deputies, or in any other way they may think proper. We forbear to
trace consequences further; the dangers are conspicuous with which this
practice is replete.

That we shall at this time also take notice of an error in the nature of our
land holdings, which crept in at a very early period of our settlement. The introduction of the feudal tenures into the kingdom of England, though antient,
is well enough understood to set this matter in a proper light. In the earlier
ages of the Saxon settlement feudal holdings were certainly altogether unknown; and very few, if any, had been introduced at the time of the Norman
conquest.[18] Our Saxon ancestors held their lands, as they did their personal

---

17. The colonial governor of Virginia repeatedly disbanded the House of Burgesses
from 1771–74 (see Introduction, p. xiii and note 7, above).
18. The Normans, led by William, Duke of Normandy in France (c. 1028–87), invaded England in 1066 and defeated the Anglo-Saxons at the Battle of Hastings.

property, in absolute dominion, disencumbered with any superior, answering nearly to the nature of those possessions which the feudalists term allodial.[19] William, the Norman,[20] first introduced that system generally. The lands which had belonged to those who fell in the battle of Hastings, and in the subsequent insurrections of his reign, formed a considerable proportion of the lands of the whole kingdom. These he granted out, subject to feudal duties, as did he also those of a great number of his new subjects, who, by persuasions or threats, were induced to surrender them for that purpose. But still much was left in the hands of his Saxon subjects; held of no superior, and not subject to feudal conditions. These, therefore, by express laws, enacted to render uniform the system of military defence, were made liable to the same military duties as if they had been feuds; and the Norman lawyers soon found means to saddle them also with all the other feudal burthens. But still they had not been surrendered to the king, they were not derived from his grant, and therefore they were not holden of him. A general principle, indeed, was introduced, that "all lands in England were held either mediately or immediately of the crown," but this was borrowed from those holdings, which were truly feudal, and only applied to others for the purposes of illustration. Feudal holdings were therefore but exceptions out of the Saxon laws of possession, under which all lands were held in absolute right. These, therefore, still form the basis, or ground-work, of the common law, to prevail wheresoever the exceptions have not taken place. America was not conquered by William the Norman, nor its lands surrendered to him, or any of his successors. Possessions there are undoubtedly of the allodial nature. Our ancestors, however, who migrated hither, were farmers, not lawyers. The fictitious principle that all lands belong originally to the king, they were early persuaded to believe real; and accordingly took grants of their own lands from the crown. And while the crown continued to grant for small sums, and on reasonable rents; there was no inducement to arrest the error, and lay it open to public view. But his majesty has lately taken on him to advance the terms of purchase, and of holding to the double of what they were; by which means the acquisition of lands being rendered difficult, the population of our country is likely to be checked. It is time, therefore, for us to lay this matter before his majesty, and to declare that he has no right to grant lands of himself. From the nature and purpose of civil institutions, all the lands within the limits which any particular society has circumscribed around itself are assumed by that society, and subject to their allotment only. This may be done by themselves, assembled

---

19. Land held freely, outright; not feudal.

20. William the Norman was also known as William the Conqueror. See note 18, above.

collectively, or by their legislature, to whom they may have delegated sovereign authority; and if they are alloted in neither of these ways, each individual of the society may appropriate to himself such lands as he finds vacant, and occupancy will give him title.

That in order to enforce the arbitrary measures before complained of, his majesty has from time to time sent among us large bodies of armed forces, not made up of the people here, nor raised by the authority of our laws. Did his majesty possess such a right as this, it might swallow up all our other rights whenever he should think proper. But his majesty has no right to land a single armed man on our shores, and those whom he sends here are liable to our laws made for the suppression and punishment of riots, routs, and unlawful assemblies; or are hostile bodies, invading us in defiance of law. When in the course of the late war it became expedient that a body of Hanoverian[21] troops should be brought over for the defence of Great Britain, his majesty's grandfather, our late sovereign, did not pretend to introduce them under any authority he possessed. Such a measure would have given just alarm to his subjects in Great Britain, whose liberties would not be safe if armed men of another country, and of another spirit, might be brought into the realm at any time without the consent of their legislature. He therefore applied to parliament, who passed an act for that purpose, limiting the number to be brought in and the time they were to continue. In like manner is his majesty restrained in every part of the empire. He possesses, indeed, the executive power of the laws in every state; but they are the laws of the particular state which he is to administer within that state, and not those of any one within the limits of another. Every state must judge for itself the number of armed men which they may safely trust among them, of whom they are to consist, and under what restrictions they shall be laid.

To render these proceedings still more criminal against our laws, instead of subjecting the military to the civil powers, his majesty has expressly made the civil subordinate to the military. But can his majesty thus put down all law under his feet? Can he erect a power superior to that which erected himself? He has done it indeed by force; but let him remember that force cannot give right.

That these are our grievances which we have thus laid before his majesty, with that freedom of language and sentiment which becomes a free people claiming their rights, as derived from the laws of nature, and not as the gift of their chief magistrate: Let those flatter who fear; it is not an American art. To

---

21. British royal house of German origin that succeeded the House of Stuart in 1714. When Stuart claimants tried unsuccessfully to regain the throne in 1715, George I called in Hanoverian soldiers.

give praise which is not due might be well from the venal,[22] but would ill beseem those who are asserting the rights of human nature. They know, and will therefore say, that kings are the servants, not the proprietors of the people. Open your breast, sire, to liberal and expanded thought. Let not the name of George the third be a blot in the page of history. You are surrounded by British counsellors, but remember that they are parties. You have no ministers for American affairs, because you have none taken from among us, nor amenable to the laws on which they are to give you advice. It behoves you, therefore, to think and to act for yourself and your people. The great principles of right and wrong are legible to every reader; to pursue them requires not the aid of many counsellors. The whole art of government consists in the art of being honest. Only aim to do your duty, and mankind will give you credit where you fail. No longer persevere in sacrificing the rights of one part of the empire to the inordinate desires of another; but deal out to all equal and impartial right. Let no act be passed by any one legislature which may infringe on the rights and liberties of another. This is the important post in which fortune has placed you, holding the balance of a great, if a well poised empire. This, sire, is the advice of your great American council, on the observance of which may perhaps depend your felicity and future fame, and the preservation of that harmony which alone can continue both to Great Britain and America the reciprocal advantages of their connection. It is neither our wish, nor our interest, to separate from her. We are willing, on our part, to sacrifice every thing which reason can ask to the restoration of that tranquillity for which all must wish. On their part, let them be ready to establish union and a generous plan. Let them name their terms, but let them be just. Accept of every commercial preference it is in our power to give for such things as we can raise for their use, or they make for ours. But let them not think to exclude us from going to other markets to dispose of those commodities which they cannot use, or to supply those wants which they cannot supply. Still less let it be proposed that our properties within our own territories shall be taxed or regulated by any power on earth but our own. The God who gave us life gave us liberty at the same time; the hand of force may destroy, but cannot disjoin them. This, sire, is our last, our determined resolution; and that you will be pleased to interpose with that efficacy which your earnest endeavours may ensure to procure redress of these our great grievances, to quiet the minds of your subjects in British America, against any apprehensions of future encroachment, to establish fraternal love and harmony through the whole empire, and that these may continue to the latest ages of time, is the fervent prayer of all British America!

---

22. Relating to corruption and successful bribery.

A DECLARATION BY THE REPRESENTATIVES OF THE UNITED STATES OF AMERICA, IN GENERAL CONGRESS ASSEMBLED[1]

(1776)[2]

When in the course of human events it becomes necessary for one people to dissolve the political bands which have connected them with another, and to assume among the powers of the earth the separate & equal station to which the laws of nature and of nature's God entitle them, a decent respect to the opinions of mankind requires that they should declare the causes which impel them to the separation.

We hold these truths to be self-evident: that all men are created equal; that they are endowed by their creator with inherent and [certain] inalienable rights; that among these are life, liberty, & the pursuit of happiness: that to secure these rights, governments are instituted among men, deriving their just powers from the consent of the governed; that whenever any form of government becomes destructive of these ends, it is the right of the people to alter or abolish it, & to institute new government, laying it's foundation on such principles, & organizing it's powers in such form, as to them shall seem most likely to effect their safety & happiness. Prudence indeed will dictate that governments long established should not be changed for light & transient causes; and accordingly all experience hath shown that mankind are more disposed to suffer while evils are sufferable, than to right themselves by abolishing the forms to which they are accustomed. But when a long train of abuses & usurpations begun at a distinguished period and pursuing invariably the same object, evinces a design to reduce them under absolute despotism, it is their right, it is their duty to throw off such government, & to provide new guards for their future security. Such has been the patient sufferance of these colonies; & such is now the necessity which constrains them to expunge [alter] their former systems of government. The history of the present king of Great Britain is a history of unremitting [repeated] injuries & usurpations, among which appears no solitary fact to contradict the uniform tenor of the rest but all have [all having] in direct object the establishment of an absolute

---

1. Underlined portions are Thomas Jefferson's original versions that were deleted by Congress. Bracketed portions are revisions made by Congress.

2. See Introduction, pp. xiv–xv.

tyranny over these states. To prove this let facts be submitted to a candid world for the truth of which we pledge a faith yet unsullied by falsehood.

He has refused his assent to laws the most wholesome & necessary for the public good.

He has forbidden his governors to pass laws of immediate & pressing importance, unless suspended in their operation till his assent should be obtained; & when so suspended, he has utterly neglected to attend to them.

He has refused to pass other laws for the accommodation of large districts of people, unless those people would relinquish the right of representation in the legislature, a right inestimable to them, & formidable to tyrants only.

He has called together legislative bodies at places unusual, uncomfortable, and distant from the depository of their public records, for the sole purpose of fatiguing them into compliance with his measures.

He has dissolved representative houses repeatedly & continually for opposing with manly firmness his invasions on the rights of the people.

He has refused for a long time after such dissolutions to cause others to be elected, whereby the legislative powers, incapable of annihilation, have returned to the people at large for their exercise, the state remaining in the meantime exposed to all the dangers of invasion from without & convulsions within.

He has endeavored to prevent the population of these states; for that purpose obstructing the laws for naturalization of foreigners, refusing to pass others to encourage their migrations hither, & raising the conditions of new appropriations of lands.

He has suffered [obstructed] the administration of justice totally to cease in some of these states [by] refusing his [assent to laws for establishing judiciary powers.

He has made our judges dependant on his will alone, for the tenure of their offices, & the amount & paiment of their salaries.

He has erected a multitude of new offices by a self assumed power and sent hither swarms of new officers to harass our people and eat out their substance.

He has kept among us in times of peace standing armies and ships of war without the consent of our legislatures.

He has affected to render the military independant of, & superior to the civil power.

He has combined with others to subject us to a jurisdiction foreign to our constitutions & unacknowledged by our laws, giving his assent to their acts of pretended legislation for quartering large bodies of armed troops among us; for protecting them by a mock-trial from punishment for any murders which they should commit on the inhabitants of these states; for cutting off our trade with all parts of the world; for imposing taxes on us without our consent; for depriving us [in many cases] of the benefits of trial by jury; for transporting us beyond seas to be tried for pretended offences; for abolishing the free system of English laws in a neighboring province, establishing therein an arbitrary government, and enlarging it's boundaries, so as to render it at once an example and fit instrument for introducing the same absolute rule into these states [colonies]; for taking away our charters, abolishing our most valuable laws, and altering fundamentally the forms of our governments; for suspending our own legislatures, & declaring themselves invested with power to legislate for us in all cases whatsoever.

He has abdicated government here withdrawing his governors, and declaring us out of his allegiance & protection. [by declaring us out of his protection, and waging war against us.]

He has plundered our seas, ravaged our coasts, burnt our towns, & destroyed the lives of our people.

He is at this time transporting large armies of foreign mercenaries to compleat the works of death, desolation & tyranny already begun with circumstances of cruelty and perfidy [scarcely paralleled in the most barbarous ages, & totally] unworthy the head of a civilized nation.

He has constrained our fellow citizens taken captive on the high seas to bear arms against their country, to become the executioners of their friends & brethren, or to fall themselves by their hands.

He has [excited domestic insurrection among us, & has] endeavored to bring on the inhabitants of our frontiers the merciless Indian savages, whose known rule of warfare is an undistinguished destruction of all ages, sexes, & conditions of existence.

He has incited treasonable insurrections of our fellow-citizens, with the allurements of forfeiture & confiscation of our property.

He has waged cruel war against human nature itself, violating it's most sacred rights of life and liberty in the persons of a distant people who never offended him, captivating & carrying them into slavery in another hemisphere, or to incur miserable death in their transportation thither. This piratical warfare, the opprobium of INFIDEL powers, is the warfare of the CHRISTIAN king of Great Britain. Determined to keep open a market where MEN should be bought & sold, he has prostituted his negative for suppressing every legislative attempt to prohibit or to restrain this execrable commerce. And that this assemblage of horrors might want no fact of distinguished die, he is now exciting those very people to rise in arms among us, and to purchase that liberty of which he has deprived them, by murdering the people on whom he also obtruded them: thus paying off former crimes committed against the LIBERTIES of one people, with crimes which he urges them to commit against the LIVES of another.

In every stage of these oppressions we have petitioned for redress in the most humble terms: our repeated petitions have been answered only by repeated injuries.

A prince whose character is thus marked by every act which may define a tyrant is unfit to be the ruler of a [free] people <u>who mean to be free. Future ages will scarcely believe that the hardiness of one man adventured, within the short compass of twelve years only, to lay a foundation so broad & so undisguised for tyranny over a people fostered & fixed in principles of freedom.</u>

Nor have we been wanting in attentions to our British brethren. We have warned them from time to time of attempts by their legislature to extend <u>a</u> [an unwarrantable] jurisdiction over <u>these our states</u> [us]. We have reminded them of the circumstances of our emigration & settlement here, <u>no one of which could warrant so strange a pretension: that these were effected at the expense of our own blood & treasure, unassisted by the wealth or the strength of Great</u> Britain: <u>that in constituting indeed our several forms of government, we had adopted one common king, thereby laying a foundation for perpetual league & amity with them: but that submission to their parliament was no part of our constitution, nor ever in idea, if history may be credited: and,</u> we [have] appealed to their native justice and magnanimity <u>as well as</u> [and we have conjured them by] to the ties of our common kindred to disavow these usurpations which <u>were likely to</u> [would inevitably] interrupt our connection and correspondence. They too have been deaf to the voice of justice & of consanguinity, <u>and when occasions have been given them, by the regular course of their laws, of removing from their councils the disturbers of our harmony, they have, by their free election, re-established them in power. At this very time too they are permitting their chief magistrate to send over not only soldiers of our common blood, but Scotch & foreign mercenaries to invade & destroy us. These facts have given the last stab to agonizing affection, and manly spirit bids us to renounce forever these unfeeling brethren. We must</u> [We must therefore] <u>endeavor to forget our former love for them, and hold them as we hold the rest of mankind, enemies in war, in peace friends. We might have been a free and a great people together; but a communication of grandeur & of freedom it seems is below their dignity. Be it so, since they will have it. The road to happiness & to glory is open to us too. We will tread it apart from them, and</u> acquiesce in the necessity which denounces our <u>eternal</u> separation [and hold them as we hold the rest of mankind, enemies in war, in peace friends.]!

We therefore the representatives of the United States of America in General Congress assembled do in the name & by authority of the good people of these states reject & renounce all allegiance & subjection to the kings of Great Britain & all others who may hereafter claim by, through or under them: we utterly dissolve all political connection which may heretofore have subsisted between us & the people or parliament of Great Britain: & finally we do assert & declare these colonies to be free & independent states, & that as free & independent states, they have full power to levy war, conclude peace, contract alliances, establish commerce, & to do all other acts & things which independent states may of right do.

And for the support of this declaration we mutually pledge to each other our lives, our fortunes, & our sacred honor.

[We therefore the representatives of the United States of America in General Congress assembled, appealing to the supreme judge of the world for the rectitude of our intentions, do in the name, & by the authority of the good people of these colonies, solemnly publish & declare that these united colonies are & of right ought to be free & independent states; that they are absolved from all allegiance to the British crown, and that all political connection between them & the state of Great Britain is, & ought to be, totally dissolved; & that as free & independent states they have full power to levy war, conclude peace, contract alliances, establish commerce & to do all other acts & things which independent states may of right do.

And for the support of this declaration, with a firm reliance on the protection of divine providence we mutually pledge to each other our lives, our fortunes, & our sacred honor.]

THE DECLARATION OF INDEPENDENCE (AS ADOPTED BY CONGRESS)

(July 4, 1776)

The unanimous Declaration of the thirteen united States of America

When, in the Course of human events, it becomes necessary for one people to dissolve the political bands which have connected them with another, and to assume among the powers of the earth, the separate and equal station to which the Laws of Nature and of Nature's God entitle them, a decent respect to the opinions of mankind requires that they should declare the causes which impel them to the separation.

We hold these truths to be self-evident, that all men are created equal, that they are endowed by their Creator with certain unalienable Rights, that among these are Life, Liberty and the pursuit of Happiness. —That to secure these rights, Governments are instituted among Men, deriving their just powers from the consent of the governed, —That whenever any Form of Government becomes destructive of these ends, it is the Right of the People to alter or to abolish it, and to institute new Government, laying its foundation on such principles and organizing its powers in such form, as to them shall seem most likely to effect their Safety and Happiness. Prudence, indeed, will dictate that Governments long established should not be changed for light and transient causes; and accordingly all experience hath shewn, that mankind are more disposed to suffer, while evils are sufferable, than to right themselves by abolishing the forms to which they are accustomed. But when a long train of abuses and usurpations, pursuing invariably the same Object evinces a design to reduce them under absolute Despotism, it is their right, it is their duty, to throw off such Government, and to provide new Guards for their future security. —Such has been the patient sufferance of these Colonies; and such is now the necessity which constrains them to alter their former Systems of Government. The history of the present King of Great Britain is a history of repeated injuries and usurpations, all having in direct object the establishment of an absolute Tyranny over these States. To prove this, let Facts be submitted to a candid world.

He has refused his Assent to Laws, the most wholesome and necessary for the public good.

He has forbidden his Governors to pass Laws of immediate and pressing importance, unless suspended in their operation till his Assent should be obtained; and when so suspended, he has utterly neglected to attend to them.

He has refused to pass other Laws for the accommodation of large districts of people, unless those people would relinquish the right of Representation in the Legislature, a right inestimable to them and formidable to tyrants only.

He has called together legislative bodies at places unusual, uncomfortable, and distant from the depository of their public Records, for the sole purpose of fatiguing them into compliance with his measures.

He has dissolved Representative Houses repeatedly, for opposing with manly firmness his invasions on the rights of the people.

He has refused for a long time, after such dissolutions, to cause others to be elected; whereby the Legislative powers, incapable of Annihilation, have returned to the People at large for their exercise; the State remaining in the mean time exposed to all the dangers of invasion from without, and convulsions within.

He has endeavoured to prevent the population of these States; for that purpose obstructing the Laws for Naturalization of Foreigners; refusing to pass others to encourage their migrations hither, and raising the conditions of new Appropriations of Lands.

He has obstructed the Administration of Justice, by refusing his Assent to Laws for establishing Judiciary powers.

He has made Judges dependent on his Will alone, for the tenure of their offices, and the amount and payment of their salaries.

He has erected a multitude of New Offices, and sent hither swarms of Officers to harrass our people, and eat out their substance.

He has kept among us, in times of peace, Standing Armies without the Consent of our legislatures.

He has affected to render the Military independent of and superior to the Civil power.

He has combined with others to subject us to a jurisdiction foreign to our constitution, and unacknowledged by our laws; giving his Assent to their Acts of pretended Legislation:

For Quartering large bodies of armed troops among us:

For protecting them, by a mock Trial, from punishment for any Murders which they should commit on the Inhabitants of these States:

For cutting off our Trade with all parts of the world:

For imposing Taxes on us without our Consent:

For depriving us in many cases, of the benefits of Trial by Jury:

For transporting us beyond Seas to be tried for pretended offences:

For abolishing the free System of English Laws in a neighbouring Province, establishing therein an Arbitrary government, and enlarging its Boundaries so as to render it at once an example and fit instrument for introducing the same absolute rule into these Colonies:

For taking away our Charters, abolishing our most valuable Laws, and altering fundamentally the Forms of our Governments:

For suspending our own Legislatures, and declaring themselves invested with power to legislate for us in all cases whatsoever.

He has abdicated Government here, by declaring us out of his Protection and waging War against us.

He has plundered our seas, ravaged our Coasts, burnt our towns, and destroyed the lives of our people.

He is at this time transporting large Armies of foreign Mercenaries to compleat the works of death, desolation and tyranny, already begun with circumstances of Cruelty & perfidy scarcely paralleled in the most barbarous ages, and totally unworthy the Head of a civilized nation.

He has constrained our fellow Citizens taken Captive on the high Seas to bear Arms against their Country, to become the executioners of their friends and Brethren, or to fall themselves by their Hands.

He has excited domestic insurrections amongst us, and has endeavoured to bring on the inhabitants of our frontiers, the merciless Indian Savages, whose known rule of warfare, is an undistinguished destruction of all ages, sexes and conditions.

In every stage of these Oppressions We have Petitioned for Redress in the most humble terms: Our repeated Petitions have been answered only by repeated injury. A Prince whose character is thus marked by every act which may define a Tyrant, is unfit to be the ruler of a free people.

Nor have We been wanting in attentions to our Brittish brethren. We have warned them from time to time of attempts by their legislature to extend an unwarrantable jurisdiction over us. We have reminded them of the circumstances of our emigration and settlement here. We have appealed to their native justice and magnanimity, and we have conjured them by the ties of our common kindred to disavow these usurpations, which, would inevitably interrupt our connections and correspondence. They too have been deaf to the voice of justice and of consanguinity. We must, therefore, acquiesce in the necessity, which denounces our Separation, and hold them, as we hold the rest of mankind, Enemies in War, in Peace Friends.

We, therefore, the Representatives of the united States of America, in General Congress, Assembled, appealing to the Supreme Judge of the world for the rectitude of our intentions, do, in the Name, and by Authority of the good People of these Colonies, solemnly publish and declare, That these United Colonies are, and of Right ought to be Free and Independent States; that they are Absolved from all Allegiance to the British Crown, and that all political connection between them and the State of Great Britain, is and ought to be totally dissolved; and that as Free and Independent States, they have full Power to levy War, conclude Peace, contract Alliances, establish Commerce, and to do all other Acts and Things which Independent States may of right do. And for the support of this Declaration, with a firm reliance on the protection of divine Providence, we mutually pledge to each other our Lives, our Fortunes and our sacred Honor.

John Hancock

New Hampshire
Josiah Bartlett
William Whipple
Matthew Thornton

Massachusetts
John Hancock
Samuel Adams
Robert Treat Paine
Elbridge Gerry

Rhode Island
Stephen Hopkins
William Ellery

Connecticut
Roger Sherman
Samuel Huntington
William Williams
Oliver Wolcott

New York
William Floyd
Philip Livingston
Francis Lewis
Lewis Morris

New Jersey
Richard Stockton
John Witherspoon
Francis Hopkinson
John Hart
Abraham Clark

Pennsylvania
Robert Morris
Benjamin Rush
Benjamin Franklin
John Morton
George Clymer
James Smith
George Taylor
James Wilson
George Ross

Delaware
Caesar Rodney
George Read
Thomas McKean

Maryland
Samuel Chase
William Paca
Thomas Stone
Charles Carroll of Carrollton

Virginia
George Wythe
Richard Henry Lee
Thomas Jefferson
Benjamin Harrison
Thomas Nelson, Jr.
Francis Lightfoot Lee
Carter Braxton

North Carolina
William Hooper
Joseph Hewes
John Penn

South Carolina
Edward Rutledge
Thomas Heyward, Jr.
Thomas Lynch, Jr.
Arthur Middleton

Georgia
Button Gwinnett
Lyman Hall
George Walton

A BILL FOR ESTABLISHING RELIGIOUS FREEDOM

(1777)[1]

SECTION I.   Well aware that the opinions and belief of men depend not on their own will, but follow involuntarily the evidence proposed to their minds; that Almighty God hath created the mind free, and manifested his supreme will that free it shall remain by making it altogether insusceptible of restraint; that all attempts to influence it by temporal punishments, or burthens, or by civil incapacitations, tend only to beget habits of hypocrisy and meanness, and are a departure from the plan of the holy author of our religion, who being lord both of body and mind, yet chose not to propagate it by coercions on either, as was in his Almighty power to do, but to extend it by its influence on reason alone; that the impious presumption of legislators and rulers, civil as well as ecclesiastical, who, being themselves but fallible and uninspired men, have assumed dominion over the faith of others, setting up their own opinions and modes of thinking as the only true and infallible, and as such endeavoring to impose them on others, hath established and maintained false religions over the greatest part of the world and through all time: That to compel a man to furnish contributions of money for the propagation of opinions which he disbelieves and abhors, is sinful and tyrannical; that even the forcing him to support this or that teacher of his own religious persuasion, is depriving him of the comfortable liberty of giving his contributions to the particular pastor whose morals he would make his pattern, and whose powers he feels most persuasive to righteousness; and is withdrawing from the ministry those temporary rewards, which proceeding from an approbation of their personal conduct, are an additional incitement to earnest and unremitting labours for the instruction of mankind; that our civil rights have no dependance on our religious opinions, any more than our opinions in physics or geometry; that therefore the proscribing any citizen as unworthy the public confidence by laying upon him an incapacity of being called to offices of trust and emolument,[2] unless he profess or renounce this or that religious opinion, is

---

1. This bill, drafted by Jefferson in 1777, was first debated by the Virginia Legislature in 1779. It was enacted, after significant revision, in 1786. See Introduction, p. xv.
2. Payment or compensation.

depriving him injuriously of those privileges and advantages to which, in common with his fellow citizens, he has a natural right; that it tends also to corrupt the principles of that very religion it is meant to encourage, by bribing, with a monopoly of worldly honours and emoluments, those who will externally profess and conform to it; that though indeed these are criminal who do not withstand such temptation, yet neither are those innocent who lay the bait in their way; that the opinions of men are not the object of civil government, nor under its jurisdiction; that to suffer the civil magistrate to intrude his powers into the field of opinion and to restrain the profession or propagation of principles on supposition of their ill tendency is a dangerous falacy, which at once destroys all religious liberty, because he being of course judge of that tendency will make his opinions the rule of judgment, and approve or condemn the sentiments of others only as they shall square with or differ from his own; that it is time enough for the rightful purposes of civil government for its officers to interfere when principles break out into overt acts against peace and good order; and finally, that truth is great and will prevail if left to herself; that she is the proper and sufficient antagonist to error, and has nothing to fear from the conflict unless by human interposition disarmed of her natural weapons, free argument and debate; errors ceasing to be dangerous when it is permitted freely to contradict them.

SECTION II.   We the General Assembly of Virginia do enact that no man shall be compelled to frequent or support any religious worship, place, or ministry whatsoever, nor shall be enforced, restrained, molested, or burthened in his body or goods, nor shall otherwise suffer, on account of his religious opinions or belief; but that all men shall be free to profess, and by argument to maintain, their opinions in matters of religion, and that the same shall in no wise diminish, enlarge, or affect their civil capacities.

SECTION III.   And though we well know that this Assembly, elected by the people for the ordinary purposes of legislation only, have no power to restrain the acts of succeeding Assemblies, constituted with powers equal to our own, and that therefore to declare this act irrevocable would be of no effect in law; yet we are free to declare, and do declare, that the rights hereby asserted are of the natural rights of mankind, and that if any act shall be hereafter passed to repeal the present or to narrow its operation, such act will be an infringement of natural right.

REPORT ON GOVERNMENT FOR WESTERN TERRITORY[1]

(Mar. 1, 1784)

THE COMMITTEE appointed to prepare a plan for the temporary Government of the Western territory have agreed to the following resolutions:

Resolved that the territory ceded or to be ceded by Individual States to the United States whensoever the same shall have been purchased of the Indian Inhabitants & offered for sale by the U. S. shall be formed into distinct States bounded in the following manner as nearly as such cessions will admit, that is to say; Northwardly & Southwardly by parallels of latitude so that each state shall comprehend from South to North two degrees of latitude beginning to count from the completion of thirty-one degrees North of the equator, but any territory Northwardly of the 47th degree shall make part of the state—below, and Eastwardly & Westwardly they shall be bounded, those on the Mississippi by that river on one side and the meridian of the lowest point of the rapids of Ohio on the other; and those adjoining on the East by the same meridian on their Western side, and on their eastern by the meridian of the Western cape of the mouth of the Great Kanhaway. And the territory eastward of this last meridian between the Ohio, Lake Erie & Pennsylvania shall be one state.

That the settlers within the territory so to be purchased & offered for sale shall, either on their own petition, or on the order of Congress, receive authority from them, with appointments of time and place for their free males of full age to meet together for the purpose of establishing a temporary government, to adopt the constitution & laws of any one of these states, so that such laws nevertheless shall be subject to alteration by their ordinary legislature, and to erect, subject to a like alteration counties or townships for the election of members for their legislature.

That such temporary government shall only continue in force in any state until it shall have acquired 20,000 free inhabitants, when, giving due proof thereof to Congress, they shall receive from them authority with appointments of time and place to call a Convention of representatives to establish a permanent Constitution & Government for themselves.

---

1. See Introduction, pp. xvii, xxiv. The plan was not adopted in this form. Although Jefferson's draft proposed a ban on slavery and involuntary servitude in the federal territories after 1800, the final 1787 ordinance banned slavery from the outset.

Provided that both the temporary & permanent Governments be established on these principles as their basis. 1, That they shall forever remain a
part of the United States of America. 2, That in their persons, property &
territory, they shall be subject to the Government of the United States in
Congress assembled and to the articles of confederation in all those cases
in which the original states shall be so subject. 3, That they shall be subject
to pay a part of the federal debts contracted or to be contracted to be appor-
tioned on them by Congress, according to the same common rule and measure by which apportionments thereof shall be made on the other states.
4, That their respective Governments shall be in republican forms, and shall
admit no person to be a citizen, who holds any hereditary title. 5, That after
the year 1800 of the Christian æra, there shall be neither slavery nor involuntary servitude in any of the said states, otherwise than in punishment of
crimes, whereof the party shall have been duly convicted to have been personally guilty.

That whenever any of the sd states shall have, of free inhabitants as many
as shall then be in any one the least numerous of the thirteen original states,
such state shall be admitted by it's delegates into the Congress of the United
States, on an equal footing with the said original states: After which the assent
of two thirds of the United States in Congress assembled shall be requisite in
all those cases, wherein by the Confederation the assent of nine States is now
required. Provided the consent of nine states to such admission may be obtained according to the eleventh of the Articles of Confederation. Until such
admission by their delegates into Congress, any of the said states, after the establishment of their temporary Government, shall have authority to keep a sit-
ting Member in Congress, with a right of debating, but not of voting.

That the territory Northward of the 45th degree, that is to say of the completion of 45° from the Equator & extending to the Lake of the Woods, shall
be called SYLVANIA.

That of the territory under the 45th & 44th degrees that which lies Westward of Lake Michigan shall be called MICHIGANIA, and that which is Eastward
thereof within the peninsula formed by the lakes & waters of Michigan,
Huron, St. Clair and Erie, shall be called CHERRONESUS, and shall include
any part of the peninsula which may extend above the 45th degree.

Of the territory under the 43d & 42d degrees, that to the Westward thro'
which the Assenisipi or Rock river runs shall be called ASSENISPIA, and that to
the Eastward in which are the fountains of the Muskingum, the two Miamis
of Ohio, the Wabash, the Illinois, the Miami of the lake and Sandusky rivers,
shall be called METROPOTAMIA.

Of the territory which lies under the 41st & 40th degrees the Western, thro
which the river Illinois runs, shall be called ILLINOIA; that next adjoining to

the Eastward SARATOGA, and that between this last & Pennsylvania & extending from the Ohio to Lake Erie shall be called WASHINGTON.

Of the territory which lies under the 39th & 38th degrees to which shall be added so much of the point of land within the fork of the Ohio & Missisipi as lies under the 37th degree, that to the Westward within & adjacent to which are the confluences of the rivers Wabash, Shawanee, Tanisse, Ohio, Illinois, Missisipi & Missouri, shall be called POLYPOTAMIA, and that to the Eastward farther up the Ohio otherwise called the PELISIPSI shall be called PELISIPIA.

That the preceding articles shall be formed into a charter of Compact, shall be duly executed by the President of the U.S. in Congress assembled under his hand and the seal of the United States, shall be promulgated, and shall stand as fundamental constitutions between the thirteen original States, & those now newly described unalterable but by the joint consent of the U.S. in Congress assembled and of the particular state within which such alteration is proposed to be made.

OPINION ON THE CONSTITUTIONALITY OF A NATIONAL BANK

(Feb. 15, 1791)

The bill for establishing a National Bank[1] undertakes among other things: —

1. To form the subscribers into a corporation.

2. To enable them in their corporate capacities to receive grants of land; and so far is against the laws of *Mortmain.*[*2] Though the Constitution controls the laws of *Mortmain* so far as to permit Congress itself to hold land for certain purposes, yet not so far as to permit them to communicate a similar right to other corporate bodies.

3. To make alien subscribers capable of holding lands; and so far is against the laws of *Alienage.*[3]

4. To transmit these lands, on the death of a proprietor, to a certain line of successors; and so far changes the course of *Descents.*[4]

---

[*]Though the Constitution controls the laws of Mortmain so far as to permit Congress itself to hold land for certain purposes, yet not so far as to permit them to communicate a similar right to other corporate bodies.

---

1. As the first Secretary of the Treasury, Alexander Hamilton (c. 1755–1804) developed a far-reaching plan to restore financial health to the new national government. Among his proposals was a plan for the government to incorporate a national bank. The bank was to be a hybrid, owned largely by private shareholders but backed by public authority. It would have the power, among other things, to control the money supply, extend credit to the government and private enterprises, collect revenues, and pay debts. Jefferson, then Secretary of State, strongly opposed the establishment of the bank on both constitutional and political grounds. He argued that the Constitution gave no power to Congress to charter a bank. He read the Necessary and Proper clause in Article I, Section 8 narrowly to mean that Congress had no power to act unless absolutely necessary. Moreover, he objected that the sale of stock would benefit wealthy (and mostly northern) citizens, while encouraging an unhealthy spirit of speculation inimical to republican government. A bitter struggle erupted between the supporters of Hamilton and Jefferson, though the measure eventually passed. The constitutionality of the bank was later affirmed by Chief Justice John Marshall (a distant relative and political enemy of Jefferson's) in *McCulloch v. Md.* in 1819. See note 2, p. 182, for more information on Hamilton.

2. Perpetual ownership of real estate by institutions such as churches that cannot transfer or sell it.

3. Laws pertaining to the right of foreigners to own land.

4. Laws pertaining to inheritance.

5. To put the lands out of the reach of forfeiture or escheat; and so far is against the laws of *Forfeiture and Escheat*.[5]

6. To transmit personal chattels[6] to successors in a certain line; and so far is against the laws of *Distribution*.[7]

7. To give them the sole and exclusive right of banking under the national authority; and so far is against the laws of Monopoly.[8]

8. To communicate to them a power to make laws paramount to the laws of the States: for so they must be construed, to protect the institution from the control of the State legislatures; and so, probably, they will be construed.

I consider the foundation of the Constitution as laid on this ground: That "all powers not delegated to the United States, by the Constitution, nor prohibited by it to the States, are reserved to the States or to the people." [XIIth Amendment][9] To take a single step beyond the boundaries thus specially drawn around the powers of Congress, is to take possession of a boundless field of power, no longer susceptible of any definition.

The incorporation of a bank, and the powers assumed by this bill, have not, in my opinion, been delegated to the United States, by the Constitution.

I. They are not among the powers specially enumerated: for these are: 1st. A power to lay taxes for the purpose of paying the debts of the United States; but no debt is paid by this bill, nor any tax laid. Were it a bill to raise money, its origination in the Senate would condemn it by the Constitution.

2d. "To borrow money." But this bill neither borrows money nor ensures the borrowing it. The proprietors of the bank will be just as free as any other money holders, to lend or not to lend their money to the public. The operation proposed in the bill, first, to lend them two millions, and then to borrow them back again, cannot change the nature of the latter act, which will still be a payment, and not a loan, call it by what name you please.

3. To "regulate commerce with foreign nations, and among the States, and with the Indian tribes." To erect a bank, and to regulate commerce, are very different acts. He who erects a bank, creates a subject of commerce in its bills; so does he who makes a bushel of wheat, or digs a dollar out of the

---

5. In English common law, a person convicted of treason forfeited his lands and property directly to the king. In other crimes, a convicted felon's land was returned (escheated) to his lord, though his chattel was given to the king. The distinction between forfeiture to the king and escheat to the lord emerged only gradually.

6. An article of movable personal property.

7. Laws governing estate distribution.

8. Laws pertaining to the circumstances under which a company or group may exercise exclusive control over a commercial activity.

9. Although Jefferson here refers to the 12th Amendment, this is actually the 10th Amendment as ratified by the states.

mines; yet neither of these persons regulates commerce thereby. To make a thing which may be bought and sold, is not to prescribe regulations for buying and selling. Besides, if this was an exercise of the power of regulating commerce, it would be void, as extending as much to the internal commerce of every State, as to its external. For the power given to Congress by the Constitution does not extend to the internal regulation of the commerce of a State, (that is to say of the commerce between citizen and citizen,) which remain exclusively with its own legislature; but to its external commerce only, that is to say, its commerce with another State, or with foreign nations, or with the Indian tribes. Accordingly the bill does not propose the measure as a regulation of trade, but as "productive of considerable advantages to trade." Still less are these powers covered by any other of the special enumerations.

II. Nor are they within either of the general phrases, which are the two following: —

1. To lay taxes to provide for the general welfare of the United States, that is to say, "to lay taxes for *the purpose* of providing for the general welfare." For the laying of taxes is the power, and the general welfare the *purpose* for which the power is to be exercised. They are not to lay taxes *ad libitum*[10] *for any purpose they please*; but only *to pay the debts or provide for the welfare of the Union*. In like manner, they are *not to do anything they please* to provide for the general welfare, but only to *lay taxes* for that purpose. To consider the latter phrase, not as describing the purpose of the first, but as giving a distinct and independent power to do any act they please, which might be for the good of the Union, would render all the preceding and subsequent enumerations of power completely useless.

It would reduce the whole instrument to a single phrase, that of instituting a Congress with power to do whatever would be for the good of the United States; and, as they would be the sole judges of the good or evil, it would be also a power to do whatever evil they please.

It is an established rule of construction where a phrase will bear either of two meanings, to give it that which will allow some meaning to the other parts of the instrument, and not that which would render all the others useless. Certainly no such universal power was meant to be given them. It was intended to lace them up straitly within the enumerated powers, and those without which, as means, these powers could not be carried into effect. It is known that the very power now proposed *as a means* was rejected as *an end* by the Convention which formed the Constitution. A proposition was made to them to authorize Congress to open canals, and an amendatory one to empower them to incorporate. But the whole was rejected, and one of the reasons for rejection urged in debate was, that then they would have a power to erect a

---

10. At the discretion of the performer, "ad lib."

bank, which would render the great cities, where there were prejudices and jealousies on the subject, adverse to the reception of the Constitution.

2. The second general phrase is, "to make all laws *necessary* and proper for carrying into execution the enumerated powers." But they can all be carried into execution without a bank. A bank therefore is not *necessary*, and consequently not authorized by this phrase.

It has been urged that a bank will give great facility or convenience in the collection of taxes. Suppose this were true: yet the Constitution allows only the means which are "*necessary*," not those which are merely "convenient" for effecting the enumerated powers. If such a latitude of construction be allowed to this phrase as to give any non-enumerated power, it will go to every one, for there is not one which ingenuity may not torture into a *convenience* in some instance *or other*, to *some one* of so long a list of enumerated powers. It would swallow up all the delegated powers, and reduce the whole to one power, as before observed. Therefore it was that the Constitution restrained them to the *necessary* means, that is to say, to those means without which the grant of power would be nugatory.[11]

But let us examine this convenience and see what it is. The report on this subject, page 3, states the only *general* convenience to be, the preventing the transportation and re-transportation of money between the States and the treasury, (for I pass over the increase of circulating medium, ascribed to it as a want, and which, according to my ideas of paper money, is clearly a demerit.) Every State will have to pay a sum of tax money into the treasury; and the treasury will have to pay, in every State, a part of the interest on the public debt, and salaries to the officers of government resident in that State. In most of the States there will still be a surplus of tax money to come up to the seat of government for the officers residing there. The payments of interest and salary in each State may be made by treasury orders on the State collector. This will take up the greater part of the money he has collected in his State, and consequently prevent the great mass of it from being drawn out of the State. If there be a balance of commerce in favor of that State against the one in which the government resides, the surplus of taxes will be remitted by the bills of exchange drawn for that commercial balance. And so it must be if there was a bank. But if there be no balance of commerce, either direct or circuitous, all the banks in the world could not bring up the surplus of taxes but in the form of money. Treasury orders then, and bills of exchange may prevent the displacement of the main mass of the money collected, without the aid of any bank; and where these fail, it cannot be prevented even with that aid.

Perhaps, indeed, bank bills may be a more *convenient* vehicle than treasury orders. But a little *difference* in the degree of *convenience*, cannot constitute

---

11. Trifling, without value.

the necessity, which the constitution makes the ground for assuming any non-enumerated power.

Besides; the existing banks will, without a doubt, enter into arrangements for lending their agency, and the more favorable, as there will be a competition among them for it; whereas the bill delivers us up bound to the national bank, who are free to refuse all arrangement, but on their own terms, and the public not free, on such refusal, to employ any other bank. That of Philadelphia, I believe, now does this business, by their post-notes, which, by an arrangement with the treasury, are paid by any State collector to whom they are presented. This expedient alone suffices to prevent the existence of that *necessity* which may justify the assumption of a non-enumerated power as a means for carrying into effect an enumerated one. The thing may be done, and has been done, and well done, without this assumption; therefore, it does not stand on that degree of *necessity* which can honestly justify it.

It may be said that a bank whose bills would have a currency all over the States, would be more convenient than one whose currency is limited to a single State. So it would be still more convenient that there should be a bank, whose bills should have a currency all over the world. But it does not follow from this superior conveniency, that there exists anywhere a power to establish such a bank; or that the world may not go on very well without it.

Can it be thought that the Constitution intended that for a shade or two of *convenience*, more or less, Congress should be authorised to break down the most ancient and fundamental laws of the several States; such as those against Mortmain, the laws of Alienage, the rules of descent, the acts of distribution, the laws of escheat and forfeiture, the laws of monopoly? Nothing but a necessity invincible by any other means, can justify such a prostitution of laws, which constitute the pillars of our whole system of jurisprudence. Will Congress be too straight-laced to carry the constitution into honest effect, unless they may pass over the foundation-laws of the State government for the slightest convenience of theirs?

The negative of the President is the shield provided by the constitution to protect against the invasions of the legislature: 1. The right of the Executive. 2. Of the Judiciary. 3. Of the States and State legislatures. The present is the case of a right remaining exclusively with the States, and consequently one of those intended by the Constitution to be placed under its protection.

It must be added, however, that unless the President's mind on a view of everything which is urged for and against this bill, is tolerably clear that it is unauthorised by the Constitution; if the pro and the con hang so even as to balance his judgment, a just respect for the wisdom of the legislature would naturally decide the balance in favor of their opinion. It is chiefly for cases where they are clearly misled by error, ambition, or interest, that the Constitution has placed a check in the negative of the President.

OPINION ON THE FRENCH TREATIES

(Apr. 28, 1793)

I proceed, in compliance with the requisition of the President,[1] to give an opinion in writing on the general Question, Whether the U S. have a right to renounce their treaties with France, or to hold them suspended till the government of that country shall be established?[2]

In the Consultation at the President's on the 19th inst. the Secretary of the Treasury took the following positions & consequences. 'France was a monarchy when we entered into treaties with it: but it has now declared itself a Republic, & is preparing a Republican form of government. As it may issue in a Republic, or a Military despotism, or in something else which may possibly render our alliance with it dangerous to ourselves, we have a right of election to renounce the treaty altogether, or to declare it suspended till their government shall be settled in the form it is ultimately to take; and then we may judge whether we will call the treaties into operation again, or declare them forever null. Having that right of election now, if we receive their minister without any qualifications, it will amount to an act of election to continue the treaties; & if the change they are undergoing should issue in a form which should bring danger on us, we shall not be then free to renounce them. To elect to continue them is equivalent to the making a new treaty at this time in the same form, that is to say, with a clause of guarantee; but to make a treaty with a clause of guarantee, during a war, is a departure from neutrality, and would make us associates in the war. To renounce or suspend the treaties therefore is a necessary act of neutrality.'

If I do not subscribe to the soundness of this reasoning, I do most fully to its ingenuity. —I shall now lay down the principles which according to my understanding govern the case.

I consider the people who constitute a society or nation as the source of all authority in that nation, as free to transact their common concerns by any

---

1. George Washington (1732–99) served as commander-in-chief of the Continental Army during the American Revolution and as the nation's first president (1789–97).

2. In 1778, the United States entered into a treaty of friendship with France (see note 6, p. 204). But in the turmoil following the outbreak of the French Revolution (1789), Secretary of State Thomas Jefferson and Secretary of the Treasury Alexander Hamilton (1757–1804) disagreed over whether the United States should continue to honor its treaty obligations. See Introduction, pp. xix–xx.

agents they think proper, to change these agents individually, or the organisation of them in form or function whenever they please: that all the acts done by those agents under the authority of the nation, are the acts of the nation, are obligatory on them, & enure[3] to their use, & can in no wise be annulled or affected by any change in the form of the government, or of the persons administering it. Consequently the Treaties between the U S. and France, were not treaties between the U.S. & Louis Capet,[4] but between the two nations of America & France, and the nations remaining in existance, tho' both of them have since changed their forms of government, the treaties are not annulled by these changes.

The Law of nations, by which this question is to be determined, is composed of three branches. 1. The Moral law of our nature. 2. The Usages of nations. 3. Their special Conventions. The first of these only, concerns this question, that is to say the Moral law to which Man has been subjected by his creator, & of which his feelings, or Conscience as it is sometimes called, are the evidence with which his creator has furnished him. The Moral duties which exist between individual and individual in a state of nature, accompany them into a state of society & the aggregate of the duties of all the individuals composing the society constitutes the duties of that society towards any other; so that between society & society the same moral duties exist as did between the individuals composing them while in an unassociated state, their maker not having released them from those duties on their forming themselves into a nation. Compacts then between nation & nation are obligatory on them by the same moral law which obliges individuals to observe their compacts. There are circumstances however which sometimes excuse the non-performance of contracts between man & man: so are there also between nation & nation. When performance, for instance, becomes *impossible*, non-performance is not immoral. So if performance becomes *self-destructive* to the party, the law of self-preservation overrules the laws of obligation to others. For the reality of these principles I appeal to the true fountains of evidence, the head & heart of every rational & honest man. It is there Nature has written her moral laws, & where every man may read them for himself. He will never read there the permission to annul his obligations for a time, or for ever, whenever they become 'dangerous, useless, or disagreeable.' Certainly not when merely *useless* or *disagreeable*, as seems to be said in an authority which has been quoted, Vattel.[5] 2. 197, and tho he may under certain degrees of danger, yet the danger must

---

3. To become accustomed to something.

4. His Royal Highness Louis XVI, King of France 1774–92.

5. Emmerich de Vattel (1714–67): Swiss philosopher, jurist, and author of *Le Droit de Gens; ou Principes de la loi naturelle appliquee a la conduitedes nations et des souverains* (*The Law of Nations or the Principles of the Law of Nature Applied to the Conduct and Affairs of Nations and Sovereigns*), 1758.

be imminent, & the degree great. Of these, it is true, that nations are to be judges for themselves, since no one nation has a right to sit in judgment over another. But the tribunal of our consciences remains, & that also of the opinion of the world. These will revise the sentence we pass in our own case, & as we respect these, we must see that in judging ourselves we have honestly done the part of impartial & vigorous judges.

But Reason, which gives this right of self-liberation from a contract in certain cases, has subjected it to certain just limitations.

I. The danger which absolves us must be great, inevitable & imminent. Is such the character of that now apprehended from our treaties with France? What is that danger. 1. Is it that if their government issues in a military despotism, an alliance with them may taint us with despotic principles? But their government, when we allied ourselves to it, was a perfect despotism, civil & military, yet the treaties were made in that very state of things, & therefore that danger can furnish no just cause. 2. Is it that their government may issue in a republic, and too much strengthen our republican principles? But this is the hope of the great mass of our constituents, & not their dread. They do not look with longing to the happy mean of a limited monarchy. 3. But says the doctrine I am combating, the change the French are undergoing may possibly end in something we know not what, and bring on us danger we know not whence. In short it may end in a Rawhead & bloody-bones in the dark.[6] Very well. Let Rawhead & bloody bones come, & then we shall be justified in making our peace with him, by renouncing our antient friends & his enemies. For observe, it is not the *possibility of danger* which absolves a party from his contract: for that possibility always exists, & in every case. It existed in the present one at the moment of making the contract. If *possibilities* would avoid contracts, there never could be a valid contract. For possibilities hang over everything. Obligation is not suspended, till the danger is become real, & the moment of it so imminent, that we can no longer avoid decision without forever losing the opportunity to do it. But can a danger which has not yet taken it's shape, which does not yet exist, & never may exist, which cannot therefore be defined, can such a danger I ask, be so imminent that if we fail to pronounce on it in this moment we can never have another opportunity of doing it?

4. The danger apprehended, is it that, the treaties remaining valid, the clause guarantying their West India islands[7] will engage us in the war? But does the Guarantee engage us to enter into the war in any event?

---

6. According to Dr. Samuel Johnson's *Dictionary*, "Rawhead & bloody-bones" is "the name of a spectre mentioned to fright children." A bogeyman.

7. France's Caribbean possessions, of which the most fractious was the island of Saint Domingue. See note 6, p. 200.

Are we to enter into it before we are called on by our allies? Have we been called on by them?—shall we ever be called on? Is it their interest to call on us?

Can they call on us before their islands are invaded, or imminently threatened?

If they can save them themselves, have they a right to call on us?

Are we obliged to go to war at once, without trying peaceable negociations with their enemy?

If all these questions be against us, there are still others behind.

Are we in a condition to go to war?

Can we be expected to begin before we are in condition?

Will the islands be lost if we do not save them? Have we the means of saving them?

If we cannot save them are we bound to go to war for a desperate object?

Will not a 10. years forbearance in us to call them into the guarantee of our posts, entitle us to some indulgence?

Many, if not most of these questions offer grounds of doubt whether the clause of guarantee will draw us into the war. Consequently if this be the danger apprehended, it is not yet certain enough to authorize us in sound morality to declare, at this moment, the treaties null.

5. Is the danger apprehended from the 17th. article of the treaty of Commerce, which admits French ships of war & privateers[8] to come and go freely, with prizes[9] made on their enemies, while their enemies are not to have the same privilege with prizes made on the French? But Holland & Prussia have approved of this article in our treaty with France, by subscribing to an express Salvo[10] of it in our treaties with them. [Dutch treaty 22. Convention 6. Prussian treaty 19.] And England in her last treaty with France [art. 40] has entered into the same stipulation verbatim, & placed us in her ports on the same footing on which she is in ours, in case of a war of either of us with France. If we are engaged in such a war, England must receive prizes made on us by the French, & exclude those made on the French by us. Nay further, in this very article of her treaty with France, is a salvo of any similar article in any anterior treaty of either party, and ours with France being anterior, this salvo confirms it expressly. Neither of these three powers then have a right to complain of this article in our treaty.

6. Is the danger apprehended from the 22d. Art. of our treaty of commerce, which prohibits the enemies of France from fitting out privateers in our ports, or selling their prizes here. But we are free to refuse the same thing

---

8. Private ships authorized by a government to attack the ships of an enemy nation.

9. Cargo of ships stolen from merchant vessels attacked by French naval vessels and privateers.

10. Exemption.

to France, there being no stipulation to the contrary, and we ought to refuse it on principles of fair neutrality.

7. But the reception of a Minister from the Republic of France, without qualifications, it is thought will bring us into danger: because this, it is said, will determine the continuance of the treaty, and take from us the right of self-liberation when at any time hereafter our safety would require us to use it. The reception of the Minister at all (in favor of which Colo. Hamilton has given his opinion, tho' reluctantly as he confessed) is an acknolegement of the legitimacy of their government: and if the qualifications meditated are to deny that legitimacy, it will be a curious compound which is to admit & deny the same thing. But I deny that the reception of a Minister has any thing to do with the treaties. There is not a word, in either of them, about sending ministers. This has been done between us under the common usage of nations, & can have no effect either to continue or annul the treaties.

But how can any act of election have the effect to continue a treaty which is acknoleged to be going on still? For it was not pretended the treaty was void, but only voidable if we chuse to declare it so. To make it void would require an act of election, but to let it go on requires only that we should do nothing, and doing nothing can hardly be an infraction of peace or neutrality.

But I go further & deny that the most explicit declaration made at this moment that we acknolege the obligation of the treatys could take from us the right of non-compliance at any future time when compliance would involve us in great & inevitable danger.

I conclude then that few of these sources threaten any danger at all; and from none of them is it inevitable: & consequently none of them give us the right at this moment of releasing ourselves from our treaties.

II. A second limitation on our right of releasing ourselves is that we are to do it from so much of the treaties only as is bringing great & inevitable danger on us, & not from the residue, allowing to the other party a right at the same time to determine whether on our non-compliance with that part they will declare the whole void. This right they would have, but we should not. Vattel. 2. 202. The only part of the treaties which can really lead us into danger is the clause of guarantee. That clause is all then we could suspend in any case, and the residue will remain or not at the will of the other party.

III. A third limitation is that where a party from necessity or danger withholds compliance with part of a treaty, it is bound to make compensation where the nature of the case admits & does not dispense with it. 2. Vattel 324. Wolf.[11] 270. 443. If actual circumstances excuse us from entering into the war

---

11. Christian Wolff (1679–1754): German Enlightenment philosopher, scientist, and mathematician. Author of *Jus gentium methodo scientifico pertractum* (*The Law of Nations Treated According to Scientific Method*), 1764.

under the clause of guarantee, it will be a question whether they excuse us from compensation. Our weight in the war admits of an estimate; & that estimate would form the measure of compensation.

If in withholding a compliance with any part of the treaties, we do it without just cause or compensation, we give to France a cause of war, and so become associated in it on the other side. An injured friend is the bitterest of foes, & France had not discovered either timidity, or over-much forbearance on the late occasions. Is this the position we wish to take for our constituents? It is certainly not the one they would take for themselves.

I will proceed now to examine the principal authority which has been relied on for establishing the right of self liberation; because tho' just in part, it would lead us far beyond justice, if taken in all the latitude of which his expressions would admit. Questions of natural right are triable by their conformity with the moral sense & reason of man. Those who write treatises of natural law, can only declare what their own moral sense & reason dictate in the several cases they state. Such of them as happen to have feelings & a reason coincident with those of the wise & honest part of mankind, are respected & quoted as witnesses of what is morally right or wrong in particular cases. Grotius,[12] Puffendorf,[13] Wolf, & Vattel are of this number. Where they agree their authority is strong. But where they differ, & they often differ, we must appeal to our own feelings and reason to decide between them.

The passages in question shall be traced through all these writers, that we may see wherein they concur, & where that concurrence is wanting. It shall be quoted from them in the order in which they wrote, that is to say, from Grotius first, as being the earliest writer, Puffendorf next, then Wolf, & lastly Vattel as latest in time.

The doctrine then of Grotius, Puffendorf & Wolf is that 'treaties remain obligatory notwithstanding any change in the form of government, except in the single case where the preservation of that form was the object of the treaty.' There the treaty extinguishes, not by the election or declaration of the party remaining in *statu quo*;[14] but independantly of that, by the evanishment[15] of the object. Vattel lays down, in fact, the same doctrine, that treaties continue obligatory, notwithstanding a change of government by the will of the other party, that to oppose that will would be a wrong, & that the ally

---

12. Hugo Grotius (1583–1645): Dutch legal scholar. Author of *De jure belli ac pacis* (*On the Law of War and Peace*), 1646.

13. Samuel Pufendorf (1632–94): German jurist and historian. Author of *De jure naturae et gentium* (*The Law of Nature and Nations*), 1774.

14. Status quo: as things are.

15. Disappearance.

remains an ally notwithstanding the change. So far he concurs with all the previous writers. But he then adds what they had not said, nor would say 'but if this change renders the alliance *useless*, dangerous, or *disagreeable* to it, it is free to renounce it.' It was unnecessary for him to have specified the exception of *danger* in this particular case, because that exception exists in all cases & it's extent has been considered. But when he adds that, because a contract is become merely *useless* or *disagreeable*, we are free to renounce it, he is in opposition to Grotius, Puffendorf, & Wolf, who admit no such licence against the obligation of treaties, & he is in opposition to the morality of every honest man, to whom we may safely appeal to decide whether he feels himself free to renounce a contract the moment it becomes merely useless or disagreeable, to him? We may appeal too to Vattel himself, in those parts of his book where he cannot be misunderstood, & to his known character, as one of the most zealous & constant advocates for the preservation of good faith in all our dealings. Let us hear him on other occasions; & first where he shews what degree of danger or injury will authorize self-liberation from a treaty. 'If simple lezion' (lezion means the loss sustained by selling a thing for less than half value, which degree of loss rendered the sale void by the Roman law), 'if simple lezion, says he, or some degree of disadvantage in a treaty does not suffice to render it invalid, it is not so as to inconveniences which would go to the *ruin* of the nation. As every treaty ought to be made by a sufficient power, a treaty pernicious to the state is null, & not at all obligatory; no governor of a nation having power to engage things capable of *destroying* the state, for the safety of which the empire is trusted to him. The nation itself, bound necessarily to whatever it's preservation & safety require, cannot enter into engagements contrary to it's indispensable obligations.' Here then we find that the degree of injury or danger which he deems sufficient to liberate us from a treaty, is that which would go to the absolute *ruin* or *destruction* of the state; not simply the lezion of the Roman law, not merely the being disadvantageous, or dangerous. For as he says himself § 158. 'lezion cannot render a treaty invalid. It is his duty, who enters into engagements, to weigh well all things before be concludes. He may do with his property what he pleases, he may relinquish his rights, renounce his advantages, as he judges proper: the acceptant is not obliged to inform himself of his motives, nor to weigh their just value. If we could free ourselves from a compact because we find ourselves injured by it, there would be nothing firm in the contracts of nations. Civil laws may set limits to lezion, & determine the degree capable of producing a nullity of the contract. But sovereigns acknolege no judge. How establish lezion among them? Who will determine the degree sufficient to invalidate a treaty? The happiness & peace of nations require manifestly that their treaties should not depend on a means of nullity so vague & so dangerous.'

Grotius. 2.16.16.

'Hither must be referred the common question, concerning personal & real treaties. If indeed it be with a free people, there can be no doubt but that the engagement is in it's nature real, because the subject is a permanent thing, and even tho the government of the state be changed into a Kingdom, the treaty remains, because the same body remains, tho' the head is changed, and, as we have before said, the government which is exercised by a King, does not cease to be the government of the people. There is an *exception*, when the object seems peculiar to the government as if free cities

Puffendorf. 8.9.6.

'It is certain that every alliance made with a republic, is real, & continues consequently to the term agreed on by the treaty, altho' the magistrates who concluded it be dead before, or that the form of government is changed, even from a democracy to a monarchy: for in this case the people does not cease to be the same, and the King, in the case supposed, being established by the consent of the people, who abolished the republican government, is understood to accept the crown with all the engagements which the people conferring it had contracted, as being free & governing them-

Wolf. 1146.

'The alliance which is made with a free people, or with a popular government, is a real alliance; and as when the form of government changes, the people remains the same, (for it is the association which forms the people, & not the manner of administering the government) this alliance subsists, tho' the form of government changes, *unless*, as is evident, the reason of the alliance was particular to the popular state.'

Vattel. 2.197.

'The same question presents itself in real alliances, & in general on every alliance made with a state, & not in particular with a King for the defense of his person. We ought without doubt to defend our ally against all invasion, against all foreign violence, & even against rebel subjects. We ought in like manner to defend a republic against the enterprises of an oppressor of the public liberty. But we ought to recollect that we are the ally of the state, or of the nation, & not it's judge. If the nation has deposed it's King in form, if the people of a republic has driven away it's magistrates, & have established

contract a league for the defence of their freedom.'

selves. There must nevertheless be an *Exception* of the alliances contracted with a view to preserve the present government. As if two Republics league for neutral defence against those who would undertake to invade their liberty: for if one of these two people consent afterwards voluntarily to change the form of their government, the alliance ends of itself, because the reason on which it was founded no longer subsists.'

themselves free, or if they have acknoleged the authority of an usurper, whether expressly or tacitly, to oppose these domestic arrangements, to contest their justice or validity, would be to meddle with the government of the nation, & to do it an injury. The ally remains the ally of the state, notwithstanding the change which has taken place. *But if this change renders the alliance useless, dangerous or disagreeable to it, it is free to renounce it. For it may say with truth, that it would not have allied itself with this nation, if it had been under the present form of it's government.'*

Let us hear him again on the general subject of the observance of treaties § 163. 'It is demonstrated in natural law that he who promises another confers on him a perfect right to require the thing promised, & that, consequently, not to observe a perfect promise, is to violate the right of another; it is as manifest injustice as to plunder any one of their right. All the tranquillity, the happiness & security of mankind rest on justice, on the obligation to respect the rights of others. The respect of others for our rights of domain & property is the security of our actual possessions; the faith of promises is our security for the things which cannot be delivered or executed on the spot. No more security, no more commerce among men, if they think themselves not obliged to preserve faith, to keep their word. This obligation then is as necessary as it is natural & indubitable, among nations who live together in a state of nature, & who acknolege no superior on earth, to maintain order & peace in their society. Nations & their governors then ought to observe inviolably their promises & their treaties. This great truth, altho' too often neglected in practice, is generally acknoleged by all nations: the reproach of perfidy is a bitter affront among sovereigns: now he who does not observe a treaty is assuredly perfidious, since he violates his faith. On the contrary nothing is so glorious to a prince & his nation, as the reputation of inviolable fidelity to his word.' Again § 219. 'Who will doubt that treaties are of the things sacred among nations? They decide matters the most important. They impose rules on the pretensions of sovereigns: they cause the rights of nations to be acknoleged, they assure their most precious interests. Among political bodies, sovereigns, who acknolege no superior on earth, treaties are the only means of adjusting their different pretensions, of establishing a rule, to know on what to count, on what to depend. But treaties are but vain words if nations do not consider them as respectable engagements, as rules, inviolable for sovereigns, & sacred through the whole earth. § 220. The faith of treaties, that firm & sincere will, that invariable constancy in fulfilling engagements, of which a declaration is made in a treaty, is there holy & sacred, among nations, whose safety & repose it ensures; & if nations will not be wanting to themselves, they will load with infamy whoever violates his faith.'

After evidence so copious & explicit of the respect of this author for the sanctity of treaties, we should hardly have expected that his authority would have been resorted to for a wanton invalidation of them whenever they should become merely *useless* or *disagreeable*. We should hardly have expected that, rejecting all the rest of his book, this scrap would have been culled, & made the hook whereon to hang such a chain of immoral consequences. Had the passage accidentally met our eye, we should have imagined it had fallen from the author's pen under some momentary view, not sufficiently developed to found a conjecture what he meant: and we may certainly affirm that a fragment like this cannot weigh against the authority of all other writers, against the uniform & systematic doctrine of every work from which it is torn, against the moral feelings & the reason of all honest men. If the terms of the fragment are not misunderstood, they are in full contradiction to all the written & unwritten evidences of morality: if they are misunderstood, they are no longer a foundation for the doctrines which have been built on them.

But even had this doctrine been as true as it is manifestly false, it would have been asked, to whom is it that the treaties with France have become *disagreeable*? How will it be proved that they are *useless*?

The conclusion of the sentence suggests a reflection too strong to be suppressed 'for the party may say with truth that it would not have allied itself with this nation, if it had been under the present form of it's government.' The Republic of the U.S. allied itself with France when under a despotic government. She changes her government, declares it shall be a Republic, prepares a form of Republic extremely free, and in the mean time is governing herself as such, and it is proposed that America shall declare the treaties void because 'it may say with truth that it would not have allied itself with that nation, if it had been under the present form of it's government!' Who is the American who can say with truth that he would not have allied himself to France if she had been a republic? or that a Republic of any form would be as disagreeable as her antient despotism?

Upon the whole I conclude

That the treaties are still binding, notwithstanding the change of government in France: that no part of them, but the clause of guarantee, holds up *danger*, even at a distance.

And consequently that a liberation from no other part could be proposed in any case: that if that clause may ever bring *danger*, it is neither extreme, nor imminent, nor even probable: that the authority for renouncing a treaty, when *useless* or *disagreeable*, is either misunderstood, or in opposition to itself, to all their writers, & to every moral feeling: that were it not so, these treaties are in fact neither useless nor disagreeable.

That the receiving a Minister from France at this time is an act of no significance with respect to the treaties, amounting neither to an admission nor a denial of them, forasmuch as he comes not under any stipulation in them:

That were it an explicit admission, or were an express declaration of this obligation now to be made, it would not take from us that right which exists at all times of liberating ourselves when an adherence to the treaties would be *ruinous* or *destructive* to the society: and that the not renouncing the treaties now is so far from being a breach of neutrality, that the doing it would be the breach, by giving just cause of war to France.

Draft of the Kentucky Resolutions[1]

(1798)

1. *Resolved*, That the several States composing the United States of America, are not united on the principle of unlimited submission to their General Government; but that, by a compact under the style and title of a Constitution for the United States, and of amendments thereto, they constituted a General Government for special purposes,—delegated to that government certain definite powers, reserving, each State to itself, the residuary mass of right to their own self-government; and that whensoever the General Government assumes undelegated powers, its acts are unauthoritative, void, and of no force; that to this compact each State acceded as a State, and is an integral party, its co-States forming, as to itself, the other party: that the government created by this compact was not made the exclusive or final judge of the extent of the powers delegated to itself; since that would have made its discretion, and not the Constitution, the measure of its powers; but that, as in all other cases of compact among powers having no common judge, each party has an equal right to judge for itself, as well of infractions as of the mode and measure of redress.

2. *Resolved*, That the Constitution of the United States, having delegated to Congress a power to punish treason, counterfeiting the securities and current coin of the United States, piracies, and felonies committed on the high seas, and offences against the law of nations, and no other crimes whatsoever; and it being true as a general principle, and one of the amendments to the Constitution having also declared, that "the powers not delegated to the United States by the Constitution, nor prohibited by it to the States, are reserved to the States respectively, or to the people,"[2] therefore the act of Congress, passed on the 14th day of July, 1798, and intituled "An Act in addition to the act intituled An Act for the punishment of certain crimes against the

---

1. In 1798, the Federalist-controlled Congress, responding to the deterioration of military and diplomatic relations with the French government, passed the Alien and Sedition Acts. These acts gave broad powers to the Federalist president John Adams to imprison or deport suspicious aliens and to punish speech critical of the government. Because many of these aliens and critics supported the pro-French policies of the Republicans, Vice President Jefferson secretly penned the Kentucky Resolutions in protest. The Kentucky Legislature adopted these resolutions, with some important revisions, on November 16, 1798. See Introduction, p. xx.

2. 10th Amendment.

United States," as also the act passed by them on the—day of June, 1798, intituled "An Act to punish frauds committed on the bank of the United States," (and all their other acts which assume to create, define, or punish crimes, other than those so enumerated in the Constitution,) are altogether void, and of no force; and that the power to create, define, and punish such other crimes is reserved, and, of right, appertains solely and exclusively to the respective States, each within its own territory.[3]

3. *Resolved,* That it is true as a general principle, and is also expressly declared by one of the amendments to the Constitution, that "the powers not delegated to the United States by the Constitution, nor prohibited by it to the States, are reserved to the States respectively, or to the people;"[4] and that no power over the freedom of religion, freedom of speech, or freedom of the press being delegated to the United States by the Constitution, nor prohibited by it to the States, all lawful powers respecting the same did of right remain, and were reserved to the States or the people: that thus was manifested their determination to retain to themselves the right of judging how far the licentiousness of speech and of the press may be abridged without lessening their useful freedom, and how far those abuses which cannot be separated from their use should be tolerated, rather than the use be destroyed. And thus also they guarded against all abridgment by the United States of the freedom of religious opinions and exercises, and retained to themselves the right of protecting the same, as this State, by a law passed on the general demand of its citizens, had already protected them from all human restraint or interference. And that in addition to this general principle and express declaration, another and more special provision has been made by one of the amendments to the Constitution, which expressly declares, that "Congress shall make no law respecting an establishment of religion, or prohibiting the free exercise thereof, or abridging the freedom of speech or of the press:"[5] thereby guarding in the same sentence, and under the same words, the freedom of religion, of speech, and of the press: insomuch, that whatever violated either, throws down the sanctuary which covers the others, and that libels, falsehood, and defamation, equally with heresy and false religion, are withheld from the cognizance of federal tribunals. That, therefore, the act of Congress of the United States, passed on the 14th day of July, 1798, intituled "An Act in addition to the act intituled An Act for the punishment of certain crimes against the United

---

3. Here, Jefferson extends his argument to cover other laws he believes the federal government has no power to enact. Having argued against the constitutionality of a national bank, it is not surprising that he objects to a law to punish frauds upon the National Bank.

4. 10th Amendment.

5. 1st Amendment.

States," which does abridge the freedom of the press, is not law, but is altogether void, and of no force.[6]

4. *Resolved,* That alien friends are under the jurisdiction and protection of the laws of the State wherein they are: that no power over them has been delegated to the United States, nor prohibited to the individual States, distinct from their power over citizens. And it being true as a general principle, and one of the amendments to the Constitution having also declared, that "the powers not delegated to the United States by the Constitution, nor prohibited by it to the States, are reserved to the States respectively, or to the people,"[7] the act of the Congress of the United States, passed on the—day of July, 1798, intituled "An Act concerning aliens," which assumes powers over alien friends, not delegated by the Constitution, is not law, but is altogether void, and of no force.

5. *Resolved,* That in addition to the general principle, as well as the express declaration, that powers not delegated are reserved, another and more special provision, inserted in the Constitution from abundant caution, has declared that "the migration or importation of such persons as any of the States now existing shall think proper to admit, shall not be prohibited by the Congress prior to the year 1808;"[8] that this commonwealth does admit the migration of alien friends, described as the subject of the said act concerning aliens: that a provision against prohibiting their migration, is a provision against all acts equivalent thereto, or it would be nugatory:[9] that to remove them when migrated, is equivalent to a prohibition of their migration, and is, therefore, contrary to the said provision of the Constitution, and void.

6. *Resolved,* That the imprisonment of a person under the protection of the laws of this commonwealth, on his failure to obey the simple *order* of the President to depart out of the United States, as is undertaken by said act intituled "An Act concerning aliens,"[10] is contrary to the Constitution, one amendment to which has provided that "no person shall be deprived of liberty without due process of law;"[11] and that another having provided that "in all criminal prosecutions the accused shall enjoy the right to public trial by an impartial jury, to be informed of the nature and cause of the accusation, to be confronted with the witnesses against him, to have compulsory process for obtaining witnesses in his favor, and to have the assistance of counsel for his

---

6. The Sedition Act.
7. The Alien Act.
8. Article I, Section 9.
9. Invalid.
10. The Alien Act.
11. 5th Amendment.

defence,"[12] the same act, undertaking to authorize the President to remove a person out of the United States, who is under the protection of the law, on his own suspicion, without accusation, without jury, without public trial, without confrontation of the witnesses against him, without hearing witnesses in his favor, without defence, without counsel, is contrary to the provision also of the Constitution, is therefore not law, but utterly void, and of no force: that transferring the power of judging any person, who is under the protection of the laws, from the courts to the President of the United States, as is undertaken by the same act concerning aliens, is against the article of the Constitution which provides that "the judicial power of the United States shall be vested in courts, the judges of which shall hold their offices during good behavior;"[13] and that the said act is void for that reason also. And it is further to be noted, that this transfer of judiciary power is to that magistrate of the General Government who already possesses all the Executive, and a negative on all legislative powers.

7. *Resolved,* That the construction applied by the General Government (as is evidenced by sundry of their proceedings) to those parts of the Constitution of the United States which delegate to Congress a power "to lay and collect taxes, duties, imports, and excises, to pay the debts, and provide for the common defence and general welfare of the United States,"[14] and "to make all laws which shall be necessary and proper for carrying into execution the powers vested by the Constitution in the government of the United States, or in any department or officer thereof,"[15] goes to the destruction of all limits prescribed to their power by the Constitution: that words meant by the instrument to be subsidiary only to the execution of limited powers, ought not to be so construed as themselves to give unlimited powers, nor a part to be so taken as to destroy the whole residue of that instrument: that the proceedings of the General Government under color of these articles, will be a fit and necessary subject of revisal and correction, at a time of greater tranquillity, while those specified in the preceding resolutions call for immediate redress.

8th. *Resolved,* That a committee of conference and correspondence be appointed, who shall have in charge to communicate the preceding resolutions to the legislatures of the several States; to assure them that this commonwealth continues in the same esteem of their friendship and union which it has manifested from that moment at which a common danger first suggested

---

12. 6th Amendment.
13. Article III, Section 1.
14. Article I, Section 8.
15. Article I, Section 8.

a common union:[16] that it considers union, for specified national purposes, and particularly to those specified in their late federal compact, to be friendly to the peace, happiness and prosperity of all the States: that faithful to that compact, according to the plain intent and meaning in which it was under-stood and acceded to by the several parties, it is sincerely anxious for its preser-vation: that it does also believe, that to take from the States all the powers of self-government and transfer them to a general and consolidated government, without regard to the special delegations and reservations solemnly agreed to in that compact, is not for the peace, happiness or prosperity of these States; and that therefore this commonwealth is determined, as it doubts not its co-States are, to submit to undelegated, and consequently unlimited powers in no man, or body of men on earth: that in cases of an abuse of the delegated powers, the members of the General Government, being chosen by the people, a change by the people would be the constitutional remedy; but, where powers are assumed which have not been delegated, a nullification of the act is the rightful remedy: that every State has a natural right in cases not within the compact, (casus non fœderis,)[17] to nullify of their own authority all assumptions of power by others within their limits: that without this right, they would be under the dominion, absolute and unlimited, of whosoever might exercise this right of judgment for them: that nevertheless, this common-wealth, from motives of regard and respect for its co-States, has wished to communicate with them on the subject: that with them alone it is proper to communicate, they alone being parties to the compact, and solely authorized to judge in the last resort of the powers exercised under it, Congress being not a party, but merely the creature of the compact, and subject as to its assump-tions of power to the final judgment of those by whom, and for whose use it-self and its powers were all created and modified: that if the acts before specified should stand, these conclusions would flow from them; that the General Government may place any act they think proper on the list of crimes, and punish it themselves whether enumerated or not enumerated by the Constitution as cognizable by them: that they may transfer its cognizance to the President, or any other person, who may himself be the accuser, coun-sel, judge and jury, whose *suspicions* may be the evidence, his *order* the sen-tence, his *officer* the executioner, and his breast the sole record of the transaction: that a very numerous and valuable description of the inhabitants of these States being, by this precedent, reduced, as outlaws, to the absolute dominion of one man, and the barrier of the Constitution thus swept away from us all, no rampart now remains against the passions and the powers of a

---

16. The American War of Independence.
17. Cases not within the compact.

majority in Congress to protect from a like exportation, or other more grievous punishment, the minority of the same body, the legislatures, judges, governors, and counsellors of the States, nor their other peaceable inhabitants, who may venture to reclaim the constitutional rights and liberties of the States and people, or who for other causes, good or bad, may be obnoxious to the views, or marked by the suspicions of the President, or be thought dangerous to his or their election, or other interests, public or personal: that the friendless alien has indeed been selected as the safest subject of a first experiment; but the citizen will soon follow, or rather, has already followed, for already has a sedition act marked him as its prey: that these and successive acts of the same character, unless arrested at the threshold, necessarily drive these States into revolution and blood, and will furnish new calumnies against republican government, and new pretexts for those who wish it to be believed that man cannot be governed but by a rod of iron: that it would be a dangerous delusion were a confidence in the men of our choice to silence our fears for the safety of our rights: that confidence is everywhere the parent of despotism—free government is founded in jealousy, and not in confidence; it is jealousy and not confidence which prescribes limited constitutions, to bind down those whom we are obliged to trust with power: that our Constitution has accordingly fixed the limits to which, and no further, our confidence may go; and let the honest advocate of confidence read the alien and sedition acts, and say if the Constitution has not been wise in fixing limits to the government it created, and whether we should be wise in destroying those limits. Let him say what the government is, if it be not a tyranny, which the men of our choice have conferred on our President, and the President of our choice has assented to, and accepted over the friendly strangers to whom the mild spirit of our country and its laws have pledged hospitality and protection: that the men of our choice have more respected the bare *suspicions* of the President, than the solid right of innocence, the claims of justification, the sacred force of truth, and the forms and substance of law and justice. In questions of power, then, let no more be heard of confidence in man, but bind him down from mischief by the chains of the Constitution. That this commonwealth does therefore call on its co-States for an expression of their sentiments on the acts concerning aliens, and for the punishment of certain crimes herein before specified, plainly declaring whether these acts are or are not authorized by the federal compact. And it doubts not that their sense will be so announced as to prove their attachment unaltered to limited government, whether general or particular. And that the rights and liberties of their co-States will be exposed to no dangers by remaining embarked in a common bottom with their own. That they will concur with this commonwealth in considering the said acts as so palpably against the Constitution as to amount to an undisguised declaration that that compact is not meant to be the measure of the powers of the

General Government, but that it will proceed in the exercise over these States, of all powers whatsoever: that they will view this as seizing the rights of the States, and consolidating them in the hands of the General Government, with a power assumed to bind the States, not merely as the cases made federal, (casus fœderis,)[18] but in all cases whatsoever, by laws made, not with their consent, but by others against their consent: that this would be to surrender the form of government we have chosen, and live under one deriving its powers from its own will, and not from our authority; and that the co-States, recurring to their natural right in cases not made federal, will concur in declaring these acts void, and of no force, and will each take measures of its own for providing that neither these acts, nor any others of the General Government not plainly and intentionally authorized by the Constitution, shall be exercised within their respective territories.

9th. *Resolved,* That the said committee be authorized to communicate by writing or personal conferences, at any times or places whatever, with any person or person who may be appointed by any one or more co-States to correspond or confer with them; and that they lay their proceedings before the next session of Assembly.

---

18. Cases within the compact.

FIRST INAUGURAL ADDRESS

(Mar. 4, 1801)

FRIENDS AND FELLOW-CITIZENS, — Called upon to undertake the duties of the first executive office of our country, I avail myself of the presence of that portion of my fellow-citizens which is here assembled to express my grateful thanks for the favor with which they have been pleased to look toward me, to declare a sincere consciousness that the task is above my talents, and that I approach it with those anxious and awful presentiments which the greatness of the charge and the weakness of my powers so justly inspire. A rising nation, spread over a wide and fruitful land, traversing all the seas with the rich productions of their industry, engaged in commerce with nations who feel power and forget right, advancing rapidly to destinies beyond the reach of mortal eye—when I contemplate these transcendent objects, and see the honor, the happiness, and the hopes of this beloved country committed to the issue and the auspices of this day, I shrink from the contemplation, and humble myself before the magnitude of the undertaking. Utterly, indeed, should I despair did not the presence of many whom I here see remind me that in the other high authorities provided by our Constitution I shall find resources of wisdom, of virtue, and of zeal on which to rely under all difficulties. To you, then, gentlemen, who are charged with the sovereign functions of legislation, and to those associated with you, I look with encouragement for that guidance and support which may enable us to steer with safety the vessel in which we are all embarked amidst the conflicting elements of a troubled world.

During the contest of opinion through which we have passed[1] the animation of discussions and of exertions has sometimes worn an aspect which might impose on strangers unused to think freely and to speak and to write what they think; but this being now decided by the voice of the nation, announced according to the rules of the Constitution, all will, of course, arrange themselves under the will of the law, and unite in common efforts for the common good. All, too, will bear in mind this sacred principle, that though the will of the majority is in all cases to prevail, that will to be rightful must be reasonable; that the minority possess their equal rights, which equal law must protect, and to violate would be oppression. Let us, then, fellow-citizens, unite with one heart and one mind. Let us restore to social intercourse that

---

1. Jefferson here refers to the recent presidential election in which he defeated incumbent President John Adams. See Introduction, p. xxi.

harmony and affection without which liberty and even life itself are but dreary things. And let us reflect that, having banished from our land that religious intolerance under which mankind so long bled and suffered, we have yet gained little if we countenance a political intolerance as despotic, as wicked, and capable of as bitter and bloody persecutions. During the throes and convulsions of the ancient world, during the agonizing spasms of infuriated man, seeking through blood and slaughter his long-lost liberty, it was not wonderful that the agitation of the billows should reach even this distant and peaceful shore; that this should be more felt and feared by some and less by others, and should divide opinions as to measures of safety. But every difference of opinion is not a difference of principle. We have called by different names brethren of the same principle. We are all Republicans,[2] we are all Federalists.[3] If there be any among us who would wish to dissolve this Union or to change its republican form, let them stand undisturbed as monuments of the safety with which error of opinion may be tolerated where reason is left free to combat it. I know, indeed, that some honest men fear that a republican government can not be strong, that this Government is not strong enough; but would the honest patriot, in the full tide of successful experiment, abandon a government which has so far kept us free and firm on the theoretic and visionary fear that this Government, the world's best hope, may by possibility want energy to preserve itself? I trust not. I believe this, on the contrary, the strongest Government on earth. I believe it the only one where every man, at the call of the law, would fly to the standard of the law, and would meet invasions of the public order as his own personal concern. Sometimes it is said that man can not be trusted with the government of himself. Can he, then, be trusted with the government of others? Or have we found angels in the forms of kings to govern him? Let history answer this question.

Let us, then, with courage and confidence pursue our own Federal and Republican principles, our attachment to union and representative government. Kindly separated by nature and a wide ocean from the exterminating havoc of

---

2. Members of the political party centered around Jefferson that came into being during Washington's first administration to oppose Hamilton's expansive economic policies and lend their support to a limited national government. Some, like James Monroe, had been Antifederalists who, in 1787, opposed the ratification of the Constitution, but others, like James Madison, were among its principal supporters.

3. Originally, the name adopted by supporters of the Constitution in 1787, and employed by Hamilton, Madison, and Jay in their essays defending the Constitution. This name later came to be associated with those supporters of a vigorous national government during Washington's first administration. Prominent federalists included George Washington, his vice president, John Adams, and, of course, Alexander Hamilton.

one quarter of the globe; too high-minded to endure the degradations of the others; possessing a chosen country, with room enough for our descendants to the thousandth and thousandth generation; entertaining a due sense of our equal right to the use of our own faculties, to the acquisitions of our own industry, to honor and confidence from our fellow-citizens, resulting not from birth, but from our actions and their sense of them; enlightened by a benign religion, professed, indeed, and practiced in various forms, yet all of them inculcating honesty, truth, temperance, gratitude, and the love of man; acknowledging and adoring an overruling Providence, which by all its dispensations proves that it delights in the happiness of man here and his greater happiness hereafter—with all these blessings, what more is necessary to make us a happy and a prosperous people? Still one thing more, fellow-citizens—a wise and frugal Government, which shall restrain men from injuring one another, shall leave them otherwise free to regulate their own pursuits of industry and improvement, and shall not take from the mouth of labor the bread it has earned. This is the sum of good government, and this is necessary to close the circle of our felicities.

About to enter, fellow-citizens, on the exercise of duties which comprehend everything dear and valuable to you, it is proper you should understand what I deem the essential principles of our Government, and consequently those which ought to shape its Administration. I will compress them within the narrowest compass they will bear, stating the general principle, but not all its limitations. Equal and exact justice to all men, of whatever state or persuasion, religious or political; peace, commerce, and honest friendship with all nations, entangling alliances with none; the support of the State governments in all their rights, as the most competent administrations for our domestic concerns and the surest bulwarks against antirepublican tendencies; the preservation of the General Government in its whole constitutional vigor, as the sheet anchor of our peace at home and safety abroad; a jealous care of the right of election by the people—a mild and safe corrective of abuses which are lopped by the sword of revolution where peaceable remedies are unprovided; absolute acquiescence in the decisions of the majority, the vital principle of republics, from which is no appeal but to force, the vital principle and immediate parent of despotism; a well-disciplined militia, our best reliance in peace and for the first moments of war till regulars may relieve them; the supremacy of the civil over the military authority; economy in the public expense, that labor may be lightly burthened; the honest payment of our debts and sacred preservation of the public faith; encouragement of agriculture, and of commerce as its handmaid; the diffusion of information and arraignment of all abuses at the bar of the public reason; freedom of religion; freedom of the press, and freedom of person under the protection of the habeas corpus,[4] and trial by juries impartially selected. These principles form the bright constellation which has gone before us and guided our steps through an age of revolution and reformation. The wisdom of our sages and blood of our heroes have been devoted to their attainment. They should be the creed of our political faith, the text of civic instruction, the touchstone by which to try the services of those we trust; and should we wander from them in moments of error or of alarm, let us hasten to retrace our steps and to regain the road which alone leads to peace, liberty, and safety.

I repair, then, fellow-citizens, to the post you have assigned me. With experience enough in subordinate offices to have seen the difficulties of this the greatest of all, I have learnt to expect that it will rarely fall to the lot of imperfect man to retire from this station with the reputation and the favor which bring him into it. Without pretensions to that high confidence you reposed in our first and greatest revolutionary character,[5] whose preeminent services had entitled him to the first place in his country's love and destined for him the fairest page in the volume of faithful history, I ask so much confidence only as may give firmness and effect to the legal administration of your affairs. I shall often go wrong through defect of judgment. When right, shall often be thought wrong by those whose positions will not command a view of the whole ground. I ask your indulgence for my own errors, which will never be intentional, and your support against the errors of others, who may condemn what they would not if seen in all its parts. The approbation implied by your suffrage is a great consolation to me for the past, and my future solicitude will be to retain the good opinion of those who have bestowed it in advance, to conciliate that of others by doing them all the good in my power, and to be instrumental to the happiness and freedom of all.

Relying, then, on the patronage of your good will, advance with obedience to the work, ready to retire from it whenever you become sensible how much better choice it is in your power to make. And may that Infinite Power which rules the destinies of the universe lead our councils to what is best, and give them a favorable issue for your peace and prosperity.

---

4. The right to obtain a writ to release an imprisoned person and bring him before a judge.
5. George Washington (1732–99), commander-in-chief of the Continental Army, and first president of the United States 1789–97.

TO MESSRS. NEHEMIAH DODGE AND OTHERS, A COMMITTEE OF THE DANBURY BAPTIST ASSOCIATION, IN THE STATE OF CONNECTICUT[1]

(Jan. 1, 1802)

GENTLEMEN,

The affectionate sentiments of esteem and approbation which you are so good as to express towards me, on behalf of the Danbury Baptist Association, give me the highest satisfaction. My duties dictate a faithful and zealous pursuit of the interests of my constituents, and in proportion as they are persuaded of my fidelity to those duties, the discharge of them becomes more and more pleasing.

Believing with you that religion is a matter which lies solely between man and his God, that he owes account to none other for his faith or his worship, that the legislative powers of government reach actions only, and not opinions, I contemplate with sovereign reverence that act of the whole American people which declared that their legislature should "make no law respecting an establishment of religion, or prohibiting the free exercise thereof," thus building a wall of separation between church and State. Adhering to this expression of the supreme will of the nation in behalf of the rights of conscience, I shall see with sincere satisfaction the progress of those sentiments which tend to restore to man all his natural rights, convinced he has no natural right in opposition to his social duties.

I reciprocate your kind prayers for the protection and blessing of the common Father and Creator of man, and tender you for yourselves and your religious association, assurances of my high respect and esteem.

---

1. Although the First Amendment to the Constitution prevented the federal government from establishing a state-supported religion, this provision did not originally apply to the states. Connecticut continued to support the Congregational Church as its official state church. Dissenting religions were required to pay taxes in support of the Congregational Church, although they could petition for tax relief. Nehemiah Dodge, a Baptist minister and fervent Republican who was a member of the executive committee of the Danbury Baptist Association, penned the letter to President Jefferson that elicited this response.

SECOND INAUGURAL ADDRESS[1]

(Mar. 4, 1805)

Proceeding, fellow citizens, to that qualification which the constitution requires, before my entrance on the charge again conferred upon me, it is my duty to express the deep sense I entertain of this new proof of confidence from my fellow citizens at large, and the zeal with which it inspires me, so to conduct myself as may best satisfy their just expectations.

On taking this station on a former occasion,[2] I declared the principles on which I believed it my duty to administer the affairs of our commonwealth. My conscience tells me that I have, on every occasion, acted up to that declaration, according to its obvious import, and to the understanding of every candid mind.

In the transaction of your foreign affairs, we have endeavored to cultivate the friendship of all nations, and especially of those with which we have the most important relations. We have done them justice on all occasions, favored where favor was lawful, and cherished mutual interests and intercourse on fair and equal terms. We are firmly convinced, and we act on that conviction, that with nations, as with individuals, our interests soundly calculated, will ever be found inseparable from our moral duties; and history bears witness to the fact, that a just nation is taken on its word, when recourse is had to armaments and wars to bridle others.

At home, fellow citizens, you best know whether we have done well or ill. The suppression of unnecessary offices, of useless establishments and expenses, enabled us to discontinue our internal taxes.[3] These covering our land with officers, and opening our doors to their intrusions, had already begun that process of domiciliary vexation which, once entered, is scarcely to be restrained from reaching successively every article of produce and property. If among these taxes some minor ones fell which had not been inconvenient, it was because their amount would not have paid the officers who collected them, and because, if they had any merit, the state authorities might adopt them, instead of others less approved.

---

1. See Introduction, pp. xxii–xxiii.

2. Jefferson's first Inaugural Address (see pp. 55–58).

3. Due to a peaceful and prosperous first term, Jefferson was able to streamline government and eliminate such internal taxes as the excise tax on whiskey.

The remaining revenue on the consumption of foreign articles, is paid cheerfully by those who can afford to add foreign luxuries to domestic comforts, being collected on our seaboards and frontiers only, and incorporated with the transactions of our mercantile citizens, it may be the pleasure and pride of an American to ask, what farmer, what mechanic, what laborer, ever sees a tax-gatherer of the United States? These contributions enable us to support the current expenses of the government, to fulfil contracts with foreign nations, to extinguish the native right of soil within our limits, to extend those limits, and to apply such a surplus to our public debts, as places at a short day their final redemption, and that redemption once effected, the revenue thereby liberated may, by a just repartition among the states, and a corresponding amendment of the constitution, be applied, *in time of peace*, to rivers, canals, roads, arts, manufactures, education, and other great objects within each state. *In time of war*, if injustice, by ourselves or others, must sometimes produce war, increased as the same revenue will be increased by population and consumption, and aided by other resources reserved for that crisis, it may meet within the year all the expenses of the year, without encroaching on the rights of future generations, by burdening them with the debts of the past. War will then be but a suspension of useful works, and a return to a state of peace, a return to the progress of improvement.

I have said, fellow citizens, that the income reserved had enabled us to extend our limits; but that extension may possibly pay for itself before we are called on, and in the meantime, may keep down the accruing interest; in all events, it will repay the advances we have made. I know that the acquisition of Louisiana[4] has been disapproved by some, from a candid apprehension that the enlargement of our territory would endanger its union. But who can limit the extent to which the federative principle may operate effectively? The larger our association, the less will it be shaken by local passions; and in any view, is it not better that the opposite bank of the Mississippi should be settled by our own brethren and children, than by strangers of another family? With which shall we be most likely to live in harmony and friendly intercourse?

In matters of religion, I have considered that its free exercise is placed by the constitution independent of the powers of the general government. I have therefore undertaken, on no occasion, to prescribe the religious exercises suited to it; but have left them, as the constitution found them, under the direction and discipline of state or church authorities acknowledged by the several religious societies.

---

4. In 1803, under President Jefferson's direction, the United States purchased the Louisiana Territory from France. See note 2, p. 198.

The aboriginal inhabitants of these countries I have regarded with the commiseration their history inspires. Endowed with the faculties and the rights of men, breathing an ardent love of liberty and independence, and occupying a country which left them no desire but to be undisturbed, the stream of overflowing population from other regions directed itself on these shores; without power to divert, or habits to contend against, they have been overwhelmed by the current, or driven before it; now reduced within limits too narrow for the hunter's state, humanity enjoins us to teach them agriculture and the domestic arts; to encourage them to that industry which alone can enable them to maintain their place in existence, and to prepare them in time for that state of society, which to bodily comforts adds the improvement of the mind and morals. We have therefore liberally furnished them with the implements of husbandry and household use; we have placed among them instructors in the arts of first necessity; and they are But the endeavors to enlighten them on the fate which awaits their present course of life, to induce them to exercise their reason, follow its dictates, and change their pursuits with the change of circumstances, have powerful obstacles to encounter; they are combated by the habits of their bodies, prejudice of their minds, ignorance, pride, and the influence of interested and crafty individuals among them, who feel themselves something in the present order of things, and fear to become nothing in any other. These persons inculcate a sanctimonious reverence for the customs of their ancestors; that whatsoever they did, must be done through all time; that reason is a false guide, and to advance under its counsel, in their physical, moral, or political condition, is perilous innovation; that their duty is to remain as their Creator made them, ignorance being safety, and knowledge full of danger; in short, my friends, among them is seen the action and counteraction of good sense and bigotry; they, too, have their anti-philosophers, who find an interest in keeping things in their present state, who dread reformation, and exert all their faculties to maintain the ascendency of habit over the duty of improving our reason, and obeying its mandates.

In giving these outlines, I do not mean, fellow citizens, to arrogate[5] to myself the merit of the measures; that is due, in the first place, to the reflecting character of our citizens at large, who, by the weight of public opinion, influence and strengthen the public measures; it is due to the sound discretion with which they select from among themselves those to whom they confide the legislative duties; it is due to the zeal and wisdom of the characters thus selected, who lay the foundations of public happiness in wholesome laws, the execution of which alone remains for others; and it is due to the able and

---

5. To take or claim for oneself without right; to appropriate.

faithful auxiliaries, whose patriotism has associated with me in the executive functions.

During this course of administration, and in order to disturb it, the artillery of the press has been levelled against us, charged with whatsoever its licentiousness could devise or dare.[6] These abuses of an institution so important to freedom and science, are deeply to be regretted, inasmuch as they tend to lessen its usefulness, and to sap its safety; they might, indeed, have been corrected by the wholesome punishments reserved and provided by the laws of the several States against falsehood and defamation; but public duties more urgent press on the time of public servants, and the offenders have therefore been left to find their punishment in the public indignation.

Nor was it uninteresting to the world, that an experiment should be fairly and fully made, whether freedom of discussion, unaided by power, is not sufficient for the propagation and protection of truth—whether a government, conducting itself in the true spirit of its constitution, with zeal and purity, and doing no act which it would be unwilling the whole world should witness, can be written down by falsehood and defamation. The experiment has been tried; you have witnessed the scene; our fellow citizens have looked on, cool and collected; they saw the latent source from which these outrages proceeded; they gathered around their public functionaries, and when the constitution called them to the decision by suffrage, they pronounced their verdict, honorable to those who had served them, and consolatory to the friend of man, who believes he may be intrusted with his own affairs.

No inference is here intended, that the laws, provided by the State against false and defamatory publications, should not be enforced; he who has time, renders a service to public morals and public tranquillity, in reforming these abuses by the salutary coercions of the law; but the experiment is noted, to prove that, since truth and reason have maintained their ground against false opinions in league with false facts, the press, confined to truth, needs no other legal restraint; the public judgment will correct false reasonings and opinions, on a full hearing of all parties; and no other definite line can be drawn between the inestimable liberty of the press and its demoralizing licentiousness. If there be still improprieties which this rule would not restrain, its supplement must be sought in the censorship of public opinion.

Contemplating the union of sentiment now manifested so generally, as auguring harmony and happiness to our future course, offer to our country sincere congratulations. With those, too, not yet rallied to the same point, the disposition to do so is gaining strength; facts are piercing through the veil

6. During his first administration, Jefferson had been scurrilously attacked in the partisan Federalist newspapers.

drawn over them; and our doubting brethren will at length see, that the mass of their fellow citizens, with whom they cannot yet resolve to act, as to principles and measures, think as they think, and desire what they desire; that our wish, as well as theirs, is, that the public efforts may be directed honestly to the public good, that peace be cultivated, civil and religious liberty unassailed, law and order preserved; equality of rights maintained, and that state of property, equal or unequal, which results to every man from his own industry, or that of his fathers. When satisfied of these views, it is not in human nature that they should not approve and support them; in the meantime, let us cherish them with patient affection; let us do them justice, and more than justice, in all competitions of interest; and we need not doubt that truth, reason, and their own interests, will at length prevail, will gather them into the fold of their country, and will complete their entire union of opinion, which gives to a nation the blessing of harmony, and the benefit of all its strength.

I shall now enter on the duties to which my fellow citizens have again called me, and shall proceed in the spirit of those principles which they have approved. I fear not that any motives of interest may lead me astray; I am sensible of no passion which could seduce me knowingly from the path of justice; but the weakness of human nature, and the limits of my own understanding, will produce errors of judgment sometimes injurious to your interests. I shall need, therefore, all the indulgence I have heretofore experienced — the want of it will certainly not lessen with increasing years. I shall need, too, the favor of that Being in whose hands we are, who led our forefathers, as Israel of old, from their native land, and planted them in a country flowing with all the necessaries and comforts of life; who has covered our infancy with his providence, and our riper years with his wisdom and power; and to whose goodness I ask you to join with me in supplications, that he will so enlighten the minds of your servants, guide their councils, and prosper their measures, that whatsoever they do, shall result in your good, and shall secure to you the peace, friendship, and approbation of all nations.

REPORT OF THE COMMISSIONERS FOR THE UNIVERSITY OF VIRGINIA

(Aug. 4, 1818)

The commissioners for the University of Virginia, having met, as by law required, at the tavern, in Rockfish Gap, on the Blue Ridge, on the first day of August, of this present year, 1818; and having formed a board, proceeded on that day to the discharge of the duties assigned to them by the act of the Legislature, entitled "An act, appropriating part of the revenue of the literary fund, and for other purposes;" and having continued their proceedings by adjournment, from day to day, to Tuesday, the 4th day of August, have agreed to a report on the several matters with which they were charged, which report they now respectfully address and submit to the Legislature of the State.

The first duty enjoined on them, was to enquire and report a site, in some convenient and proper part of the State, for an university, to be called the "University of Virginia." In this enquiry, they supposed that the governing considerations should be the healthiness of the site, the fertility of the neighboring country, and its centrality to the white population of the whole State. For, although the act authorized and required them to receive any voluntary contributions, whether conditional or absolute, which might be offered through them to the President and Directors of the Literary Fund, for the benefit of the University, yet they did not consider this as establishing an auction, or as pledging the location to the highest bidder.

Three places were proposed, to wit: Lexington, in the county of Rockbridge, Staunton, in the county of Augusta, and the Central College, in the county of Albemarle. Each of these was unexceptionable as to healthiness and fertility. It was the degree of centrality to the white population of the State which alone then constituted the important point of comparison between these places; and the Board, after full enquiry, and impartial and mature consideration, are of opinion, that the central point of the white population of the State is nearer to the Central College than to either Lexington or Staunton, by great and important differences; and all other circumstances of the place in general being favorable to it, as a position for an university, they do report the Central College, in Albemarle, to be a convenient and proper part of the State for the University of Virginia.

2. The Board having thus agreed on a proper site for the University, to be reported to the Legislature, proceed to the second of the duties assigned to them—that of proposing a plan for its buildings—and they are of opinion that

it should consist of distinct houses or pavilions, arranged at proper distances on each side of a lawn of a proper breadth, and of indefinite extent, in one direction, at least; in each of which should be a lecturing room, with from two to four apartments, for the accommodation of a professor and his family; that these pavilions should be united by a range of dormitories, sufficient each for the accommodation of two students only, this provision being deemed advantageous to morals, to order, and to uninterrupted study; and that a passage of some kind, under cover from the weather, should give a communication along the whole range. It is supposed that such pavilions, on an average of the larger and smaller, will cost each about $5,000; each dormitory about $350, and hotels of a single room, for a refectory,[1] and two rooms for the tenant, necessary for dieting the students, will cost about $3500 each. The number of these pavilions will depend on the number of professors, and that of the dormitories and hotels on the number of students to be lodged and dieted. The advantages of this plan are: greater security against fire and infection; tranquillity and comfort to the professors and their families thus insulated; retirement to the students; and the admission of enlargement to any degree to which the institution may extend in future times. It is supposed probable, that a building of somewhat more size in the middle of the grounds may be called for in time, in which may be rooms for religious worship, under such impartial regulations as the Visitors shall prescribe, for public examinations, for a library, for the schools of music, drawing, and other associated purposes.

3, 4. In proceeding to the third and fourth duties prescribed by the Legislature, of reporting "the branches of learning, which should be taught in the University, and the number and description of the professorships they will require," the Commissioners were first to consider at what point it was understood that university education should commence? Certainly not with the alphabet, for reasons of expediency and impracticability, as well from the obvious sense of the Legislature, who, in the same act, make other provision for the primary instruction of the poor children, expecting, doubtless, that in other cases it would be provided by the parent, or become, perhaps, subject of future and further attention of the Legislature. The objects of this primary education determine its character and limits. These objects would be,

To give to every citizen the information he needs for the transaction of his own business;

To enable him to calculate for himself, and to express and preserve his ideas, his contracts and accounts, in writing;

To improve, by reading, his morals and faculties;

---

1. A dining hall.

To understand his duties to his neighbors and country, and to discharge with competence the functions confided to him by either;

To know his rights; to exercise with order and justice those he retains; to choose with discretion the fiduciary of those he delegates; and to notice their conduct with diligence, with candor, and judgment;

And, in general, to observe with intelligence and faithfulness all the social relations under which he shall be placed.

To instruct the mass of our citizens in these, their rights, interests and duties, as men and citizens, being then the objects of education in the primary schools, whether private or public, in them should be taught reading, writing and numerical arithmetic, the elements of mensuration,[2] (useful in so many callings,) and the outlines of geography and history. And this brings us to the point at which are to commence the higher branches of education, of which the Legislature require the development; those, for example, which are,

To form the statesmen, legislators and judges, on whom public prosperity and individual happiness are so much to depend;

To expound the principles and structure of government, the laws which regulate the intercourse of nations, those formed municipally for our own government, and a sound spirit of legislation, which, banishing all arbitrary and unnecessary restraint on individual action, shall leave us free to do whatever does not violate the equal rights of another;

To harmonize and promote the interests of agriculture, manufactures and commerce, and by well informed views of political economy to give a free scope to the public industry;

To develop the reasoning faculties of our youth, enlarge their minds, cultivate their morals, and instill into them the precepts of virtue and order;

To enlighten them with mathematical and physical sciences, which advance the arts, and administer to the health, the subsistence, and comforts of human life;

And, generally, to form them to habits of reflection and correct action, rendering them examples of virtue to others, and of happiness within themselves.

These are the objects of that higher grade of education, the benefits and blessings of which the Legislature now propose to provide for the good and ornament of their country, the gratification and happiness of their fellow-citizens, of the parent especially, and his progeny, on which all his affections are concentrated.

In entering on this field, the Commissioners are aware that they have to encounter much difference of opinion as to the extent which it is expedient that

---

2. The science of geometric measurement.

this institution should occupy. Some good men, and even of respectable information, consider the learned sciences as useless acquirements; some think
that they do not better the condition of man; and others that education, like
private and individual concerns, should be left to private individual effort; not
reflecting that an establishment embracing all the sciences which may be useful and even necessary in the various vocations of life, with the buildings and
apparatus belonging to each, are far beyond the reach of individual means,
and must either derive existence from public patronage, or not exist at all.
This would leave us, then, without those callings which depend on education, or send us to other countries to seek the instruction they require. But the
Commissioners are happy in considering the statute under which they are assembled as proof that the Legislature is far from the abandonment of objects
so interesting. They are sensible that the advantages of well-directed education, moral, political and economical, are truly above all estimate. Education
generates habits of application, of order, and the love of virtue; and controls,
by the force of habit, any innate obliquities in our moral organization. We
should be far, too, from the discouraging persuasion that man is fixed, by the
law of his nature, at a given point; that his improvement is a chimera,[3] and the
hope delusive of rendering ourselves wiser, happier or better than our forefathers were. As well might it be urged that the wild and uncultivated tree, hitherto yielding sour and bitter fruit only, can never be made to yield better; yet
we know that the grafting art implants a new tree on the savage stock, producing what is most estimable both in kind and degree. Education, in like manner, engrafts a new man on the native stock, and improves what in his nature
was vicious and perverse into qualities of virtue and social worth. And it cannot
be but that each generation succeeding to the knowledge acquired by all those
who preceded it, adding to it their own acquisitions and discoveries, and hand-
ing the mass down for successive and constant accumulation, must advance
the knowledge and well-being of mankind, not *infinitely*, as some have said,
but *indefinitely*, and to a term which no one can fix and foresee. Indeed, we
need look back half a century, to times which many now living remember
well, and see the wonderful advances in the sciences and arts which have been
made within that period. Some of these have rendered the elements themselves subservient to the purposes of man, have harnessed them to the yoke of
his labors, and effected the great blessings of moderating his own, of accomplishing what was beyond his feeble force, and extending the comforts of life to
a much enlarged circle, to those who had before known its necessaries only.
That these are not the vain dreams of sanguine hope, we have before our eyes
real and living examples. What, but education, has advanced us beyond the
condition of our indigenous neighbors? And what chains them to their present

3. A fanciful mental illusion or fabrication.

state of barbarism and wretchedness, but a bigotted veneration for the supposed superlative wisdom of their fathers, and the preposterous idea that they are to look backward for better things, and not forward, longing, as it should seem, to return to the days of eating acorns and roots, rather than indulge in the degeneracies of civilization? And how much more encouraging to the achievements of science and improvement is this, than the desponding view that the condition of man cannot be ameliorated, that what has been must ever be, and that to secure ourselves where we are, we must tread with awful reverence in the footsteps of our fathers. This doctrine is the genuine fruit of the alliance between Church and State; the tenants of which, finding themselves but too well in their present condition, oppose all advances which might unmask their usurpations, and monopolies of honors, wealth, and power, and fear every change, as endangering the comforts they now hold. Nor must we omit to mention, among the benefits of education, the incalculable advantage of training up able counsellors to administer the affairs of our country in all its departments, legislative, executive and judiciary, and to bear their proper share in the councils of our national government; nothing more than education advancing the prosperity, the power, and the happiness of a nation.

Encouraged, therefore, by the sentiments of the Legislature, manifested in this statute, we present the following tabular statement of the branches of learning which we think should be taught in the University, forming them into groups, each of which are within the powers of a single professor:

I.   Languages, ancient: Latin, Greek, Hebrew.
II. Languages, modern: French, Spanish, Italian, German, Anglo-Saxon.[4]
III. Mathematics, pure: Algebra, Fluxions,[5] Geometry, Elementary, Transcendental. Architecture, Military, Naval.
IV. Physico-Mathematics: Mechanics, Statics, Dynamics, Pneumatics, Acoustics, Optics, Astronomy, Geography.
V.   Physics, or Natural Philosophy: Chemistry, Mineralogy.
VI. Botany, Zoology.
VII. Anatomy, Medicine.
VIII. Government, Political Economy, Law of Nature and Nations, History, being interwoven with Politics and Law.
IX. Law, municipal.
X.   Ideology, General Grammar, Ethics, Rhetoric, Belles Lettres, and the fine arts.

---

4. See note 4, p. 4.
5. Differential calculus.

Some of the terms used in this table being subject to a difference of accep-
tation, it is proper to define the meaning and comprehension intended to be
given them here:

Geometry, Elementary, is that of straight lines and of the circle. Transcen-
    dental, is that of all other curves; it includes, of course, *Projectiles*, a
    leading branch of the military art.
Military Architecture includes Fortification, another branch of that art.
Statics respect matter generally, in a state of rest, and include Hydrostatics, or
    the laws of fluids particularly, at rest or in equilibrio.[6]
Dynamics, used as a general term, include Dynamics proper, or the laws of
    solids in motion; and Hydrodynamics, or Hydraulics, those of *fluids* in
    motion.
Pneumatics teach the theory of air, its weight, motion, condensation, rarefac-
    tion, &c.
Acoustics, or Phonics, the theory of sound.
Optics, the laws of light and vision.
Physics, or Physiology, in a general sense, mean the doctrine of the physical
    objects of our senses.
Chemistry is meant, with its other usual branches, to comprehend the theory
    of agriculture.
Mineralogy, in addition to its peculiar subjects, is here understood to embrace
    what is real in geology.
Ideology is the doctrine of thought.
General Grammar explains the construction of language.

Some articles in this distribution of sciences will need observation. A professor is proposed for ancient languages, the Latin, Greek, and Hebrew, particularly; but these languages being the foundation common to all the
sciences, it is difficult to foresee what may be the extent of this school. At the
same time, no greater obstruction to industrious study could be proposed than
the presence, the intrusions and the noisy turbulence of a multitude of small
boys; and if they are to be placed here for the rudiments of the languages, they
may be so numerous that its character and value as an University will be
merged in those of a Grammar school. It is, therefore, greatly to be wished,
that preliminary schools, either on private or public establishment, could be
distributed in districts through the State, as preparatory to the entrance of students into the University. The tender age at which this part of education com-
mences, generally about the tenth year, would weigh heavily with parents in

6. Balanced.

sending their sons to a school so distant as the central establishment would be from most of them. Districts of such extent as that every parent should be within a day's journey of his son at school, would be desirable in cases of sickness, and convenient for supplying their ordinary wants, and might be made to lessen sensibly the expense of this part of their education. And where a sparse population would not, within such a compass, furnish subjects sufficient to maintain a school, a competent enlargement of district must, of necessity, there be submitted to. At these district schools or colleges, boys should be rendered able to read the easier authors, Latin and Greek. This would be useful and sufficient for many not intended for an University education. At these, too, might be taught English grammar, the higher branches of numerical arithmetic, the geometry of straight lines and of the circle, the elements of navigation, and geography to a sufficient degree, and thus afford to greater numbers the means of being qualified for the various vocations of life, needing more instruction than merely menial or praedial[7] labor, and the same advantages to youths whose education may have been neglected until too late to lay a foundation in the learned languages. These institutions, intermediate between the primary schools and University, might then be the passage of entrance for youths into the University, where their classical learning might be critically completed, by a study of the authors of highest degree; and it is at this stage only that they should be received at the University. Giving then a portion of their time to a finished knowledge of the Latin and Greek, the rest might be appropriated to the modern languages, or to the commencement of the course of science for which they should be destined. This would generally be about the fifteenth year of their age, when they might go with more safety and contentment to that distance from their parents. Until this preparatory provision shall be made, either the University will be overwhelmed with the grammar school, or a separate establishment, under one or more ushers, for its lower classes, will be advisable, at a mile or two distant from the general one; where, too, may be exercised the stricter government necessary for young boys, but unsuitable for youths arrived at years of discretion.

The considerations which have governed the specification of languages to be taught by the professor of modern languages were, that the French is the language of general intercourse among nations, and as a depository of human science, is unsurpassed by any other language, living or dead; that the Spanish is highly interesting to us, as the language spoken by so great a portion of the inhabitants of our continents, with whom we shall probably have great intercourse ere long, and is that also in which is written the greater part of the earlier history of America. The Italian abounds with works of very superior order,

---

7. Agricultural.

valuable for their matter, and still more distinguished as models of the finest taste in style and composition. And the German now stands in a line with that of the most learned nations in richness of erudition and advance in the sciences. It is too of common descent with the language of our own country, a branch of the same original Gothic stock,[8] and furnishes valuable illustrations for us. But in this point of view, the Anglo-Saxon is of peculiar value. We have placed it among the modern languages, because it is in fact that which we speak, in the earliest form in which we have knowledge of it. It has been undergoing, with time, those gradual changes which all languages, ancient and modern, have experienced; and even now needs only to be printed in the modern character and orthography[9] to be intelligible, in a considerable degree, to an English reader. It has this value, too, above the Greek and Latin, that while it gives the radix[10] of the mass of our language, they explain its innovations only. Obvious proofs of this have been presented to the modern reader in the disquisitions of Horn Tooke;[11] and Fortescue Aland[12] has well explained the great instruction which may be derived from it to a full understanding of our ancient common law, on which, as a stock, our whole system of law is engrafted. It will form the first link in the chain of an historical review of our language through all its successive changes to the present day, will constitute the foundation of that critical instruction in it which ought to be found in a seminary of general learning, and thus reward amply the few weeks of attention which would alone be requisite for its attainment; a language already fraught with all the eminent science of our parent country, the future vehicle of whatever we may ourselves achieve, and destined to occupy so much space on the globe, claims distinguished attention in American education.

Medicine, where fully taught, is usually subdivided into several professorships, but this cannot well be without the accessory of an hospital, where the student can have the benefit of attending clinical lectures, and of assisting at operations of surgery. With this accessory, the seat of our University is not yet prepared, either by its population or by the numbers of poor who would leave their own houses, and accept of the charities of an hospital. For the present, therefore, we propose but a single professor for both medicine and anatomy. By him the medical science may be taught, with a history and explanations of

---

8. The language of the Goths; Germanic and medieval, not classical.

9. Correct spelling.

10. Root.

11. John Horn Tooke (1736–1812): a British radical and pamphleteer.

12. John Fortescue-Aland (1670–1746): a British Justice whom Jefferson admired for his Saxon learning.

all its successive theories from Hippocrates[13] to the present day; and anatomy may be fully treated. Vegetable pharmacy will make a part of the botanical course, and mineral and chemical pharmacy of those of mineralogy and chemistry.[14] This degree of medical information is such as the mass of scientific students would wish to possess, as enabling them in their course through life, to estimate with satisfaction the extent and limits of the aid to human life and health, which they may understandingly expect from that art; and it constitutes such a foundation for those intended for the profession, that the finishing course of practice at the bed-sides of the sick, and at the operations of surgery in a hospital, can neither be long nor expensive. To seek this finishing elsewhere, must therefore be submitted to for a while.

In conformity with the principles of our Constitution, which places all sects of religion on an equal footing, with the jealousies of the different sects in guarding that equality from encroachment and surprise, and with the sentiments of the Legislature in favor of freedom of religion, manifested on former occasions, we have proposed no professor of divinity; and the rather as the proofs of the being of a God, the creator, preserver, and supreme ruler of the universe, the author of all the relations of morality, and of the laws and obligations these infer, will be within the province of the professor of ethics; to which adding the developments of these moral obligations, of those in which all sects agree, with a knowledge of the languages, Hebrew, Greek, and Latin, a basis will be formed common to all sects. Proceeding thus far without offence to the Constitution, we have thought it proper at this point to leave every sect to provide, as they think fittest, the means of further instruction in their own peculiar tenets.

We are further of opinion, that after declaring by law that certain sciences shall be taught in the University, fixing the number of professors they require, which we think should, at present, be ten, limiting (except as to the professors who shall be first engaged in each branch,) a maximum for their salaries, (which should be a certain but moderate subsistence, to be made up by liberal tuition fees, as an excitement to assiduity,) it will be best to leave to the discretion of the visitors, the grouping of these sciences together, according to the accidental qualifications of the professors; and the introduction also of other branches of science, when enabled by private donations, or by public provision, and called for by the increase of population, or other change of circumstances; to establish beginnings, in short, to be developed by time, as

---

13. Hippocrates (460–377 BC): Greek physician regarded as the founder of medicine.
14. Jefferson is referring to the study of how different vegetables, minerals, and chemicals might be used as medicines.

those who come after us shall find expedient. They will be more advanced than we are in science and in useful arts, and will know best what will suit the circumstances of their day.

We have proposed no formal provision for the gymnastics of the school, although a proper object of attention for every institution of youth. These exercises with ancient nations, constituted the principal part of the education of their youth. Their arms and mode of warfare rendered them severe in the extreme; ours, on the same correct principle, should be adapted to our arms and warfare; and the manual exercise, military manœuvres, and tactics generally, should be the frequent exercises of the students, in their hours of recreation. It is at that age of aptness, docility, and emulation of the practices of manhood, that such things are soonest learnt and longest remembered. The use of tools too in the manual arts is worthy of encouragement, by facilitating to such as choose it, an admission into the neighboring workshops. To these should be added the arts which embellish life, dancing, music, and drawing; the last more especially, as an important part of military education. These innocent arts furnish amusement and happiness to those who, having time on their hands, might less inoffensively employ it. Needing, at the same time, no regular incorporation with the institution, they may be left to accessory teachers, who will be paid by the individuals employing them, the University only providing proper apartments for their exercise.

The fifth duty prescribed to the Commissioners, is to propose such general provisions as may be properly enacted by the Legislature, for the better organizing and governing the University.

In the education of youth, provision is to be made for, 1, tuition; 2, diet; 3, lodging; 4, government; and 5, honorary excitements. The first of these constitutes the proper functions of the professors; 2, the dieting of the students should be left to private boarding houses of their own choice, and at their own expense; to be regulated by the Visitors from time to time, the house only being provided by the University within its own precincts, and thereby of course subjected to the general regimen, moral or sumptuary,[15] which they shall prescribe. 3. They should be lodged in dormitories, making a part of the general system of buildings. 4. The best mode of government for youth, in large collections, is certainly a desideratum not yet attained with us. It may be well questioned whether *fear* after a certain age, is a motive to which we should have ordinary recourse. The human character is susceptible of other incitements to correct conduct, more worthy of employ, and of better effect. Pride of character, laudable ambition, and moral dispositions are innate correctives of the indiscretions of that lively age; and when strengthened by

---

15. Regulating or limiting personal expenditures.

habitual appeal and exercise, have a happier effect on future character than the degrading motive of fear. Hardening them to disgrace, to corporal punishments, and servile humiliations cannot be the best process for producing erect character. The affectionate deportment between father and son, offers in truth the best example for that of tutor and pupil; and the experience and practice of other countries,* in this respect, may be worthy of enquiry and consideration with us. It will then be for the wisdom and discretion of the Visitors to devise and perfect a proper system of government, which, if it be founded in reason and comity, will be more likely to nourish in the minds of our youth the combined spirit of order and self-respect, so congenial with our political institutions, and so important to be woven into the American character. 5. What qualifications shall be required to entitle to entrance into the University, the arrangement of the days and hours of lecturing for the different schools, so as to facilitate to the students the circle of attendance on them; the establishment of periodical and public examinations, the premiums to be given for distinguished merit; whether honorary degrees shall be conferred, and by what appellations; whether the title to these shall depend on the time the candidate has been at the University, or, where nature has given a greater share of understanding, attention, and application; whether he shall not be allowed the advantages resulting from these endowments, with other minor items of government, we are of opinion should be entrusted to the Visitors. . . .

Signed and certified by the members present, each in his proper handwriting, this 4th day of August, 1818.

PHIL. JEFFERSON,	WM. H. CABELL,
C. PENDLETON,	JAMES BRECKENRIDGE,
CREED TAYLOR,	NAT. H. CLAIBORNE,
SPENCER ROANE,	HENRY E. WATKINS,
PETER RANDOLPH,	WM. A. C. DADE,
JOHN M. C. TAYLOR,	JAMES MADISON,
WM. BROCKENBROUGH,	WILLIAM JONES,
J. G. JACKSON,	A. T. MASON,
ARCH'D RUTHERFORD,	THOMAS WILSON,
PHIL. SLAUGHTER,	HUGH HOLMES
ARDH'D STUART,	

*A police exercised by the students themselves, under proper discretion, has been tried with success in some countries, and the rather as forming them for initiation into the duties and practices of civil life.

Excerpts from *Notes on Virginia* (1782)

QUERY VI[1]

A notice of the mines and other subterraneous riches; its trees, plants, fruits, &c.

. . . The opinion advanced by the Count de Buffon,[2] is 1. That the animals common both to the old and new world, are smaller in the latter. 2. That those peculiar to the new, are on a smaller scale. 3. That those which have been domesticated in both, have degenerated in America: and 4. That on the whole it exhibits fewer species. And the reason he thinks is, that the heats of America are less; that more waters are spread over its surface by nature, and fewer of these drained off by the hand of man. In other words, that *heat* is friendly, and *moisture* adverse to the production and developement of large quadrupeds. . . .

Hitherto I have considered this hypothesis as applied to brute animals only, and not in its extension to the man of America, whether aboriginal or transplanted. It is the opinion of Mons. de Buffon that the former furnishes no exception to it. . . . Of the Indian of South America I know nothing; for I would not honor with the appellation of knowledge, what I derive from the fables published of them. These I believe to be just as true as the fables of Æsop.[3] This belief is founded on what I have seen of man, white, red, and black, and what has been written of him by authors, enlightened themselves, and writing amidst an enlightened people. The Indian of North America being more within our reach, I can speak of him somewhat from my own knowledge, but more from the information of others better acquainted with him, and on whose truth and judgment I can rely. From these sources I am able to say, in contradiction to this representation, that he is neither more defective in ardor, nor more impotent with his female, than the white reduced to the same diet and exercise: that he is brave, when an enterprize depends on bravery; education with him making the point of honor consist in the destruction of an enemy by stratagem, and in the preservation of his own person free from injury; or perhaps this is nature; while it is education which

---

1. See Introduction, pp. xvi–xvii.

2. George-Louis Leclerc, Count of Buffon (1707–88): a noted French naturalist. His massive *Histoire Naturelle*, published in 44 volumes over 40 years (1749–88; 1804), became the basis for many branches of modern natural science.

3. Aesop (sixth century BC): Greek author whose fables—in which animals talked and acted like humans—illustrated moral points.

teaches us to° honor force more than finesse: that he will defend himself against an host of enemies, always chusing to be killed, rather than to surrender,† though it be to the whites, who he knows will treat him well: that in other situations also he meets death with more deliberation, and endures tortures with a firmness unknown almost to religious enthusiasm with us: that he is affectionate to his children, careful of them, and indulgent in the extreme: that his affections comprehend his other connections, weakening, as with us, from circle to circle, as they recede from the center: that his friendships are

°Sol Rodomonte sprezza di venire Se non, dove la via meno sicura. Ariosto. 14. 117.

†In so judicious an author as Don Ulloa,[4] and one to whom we are indebted for the most precise information we have of South America, I did not expect to find such assertions as the following. 'Los Indios vencidos son los mas cobardes y pusilanimes que se peuden vér: — se hacen inöcentes, se humillan hasta el desprecio, disculpan su inconsiderado arrojo, y con las súplicas y los ruegos dán seguras pruebas de su pusilanimidad. — ó lo que resieren las historias de la Conquista, sobre sus grandes acciones, es en un sentido figurado, ó el caracter de estas gentes no es ahora segun era entonces; pero lo que no tiene duda es, que las Naciones de la parte Septentrional subsisten en la misma libertad que siempre han tenido, sin haber sido sojuzgados por algun Principe extraño, y que viven segun su régimen y costumbres de toda la vida, sin que haya habido motivo para que muden de caracter; y en estos se vé lo mismo, que sucede en los del Perú, y de toda la América Meridional, reducidos, y que nunca lo han estado.'[5] *Noticias Americanas. Entretenimiento* XVIII, § 1. Don Ulloa here admits, that the authors who have described the Indians of South America, before they were enslaved, had represented them as a brave people, and therefore seems to

---

4. Antonio de Ulloa (1716–95): Spanish scientist, explorer, and colonial administrator. In 1748, Ulloa and Jorge Juan published *Relación histórica del viaje á la América Meridional*, an account of their travels in South America. In 1766 Ulloa served as Governor of Louisiana, which had been ceded by France to Spain. See Jefferson's letter to Livingston, note 2, p. 198.

5. "Indians, when defeated, are the most craven and cowardly men one can see. They protest their innocence, humble themselves to the point of self-contempt, beg forgiveness for their ill-considered boldness, and with their pleas and supplication render manifest their cowardice. Either the accounts of the Indians' brave deeds, in the histories of the conquest, are to be taken figuratively, or the character of these peoples is not today what is was then. But it is clear that the nations of North America remain in the same state of liberty as always, never having been subjugated by any foreign ruler, and maintain their traditional customs and way of life, nothing having occurred to cause a change in their character; and among them, though they have never been conquered, one sees the same behavior as in the subjugated peoples of Peru and all of South America." (A mistake appears in the Spanish text, perhaps as a result of Jefferson's own faulty transcription: *resieren* should be *refieren*.)

strong and faithful to the uttermost extremity:* that his sensibility is keen, even the warriors weeping most bitterly on the loss of their children, though in general they endeavour to appear superior to human events: that his vivacity and activity of mind is equal to ours in the same situation; hence his eagerness for hunting, and for games of chance. The women are submitted to unjust drudgery. This I believe is the case with every barbarous people. With such, force is law. The stronger sex therefore imposes on the weaker. It is civilization

---

have suspected that the cowardice which he had observed in those of the present race might be the effect of subjugation. But, supposing the Indians of North America to be cowards also, he concludes the ancestors of those of South America to have been so too, and therefore that those authors have given fictions for truths. He was probably not acquainted himself with the Indians of North America, and had formed his opinion of them from hear-say. Great numbers of French, of English, and of Americans, are perfectly acquainted with these people. Had he had an opportunity of enquiring of any of these, they would have told him, that there never was an instance known of an Indian begging his life when in the power of his enemies: on the contrary, that he courts death by every possible insult and provocation. His reasoning then would have been reversed thus. 'Since the present Indian of North America is brave, and authors tell us, that the ancestors of those of South America were brave also; it must follow, that the cowardice of their descendants is the effect of subjugation and ill treatment.' For he observes, *ib*. §. 27, that 'los obrages los aniquilan por la inhumanidad con que se les trata.'[6]

*A remarkable instance of this appeared in the case of the late Col. Byrd,[7] who was sent to the Cherokee nation to transact some business with them. It happened that some of our disorderly people had just killed one or two of that nation. It was therefore proposed in the council of the Cherokees that Col. Byrd should be put to death, in revenge for the loss of their countrymen. Among them was a chief called Silòuee, who, on some former occasion, had contracted an acquaintance and friendship with Col. Byrd. He came to him every night in his tent, and told him not to be afraid, they should not kill him. After many days deliberation, however, the determination was, contrary to Silòuee's expectation, that Byrd should be put to death, and some warriors were dispatched as executioners. Silòuee attended them, and when they entered the tent, he threw himself between them and Byrd, and said to the warriors, 'this man is my friend: before you get at him, you must kill me.' On which they returned, and the council respected the principle so much as to recede from their determination.

---

6. ". . . the forced labor imposed on the Indians destroys them, such is the inhumanity with which they are treated."
7. Colonel William Byrd II (1674–1744) surveyed the wilderness between Virginia and North Carolina and provided the land on which Richmond, Virginia was built.

alone which replaces women in the enjoyment of their natural equality. That first teaches us to subdue the selfish passions, and to respect those rights in others which we value in ourselves. Were we in equal barbarism, our females would be equal drudges. The man with them is less strong than with us, but their woman stronger than ours; and both for the same obvious reason; because our man and their woman is habituated to labour, and formed by it. With both races the sex which is indulged with ease is least athletic. An Indian man is small in the hand and wrist for the same reason for which a sailor is large and strong in the arms and shoulders, and a porter in the legs and thighs. —They raise fewer children than we do. The causes of this are to be found, not in a difference of nature, but of circumstance. The women very frequently attending the men in their parties of war and of hunting, childbearing becomes extremely inconvenient to them. It is said, therefore, that they have learnt the practice of procuring abortion by the use of some vegetable; and that it even extends to prevent conception for a considerable time after. During these parties they are exposed to numerous hazards, to excessive exertions, to the greatest extremities of hunger. Even at their homes the nation depends for food, through a certain part of every year, on the gleanings of the forest: that is, they experience a famine once in every year. With all animals, if the female be badly fed, or not fed at all, her young perish: and if both male and female be reduced to like want, generation becomes less active, less productive. To the obstacles then of want and hazard, which nature has opposed to the multiplication of wild animals, for the purpose of restraining their numbers within certain bounds, those of labour and of voluntary abortion are added with the Indian. No wonder then if they multiply less than we do. Where food is regularly supplied, a single farm will shew more of cattle, than a whole country of forests can of buffaloes. The same Indian women, when married to white traders, who feed them and their children plentifully and regularly, who exempt them from excessive drudgery, who keep them stationary and unexposed to accident, produce and raise as many children as the white women. Instances are known, under these circumstances, of their rearing a dozen children. An inhuman practice once prevailed in this country of making slaves of the Indians. It is a fact well known with us, that the Indian women so enslaved produced and raised as numerous families as either the whites or blacks among whom they lived. —It has been said, that Indians have less hair than the whites, except on the head. But this is a fact of which fair proof can scarcely be had. With them it is disgraceful to be hairy on the body. They say it likens them to hogs. They therefore pluck the hair as fast as it appears. But the traders who marry their women, and prevail on them to discontinue this practice, say, that nature is the same with them as with the whites. Nor, if the fact be true, is the consequence necessary which has been drawn from it. Negroes have notoriously less hair than the whites; yet they are more ardent. But if cold and moisture be the agents of nature for diminishing the races of animals, how comes she all at once to suspend their operation as to the physical man of the new world, whom the Count acknowledges to be 'à peu près de même stature que l'homme de notre monde,'[8] and to let loose their influence on his moral faculties? How has this 'combination of the elements and other physical causes, so contrary to the enlargement of animal nature in this new world, these obstacles to the developement and formation of great germs,' been arrested and suspended, so as to permit the human body to acquire its just dimensions, and by what inconceivable process has their action been directed on his mind alone? To judge of the truth of this, to form a just estimate of their genius and mental powers, more facts are wanting, and great allowance to be made for those circumstances of their situation which call for a display of particular talents only. This done, we shall probably find that they are formed in mind as well as in body, on the same module with the 'Homo sapiens Europaeus.'* The principles of their society forbidding all compulsion, they are to be led to duty and to enterprize by personal influence and persuasion. Hence eloquence in council, bravery and address in war, become the foundations of all consequence with them. To these acquirements all their faculties are directed. Of their bravery and address in war we have multiplied proofs, because we have been the subjects on which they were exercised. Of their eminence in oratory we have fewer examples, because it is displayed chiefly in their own councils. Some, however, we have of very superior lustre. I may challenge the whole orations of Demosthenes[9] and Cicero,[10] and of any more eminent orator, if Europe has furnished more eminent, to produce a single passage, superior to the speech of Logan, a Mingo chief, to Lord Dunmore,[11] when governor of this state. And, as a testimony of their talents in this line, I beg leave to introduce it, first stating the incidents necessary for understanding it. In the spring of the year 1774, a robbery and murder were committed on an inhabitant of the frontiers of Virginia, by two Indians of the Shawanee tribe. The neighbouring whites, according to their custom,

*Linn. Syst. Definition of a Man.

---

8. "of about the same height as men of our world [i.e., Europe]"
9. Demosthenes (fourth century BC): Greek orator who warned his countrymen that Philip of Macedon was planning to conquer Greece.
10. Marcus Tullius Cicero (106–43 BC): statesman, philosopher, and orator who lived in Rome at the end of the Republic.
11. John Murray, Fourth Earl of Dunmore, was colonial governor of Virginia from 1771–76. See note 15, p. 13.

undertook to punish this outrage in a summary way. Col. Cresap,[12] a man infamous for the many murders he had committed on those much-injured people, collected a party, and proceeded down the Kanhaway in quest of vengeance. Unfortunately a canoe of women and children, with one man only, was seen coming from the opposite shore, unarmed, and unsuspecting an hostile attack from the whites. Cresap and his party concealed themselves on the bank of the river, and the moment the canoe reached the shore, singled out their objects, and, at one fire, killed every person in it. This happened to be the family of Logan, who had long been distinguished as a friend of the whites. This unworthy return provoked his vengeance. He accordingly signalized himself in the war which ensued. In the autumn of the same year, a decisive battle was fought at the mouth of the Great Kanhaway, between the collected forces of the Shawanees, Mingoes, and Delawares, and a detachment of the Virginia militia. The Indians were defeated, and sued for peace. Logan however disdained to be seen among the suppliants. But, lest the sincerity of a treaty should be distrusted, from which so distinguished a chief absented himself, he sent by a messenger the following speech to be delivered to Lord Dunmore.

"I appeal to any white man to say, if ever he entered Logan's cabin hungry, and he gave him not meat; if ever he came cold and naked, and he clothed him not. During the course of the last long and bloody war, Logan remained idle in his cabin, an advocate for peace. Such was my love for the whites, that my countrymen pointed as they passed, and said, 'Logan is the friend of white men.' I had even thought to have lived with you, but for the injuries of one man. Col. Cresap, the last spring, in cold blood, and unprovoked, murdered all the relations of Logan, not sparing even my women and children. There runs not a drop of my blood in the veins of any living creature. This called on me for revenge. I have sought it: I have killed many: I have fully glutted my

---

12. Colonel Michael Cresap (1742–75): a Virginia frontiersman, surveyor, and American Revolutionary soldier. Ohioan Indians, resisting the westward expansion of the whites, attacked a surveying party of which Cresap was a member. Cresap led several raids in retaliation and was part of the raid—later known as "Cresap's War"—that resulted in the brutal murder of Logan's family. Jefferson's Federalist enemies claimed that Cresap was not responsible for the incident and that Jefferson, in publishing Chief Logan's speech in the *Notes*, was slandering an innocent man; this controversy had serious political implications for Jefferson. He conducted his own investigation into the matter and collected, in an appendix to the 1800 edition of the *Notes*, a body of documentary evidence that seemed to prove Cresap's guilt once and for all. But eyewitness testimony discovered after Jefferson's death (and of which he might have been aware) revealed that Daniel Greathouse—Cresap's second-in-command—was probably responsible for the massacre.

vengeance. For my country, I rejoice at the beams of peace. But do not harbour a thought that mine is the joy of fear. Logan never felt fear. He will not turn on his heel to save his life. Who is there to mourn for Logan? —Not one."

Before we condemn the Indians of this continent as wanting genius, we must consider that letters have not yet been introduced among them. Were we to compare them in their present state with the Europeans North of the Alps, when the Roman arms and arts first crossed those mountains, the comparison would be unequal, because, at that time, those parts of Europe were swarming with numbers; because numbers produce emulation, and multiply the chances of improvement, and one improvement begets another. Yet I may safely ask, How many good poets, how many able mathematicians, how many great inventors in arts or sciences, had Europe North of the Alps then produced? And it was sixteen centuries after this before a Newton[13] could be formed. I do not mean to deny, that there are varieties in the race of man, distinguished by their powers both of body and mind. I believe there are, as I see to be the case in the races of other animals. I only mean to suggest a doubt, whether the bulk and faculties of animals depend on the side of the Atlantic on which their food happens to grow, or which furnishes the elements of which they are compounded? Whether nature has enlisted herself as a Cis- or Trans-Atlantic partisan? I am induced to suspect, there has been more eloquence than sound reasoning displayed in support of this theory; that it is one of those cases where the judgment has been seduced by a glowing pen: and whilst I render every tribute of honor and esteem to the celebrated Zoologist, who has added, and is still adding, so many precious things to the treasures of science, I must doubt whether in this instance he has not cherished error also, by lending her for a moment his vivid imagination and bewitching language.

So far the Count de Buffon has carried this new theory of the tendency of nature to belittle her productions on this side the Atlantic. Its application to the race of whites, transplanted from Europe, remained for the Abbé Raynal.[14] 'On doit etre etonné (he says) que l'Amerique n'ait pas encore produit un bon poëte, un habile mathematicien, un homme de genie dans un seul art, ou une seule science.' 7. Hist. Philos. p. 92. ed. Maestricht. 1774. 'America has not yet produced one good poet.' When we shall have existed as a people as long as the Greeks did before they produced a Homer,[15] the

---

13. Sir Isaac Newton (1642–1727): prominent mathematician, physicist, and scientist.

14. Guillaume-Thomas-François Raynal (1713–96): a French priest who wrote a philosophical history of the European colonies in the Indies and America, published in 1770.

15. Homer (c. eighth century BC): Greek poet, author of the epics *Iliad* and *Odyssey*.

Romans a Virgil,[16] the French a Racine[17] and Voltaire,[18] the English a Shakespeare[19] and Milton,[20] should this reproach be still true, we will enquire from what unfriendly causes it has proceeded, that the other countries of Europe and quarters of the earth shall not have inscribed any name in the roll of poets.* But neither has America produced 'one able mathematician, one man of genius in a single art or a single science.' In war we have produced a Washington,[21] whose memory will be adored while liberty shall have votaries, whose name will triumph over time, and will in future ages assume its just station among the most celebrated worthies of the world, when that wretched philosophy shall be forgotten which would have arranged him among the degeneracies of nature. In physics we have produced a Franklin,[22] than whom no one of the present age has made more important discoveries, nor has en-

---

*Has the world as yet produced more than two poets, acknowledged to be such by all nations? An Englishman, only, reads Milton with delight, an Italian Tasso,[23] a Frenchman the Henriade,[24] a Portuguese Camouens:[25] but Homer and Virgil have been the rapture of every age and nation: they are read with enthusiasm in their originals by those who can read the originals, and in translations by those who cannot.

---

16. Virgil (70–19 BC): Roman poet, author of the epic *Aeneid*.

17. Jean Baptiste Racine (1639–99): French tragic dramatist who later became royal historiographer to Louis XIV. His major works included *Britannicus* (1669) and *Phédre* (1677).

18. François Marie Arouet de Voltaire (1694–1778): French writer, satirist, and champion of the Enlightenment, best known as the author of *Candide* (1759).

19. William Shakespeare (1564–1616): English playwright and poet.

20. John Milton (1608–74): English author and poet. A Puritan, Milton sided with Cromwell during the English Civil War. Best known for his poem *Paradise Lost* (1667) and *Areopagitica* (1644), his defense of free speech.

21. George Washington (1732–99): commander-in-chief of the Continental Army during the American Revolution and first president of the United States, 1789–97.

22. Benjamin Franklin (1706–90): American printer, author, inventor, revolutionary, and politician. As the American ambassador to France from 1776 to 1785, Franklin negotiated French support for the American Revolution; in his later years, he served as a delegate to the Constitutional Convention. Along the way, he edited and published the hugely popular *Poor Richard's Almanac*, created early prototypes of the modern fire department and library, wrote his well-known *Autobiography*, and was elected a Fellow of the Royal Society, among other notable achievements.

23. Torquato Tasso (1544–1595): Italian poet, author of the epic *Gerusalemme Liberata* (1581).

24. Poem by Voltaire (see note 18, above).

25. Luiz vaz de Camões (c. 1524–1580): Portuguese poet, author of epic poem *Os Luisíadas*.

riched philosophy with more, or more ingenious solutions of the phænomena of nature. We have supposed Mr. Rittenhouse[26] second to no astronomer living: that in genius he must be the first, because he is self-taught. As an artist he has exhibited as great a proof of mechanical genius as the world has ever produced. He has not indeed made a world; but he has by imitation approached nearer its Maker than any man who has lived from the creation to this day.* As in philosophy and war, so in government, in oratory, in painting, in the plastic art, we might shew that America, though but a child of yesterday, has already given hopeful proofs of genius, as well of the nobler kinds, which arouse the best feelings of man, which call him into action, which substantiate his freedom, and conduct him to happiness, as of the subordinate, which serve to amuse him only. We therefore suppose, that this reproach is as unjust as it is unkind; and that, of the geniuses which adorn the present age, America contributes its full share. For comparing it with those countries, where genius is most cultivated, where are the most excellent models for art, and scaffoldings for the attainment of science, as France and England for instance, we calculate thus. The United States contain three millions of inhabitants; France twenty millions; and the British islands ten. We produce a Washington, a Franklin, a Rittenhouse. France then should have half a dozen in each of these lines, and Great-Britain half that number, equally eminent. It may be true, that France has: we are but just becoming acquainted with her, and our acquaintance so far gives us high ideas of the genius of her inhabitants. It would be injuring too many of them to name particularly a Voltaire, a Buffon, the constellation of Encyclopedists,[27] the Abbé Raynal himself, &c. &c. We therefore have reason to believe she can produce her full quota of genius. The present war having so long cut off all communication with Great-Britain, we are not able to make a fair estimate of the state of science in that

*There are various ways of keeping truth out of sight. Mr. Rittenhouse's model of the planetary system has the plagiary appellation of an Orrery;[28]and the quadrant invented by Godfrey, an American also, and with the aid of which the European nations traverse the globe, is called Hadley's quadrant.[29]

---

26. David Rittenhouse (1732–96): American astronomer and mathematician. See note 28 below, and Jefferson's letter to Rittenhouse, p. 143.

27. A group of French Enlightenment thinkers, who, in the middle of the eighteenth century, compiled articles on philosophic, religious, scientific, moral, and economic questions in order to promote the spread of general knowledge.

28. A clockwork model of the solar system invented by American astronomer David Rittenhouse but subsequently named for Charles Boyle, the Fourth Earl of Orrery.

29. Thomas Godfrey (1704–49): American artisan and mathematician who invented the quadrant, even though it was named for the British mathematician, John Hadley (1682–1744).

country. The spirit in which she wages war is the only sample before our eyes, and that does not seem the legitimate offspring either of science or of civilization. The sun of her glory is fast descending to the horizon. Her philosophy has crossed the Channel, her freedom the Atlantic, and herself seems passing to that awful dissolution, whose issue is not given human foresight to scan.[*]

[*]In a later edition of the Abbé Raynal's work, he has withdrawn his censure from that part of the new world inhabited by the Federo-Americans; but has left it still on the other parts. North America has always been more accessible to strangers than South. If he was mistaken then as to the former, he may be so as to the latter. The glimmerings which reach us from South America enable us only to see that its inhabitants are held under the accumulated pressure of slavery, superstition, and ignorance. Whenever they shall be able to rise under this weight, and to shew themselves to the rest of the world, they will probably shew they are like the rest of the world. We have not yet sufficient evidence that there are more lakes and fogs in South America than in other parts of the earth. As little do we know what would be their operation on the mind of man. That country has been visited by Spaniards and Portugueze chiefly, and almost exclusively. These, going from a country of the old world remarkably dry in its soil and climate, fancied there were more lakes and fogs in South America than in Europe. An inhabitant of Ireland, Sweden, or Finland, would have formed the contrary opinion. Had South America then been discovered and seated by a people from a fenny[30] country, it would probably have been represented as much drier than the old world. A patient pursuit of facts, and cautious combination and comparison of them, is the drudgery to which man is subjected by his Maker, if he wishes to attain sure knowledge.

---

30. Marshy, boggy.

QUERY VIII[1]

The number of its inhabitants?

POPULATION. The following table[2] shews the number of persons imported for the establishment of our colony in its infant state, and the census of inhabitants at different periods, extracted from our historians and public records, as particularly as I have had opportunities and leisure to examine them. Successive lines in the same year shew successive periods of time in that year. I have stated the census in two different columns, the whole inhabitants having been sometimes numbered, and sometimes the *tythes* only. This term, with us, includes the free males above 16 years of age, and slaves above that age of both sexes. A further examination of our records would render this history of our population much more satisfactory and perfect, by furnishing a greater number of intermediate terms. Those however which are here stated will enable us to calculate, with a considerable degree of precision, the rate at which we have increased. During the infancy of the colony, while numbers were small, wars, importations, and other accidental circumstances render the progression fluctuating and irregular. By the year 1654, however, it becomes tolerably uniform, importations having in a great measure ceased from the dissolution of the company,[3] and the inhabitants become too numerous to be sensibly affected by Indian wars. Beginning at that period, therefore, we find that from thence to the year 1772, our tythes had increased from 7209 to 153,000. The whole term being of 118 years, yields a duplication once in every 27 1/4 years. The intermediate enumerations taken in 1700, 1748, and 1759, furnish proofs of the uniformity of this progression. Should this rate of increase continue, we shall have between six and seven millions of inhabitants within 95 years. If we suppose our country to be bounded, at some future day, by the meridian of the mouth of the Great Kanhaway, (within which it has been before conjectured, are 64,491 square miles) there will then be 100 inhabitants for every square mile, which is nearly the state of population in the British islands.

---

1. See Introduction, pp. xvi–xvii.

2. Omitted here.

3. Virginia was first settled by the Virginia Company of London, which was chartered by King James in 1606. But the company failed to make a profit for its stockholders, and the colony was beset with political division and financial mismanagement. In 1624, King James dissolved the company and declared Virginia a royal colony, which placed it on a more stable footing.

Here I will beg leave to propose a doubt. The present desire of America is to produce rapid population by as great importations of foreigners as possible. But is this founded in good policy? The advantage proposed is the multiplication of numbers. Now let us suppose (for example only) that, in this state, we could double our numbers in one year by the importation of foreigners; and this is a greater accession than the most sanguine advocate for emigration has a right to expect. Then I say, beginning with a double stock, we shall attain any given degree of population only 27 years and 3 months sooner than if we proceed on our single stock. If we propose four millions and a half as a competent population for this state, we should be 54 1/2 years attaining it, could we at once double our numbers; and 81 3/4 years, if we rely on natural propagation, as may be seen by the following table.[4]

In the first column are stated periods of 27 1/4 years; in the second are our numbers, at each period, as they will be if we proceed on our actual stock; and in the third are what they would be, at the same periods, were we to set out from the double of our present stock. I have taken the term of four millions and a half of inhabitants for example's sake only. Yet I am persuaded it is a greater number than the country spoken of, considering how much inarrable[5] land it contains, can clothe and feed, without a material change in the quality of their diet. But are there no inconveniences to be thrown into the scale against the advantage expected from a multiplication of numbers by the importation of foreigners? It is for the happiness of those united in society to harmonize as much as possible in matters which they must of necessity transact together. Civil government being the sole object of forming societies, its administration must be conducted by common consent. Every species of government has its specific principles. Ours perhaps are more peculiar than those of any other in the universe. It is a composition of the freest principles of the English constitution, with others derived from natural right and natural reason. To these nothing can be more opposed than the maxims of absolute monarchies. Yet, from such, we are to expect the greatest number of emigrants. They will bring with them the principles of the governments they leave, imbibed in their early youth; or, if able to throw them off, it will be in exchange for an unbounded licentiousness, passing, as is usual, from one extreme to another. It would be a miracle were they to stop precisely at the point of temperate liberty. These principles, with their language, they will transmit to their children. In proportion to their numbers, they will share with us the legislation. They will infuse into it their spirit, warp and bias its direction, and render it a heterogeneous, incoherent, distracted mass. I may appeal to expe-

---

4. Omitted here.
5. Not fit to be cultivated.

rience, during the present contest, for a verification of these conjectures. But, if they be not certain in event, are they not possible, are they not probable? Is it not safer to wait with patience 27 years and three months longer, for the attainment of any degree of population desired, or expected? May not our government be more homogeneous, more peaceable, more durable? Suppose 20 millions of republican Americans thrown all of a sudden into France, what would be the condition of that kingdom? If it would be more turbulent, less happy, less strong, we may believe that the addition of half a million of foreigners to our present numbers would produce a similar effect here. If they come of themselves, they are entitled to all the rights of citizenship: but I doubt the expediency of inviting them by extraordinary encouragements. I mean not that these doubts should be extended to the importation of useful artificers.[6] The policy of that measure depends on very different considerations. Spare no expence in obtaining them. They will after a while go to the plough and the hoe; but, in the mean time, they will teach us something we do not know. It is not so in agriculture. The indifferent state of that among us does not proceed from a want of knowledge merely; it is from our having such quantities of land to waste as we please. In Europe the object is to make the most of their land, labour being abundant: here it is to make the most of our labour, land being abundant.

It will be proper to explain how the numbers for the year 1782 have been obtained; as it was not from a perfect census of the inhabitants. It will at the same time develope the proportion between the free inhabitants and slaves. The following return of taxable articles for that year was given in.

53,289	free males above 21 years of age.
211,698	slaves of all ages and sexes.
23,766	not distinguished in the returns, but said to be titheable[7] slaves.
195,439	horses.
609,734	cattle.
5,126	wheels of riding-carriages.
191	taverns.

There were no returns from the 8 counties of Lincoln, Jefferson, Fayette, Monongalia, Yohogania, Ohio, Northampton, and York. To find the number of slaves which should have been returned instead of the 23,766 titheables, we must mention that some observations on a former census had given reason

6. Manufacturers.

7. Subject or liable to the payment of tithes, i.e., one-tenth of one's property for the support of the church.

to believe that the numbers above and below 16 years of age were equal. The double of this number, therefore, to wit, 47,532 must be added to 211,698, which will give us 259,230 slaves of all ages and sexes. To find the number of free inhabitants, we must repeat the observation, that those above and below 16 are nearly equal. But as the number 53,289 omits the males between 16 and 21, we must supply them from conjecture. On a former experiment it had appeared that about one-third of our militia, that is, of the males between 16 and 50, were unmarried. Knowing how early marriage takes place here, we shall not be far wrong in supposing that the unmarried part of our militia are those between 16 and 21. If there be young men who do not marry till after 21, there are as many who marry before that age. But as the men above 50 were not included in the militia, we will suppose the unmarried, or those between 16 and 21, to be one-fourth of the whole number above 16, then we have the following calculation:

53,289	free males above 21 years of age.
17,763	free males between 16 and 21.
71,052	free males under 16.
142,104	free females of all ages.
284,208	free inhabitants of all ages.
259,230	slaves of all ages.
543,438	inhabitants, exclusive of the 8 counties from which were no returns. In these 8 counties in the years 1779 and 1780 were 3,161 militia. Say then,
3,161	free males above the age of 16.
3,161	ditto under 16.
6,322	free females.
12,644	free inhabitants in these 8 counties. To find the number of slaves, say, as 284,208 to 259,230, so is 12,644 to 11,532. Adding the third of these numbers to the first, and the fourth to the second, we have,
296,852	free inhabitants.
270,762	slaves.
567,614	inhabitants of every age, sex, and condition.

But 296,852, the number of free inhabitants, are to 270,762, the number of slaves, nearly as 11 to 10. Under the mild treatment our slaves experience, and their wholesome, though coarse, food, this blot in our country increases as fast, or faster, than the whites. During the regal government, we had at one time obtained a law, which imposed such a duty on the importation of slaves, as amounted nearly to a prohibition, when one inconsiderate assembly, placed under a peculiarity of circumstance, repealed the law. This repeal met a joyful sanction from the then sovereign, and no devices, no expedients, which could ever after be attempted by subsequent assemblies, and they seldom met without attempting them, could succeed in getting the royal assent to a renewal of the duty. In the very first session held under the republican government, the assembly passed a law for the perpetual prohibition of the importation of slaves. This will in some measure stop the increase of this great political and moral evil, while the minds of our citizens may be ripening for a complete emancipation of human nature.

QUERY XI[1]

A description of the Indians established in that state?

ABORIGINES.   When the first effectual settlement of our colony was made, which was in 1607, the country from the sea-coast to the mountains, and from Patowmac to the most southern waters of James river, was occupied by upwards of forty different tribes of Indians. Of these the *Powhatans*, the *Mannahoacs*, and *Monacans*, were the most powerful. Those between the sea-coast and falls of the rivers, were in amity with one another, and attached to the *Powhatans* as their link of union. Those between the falls of the rivers and the mountains, were divided into two confederacies; the tribes inhabiting the head waters of Patowmac and Rappahanoc being attached to the *Mannahoacs*; and those on the upper parts of James river to the *Monacans*. But the *Monacans* and their friends were in amity with the *Mannahoacs* and their friends, and waged joint and perpetual war against the *Powhatans*. We are told that the *Powhatans*, *Mannahoacs*, and *Monacans*, spoke languages so radically different, that interpreters were necessary when they transacted business. Hence we may conjecture, that this was not the case between all the tribes, and probably that each spoke the language of the nation to which it was attached; which we know to have been the case in many particular instances. Very possibly there may have been antiently three different stocks, each of which multiplying in a long course of time, had separated into so many little societies. [This practice results from the circumstance of their having never submitted themselves to any laws, any coercive power, any shadow of government. Their only controuls are their manners, and that moral sense of right and wrong, which, like the sense of tasting and feeling, in every man makes a part of his nature. An offence against these is punished by contempt, by exclusion from society, or, where the case is serious, as that of murder, by the individuals whom it concerns. Imperfect as this species of coercion may seem, crimes are very rare among them: insomuch that were it made a question, whether no law, as among the savage Americans, or too much law, as among the civilized Europeans, submits man to the greatest evil, one who has seen both conditions of existence would pronounce it to be the last: and that the sheep are happier of themselves, than under care of the wolves. It will be said,

---

1. See Introduction, pp. xvi–xvii.

that great societies cannot exist without government. The Savages therefore break them into small ones.][2]

The territories of the *Powhatan* confederacy, south of the Patowmac, comprehended about 8000 square miles, 30 tribes, and 2400 warriors. Capt. Smith[3] tells us, that within 60 miles of James town were 5000 people, of whom 1500 were warriors. From this we find the proportion of their warriors to their whole inhabitants, was as 3 to 10. The *Powhatan* confederacy then would consist of about 8000 inhabitants, which was one for every square mile; being about the twentieth part of our present population in the same territory, and the hundredth of that of the British islands.

Besides these, were the *Nottoways*, living on Nottoway river, the *Meherrins* and *Tuteloes* on Meherrin river, who were connected with the Indians of Carolina, probably with the *Chowanocs*.

The preceding table[4] contains a state of these several tribes, according to their confederacies and geographical situation, with their numbers when we first became acquainted with them, where these numbers are known. The numbers of some of them are again stated as they were in the year 1669, when an attempt was made by the assembly to enumerate them. Probably the enumeration is imperfect, and in some measure conjectural, and that a further search into the records would furnish many more particulars. What would be the melancholy sequel of their history, may however be augured[5] from the census of 1669; by which we discover that the tribes therein enumerated were, in the space of 62 years, reduced to about one-third of their former numbers. Spirituous liquors, the small-pox, war, and an abridgment of territory, to a people who lived principally on the spontaneous productions of nature, had committed terrible havock among them, which generation, under the obstacles opposed to it among them, was not likely to make good. That the lands of this country were taken from them by conquest, is not so general a truth as is supposed. I find in our historians and records, repeated proofs of purchase, which cover a considerable part of the lower country; and many more would

---

2. The bracketed section above was added to the 1787 and subsequent editions of the *Notes on Virginia*. In the original version, the preceding sentence read, "Very possibly there may have been antiently three different stocks, each of which multiplying in a long course of time, had separated into so many little societies the principles of their governments being so weak as to this liberty to all its members."

3. Captain John Smith (1580–1631): one of the founders of the first permanent English settlement at Jamestown, Virginia. Smith was later taken captive by the Powhatan Indians and condemned to death. He was saved by Pocahontas, daughter of the Indian chief.

4. Omitted here.

5. Predicted from signs or tokens.

doubtless be found on further search. The upper country we know has been acquired altogether by purchases made in the most unexceptionable form.

Westward of all these tribes, beyond the mountains, and extending to the great lakes, were the *Massawomecs*, a most powerful confederacy, who harrassed unremittingly the *Powhatans* and *Manahoacs*. These were probably the ancestors of the tribes known at present by the name of the *Six Nations*.

. . . . Great question has arisen from whence came those aboriginal inhabitants of America? Discoveries, long ago made, were sufficient to shew that a passage from Europe to America was always practicable, even to the imperfect navigation of ancient times. In going from Norway to Iceland, from Iceland to Groenland, from Groenland to Labrador, the first traject[6] is the widest: and this having been practised from the earliest times of which we have any account of that part of the earth, it is not difficult to suppose that the subsequent trajects may have been sometimes passed. Again, the late discoveries of Captain Cook,[7] coasting from Kamschatka[8] to California, have proved that, if the two continents of Asia and America be separated at all, it is only by a narrow streight. So that from this side also, inhabitants may have passed into America: and the resemblance between the Indians of America and the Eastern inhabitants of Asia, would induce us to conjecture, that the former are the descendants of the latter, or the latter of the former: excepting indeed the Eskimaux, who, from the same circumstance of resemblance, and from identity of language, must be derived from the Groenlanders, and these probably from some of the northern parts of the old continent. A knowledge of their several languages would be the most certain evidence of their derivation which could be produced. In fact, it is the best proof of the affinity of nations which ever can be referred to. How many ages have elapsed since the English, the Dutch, the Germans, the Swiss, the Norwegians, Danes and Swedes have separated from their common stock? Yet how many more must elapse before the proofs of their common origin, which exist in their several languages, will disappear? It is to be lamented then, very much to be lamented, that we have suffered so many of the Indian tribes already to extinguish, without our having previously collected and deposited in the records of literature, the general rudiments at least of the languages they spoke. Were vocabularies formed of all the languages spoken in North and South America, preserving their appellations of the most common objects in nature, of those which must be present to every

---

6. Crossing route.

7. Captain James Cook (1728–79): British navigator and explorer. He sailed around the world twice and made possible the establishment of colonies throughout the Pacific.

8. Territory in western Russia on the Pacific coast.

nation barbarous or civilised, with the inflections of their nouns and verbs, their principles of regimen and concord, and these deposited in all the public libraries, it would furnish opportunities to those skilled in the languages of the old world to compare them with these, now, or at any future time, and hence to construct the best evidence of the derivation of this part of the human race.

QUERY XIII[1]

The constitution of the state, and its several charters?

. . . . In each state separately a new form of government was established. Of ours particularly the following are the outlines. The executive powers are lodged in the hands of a governor, chosen annually, and incapable of acting more than three years in seven. He is assisted by a council of eight members. The judiciary powers are divided among several courts, as will be hereafter explained. Legislation is exercised by two houses of assembly, the one called the house of Delegates, composed of two members from each county, chosen annually by the citizens possessing an estate for life in 100 acres of uninhabited land, or 25 acres with a house on it, or in a house or lot in some town: the other called the Senate, consisting of 24 members, chosen quadrennially[2] by the same electors, who for this purpose are distributed into 24 districts. The concurrence of both houses is necessary to the passage of a law. They have the appointment of the governor and council, the judges of the superior courts, auditors, attorney-general, treasurer, register of the land office, and delegates to congress. As the dismemberment of the state had never had its confirmation, but, on the contrary, had always been the subject of protestation and complaint, that it might never be in our own power to raise scruples on that subject, or to disturb the harmony of our new confederacy, the grants to Maryland, Pennsylvania, and the two Carolinas, were ratified.[3]

This constitution was formed when we were new and unexperienced in the science of government. It was the first too which was formed in the whole United States. No wonder then that time and trial have discovered very capital defects in it.

1. The majority of the men in the state, who pay and fight for its support, are unrepresented in the legislature, the roll of freeholders intitled to vote, not including generally the half of those on the roll of the militia, or of the tax-gatherers.

2. Among those who share the representation, the shares are very unequal. Thus the county of Warwick, with only one hundred fighting men, has an equal representation with the county of Loudon, which has 1746. So that

---

1. See Introduction, pp. xvi–xvii, xxxi.
2. Once every four years.
3. Virginia declined to contest the territorial claims of neighboring states.

every man in Warwick has as much influence in the government as 17 men in Loudon. But lest it should be thought that an equal interspersion[4] of small among large counties, through the whole state, may prevent any danger of injury to particular parts of it, we will divide it into districts, and shew the proportions of land, of fighting men, and of representation in each.

An inspection of this table[5] will supply the place of commentaries on it. It will appear at once that nineteen thousand men, living below the falls of the rivers, possess half the senate, and want four members only of possessing a majority of the house of delegates; a want more than supplied by the vicinity of their situation to the seat of government, and of course the greater degree of convenience and punctuality with which their members may and will attend in the legislature. These nineteen thousand, therefore, living in one part of the country, give law to upwards of thirty thousand, living in another, and appoint all their chief officers executive and judiciary. From the difference of their situation and circumstances, their interests will often be very different.

3. The senate is, by its constitution, too homogeneous with the house of delegates. Being chosen by the same electors, at the same time, and out of the same subjects, the choice falls of course on men of the same description. The purpose of establishing different houses of legislation is to introduce the influence of different interests or different principles. Thus in Great-Britain it is said their constitution relies on the house of commons for honesty, and the lords for wisdom; which would be a rational reliance if honesty were to be bought with money, and if wisdom were hereditary. In some of the American states the delegates and senators are so chosen, as that the first represent the persons, and the second the property of the state. But with us, wealth and wisdom have equal chance for admission into both houses. We do not therefore derive from the separation of our legislature into two houses, those benefits which a proper complication of principles is capable of producing, and those which alone can compensate the evils which may be produced by their dissensions.

4. All the powers of government, legislative, executive, and judiciary, result to the legislative body. The concentrating these in the same hands is precisely the definition of despotic government. It will be no alleviation that these powers will be exercised by a plurality of hands, and not by a single one. 173 despots would surely be as oppressive as one. Let those who doubt it turn their eyes on the republic of Venice.[6] As little will it avail us that they are

---

4. Intermingling.

5. Omitted here.

6. From the twelfth century onward, the republic of Venice was governed by a small number of aristocratic families.

chosen by ourselves. An *elective despotism* was not the government we fought for; but one which should not only be founded on free principles, but in which the powers of government should be so divided and balanced among several bodies of magistracy, as that no one could transcend their legal limits, without being effectually checked and restrained by the others. For this reason that convention, which passed the ordinance of government, laid its foundation on this basis, that the legislative, executive and judiciary departments should be separate and distinct, so that no person should exercise the powers of more than one of them at the same time. But no barrier was provided between these several powers. The judiciary and executive members were left dependant on the legislative, for their subsistence in office, and some of them for their continuance in it. If therefore the legislature assumes executive and judiciary powers, no opposition is likely to be made; nor, if made, can it be effectual; because in that case they may put their proceedings into the form of an act of assembly, which will render them obligatory on the other branches. They have accordingly, in many instances, decided rights which should have been left to judiciary controversy:[7] and the direction of the executive, during the whole time of their session, is becoming habitual and familiar. And this is done with no ill intention. The views of the present members are perfectly upright. When they are led out of their regular province, it is by art in others, and inadvertence in themselves. And this will probably be the case for some time to come. But it will not be a very long time. Mankind soon learn to make interested uses of every right and power which they possess, or may assume. The public money and public liberty, intended to have been deposited with three branches of magistracy, but found inadvertently to be in the hands of one only, will soon be discovered to be sources of wealth and dominion to those who hold them; distinguished too by this tempting circumstance, that they are the instrument, as well as the object of acquisition. With money we will get men, said Cæsar,[8] and with men we will get money. Nor should our assembly be deluded by the integrity of their own purposes, and conclude that these unlimited powers will never be abused, because themselves are not disposed to abuse them. They should look forward to a time, and that not a distant one, when corruption in this, as in the country from which we derive our origin, will have seized the heads of government, and be spread by them through the body of the people; when they will purchase the voices of the people, and make them pay the price. Human nature is the same on every side of the Atlantic, and will be alike influenced by the same causes. The time

---

7. Judgment by the judicial branch.
8. Julius Caesar (100–44 BC): Roman general and statesman who became dictator, thereby ending the Roman republic.

to guard against corruption and tyranny, is before they shall have gotten hold on us. It is better to keep the wolf out of the fold, than to trust to drawing his teeth and talons after he shall have entered. To render these considerations the more cogent, we must observe in addition,

5. That the ordinary legislature may alter the constitution itself. On the discontinuance of assemblies, it became necessary to substitute in their place some other body, competent to the ordinary business of government, and to the calling forth the powers of the state for the maintenance of our opposition to Great-Britain.[9] Conventions were therefore introduced, consisting of two delegates from each county, meeting together and forming one house, on the plan of the former house of Burgesses,[10] to whose places they succeeded. These were at first chosen anew for every particular session. But in March 1775, they recommended to the people to chuse a convention, which should continue in office a year. This was done accordingly in April 1775, and in the July following that convention passed an ordinance for the election of delegates in the month of April annually. It is well known, that in July 1775, a separation from Great-Britain and establishment of Republican government had never yet entered into any person's mind. A convention therefore, chosen under that ordinance, cannot be said to have been chosen for purposes which certainly did not exist in the minds of those who passed it. Under this ordinance, at the annual election in April 1776, a convention for the year was chosen. Independance, and the establishment of a new form of government, were not even yet the objects of the people at large. One extract from the pamphlet called Common Sense[11] had appeared in the Virginia papers in February, and copies of the pamphlet itself had got into a few hands. But the idea had not been opened to the mass of the people in April, much less can it be said that they had made up their minds in its favor. So that the electors of April 1776, no more than the legislators of July 1775, not thinking of independance and a permanent republic, could not mean to vest in these delegates powers of establishing them, or any authorities other than those of the ordinary legislature. So far as a temporary organization of government was necessary to render our opposition energetic, so far their organization was valid. But they received in their creation no powers but what were given to

---

9. Jefferson is here referring to the revolutionary assemblies that convened after the King dissolved the colonial legislatures.

10. The lower house of the colonial Virginia legislature that had been disbanded by British colonial authorities.

11. An influential pamphlet, published anonymously in 1776 by Thomas Paine (1737–1809), that made the case for American independence and helped ignite the revolution.

every legislature before and since. They could not therefore pass an act transcendant to the powers of other legislatures. If the present assembly pass any act, and declare it shall be irrevocable by subsequent assemblies, the declaration is merely void, and the act repealable, as other acts are. So far, and no farther authorized, they organized the government by the ordinance entitled a Constitution or Form of government. It pretends to no higher authority than the other ordinances of the same session; it does not say, that it shall be perpetual; that it shall be unalterable by other legislatures; that it shall be transcendant above the powers of those, who they knew would have equal power with themselves. Not only the silence of the instrument is a proof they thought it would be alterable, but their own practice also: for this very convention, meeting as a House of Delegates in General Assembly with the new Senate in the autumn of that year, passed acts of assembly in contradiction to their ordinance of government; and every assembly from that time to this has done the same. I am safe therefore in the position, that the constitution itself is alterable by the ordinary legislature. Though this opinion seems founded on the first elements of common sense, yet is the contrary maintained by some persons. 1. Because, say they, the conventions were vested with every power necessary to make effectual opposition to Great-Britain. But to complete this argument, they must go on, and say further, that effectual opposition could not be made to Great-Britain, without establishing a form of government perpetual and unalterable by the legislature; which is not true. An opposition which at some time or other was to come to an end, could not need a perpetual institution to carry it on: and a government, amendable as its defects should be discovered, was as likely to make effectual resistance, as one which should be unalterably wrong. Besides, the assemblies were as much vested with all powers requisite for resistance as the conventions were. If therefore these powers included that of modelling the form of government in the one case, they did so in the other. The assemblies then as well as the conventions may model the government; that is, they may alter the ordinance of government. 2. They urge, that if the convention had meant that this instrument should be alterable, as their other ordinances were, they would have called it an ordinance: but they have called it a *constitution*, which ex vi termini[12] means 'an act above the power of the ordinary legislature.' I answer that *constitutio, constitutum, statutum, lex*, are convertible terms. 'Constitutio dicitur jus quod a principe conditur.'[13] '*Constitutum*, quod ab imperatoribus rescriptum statutumve est.'[14] '*Statutum*, idem quod lex.'[15] Calvini Lexicon

---

12. By the force of the term.
13. "The term *constitutio* is used of law established by the prince."
14. "The term *constitutum* is used of legal decisions and decrees of emperors."
15. "The term *statutum* has the same meaning as 'law.'"

juridicum. *Constitution* and *statute* were originally terms of the civil law,* and from thence introduced by Ecclesiastics into the English law. Thus in the statute 25 Hen. 8. c. 19. § 1. '*Constitutions* and *ordinances*' are used as synonimous. The term *constitution* has many other significations in physics and in politics; but in Jurisprudence, whenever it is applied to any act of the legislature, it invariably means a statute, law, or ordinance, which is the present case. No inference then of a different meaning can be drawn from the adoption of this title: on the contrary, we might conclude, that, by their affixing to it a term synonimous with ordinance, or statute, they meant it to be an ordinance or statute. But of what consequence is their meaning, where their power is denied? If they meant to do more than they had power to do, did this give them power? It is not the name, but the authority which renders an act obligatory. Lord Coke[16] says, 'an article of the statute 11 R. 2. c. 5. that no person should attempt to revoke any ordinance then made, is repealed, for that such restraint is against the jurisdiction and power of the parliament.' 4. inst. 42. and again, 'though divers parliaments have attempted to restrain subsequent parliaments, yet could they never effect it; for the latter parliament hath ever power to abrogate,[17] suspend, qualify, explain, or make void the former in the whole or in any part thereof, notwithstanding any words of restraint, prohibition, or penalty, in the former: for it is a maxim in the laws of the parliament, quod leges posteriores priores contrarias abrogant.'[18] 4. inst. 43. — To get rid of the magic supposed to be in the word *constitution*, let us translate it into its definition as given by those who think it above the power of the law; and let us suppose the convention instead of saying, 'We, the ordinary legislature, establish a *constitution*,' had said, 'We, the ordinary legislature, establish an act *above the power of the ordinary legislature*.' Does not this expose the absurdity of the attempt? 3. But, say they, the people have acquiesced, and this has given it an authority superior to the laws. It is true, that the people did not rebel against it: and was that a time for the people to rise in rebellion? Should a prudent acquiescence, at a critical time, be construed into a confirmation of every illegal thing done during that period? Besides, why should they rebel? At an annual election, they had chosen delegates for the year, to exercise the ordinary powers of legislation, and to manage the great contest in which they

---

*To *bid*, to *set*, was the antient legislative word of the English. Ll. Hlotharii & Eadrici. Ll. Inae. Ll. Eadwerdi. Ll. Aathelstani.

---

16. Sir Edward Coke (1552–1634): English jurist who defended the common law against the prerogatives of the Crown.

17. To abolish.

18. "That later laws supersede earlier ones."

were engaged. These delegates thought the contest would be best managed by an organized government. They therefore, among others, passed an ordinance of government. They did not presume to call it perpetual and unalterable. They well knew they had no power to make it so; that our choice of them had been for no such purpose, and at a time when we could have no such purpose in contemplation. Had an unalterable form of government been meditated, perhaps we should have chosen a different set of people. There was no cause then for the people to rise in rebellion. But to what dangerous lengths will this argument lead? Did the acquiescence of the colonies under the various acts of power exercised by Great-Britain in our infant state, confirm these acts, and so far invest them with the authority of the people as to render them unalterable, and our present resistance wrong? On every unauthoritative exercise of power by the legislature, must the people rise in rebellion, or their silence be construed into a surrender of that power to them? If so, how many rebellions should we have had already? One certainly for every session of assembly. The other states in the Union have been of opinion, that to render a form of government unalterable by ordinary acts of assembly, the people must delegate persons with special powers. They have accordingly chosen special conventions to form and fix their governments. The individuals then who maintain the contrary opinion in this country, should have the modesty to suppose it possible that they may be wrong and the rest of America right. But if there be only a possibility of their being wrong, if only a plausible doubt remains of the validity of the ordinance of government, is it not better to remove that doubt, by placing it on a bottom which none will dispute? If they be right, we shall only have the unnecessary trouble of meeting once in convention. If they be wrong, they expose us to the hazard of having no fundamental rights at all. True it is, this is no time for deliberating on forms of government. While an enemy is within our bowels, the first object is to expel him. But when this shall be done, when peace shall be established, and leisure given us for intrenching within good forms, the rights for which we have bled, let no man be found indolent enough to decline a little more trouble for placing them beyond the reach of question. If any thing more be requisite to produce a conviction of the expediency of calling a convention, at a proper season, to fix our form of government, let it be the reflection,

6. That the assembly exercises a power of determining the Quorum[19] of their own body which may legislate for us. After the establishment of the new form they adhered to the *Lex majoris partis*,[20] founded in common law[*] as

[*]Bro. abr. Corporations. 31.34. Hakewell, 93.

---

19. The minimum number of members needed for the valid transaction of business.
20. The law of the majority, i.e., majority rule.

well as common right. It is the natural law* of every assembly of men, whose numbers are not fixed by any other law. They continued for some time to require the presence of a majority of their whole number, to pass an act. But the British parliament fixes its own quorum: our former assemblies fixed their own quorum: and one precedent in favour of power is stronger than an hundred against it. The house of delegates therefore have lately† voted that, during the present dangerous invasion,[21] forty members shall be a house to proceed to business. They have been moved to this by the fear of not being able to collect a house. But this danger could not authorize them to call that a house which was none: and if they may fix it at one number, they may at another, till it loses its fundamental character of being a representative body. As this vote expires with the present invasion, it is probable the former rule will be permitted to revive: because at present no ill is meant. The power however of fixing their own quorum has been avowed, and a precedent set. From forty it may be reduced to four, and from four to one: from a house to a committee, from a committee to a chairman or speaker, and thus an oligarchy or monarchy be substituted under forms supposed to be regular. 'Omnia mala exempla ex bonis orta sunt: sed ubi imperium ad ignaros aut minus bonos pervenit, novum illud exemplum ab dignis et idoneis ad indignos et non idoneos fertur.'[22] When therefore it is considered, that there is no legal obstacle to the assumption by the assembly of all the powers legislative, executive, and judiciary, and that these may come to the hands of the smallest rag of delegation, surely the people will say, and their representatives, while yet they have honest representatives, will advise them to say, that they will not acknowledge as laws any acts not considered and assented to by the major part of their delegates.

In enumerating the defects of the constitution, it would be wrong to count among them what is only the error of particular persons. In December 1776, our circumstances being much distressed, it was proposed in the house of

---

*Puff. Off. hom. l. 2. c. 6. 12.
†June 4, 1781.

---

21. The British army invaded Virginia in 1781 and, led by the traitorous American general Benedict Arnold (1741–1801), burned the capital at Richmond. Later that year, troops under British Colonel Banastre Tarleton (1754–1833) advanced to Charlottesville, where they captured seven legislators and just missed capturing Governor Thomas Jefferson. See Introduction, pp. xv–xvi.

22. "All bad examples have their origin in good ones: when power passes to the ignorant and unprincipled, new examples [of severity in punishment] are transferred from those deserving [of such punishment] to those not deserving" (Sallust, *De Conjuratione Catalinae,* 51, in a speech attributed to Julius Caesar).

delegates to create a *dictator*, invested with every power legislative, executive and judiciary, civil and military, of life and of death, over our persons and over our properties: and in June 1781, again under calamity, the same proposition was repeated, and wanted a few votes only of being passed. —One who entered into this contest from a pure love of liberty, and a sense of injured rights, who determined to make every sacrifice, and to meet every danger, for the re-establishment of those rights on a firm basis, who did not mean to expend his blood and substance for the wretched purpose of changing this master for that, but to place the powers of governing him in a plurality of hands of his own choice, so that the corrupt will of no one man might in future oppress him, must stand confounded and dismayed when he is told, that a considerable portion of that plurality had meditated the surrender of them into a single hand, and, in lieu of a limited monarch, to deliver him over to a despotic one! How must we find his efforts and sacrifices abused and baffled, if he may still by a single vote be laid prostrate at the feet of one man! In God's name, from whence have they derived this power? Is it from our ancient laws? None such can be produced. Is it from any principle in our new constitution, expressed or implied? Every lineament of that expressed or implied, is in full opposition to it. Its fundamental principle is, that the state shall be governed as a commonwealth. It provides a republican organization, proscribes under the name of *prerogative* the exercise of all powers undefined by the laws; places on this basis the whole system of our laws; and, by consolidating them together, chuses that they shall be left to stand or fall together, never providing for any circumstances, nor admitting that such could arise, wherein either should be suspended, no, not for a moment. Our antient laws expressly declare, that those who are but delegates themselves shall not delegate to others powers which require judgment and integrity in their exercise. —Or was this proposition moved on a supposed right in the movers of abandoning their posts in a moment of distress? The same laws forbid the abandonment of that post, even on ordinary occasions; and much more a transfer of their powers into other hands and other forms, without consulting the people. They never admit the idea that these, like sheep or cattle, may be given from hand to hand without an appeal to their own will. —Was it from the necessity of the case? Necessities which dissolve a government, do not convey its authority to an oligarchy or a monarchy. They throw back, into the hands of the people, the powers they had delegated, and leave them as individuals to shift for themselves. A leader may offer, but not impose himself, nor be imposed on them. Much less can their necks be submitted to his sword, their breath be held at his will or caprice. The necessity which should operate these tremendous effects should at least be palpable and irresistible. Yet in both instances, where it was feared, or pretended with us, it was belied by the event. It was belied too by the preceding experience of our sister states, several of whom had grappled through greater difficulties without abandoning their forms of government. When the proposition was first made, Massachusets had found even the government of committees sufficient to carry them through an invasion.[23] But we at the time of that proposition were under no invasion. When the second was made, there had been added to this example those of Rhode-Island, New-York, New-Jersey, and Pennsylvania, in all of which the republican form had been found equal to the task of carrying them through the severest trials. In this state alone did there exist so little virtue, that fear was to be fixed in the hearts of the people, and to become the motive of their exertions and the principle of their government? The very thought alone was treason against the people; was treason against mankind in general; as rivetting for ever the chains which bow down their necks, by giving to their oppressors a proof, which they would have trumpeted through the universe, of the imbecility of republican government, in times of pressing danger, to shield them from harm. Those who assume the right of giving away the reins of government in any case, must be sure that the herd, whom they hand on to the rods and hatchet of the dictator, will lay their necks on the block when he shall nod to them. But if our assemblies supposed such a resignation in the people, I hope they mistook their character. I am of opinion, that the government, instead of being braced and invigorated for greater exertions under their difficulties, would have been thrown back upon the bungling machinery of county committees for administration, till a convention could have been called, and its wheels again set into regular motion. What a cruel moment was this for creating such an embarrassment, for putting to the proof the attachment of our countrymen to republican government! Those who meant well, of the advocates for this measure, (and most of them meant well, for I know them personally, had been their fellow-labourers in the common cause, and had often proved the purity of their principles), had been seduced in their judgment by the example of an ancient republic, whose constitution and circumstances were fundamentally different. They had sought this precedent in the history of Rome, where alone it was to be found, and where at length too it had proved fatal.[24] They had taken it from a republic, rent by the most bitter factions and tumults, where the government was of a heavy-handed unfeeling aristocracy, over a people ferocious, and rendered desperate by poverty and

23. By 1776, when the Virginians first proposed a dictator, the state had not yet seen any military action; Massachusetts, by contrast, had already experienced the battles of Lexington, Concord, and Bunker Hill.

24. The Roman Republic had a system in place to appoint dictators in times of crisis. The extended dictatorship of Julius Caesar eventually led to the overthrow of the Roman Republic and the reinstitution of rule by a single man.

wretchedness; tumults which could not be allayed under the most trying circumstances, but by the omnipotent hand of a single despot. Their constitution therefore allowed a temporary tyrant to be erected, under the name of a Dictator; and that temporary tyrant, after a few examples, became perpetual. They misapplied this precedent to a people, mild in their dispositions, patient under their trial, united for the public liberty, and affectionate to their leaders. But if from the constitution of the Roman government there resulted to their Senate a power of submitting all their rights to the will of one man, does it follow, that the assembly of Virginia have the same authority? What clause in our constitution has substituted that of Rome, by way of residuary provision, for all cases not otherwise provided for? Or if they may step ad libitum[25] into any other form of government for precedents to rule us by, for what oppression may not a precedent be found in this world of the bellum omnium in omnia?[26] —Searching for the foundations of this proposition, I can find none which may pretend a colour of right or reason, but the defect before developed, that there being no barrier between the legislative, executive, and judiciary departments, the legislature may seize the whole: that having seized it, and possessing a right to fix their own quorum, they may reduce that quorum to one, whom they may call a chairman, speaker, dictator, or by any other name they please. —Our situation is indeed perilous, and I hope my countrymen will be sensible of it, and will apply, at a proper season, the proper remedy; which is a convention to fix the constitution, to amend its defects, to bind up the several branches of government by certain laws, which when they transgress their acts shall become nullities; to render unnecessary an appeal to the people, or in other words a rebellion, on every infraction of their rights, on the peril that their acquiescence shall be construed into an intention to surrender those rights.

---

25. At one's own discretion, to the extent one desires.
26. "War of all against all," a reference to Hobbes' "war of every man against every man" (*Leviathan*, ch. 13). In his own Latin version of *Leviathan*, Hobbes uses in this passage the expression "bellum omnium contra omnes" ("war of all men against all men"). See note 5, p. 237.

QUERY XIV[1]

The administration of justice and description of the laws?

.... A description of the laws.

.... It will be unnecessary to attempt a description of the laws of England, as that may be found in English publications. To those which were established here, by the adoption of the legislature, have been since added a number of acts of assembly passed during the monarchy, and ordinances of convention and acts of assembly enacted since the establishment of the republic. The following variations from the British model are perhaps worthy of being specified.

Debtors unable to pay their debts, and making faithful delivery of their whole effects, are released from confinement, and their persons for ever discharged from restraint for such previous debts: but any property they may afterwards acquire will be subject to their creditors.

The poor, unable to support themselves, are maintained by an assessment on the titheable persons[2] in their parish. This assessment is levied and administered by twelve persons in each parish, called vestrymen, originally chosen by the housekeepers of the parish, but afterwards filling vacancies in their own body by their own choice. These are usually the most discreet farmers, so distributed through their parish, that every part of it may be under the immediate eye of some one of them. They are well acquainted with the details and œconomy of private life, and they find sufficient inducements to execute their charge well, in their philanthropy, in the approbation of their neighbours, and the distinction which that gives them. The poor who have neither property, friends, nor strength to labour, are boarded in the houses of good farmers, to whom a stipulated sum is annually paid. To those who are able to help themselves a little, or have friends from whom they derive some succours, inadequate however to their full maintenance, supplementory aids are given, which enable them to live comfortably in their own houses, or in the houses of their friends. Vagabonds, without visible property or vocation, are placed in workhouses, where they are well cloathed, fed, lodged, and made to labour. Nearly the same method of providing for the poor prevails through all our states; and

---

1. See Introduction, pp. xvi, xxxiii.
2. Taxpayers.

from Savannah to Portsmouth you will seldom meet a beggar. In the larger towns indeed they sometimes present themselves. These are usually foreigners, who have never obtained a settlement in any parish. I never yet saw a native American begging in the streets or highways. A subsistence is easily gained here: and if, by misfortunes, they are thrown on the charities of the world, those provided by their own country are so comfortable and so certain, that they never think of relinquishing them to become strolling beggars. Their situation too, when sick, in the family of a good farmer, where every member is emulous[3] to do them kind offices, where they are visited by all the neighbours, who bring them the little rarities which their sickly appetites may crave, and who take by rotation the nightly watch over them, when their condition requires it, is without comparison better than in a general hospital, where the sick, the dying, and the dead are crammed together, in the same rooms, and often in the same beds. The disadvantages, inseparable from general hospitals, are such as can never be counterpoised[4] by all the regularities of medicine and regimen. Nature and kind nursing save a much greater proportion in our plain way, at a smaller expence, and with less abuse. One branch only of hospital institution is wanting with us; that is, a general establishment for those labouring under difficult cases of chirurgery.[5] The aids of this art are not equivocal. But an able chirurgeon cannot be had in every parish. Such a receptacle should therefore be provided for those patients: but no others should be admitted.

Marriages must be solemnized either on special licence, granted by the first magistrate of the county, on proof of the consent of the parent or guardian of either party under age, or after solemn publication, on three several Sundays, at some place of religious worship, in the parishes where the parties reside. The act of solemnization may be by the minister of any society of Christians, who shall have been previously licensed for this purpose by the court of the county. Quakers and Menonists[6] however are exempted from all these conditions, and marriage among them is to be solemnized by the society itself.

A foreigner of any nation, not in open war with us, becomes naturalized by removing to the state to reside, and taking an oath of fidelity: and thereupon acquires every right of a native citizen: and citizens may divest themselves of that character, by declaring, by solemn deed, or in open court, that they mean to expatriate themselves, and no longer to be citizens of this state.

---

3. Characterized or prompted by a spirit of rivalry to excel.
4. Balanced by a counterweight.
5. Surgery.
6. Quakers and Menonists [or Mennonites] were (and are) two dissenting Christian sects characterized by simplicity of life, pacifism, and nonresistance.

Conveyances of land must be registered in the court of the county wherein they lie, or in the general court, or they are void, as to creditors, and subsequent purchasers.

Slaves pass by descent and dower[7] as lands do. Where the descent is from a parent, the heir is bound to pay an equal share of their value in money to each of his brothers and sisters.

Slaves, as well as lands, were entailable[8] during the monarchy: but, by an act of the first republican assembly, all donees in tail,[9] present and future, were vested with the absolute dominion of the entailed subject.

Bills of exchange, being protested, carry 10 per cent. interest from their date. No person is allowed, in any other case, to take more than five per cent. per annum simple interest, for the loan of monies.

Gaming debts are made void, and monies actually paid to discharge such debts (if they exceeded 40 shillings) may be recovered by the payer within three months, or by any other person afterwards.

Tobacco, flour, beef, pork, tar, pitch, and turpentine, must be inspected by persons publicly appointed, before they can be exported.

The erecting [of] iron-works and mills is encouraged by many privileges; with necessary cautions however to prevent their dams from obstructing the navigation of the water-courses. The general assembly have on several occasions shewn a great desire to encourage the opening the great falls of James and Patowmac rivers. As yet, however, neither of these have been effected.

The laws have also descended to the preservation and improvement of the races of useful animals, such as horses, cattle, deer; to the extirpation[10] of those which are noxious, as wolves, squirrels, crows, blackbirds; and to the guarding our citizens against infectious disorders, by obliging suspected vessels coming into the state, to perform quarantine, and by regulating the conduct of persons having such disorders within the state.

The mode of acquiring lands, in the earliest times of our settlement, was by petition to the general assembly. If the lands prayed for were already cleared of the Indian title, and the assembly thought the prayer reasonable, they passed the property by their vote to the petitioner. But if they had not yet been ceded by the Indians, it was necessary that the petitioner should previously purchase their right. This purchase the assembly verified, by enquiries of the Indian proprietors; and being satisfied of its reality and fairness, proceeded

---

7. That part of her husband's property that a widow inherits at his death.

8. The inheritance of entailed property was, by law, limited to a specific succession of heirs. This was a means of preserving property by restricting inheritance.

9. Beneficiaries whose land is entailed.

10. Eradication.

further to examine the reasonableness of the petition, and its consistence with policy; and, according to the result, either granted or rejected the petition. The company also sometimes, though very rarely, granted lands, independantly of the general assembly. As the colony increased, and individual applications for land multiplied, it was found to give too much occupation to the general assembly to enquire into and execute the grant in every special case. They therefore thought it better to establish general rules, according to which all grants should be made, and to leave to the governor the execution of them, under these rules. This they did by what have been usually called the land laws, amending them from time to time, as their defects were developed. According to these laws, when an individual wished a portion of unappropriated land, he was to locate and survey it by a public officer, appointed for that purpose: its breadth was to bear a certain proportion to its length: the grant was to be executed by the governor: and the lands were to be improved in a certain manner, within a given time. From these regulations there resulted to the state a sole and exclusive power of taking conveyances of the Indian right of soil: since, according to them, an Indian conveyance alone could give no right to an individual, which the laws would acknowledge. The state, or the crown, thereafter, made general purchases of the Indians from time to time, and the governor parcelled them out by special grants, conformed to the rules before described, which it was not in his power, or in that of the crown, to dispense with. Grants, unaccompanied by their proper legal circumstances, were set aside regularly by *scire facias*,[11] or by bill in Chancery.[12] Since the establishment of our new government, this order of things is but little changed. An individual, wishing to appropriate to himself lands still unappropriated by any other, pays to the public treasurer a sum of money proportioned to the quantity he wants. He carries the treasurer's receipt to the auditors of public accompts, who thereupon debit the treasurer with the sum, and order the register of the land-office to give the party a warrant for his land. With this warrant from the register, he goes to the surveyor of the county where the land lies on which he has cast his eye. The surveyor lays it off for him, gives him its exact description, in the form of a certificate, which certificate he returns to the land-office, where a grant is made out, and is signed by the governor. This vests in him a perfect dominion in his lands, transmissible to whom he pleases by deed or will, or by descent to his heirs if he die intestate.[13]

Many of the laws which were in force during the monarchy being relative merely to that form of government, or inculcating principles inconsistent with

---

11. A writ requiring the party against whom it is brought to show why a judgment should not be executed, vacated, or annulled.

12. A court with equity (non-common-law) jurisdiction.

13. Without a will.

republicanism, the first assembly which met after the establishment of the commonwealth appointed a committee to revise the whole code, to reduce it into proper form and volume, and report it to the assembly. This work has been executed by three gentlemen, and reported; but probably will not be taken up till a restoration of peace shall leave to the legislature leisure to go through such a work.

The plan of the revisal was this. The common law of England, by which is meant, that part of the English law which was anterior to the date of the oldest statutes extant, is made the basis of the work. It was thought dangerous to attempt to reduce it to a text: it was therefore left to be collected from the usual monuments of it.[14] Necessary alterations in that, and so much of the whole body of the British statutes, and of acts of assembly, as were thought proper to be retained, were digested into 126 new acts, in which simplicity of stile was aimed at, as far as was safe. The following are the most remarkable alterations proposed:

To change the rules of descent, so as that the lands of any person dying intestate shall be divisible equally among all his children, or other representatives, in equal degree.

To make slaves distributable among the next of kin, as other moveables.

To have all public expences, whether of the general treasury, or of a parish or county, (as for the maintenance of the poor, building bridges, court-houses, &c.) supplied by assessments on the citizens, in proportion to their property.

To hire undertakers for keeping the public roads in repair, and indemnify individuals through whose lands new roads shall be opened.

To define with precision the rules whereby aliens should become citizens, and citizens make themselves aliens.

To establish religious freedom on the broadest bottom.

To emancipate all slaves born after passing the act. The bill reported by the revisors does not itself contain this proposition; but an amendment containing it was prepared, to be offered to the legislature whenever the bill should be taken up, and further directing, that they should continue with their parents to a certain age, then be brought up, at the public expence, to tillage,[15] arts or sciences, according to their geniusses,[16] till the females should be eighteen,

---

14. The common law of England formed the basis for the revisal of Virginia's laws. Common law refers to law developed through custom before the establishment of written laws and applied by judges even after the development of written laws. According to the English jurist William Blackstone, the "monuments" of these customs are found in court records, reports, and judicial decisions, as well as "the treatises of learned sages."

15. Farming.

16. Natural abilities.

and the males twenty-one years of age, when they should be colonized to such place as the circumstances of the time should render most proper, sending them out with arms, implements of houshold and of the handicraft arts, feeds, pairs of the useful domestic animals, &c. to declare them a free and independant people, and extend to them our alliance and protection, till they shall have acquired strength; and to send vessels at the same time to other parts of the world for an equal number of white inhabitants; to induce whom to migrate hither, proper encouragements were to be proposed. It will probably be asked, Why not retain and incorporate the blacks into the state, and thus save the expence of supplying, by importation of white settlers, the vacancies they will leave? Deep rooted prejudices entertained by the whites; ten thousand recollections, by the blacks, of the injuries they have sustained; new provocations; the real distinctions which nature has made; and many other circumstances, will divide us into parties, and produce convulsions which will probably never end but in the extermination of the one or the other race. — To these objections, which are political, may be added others, which are physical and moral. The first difference which strikes us is that of colour. Whether the black of the negro resides in the reticular membrane between the skin and scarf-skin,[17] or in the scarf-skin itself; whether it proceeds from the colour of the blood, the colour of the bile, or from that of some other secretion, the difference is fixed in nature, and is as real as if its seat and cause were better known to us. And is this difference of no importance? Is it not the foundation of a greater or less share of beauty in the two races? Are not the fine mixtures of red and white, the expressions of every passion by greater or less suffusions of colour in the one, preferable to that eternal monotony, which reigns in the countenances, that immoveable veil of black which covers all the emotions of the other race?[18] Add to these, flowing hair, a more elegant symmetry of form, their own judgment in favour of the whites, declared by their preference of them, as uniformly as is the preference of the Oranootan[19] for the black women over those of his own species. The circumstance of superior beauty, is thought worthy attention in the propagation of our horses, dogs, and other domestic animals; why not in that of man? Besides those of colour, figure, and hair, there are other physical distinctions proving a difference of race. They have less hair on the face and body. They secrete less by the kidnies, and more by the glands of the skin, which gives them a

---

17. Outermost layer of skin.

18. Jefferson is here referring to blushing, displays of anger, fear, and other emotions that cause Caucasians to turn red or grow pale.

19. Orangutan.

very strong and disagreeable odour. This greater degree of transpiration[20] renders them more tolerant of heat, and less so of cold, than the whites. Perhaps too a difference of structure in the pulmonary apparatus, which a late ingenious experimentalist[*][21] has discovered to be the principal regulator of animal heat, may have disabled them from extricating, in the act of inspiration, so much of that fluid from the outer air, or obliged them in expiration, to part with more of it. They seem to require less sleep. A black, after hard labour through the day, will be induced by the slightest amusements to sit up till midnight, or later, though knowing he must be out with the first dawn of the morning. They are at least as brave, and more adventuresome. But this may perhaps proceed from a want of forethought, which prevents their seeing a danger till it be present. When present, they do not go through it with more coolness or steadiness than the whites. They are more ardent after their female: but love seems with them to be more an eager desire, than a tender delicate mixture of sentiment and sensation. Their griefs are transient. Those numberless afflictions, which render it doubtful whether heaven has given life to us in mercy or in wrath, are less felt, and sooner forgotten with them. In general, their existence appears to participate more of sensation than reflection. To this must be ascribed their disposition to sleep when abstracted from their diversions, and unemployed in labour. An animal whose body is at rest, and who does not reflect, must be disposed to sleep of course. Comparing them by their faculties of memory, reason, and imagination, it appears to me, that in memory they are equal to the whites; in reason much inferior, as I think one could scarcely be found capable of tracing and comprehending the investigations of Euclid[22]; and that in imagination they are dull, tasteless, and anomalous. It would be unfair to follow them to Africa for this investigation. We will consider them here, on the same stage with the whites, and where the facts are not apocryphal on which a judgment is to be formed. It will be right to make great allowances for the difference of condition, of education, of conversation, of the sphere in which they move. Many millions of them have been brought to, and born in America. Most of them indeed have been confined to tillage, to their own homes, and their own society: yet many have been so situated, that they might have availed themselves of the conversation

[*]Crawford.

---

20. Perspiration.

21. Adair Crawford (1748–95): Irish chemist, author of *Experiments and Observations on Animal Heat* (1779). In 1790, he discovered the element Strontium.

22. Euclid (c. 325–265 BC): Greek mathematician best known for *The Elements*, which set forth the logical development of geometry and other branches of mathematics.

of their masters; many have been brought up to the handicraft arts, and from that circumstance have always been associated with the whites. Some have been liberally educated, and all have lived in countries where the arts and sciences are cultivated to a considerable degree, and have had before their eyes samples of the best works from abroad. The Indians, with no advantages of this kind, will often carve figures on their pipes not destitute of design and merit. They will crayon[23] out an animal, a plant, or a country, so as to prove the existence of a germ in their minds which only wants cultivation. They astonish you with strokes of the most sublime oratory; such as prove their reason and sentiment strong, their imagination glowing and elevated. But never yet could I find that a black had uttered a thought above the level of plain narration; never see even an elementary trait of painting or sculpture. In music they are more generally gifted than the whites with accurate ears for tune and time, and they have been found capable of imagining a small catch.[*24] Whether they will be equal to the composition of a more extensive run of melody, or of complicated harmony, is yet to be proved. Misery is often the parent of the most affecting touches in poetry. —Among the blacks is misery enough, God knows, but no poetry. Love is the peculiar œstrum[25] of the poet. Their love is ardent, but it kindles the senses only, not the imagination. Religion indeed has produced a Phyllis Whately;[26] but it could not produce a poet. The compositions published under her name are below the dignity of criticism. The heroes of the Dunciad[27] are to her, as Hercules to the author of that poem. Ignatius Sancho[28] has approached nearer to merit in composition; yet his letters do more honour to the heart than the head. They breathe the purest effusions of friendship and general philanthropy, and shew how great a degree of the latter may be compounded with strong religious zeal. He is

*The instrument proper to them is the Banjar, which they brought hither from Africa, and which is the original of the guitar, its chords being precisely the four lower chords of the guitar.

---

23. Draw or color.

24. A musical round for several unaccompanied voices.

25. State of readiness for love.

26. Phyllis Wheatley (1753–84): a slave, taught to read English, Greek, and Latin by her owners. She began composing poetry as a teenager and eventually published a book of poetry.

27. A satirical poem by Alexander Pope (1688–1744) in which he attacks all of his many detractors.

28. Ignatius Sancho (1729–80): African slave who served as butler to the Montagu family in England. He composed music, performed on stage, and carried on a wide correspondence that was collected and published after his death.

often happy in the turn of his compliments, and his stile is easy and familiar, except when he affects a Shandean[29] fabrication of words. But his imagination is wild and extravagant, escapes incessantly from every restraint of reason and taste, and, in the course of its vagaries, leaves a tract of thought as incoherent and eccentric, as is the course of a meteor through the sky. His subjects should often have led him to a process of sober reasoning: yet we find him always substituting sentiment for demonstration. Upon the whole, though we admit him to the first place among those of his own colour who have presented themselves to the public judgment, yet when we compare him with the writers of the race among whom he lived, and particularly with the epistolary class,[30] in which he has taken his own stand, we are compelled to enroll him at the bottom of the column. This criticism supposes the letters published under his name to be genuine, and to have received amendment from no other hand; points which would not be of easy investigation. The improvement of the blacks in body and mind, in the first instance of their mixture with the whites, has been observed by every one, and proves that their inferiority is not the effect merely of their condition of life. We know that among the Romans, about the Augustan age[31] especially, the condition of their slaves was much more deplorable than that of the blacks on the continent of America. The two sexes were confined in separate apartments, because to raise a child cost the master more than to buy one. Cato,[32] for a very restricted indulgence to his slaves in this particular,* took from them a certain price. But in this country the slaves multiply as fast as the free inhabitants. Their situation and manners place the commerce between the two sexes almost without restraint. —The same Cato, on a principle of œconomy, always sold his sick and superannuated[33] slaves. He gives it as a standing precept to a master visiting his farm, to sell his old oxen, old waggons, old tools, old and diseased servants,

---

*Τὸς δὸλὸς εταξεν ὡρισμενὸ νομισματος ὁμιλειν ταις θεραπαινισιν.
—Plutarch. Cato.

---

29. In the style of Laurence Sterne's eponymous hero *Tristam Shandy*. See note 3, p. 162.

30. Those who write letters; the educated class.

31. Octavian (63 BC–14 AD) was given the honorary name Augustus after he defeated Marc Antony and Cleopatra in 31 BC to become the first emperor of Rome (27 BC–14 AD).

32. Marcus Porcius Cato (234–149 BC): Cato the Elder, Roman orator and author of the first history of Rome. As Censor, he sought to improve Rome's morals and was honored for his stern Roman virtues.

33. Too old to work. In his *Life of Cato*, Plutarch criticizes Cato for this harsh policy.

and every thing else become useless. 'Vendat boves vetulos, plaustrum vetus, ferramenta vetera, servum senem, servum morbosum, & si quid aliud supersit vendat.'[34] Cato de re rustic. c. 2. The American slaves cannot enumerate this among the injuries and insults they receive. It was the common practice to expose in the island [Suet. Claud. 25.] of Æsculapius,[35] in the Tyber, diseased slaves, whose cure was like to become tedious. The Emperor Claudius,[36] by an edict, gave freedom to such of them as should recover, and first declared, that if any person chose to kill rather than to expose them, it should be deemed homicide. The exposing them is a crime of which no instance has existed with us; and were it to be followed by death, it would be punished capitally. We are told of a certain Vedius Pollio, who, in the presence of Augustus,[37] would have given a slave as food to his fish, for having broken a glass. With the Romans, the regular method of taking the evidence of their slaves was under torture. Here it has been thought better never to resort to their evidence. When a master was murdered, all his slaves, in the same house, or within hearing, were condemned to death. Here punishment falls on the guilty only, and as precise proof is required against him as against a freeman. Yet notwithstanding these and other discouraging circumstances among the Romans, their slaves were often their rarest artists. They excelled too in science, insomuch as to be usually employed as tutors to their master's children. Epictetus,[38] Terence,[39] and Phaedrus,[40] were slaves. But they were of the race of whites. It is not their condition then, but nature, which has produced the distinction. —Whether further observation will or will not verify the conjecture, that nature has been less bountiful to them in the endowments of the head, I believe that in those of the heart she will be found to have done them justice. That disposition to theft with which they have been branded, must be ascribed to their situation, and not to any depravity of the

---

34. "Let him sell his old oxen, old wagon, old tools, old servant, sick servant, and anything else that is not needed." (Jefferson translates this quote accurately in the preceding sentence.)

35. Mythical Greek and Roman god of healing. Diseased slaves were left to die ("exposed") on an island in the Tiber River honoring him.

36. Claudius I (Tiberius Claudius Drusus Nero Germanicus) (10 BC–54 AD): Emperor of Rome from 41 BC–54 AD.

37. See note 31 on Octavian, above.

38. Epictetus (c. 55–c. 135 AD): Roman slave and Stoic philosopher, author of the *Encheridion*.

39. Publius Terentius (c. 185–c. 159 BC): Greek-born Roman slave who was educated, then freed, by his master. He became one of the best-known Roman playwrights on the strength of such comedies as *Phormio* and *Adelphi*.

40. Phaedrus (first century AD) a Roman slave and fabulist who was freed during the reign of Augustus.

moral sense. The man, in whose favour no laws of property exist, probably feels himself less bound to respect those made in favour of others. When arguing for ourselves, we lay it down as a fundamental, that laws, to be just, must give a reciprocation of right: that, without this, they are mere arbitrary rules of conduct, founded in force, and not in conscience: and it is a problem which give to the master to solve, whether the religious precepts against the violation of property were not framed for him as well as his slave? And whether the slave may not as justifiably take a little from one, who has taken all from him, as he may slay one who would slay him? That a change in the relations in which a man is placed should change his ideas of moral right and wrong, is neither new, nor peculiar to the colour of the blacks. Homer[41] tells us it was so 2600 years ago.

Ἥμισυ, γαζ τ' ἀρετῆς ἀποαίνυlαι εὐρύθπα Ζεὺς
Ἀνερος, ευτ' ἄν μιν κατὰ δόλιον ἦμαζ ἕλησιν.
Od. 17. 323.

Jove fix'd it certain, that whatever day
Makes man a slave, takes half his worth away.

But the slaves of which Homer speaks were whites. Notwithstanding these considerations which must weaken their respect for the laws of property, we find among them numerous instances of the most rigid integrity, and as many as among their better instructed masters, of benevolence, gratitude, and unshaken fidelity. —The opinion, that they are inferior in the faculties of reason and imagination, must be hazarded with great diffidence. To justify a general conclusion, requires many observations, even where the subject may be submitted to the Anatomical knife, to Optical glasses, to analysis by fire, or by solvents. How much more then where it is a faculty, not a substance, we are examining; where it eludes the research of all the senses; where the conditions of its existence are various and variously combined; where the effects of those which are present or absent bid defiance to calculation; let me add too, as a circumstance of great tenderness, where our conclusion would degrade a whole race of men from the rank in the scale of beings which their Creator may perhaps have given them. To our reproach it must be said, that though for a century and a half we have had under our eyes the races of black and of red men, they have never yet been viewed by us as subjects of natural history. I advance it therefore as a suspicion only, that the blacks, whether originally a distinct race, or made distinct by time and circumstances, are inferior to the

---

41. Homer: See note 15, p. 85.

whites in the endowments both of body and mind. It is not against experience to suppose, that different species of the same genus, or varieties of the same species, may possess different qualifications. Will not a lover of natural history then, one who views the gradations in all the races of animals with the eye of philosophy, excuse an effort to keep those in the department of man as distinct as nature has formed them? This unfortunate difference of colour, and perhaps of faculty, is a powerful obstacle to the emancipation of these people. Many of their advocates, while they wish to vindicate the liberty of human nature, are anxious also to preserve its dignity and beauty. Some of these, embarrassed by the question 'What further is to be done with them?' join themselves in opposition with those who are actuated by sordid avarice only.[42] Among the Romans emancipation required but one effort.[43] The slave, when made free, might mix with, without staining the blood of his master. But with us a second is necessary, unknown to history. When freed, he is to be removed beyond the reach of mixture.

The revised code further proposes to proportion crimes and punishments. This is attempted on the following scale.

I.   Crimes whose punishment extends to *Life*.
    1. High treason.   Death by hanging.
                       Forfeiture of lands and goods to the commonwealth
    2. Petty treason   Death by hanging.   Dissection.
                       Forfeiture of half the lands and goods to the representatives of the party slain.
    3. Murder   1. by poison.   Death by poison.
                                   Forfeiture of one-half as before.
                       2. in Duel.   Death by hanging.
                                   Gibbeting, if the challenger
                                   Forfeiture of one-half as before, unless it be the party challenged, then the forfeiture is to the commonwealth.
                       3. in any other way.   Death by hanging.
                                   Forfeiture of one-half as before.
    4. Manslaughter.   The second offense is Murder.

---

42. Immoderate desire for wealth.

43. Because the Roman slaves were of the same race as their masters, all that was required was that they be set free. In Jefferson's America, emancipation was not enough; because the slaves were of a different race, they also had to be expatriated.

II.   Crimes whose punishment goes to *Limb*.

1. Rape,
2. Sodomy, } Dismemberment

3. Maiming,
4. Disfiguring, } Retaliation, and the forfeiture of half the lands and goods to the sufferer.

III. Crimes punishable by *Labour*.

1. Manslaughter, 1st offence.	Labour VII. years for the public.	Forfeiture of half as in murder.
2. Counterfeiting money	Labour VI. years	Forfeiture of lands and goods to the commonwealth
3. Arson. 4. Asportation of vessels. }	Labour V. years	Reparation three-fold
5. Robbery. 6. Burglary. }	Labour IV. years	Reparation double
7. Housebreaking. 8. Horse-stealing. }	Labour III. years	Reparation
9. Grand Larceny.	Labour II. years	Reparation. Pillory.
10. Petty Larceny	Labour I. year	Reparation. Pillory.
11. Pretensions to witchcraft, &c.	Ducking.	Stripes.[44]
12. Excusable homicide. 13. Suicide. 14. Apostacy. Hersey. }	to be pitied, not punished.	

Pardon and privilege of clergy are proposed to be abolished; but if the verdict be against the defendant, the court in their discretion, may allow a new trial. No attainder to cause a corruption of blood, or forfeiture of dower.[45] Slaves guilty of offences punishable in others by labour, to be transported to Africa, or elsewhere, as the circumstances of the time admit, there to be continued in slavery. A rigorous regimen proposed for those condemned to labour.

Another object of the revisal is, to diffuse knowledge more generally through the mass of the people. This bill proposes to lay off every county into small districts of five or six miles square, called hundreds,[46] and in each of them to establish a school for teaching reading, writing, and arithmetic. The tutor to be supported by the hundred, and every person in it entitled to send their children three years gratis, and as much longer as they please, paying for it. These schools to be under a visitor, who is annually to chuse the boy, of

---

44. Stripes (these are punishments listed in the table of punishments).
45. The part of, or interest in, a deceased man's estate allowed to his widow.
46. Jefferson later called these "wards."

best genius in the school, of those whose parents are too poor to give them further education, and to send him forward to one of the grammar schools, of which twenty are proposed to be erected in different parts of the country, for teaching Greek, Latin, geography, and the higher branches of numerical arithmetic. Of the boys thus sent in any one year, trial is to be made at the grammar schools one or two years, and the best genius of the whole selected, and continued six years, and the residue dismissed. By this means twenty of the best geniusses will be raked from the rubbish annually, and be instructed, at the public expence, so far as the grammer schools go. At the end of six years instruction, one half are to be discontinued (from among whom the grammar schools will probably be supplied with future masters); and the other half, who are to be chosen for the superiority of their parts and disposition, are to be sent and continued three years in the study of such sciences as they shall chuse, at William and Mary college, the plan of which is proposed to be enlarged, as will be hereafter explained, and extended to all the useful sciences. The ultimate result of the whole scheme of education would be the teaching all the children of the state reading, writing, and common arithmetic: turning out ten annually of superior genius, well taught in Greek, Latin, geography, and the higher branches of arithmetic: turning out ten others annually, of still superior parts, who, to those branches of learning, shall have added such of the sciences as their genius shall have led them to: the furnishing to the wealthier part of the people convenient schools, at which their children may be educated, at their own expence. —The general objects of this law are to provide an education adapted to the years, to the capacity, and the condition of every one, and directed to their freedom and happiness. Specific details were not proper for the law. These must be the business of the visitors entrusted with its execution. The first stage of this education being the schools of the hundreds, wherein the great mass of the people will receive their instruction, the principal foundations of future order will be laid here. Instead therefore of putting the Bible and Testament into the hands of the children, at an age when their judgments are not sufficiently matured for religious enquiries, their memories may here be stored with the most useful facts from Grecian, Roman, European and American history. The first elements of morality too may be instilled into their minds; such as, when further developed as their judgments advance in strength, may teach them how to work out their own greatest happiness, by shewing them that it does not depend on the condition of life in which chance has placed them, but is always the result of a good conscience, good health, occupation, and freedom in all just pursuits. — Those whom either the wealth of their parents or the adoption of the state shall destine to higher degrees of learning, will go on to the grammar schools, which constitute the next stage, there to be instructed in the languages. The learning Greek and Latin, I am told, is going into disuse in Europe. I know not what their manners and occupations may call for: but it would be very ill-judged in us to follow their example in this instance. There is a certain period of life, say from eight to fifteen or sixteen years of age, when the mind, like the body, is not yet firm enough for laborious and close operations. If applied to such, it falls an early victim to premature exertion; exhibiting indeed at first, in these young and tender subjects, the flattering appearance of their being men while they are yet children, but ending in reducing them to be children when they should be men. The memory is then most susceptible and tenacious of impressions; and the learning of languages being chiefly a work of memory, it seems precisely fitted to the powers of this period, which is long enough too for acquiring the most useful languages antient and modern. I do not pretend that language is science. It is only an instrument for the attainment of science. But that time is not lost which is employed in providing tools for future operation: more especially as in this case the books put into the hands of the youth for this purpose may be such as will at the same time impress their minds with useful facts and good principles. If this period be suffered to pass in idleness, the mind becomes lethargic and impotent, as would the body it inhabits if unexercised during the same time. The sympathy between body and mind during their rise, progress and decline, is too strict and obvious to endanger our being misled while we reason from the one to the other. —As soon as they are of sufficient age, it is supposed they will be sent on from the grammar schools to the university, which constitutes our third and last stage, there to study those sciences which may be adapted to their views. —By that part of our plan which prescribes the selection of the youths of genius from among the classes of the poor, we hope to avail the state of those talents which nature has sown as liberally among the poor as the rich, but which perish without use, if not sought for and cultivated. —But of all the views of this law none is more important, none more legitimate, than that of rendering the people the safe, as they are the ultimate, guardians of their own liberty. For this purpose the reading in the first stage, where *they* will receive their whole education, is proposed, as has been said, to be chiefly historical. History by apprising them of the past will enable them to judge of the future; it will avail them of the experience of other times and other nations; it will qualify them as judges of the actions and designs of men; it will enable them to know ambition under every disguise it may assume; and knowing it, to defeat its views. In every government on earth is some trace of human weakness, some germ of corruption and degeneracy, which cunning will discover, and wickedness insensibly open, cultivate, and improve. Every government degenerates when trusted to the rulers of the people alone. The people themselves therefore are its only safe depositories. And to render even them safe their minds must be improved to a certain degree. This indeed is not all that is necessary, though it be essentially necessary. An amendment of our constitution must here come in aid of the public education. The influence over government must be shared among all the people. If every individual which composes their mass participates of the ultimate authority, the government will be safe; because the corrupting the whole mass will exceed any private resources of wealth: and public ones cannot be provided but by levies on the people. In this case every man would have to pay his own price. The government of Great-Britain has been corrupted, because but one man in ten has a right to vote for members of parliament. The sellers of the government therefore get nine-tenths of their price clear. It has been thought that corruption is restrained by confining the right of suffrage to a few of the wealthier of the people: but it would be more effectually restrained by an extension of that right to such numbers as would bid defiance to the means of corruption.

Lastly, it is proposed, by a bill in this revisal, to begin a public library and gallery, by laying out a certain sum annually in books, paintings, and statues.

QUERY XVII[1]

The different religions received into that state?

RELIGION. The first settlers in this country[2] were emigrants from England, of the English church, just at a point of time when it was flushed with complete victory over the religious of all other persuasions.[3] Possessed, as they became, of the powers of making, administering, and executing the laws, they shewed equal intolerance in this country with their Presbyterian brethren, who had emigrated to the northern government. The poor Quakers[4] were flying from persecution in England. They cast their eyes on these new countries as asylums of civil and religious freedom; but they found them free only for the reigning sect. Several acts of the Virginia assembly of 1659, 1662, and 1693, had made it penal in parents to refuse to have their children baptized; had prohibited the unlawful assembling of Quakers; had made it penal[5] for any master of a vessel to bring a Quaker into the state; had ordered those already here, and such as should come thereafter, to be imprisoned till they should abjure[6] the country; provided a milder punishment for their first and second return, but death for their third; had inhibited all persons from suffering their meetings in or near their houses, entertaining them individually, or disposing of books which supported their tenets. If no capital execution took place here, as did in New-England, it was not owing to the moderation of the church, or spirit of the legislature, as may be inferred from the law itself; but to historical circumstances which have not been handed down to us. The Anglicans[7] retained full possession of the country about a century. Other opinions began then to creep in, and the great care of the government to support their own church, having begotten an equal degree of indolence in its clergy,

---

1. See Introduction, pp. xvi–xxxiii.

2. I.e., Virginia.

3. At the time of American colonization, in the reign of James I, the Church of England (known as Anglicanism) had prevailed over both Catholicism and more reformed Protestant sects.

4. A Christian sect that developed during the English Civil Wars (1642–49) and was influenced by radical Puritanism. Perhaps best known for its pacifism and opposition to violence. (See note 6, p. 110.)

5. Illegal, punishable by law.

6. To renounce an oath or belief; here, Jefferson seems to be using the word to mean "leave the country."

7. Members of the Church of England. See note 3, above.

two-thirds of the people had become dissenters at the commencement of the present revolution.[8] The laws indeed were still oppressive on them, but the spirit of the one party had subsided into moderation, and of the other had risen to a degree of determination which commanded respect.

The present state of our laws on the subject of religion is this. The convention of May 1776, in their declaration of rights, declared it to be a truth, and a natural right, that the exercise of religion should be free; but when they proceeded to form on that declaration the ordinance of government, instead of taking up every principle declared in the bill of rights, and guarding it by legislative sanction, they passed over that which asserted our religious rights, leaving them as they found them. The same convention, however, when they met as a member of the general assembly in October 1776, repealed all *acts of parliament* which had rendered criminal the maintaining any opinions in matters of religion, the forbearing to repair to church, and the exercising any mode of worship; and suspended the laws giving salaries to the clergy, which suspension was made perpetual in October 1779. Statutory oppressions in religion being thus wiped away, we remain at present under those only imposed by the common law,[9] or by our own acts of assembly. At the common law, *heresy*[10] was a capital offence, punishable by burning. Its definition was left to the ecclesiastical judges, before whom the conviction was, till the statute of the 1 El. c. 1. circumscribed it, by declaring, that nothing should be deemed heresy, but what had been so determined by authority of the canonical scriptures, or by one of the four first general councils, or by some other council having for the grounds of their declaration the express and plain words of the scriptures. Heresy, thus circumscribed, being an offence at the common law, our act of assembly of October 1777, c. 17. gives cognizance of it to the general court, by declaring, that the jurisdiction of that court shall be general in all matters at the common law. The execution is by the writ *De haeretico comburendo*.[11] By our own act of assembly of 1705, c. 30, if a person brought up in the Christian religion denies the being of a God, or the Trinity, or asserts there are more Gods than one, or denies the Christian religion to be true, or the scriptures to be of divine authority, he is punishable on the first offence by

---

8. The First Great Awakening, a period of intense religious revival in the decades leading up to the Revolution, in which many Virginians turned to dissenting Protestant sects.

9. See notes 4, p. 113, and 16, p. 264.

10. Rejection of orthodox religious belief, at one time a crime punishable by death.

11. Literally: burning the heretics. A writ issued by the English secular courts to burn at the stake any heretics condemned as such by the ecclesiastical courts. It was first enacted in 1401 against the anti-Catholic followers of John Wycliffe (c. 1328–84), known as the Lollards, and was used as late as 1611.

incapacity to hold any office or employment ecclesiastical, civil, or military; on the second by disability to sue, to take any gift or legacy, to be guardian, executor, or administrator, and by three years imprisonment, without bail. A father's right to the custody of his own children being founded in law on his right of guardianship, this being taken away, they may of course be severed from him, and put, by the authority of a court, into more orthodox hands. This is a summary view of that religious slavery, under which a people have been willing to remain, who have lavished their lives and fortunes for the establishment of their civil freedom.* The error seems not sufficiently eradicated, that the operations of the mind, as well as the acts of the body, are subject to the coercion of the laws. But our rulers can have authority over such natural rights only as we have submitted to them. The rights of conscience we never submitted, we could not submit. We are answerable for them to our God. The legitimate powers of government extend to such acts only as are injurious to others. But it does me no injury for my neighbour to say there are twenty gods, or no god. It neither picks my pocket nor breaks my leg. If it be said, his testimony in a court of justice cannot be relied on, reject it then, and be the stigma on him. Constraint may make him worse by making him a hypocrite, but it will never make him a truer man. It may fix him obstinately in his errors, but will not cure them. Reason and free enquiry are the only effectual agents against error. Give a loose to them, they will support the true religion, by bringing every false one to their tribunal, to the test of their investigation. They are the natural enemies of error, and of error only. Had not the Roman government permitted free enquiry, Christianity could never have been introduced. Had not free enquiry been indulged, at the æra of the reformation, the corruptions of Christianity could not have been purged away. If it be restrained now, the present corruptions will be protected, and new ones encouraged. Was the government to prescribe to us our medicine and diet, our bodies would be in such keeping as our souls are now. Thus in France the emetic[12] was once forbidden as a medicine, and the potatoe as an article of food. Government is just as infallible too when it fixes systems in physics. Galileo[13] was sent to the inquisition for affirming that the earth was a sphere: the government had declared it to be as flat as a trencher,[14] and

*Furneaux passim.

---

12. Substance that causes vomiting.
13. Galileo Galilei (1564–1642): Italian astronomer who challenged the accepted theory that the sun and planets all revolve around the earth. He was convicted of heresy in 1633 by the Inquisition and publicly forced to withdraw his statements.
14. Wooden board on which food was served.

Galileo was obliged to abjure his error. This error however at length prevailed, the earth became a globe, and Descartes[15] declared it was whirled round its axis by a vortex. The government in which he lived was wise enough to see that this was no question of civil jurisdiction, or we should all have been involved by authority in vortices. In fact, the vortices have been exploded, and the Newtonian principle of gravitation[16] is now more firmly established, on the basis of reason, than it would be were the government to step in, and to make it an article of necessary faith. Reason and experiment have been indulged, and error has fled before them. It is error alone which needs the support of government. Truth can stand by itself. Subject opinion to coercion: whom will you make your inquisitors? Fallible men; men governed by bad passions, by private as well as public reasons. And why subject it to coercion? To produce uniformity. But is uniformity of opinion desireable? No more than of face and stature. Introduce the bed of Procrustes[17] then, and as there is danger that the large men may beat the small, make us all of a size, by lopping the former and stretching the latter. Difference of opinion is advantageous in religion. The several sects perform the office of a Censor morum[18] over each other. Is uniformity attainable? Millions of innocent men, women, and children, since the introduction of Christianity, have been burnt, tortured, fined, imprisoned; yet we have not advanced one inch towards uniformity. What has been the effect of coercion? To make one half the world fools, and the other half hypocrites. To support roguery and error all over the earth. Let us reflect that it is inhabited by a thousand millions of people. That these profess probably a thousand different systems of religion. That ours is but one of that thousand. That if there be but one right, and ours that one, we should wish to see the 999 wandering sects gathered into the fold of truth. But against such a majority we cannot effect this by force. Reason and persuasion are the only practicable instruments. To make way for these, free enquiry must be indulged; and how can we wish others to indulge it while we refuse it ourselves.

---

15. René Descartes (1596–1650): French philosopher and mathematician who tried to explain the origin of the universe and the movement of bodies within it by a theory of vortices. He is perhaps best known for his *Meditationes de Prima Philosophia* (*Meditations on First Philosophy*) (1641) and for his argument *"cogito ergo sum"* ("I think, therefore I am").

16. Sir Isaac Newton (1642–1727): English scientist and mathematician. In contrast to Descartes, Newton hypothesized that the movement of bodies resulted from gravitational force.

17. A character in Greek myth who lured people into his bed by telling them it would be the perfect length for them. He then either stretched or hacked his victims to the perfect size.

18. Moral censor.

But every state, says an inquisitor, has established some religion. No two, say I, have established the same. Is this a proof of the infallibility of establishments? Our sister states of Pennsylvania and New York, however, have long subsisted without any establishment at all. The experiment was new and doubtful when they made it. It has answered beyond conception. They flourish infinitely. Religion is well supported; of various kinds, indeed, but all good enough; all sufficient to preserve peace and order: or if a sect arises, whose tenets would subvert morals, good sense has fair play, and reasons and laughs it out of doors, without suffering the state to be troubled with it. They do not hang more malefactors[19] than we do. They are not more disturbed with religious dissensions. On the contrary, their harmony is unparalleled, and can be ascribed to nothing but their unbounded tolerance, because there is no other circumstance in which they differ from every nation on earth. They have made the happy discovery, that the way to silence religious disputes, is to take no notice of them. Let us too give this experiment fair play, and get rid, while we may, of those tyrannical laws. It is true, we are as yet secured against them by the spirit of the times. I doubt whether the people of this country would suffer an execution for heresy, or a three years imprisonment for not comprehending the mysteries of the Trinity.[20] But is the spirit of the people an infallible, a permanent reliance? Is it government? Is this the kind of protection we receive in return for the rights we give up? Besides, the spirit of the times may alter, will alter. Our rulers will become corrupt, our people careless. A single zealot may commence persecutor, and better men be his victims. It can never be too often repeated, that the time for fixing every essential right on a legal basis is while our rulers are honest, and ourselves united. From the conclusion of this war we shall be going down hill. It will not then be necessary to resort every moment to the people for support. They will be forgotten, therefore, and their rights disregarded. They will forget themselves, but in the sole faculty of making money, and will never think of uniting to effect a due respect for their rights. The shackles, therefore, which shall not be knocked off at the conclusion of this war, will remain on us long, will be made heavier and heavier, till our rights shall revive or expire in a convulsion.

---

19. Evildoers.

20. In traditional Christian teachings, the Father (God), the Son (Jesus Christ), and the Holy Spirit.

QUERY XVIII[1]

The particular customs and manners that may happen to be received in that state?

MANNERS.[2]   It is difficult to determine on the standard by which the manners of a nation may be tried, whether *catholic*,[3] or *particular*. It is more difficult for a native to bring to that standard the manners of his own nation, familiarized to him by habit. There must doubtless be an unhappy influence on the manners of our people produced by the existence of slavery among us. The whole commerce between master and slave is a perpetual exercise of the most boisterous passions, the most unremitting despotism on the one part, and degrading submissions on the other. Our children see this, and learn to imitate it; for man is an imitative animal. This quality is the germ of all education in him. From his cradle to his grave he is learning to do what he sees others do. If a parent could find no motive either in his philanthropy or his self-love, for restraining the intemperance of passion towards his slave, it should always be a sufficient one that his child is present. But generally it is not sufficient. The parent storms, the child looks on, catches the lineaments[4] of wrath, puts on the same airs in the circle of smaller slaves, gives a loose to his worst of passions, and thus nursed, educated, and daily exercised in tyranny, cannot but be stamped by it with odious peculiarities. The man must be a prodigy who can retain his manners and morals undepraved by such circumstances. And with what execration[5] should the statesman be loaded, who permitting one half the citizens thus to trample on the rights of the other, transforms those into despots, and these into enemies, destroys the morals of the one part, and the amor patriae[6] of the other. For if a slave can have a country in this world, it must be any other in preference to that in which he is born to live and labour for another: in which he must lock up the faculties of his nature, contribute as far as depends on his individual endeavours to the

---

1. See Introduction, pp. xvi–xxxiii.
2. In the broader sense of the word, the habits, customs, beliefs, and actions of a particular people.
3. Universal.
4. Character or lines of the face.
5. Curse.
6. Love of country.

evanishment[7] of the human race, or entail[8] his own miserable condition on the endless generations proceeding from him. With the morals of the people, their industry also is destroyed. For in a warm climate, no man will labour for himself who can make another labour for him. This is so true, that of the proprietors of slaves a very small proportion indeed are ever seen to labour. And can the liberties of a nation be thought secure when we have removed their only firm basis, a conviction in the minds of the people that these liberties are of the gift of God? That they are not to be violated but with his wrath? Indeed I tremble for my country when reflect that God is just: that his justice cannot sleep for ever: that considering numbers, nature and natural means only, a revolution of the wheel of fortune, an exchange of situation, is among possible events: that it may become probable by supernatural interference! The Almighty has no attribute which can take side with us in such a contest. —But it is impossible to be temperate and to pursue this subject through the various considerations of policy, of morals, of history natural and civil. We must be contented to hope they will force their way into every one's mind. I think a change already perceptible, since the origin of the present revolution. The spirit of the master is abating, that of the slave rising from the dust, his condition mollifying, the way I hope preparing, under the auspices of heaven, for a total emancipation, and that this is disposed, in the order of events, to be with the consent of the masters, rather than by their extirpation.[9]

---

7. Disappearance.
8. Bequeath. See note 8, p. 111.
9. Eradication.

QUERY XIX[1]

The present state of manufactures, commerce, interior and exterior trade?

MANUFACTURES. We never had an interior trade of any importance. Our exterior commerce has suffered very much from the beginning of the present contest.[2] During this time we have manufactured within our families the most necessary articles of cloathing. Those of cotton will bear some comparison with the same kinds of manufacture in Europe; but those of wool, flax and hemp are very coarse, unsightly, and unpleasant: and such is our attachment to agriculture, and such our preference for foreign manufactures, that be it wise or unwise, our people will certainly return as soon as they can, to the raising raw materials, and exchanging them for finer manufactures than they are able to execute themselves.

The political œconomists of Europe have established it as a principle that every state should endeavour to manufacture for itself: and this principle, like many others, we transfer to America, without calculating the difference of circumstance which should often produce a difference of result. In Europe the lands are either cultivated, or locked up against the cultivator. Manufacture must therefore be resorted to of necessity not of choice, to support the surplus of their people. But we have an immensity of land courting the industry of the husbandman.[3] Is it best then that all our citizens should be employed in its improvement, or that one half should be called off from that to exercise manufactures and handicraft arts for the other? Those who labour in the earth are the chosen people of God, if ever he had a chosen people, whose breasts he has made his peculiar deposit for substantial and genuine virtue. It is the focus in which he keeps alive that sacred fire, which otherwise might escape from the face of the earth. Corruption of morals in the mass of cultivators is a phænomenon of which no age nor nation has furnished an example. It is the mark set on those, who not looking up to heaven, to their own soil and industry, as does the husbandman, for their subsistance, depend for it on the casualties and caprice of customers. Dependance begets subservience and

---

1. See Introduction, pp. xvi–xxxiii.
2. The American War of Independence was ongoing when Jefferson composed the *Notes*.
3. Farmer or breeder of livestock.

132

venality,[4] suffocates the germ of virtue, and prepares fit tools for the designs of ambition. This, the natural progress and consequence of the arts, has sometimes perhaps been retarded by accidental circumstances: but, generally speaking, the proportion which the aggregate of the other classes of citizens bears in any state to that of its husbandmen, is the proportion of its unsound to its healthy parts, and is a good-enough barometer whereby to measure its degree of corruption. While we have land to labour then, let us never wish to see our citizens occupied at a work-bench, or twirling a distaff.[5] Carpenters, masons, smiths, are wanting in husbandry: but, for the general operations of manufacture, let our work-shops remain in Europe. It is better to carry provisions and materials to workmen there, than bring them to the provisions and materials, and with them their manners and principles. The loss by the transportation of commodities across the Atlantic will be made up in happiness and permanence of government. The mobs of great cities add just so much to the support of pure government, as sores do to the strength of the human body. It is the manners and spirit of a people which preserve a republic in vigour. A degeneracy in these is a canker which soon eats to the heart of its laws and constitution.

---

4. Jefferson is here using the word to refer to a willingness to sell one's opinions or vote for money.
5. Staff from which flax is drawn in spinning.

QUERY XXII[1]

The Public Income and Expenses?

REVENUE.   The nominal amount of these varying constantly and rapidly, with the constant and rapid depreciation of our paper-money,[2] it becomes impracticable to say what they are. We find ourselves cheated in every essay[3] by the depreciation intervening between the declaration of the tax and its actual receipt. It will therefore be more satisfactory to consider what our income may be when we shall find means of collecting what the people may spare. I should estimate the whole taxable property of this state at an hundred millions of dollars, or thirty millions of pounds our money. One per cent on this, compared with any thing we ever yet paid, would be deemed a very heavy tax. Yet I think that those who manage well, and use reasonable œconomy, could pay one and a half per cent, and maintain their houshould comfortably in the mean time, without aliening[4] any part of their principal, and that the people would submit to this willingly for the purpose of supporting their present contest.[5] We may say then, that we could raise, and ought to raise, from one million to one million and a half of dollars annually, that is from three hundred to four hundred and fifty thousand pounds, Virginia money.[6]

Of our expences it is equally difficult to give an exact state, and for the same reason. They are mostly stated in paper money, which varying continually, the legislature endeavours at every session, by new corrections, to adapt the nominal sums to the value it is wished they should bear. I will state them therefore in real coin,[7] at the point at which they endeavour to keep them.

---

1. See Introduction, pp. xvi–xxxiii.
2. See note 7, below.
3. Attempt.
4. Cutting into.
5. The American War of Independence.
6. In the period immediately following the War of Independence—when the new nation was governed by the Articles of Confederation—Virginia, like most states, issued its own paper currency.
7. Gold coins (as opposed to the varied American paper currencies).

	Dollars
The annual expences of the general assembly are about	20,000
The governor	$3,333^1/_3$
The council of state	$10,666^2/_3$
Their clerks	1,166 2/3
Eleven judges	11,000
The clerk of the chancery	$666^2/_3$
The attorney general	1,000
Three auditors and a solicitor	$5,333^1/_3$
Their clerks	2,000
The treasurer	2,000
His clerks	2,000
The keeper of the public jail	1,000
The public printer	$1,666^2/_3$
Clerks of the inferior courts	$43,333^1/_3$
Public levy: this is chiefly for the expences of criminal justice	40,000
County levy, for bridges, court houses, prisons, &c.	40,000
Members of congress	7,000
Quota of the Federal civil list,[8] supposed 1/6 of about 78,000 dollars	13,000
Expences of collection, 6 per cent. on the above	12,310
The clergy receive only voluntary contributions: suppose them on an average 1/8 of a dollar a tythe[9] on 200,000 tythes	25,000
Contingencies, to make round numbers not far from truth	$7,523^1/_3$
	250,000

Dollars, or 53,571 guineas. This estimate is exclusive of the military expence. That varies with the force actually employed, and in time of peace will probably be little or nothing. It is exclusive also of the public debts, which are growing while I am writing, and cannot therefore be now fixed. So it is of the maintenance of the poor, which being merely a matter of charity, cannot be deemed expended in the administration of government. And if we strike out the 25,000 dollars for the services of the clergy, which neither makes part of that administration, more than what is paid to physicians or lawyers, and being voluntary, is either much or nothing as every one pleases, it leaves 225,000

---

8. All those on the federal government payroll.

9. A tax; here, Jefferson is referring to a tax on church income generated by tithes.

dollars, equal to 48,208 guineas,[10] the real cost of the apparatus of government with us. This, divided among the actual inhabitants of our country, comes to about two-fifths of a dollar, 21d sterling, or 42 sols, the price which each pays annually for the protection of the residue of his property, that of his person, and the other advantages of a free government. The public revenues of Great Britain divided in like manner on its inhabitants would be sixteen times greater. Deducting even the double of the expences of government, as before estimated, from the million and a half of dollars which we before supposed might be annually paid without distress, we may conclude that this state can contribute one million of dollars annually towards supporting the federal army, paying the federal debt, building a federal navy, or opening roads, clearing rivers, forming safe ports, and other useful works.

To this estimate of our abilities, let me add a word as to the application of them, if, when cleared of the present contest, and of the debts with which that will charge us, we come to measure force hereafter with any European power. Such events are devoutly to be deprecated. Young as we are, and with such a country before us to fill with people and with happiness, we should point in that direction the whole generative force of nature, wasting none of it in efforts of mutual destruction. It should be our endeavour to cultivate the peace and friendship of every nation, even of that which has injured us most, when we shall have carried our point against her. Our interest will be to throw open the doors of commerce, and to knock off all its shackles, giving perfect freedom to all persons for the vent of whatever they may chuse to bring into our ports, and asking the same in theirs. Never was so much false arithmetic employed on any subject, as that which has been employed to persuade nations that it is their interest to go to war. Were the money which it has cost to gain, at the close of a long war, a little town, or a little territory, the right to cut wood here, or to catch fish there, expended in improving what they already possess, in making roads, opening rivers, building ports, improving the arts, and finding employment for their idle poor, it would render them much stronger, much wealthier and happier. This I hope will be our wisdom. And, perhaps, to remove as much as possible the occasions of making war, it might be better for us to abandon the ocean altogether, that being the element whereon we shall be principally exposed to jostle with other nations: to leave to others to bring what we shall want, and to carry what we can spare. This would make us invulnerable to Europe, by offering none of our property to their prize, and would turn all our citizens to the cultivation of the earth; and, I repeat it again, cultivators of the earth are the most virtuous and independant citizens.

---

10. Gold coins, issued in England from 1663 to 1813, worth one British pound, one shilling.

It might be time enough to seek employment for them at sea, when the land no longer offers it. But the actual habits of our countrymen attach them to commerce. They will exercise it for themselves. Wars then must sometimes be our lot; and all the wise can do, will be to avoid that half of them which would be produced by our own follies, and our own acts of injustice; and to make for the other half the best preparations we can. Of what nature should these be? A land army would be useless for offence, and not the best nor safest instrument of defence. For either of these purposes, the sea is the field on which we should meet an European enemy. On that element it is necessary we should possess some power. To aim at such a navy as the greater nations of Europe possess, would be a foolish and wicked waste of the energies of our countrymen. It would be to pull on our own heads that load of military expence, which makes the European labourer go supperless to bed, and moistens his bread with the sweat of his brows. It will be enough if we enable ourselves to prevent insults from those nations of Europe which are weak on the sea, because circumstances exist, which render even the stronger ones weak as to us. Providence has placed their richest and most defenceless possessions at our door; has obliged their most precious commerce to pass as it were in review before us. To protect this, or to assail us, a small part only of their naval force will ever be risqued across the Atlantic. The dangers to which the elements expose them here are too well known, and the greater dangers to which they would be exposed at home, were any general calamity to involve their whole fleet. They can attack us by detachment only; and it will suffice to make ourselves equal to what they may detach. Even a smaller force than they may detach will be rendered equal or superior by the quickness with which any check may be repaired with us, while losses with them will be irreparable till too late. A small naval force then is sufficient for us, and a small one is necessary. What this should be, I will not undertake to say. I will only say, it should by no means be so great as we are able to make it. Suppose the million of dollars, or 300,000 pounds, which Virginia could annually spare without distress, to be applied to the creating a navy. A single year's contribution would build, equip, man, and send to sea a force which should carry 300 guns. The rest of the confederacy, exerting themselves in the same proportion, would equip in the same time 1500 guns more. So that one year's contributions would set up a navy of 1800 guns. The British ships of the line average 76 guns; their frigates[11] 38. 1800 guns then would form a fleet of 30 ships, 18 of which might be of the line, and 12 frigates. Allowing 8 men, the British average, for every gun, their annual expence, including subsistence, cloathing, pay, and ordinary repairs, would be about 1280 dollars for every

---

11. High-speed, medium-sized warships.

gun, or 2,304,000 dollars for the whole. I state this only as one year's possible exertion, without deciding whether more or less than a year's exertion should be thus applied.

The value of our lands and slaves, taken conjunctly, doubles in about twenty years. This arises from the multiplication of our slaves, from the extension of culture, and increased demand for lands. The amount of what may be raised will of course rise in the same proportion.

Correspondence

To Edmund Pendleton[1]

Philadelphia, Aug. 26, 1776

DEAR SIR—Your's of the 10th inst. came to hand about three days ago, the post having brought no mail with him the last week. You seem to have misapprehended my proposition for the choice of a Senate. I had two things in view: to get the wisest men chosen, & to make them perfectly independent when chosen. I have ever observed that a choice by the people themselves is not generally distinguished for it's wisdom. This first secretion from them is usually crude & heterogeneous. But give to those so chosen by the people a second choice themselves, & they generally will chuse wise men. For this reason it was that I proposed the representatives (& not the people) should chuse the Senate, & thought I had notwithstanding that made the Senators (when chosen) perfectly independant of their electors. However I should have no objection to the mode of election proposed in the printed plan of your committee, to wit, that the people of each county should chuse twelve electors, who should meet those of the other counties in the same district & chuse a senator. I should prefer this too for another reason, that the upper as well as lower house should have an opportunity of superintending & judging of the situation of the whole state & be not all of one neighborhood as our upper house used to be. So much for the wisdom of the Senate. To make them independent, I had proposed that they should hold their places for nine years, & then go out (one third every three years) & be incapable for ever of being re-elected to that house. My idea was that if they might be re-elected, they would be casting their eye forward to the period of election (however distant) & be currying favor with the electors, & consequently dependant on them. My reason for fixing them in office for a term of years rather than for life, was that they might have in idea that they were at a certain period to return into the mass of the people & become the governed instead of the governor which might still keep alive that regard to the public good that otherwise they might perhaps be induced by their independance to forget. Yet I could submit, tho' not so willingly to an appointment for life, or to any thing rather than a mere creation by & dependance on the people. I think the present mode of election objectionable because the larger county will be able to send & will always send a man

---

1. Edmund Pendleton (1751–1803): a Revolutionary War patriot and jurist who worked closely with Thomas Jefferson to revise the laws under Virginia's first revolutionary constitution. He was a supporter of the U.S. Constitution.

(less fit perhaps) of their own county to the exclusion of a fitter who may chance to live in a smaller county. — I wish experience may contradict my fears. — That the Senate as well as lower [or shall I speak truth & call it upper] house should hold no office of profit I am clear; but not that they should of necessity possess distinguished property. You have lived longer than I have and perhaps may have formed a different judgment on better grounds; but my observations do not enable me to say think integrity the characteristic of wealth. In general I beleive the decisions of the people, in a body, will be more honest & more disinterested than those of wealthy men: & I can never doubt an attachment to his country in any man who has his family & peculium[2] in it: — Now as to the representative house which ought to be so constructed as to answer that character truly. I was for extending the right of suffrage (or in other words the rights of a citizen) to all who had a permanent intention of living in the country. Take what circumstances you please as evidence of this, either the having resided a certain time, or having a family, or having property, any or all of them. Whoever intends to live in a country must wish that country well, & has a natural right of assisting in the preservation of it. I think you cannot distinguish between such a person residing in the country & having no fixed property, & one residing in a township whom you say you would admit to a vote. — The other point of equal representation I think capital & fundamental. I am glad you think an alteration may be attempted in that matter. — The fantastical idea of virtue & the public good being a sufficient security to the state against the commission of crimes, which you say you have heard insisted on by some, assure you was never mine. It is only the sanguinary hue of our penal laws which I meant to object to. Punishments I know are necessary, & I would provide them, strict & inflexible, but proportioned to the crime. Death might be inflicted for murther & perhaps for treason if you would take out of the description of treason all crimes which are not such in their nature. Rape, buggery &c —punish by castration. All other crimes by working on high roads, rivers, gallies &c. a certain time proportioned to the offence. But as this would be no punishment or change of condition to slaves (me miserum!)[3] let them be sent to other countries. By these means we should be freed from the wickedness of the latter, & the former would be living monuments of public vengeance. Laws thus proportionate & mild should never be dispensed with. Let mercy be the character of the lawgiver, but let the judge be a mere machine. The mercies of the law will be dispensed equally & impartially to every description of men; those of the judge, or of the executive power, will be the eccentric impulses of whimsical, capricious designing man. . . .

---

2. Property.
3. Wretched me!

TO DAVID RITTENHOUSE[1]

Monticello in Albemarle, July 19, 1778

DEAR SIR, —I sincerely congratulate you on the recovery of Philadelphia,[2] and wish it may be found uninjured by the enemy—how far the interests of literature may have suffered by the injury or removal of the Orrery (as it is miscalled)[3] the publick libraries, your papers & implements, are doubts which still excite anxiety. We were much disappointed in Virginia generally on the day of the great eclipse, which proved to be cloudy. In Williamsburgh, where it was total, I understand only the beginning was seen. At this place which is in Lat. 38°–8' and Longitude West from Williamsburgh about 1°–45' as is conjectured, eleven digits only were supposed to be covered, as it was not seen at all till the moon had advanced nearly one third over the sun's disc. Afterwards it was seen at intervals through the whole. The egress[4] particularly was visible. It proved however of little use to me for want of a time piece that could be depended on; which circumstance, together with the subsequent restoration of Philadelphia to you, has induced me to trouble you with this letter to remind you of your kind promise of making me an accurate clock; which being intended for astronomical purposes only, I would have divested of all apparatus for striking or for any other purpose, which by increasing it's complication might disturb it's accuracy. A companion to it, for keeping seconds, and which might be moved easily, would greatly add to it's value. The theodolite,[5] for which I spoke to you also, I can now dispense with, having since purchased a most excellent one.

Writing to a philosopher, I may hope to be pardoned for intruding some thoughts of my own tho' they relate to him personally. Your time for two years past has, I believe, been principally employed in the civil government of your country. Tho' I have been aware of the authority our cause would acquire

---

1. David Rittenhouse (1732–96): a celebrated instrument maker, astronomer, and mathemetician. See note 26, Query VI, p. 87.

2. General Howe's British troops had occupied Philadelphia.

3. Although Rittenhouse invented a mechanical device that showed the motions and positions of the planets and satellites in the solar system, Charles Boyle, 4th Earl of Orrery, claimed to have invented it, and it was named after him. See note 28, Query VI, p. 87.

4. The emergence of a celestial body from eclipse or occultation.

5. A surveying instrument.

with the world from it's being known that yourself & Doct. Franklin[6] were
zealous friends to it and am myself duly impressed with a sense of the ardu-
ousness of government, and the obligation those are under who are able to
conduct it, yet I am also satisfied there is an order of geniusses above that obligation, & therefore exempted from it, nobody can conceive that nature ever
intended to throw away a Newton[7] upon the occupations of a crown. It would
have been a prodigality for which even the conduct of providence might have
been arraigned, had he been by birth annexed to what was so far below him.
Cooperating with nature in her ordinary economy we should dispose of and
employ the geniusses of men according to their several orders and degrees. I
doubt not there are in your country many persons equal to the task of conducting government: but you should consider that the world has but one Ryt-
tenhouse, & that it never had one before. The amazing mechanical
representation of the solar system which you conceived & executed, has never
been surpassed by any but the work of which it is a copy. Are those powers
then, which being intended for the erudition of the world are, like air and
light, the world's common property, to be taken from their proper pursuit to
do the commonplace drudgery of governing a single state, a work which my
be executed by men of an ordinary stature, such as are always & everywhere to
be found? Without having ascended mount Sinai[8] for inspiration, I can pronounce that the precept, in the decalogue[9] of the vulgar, that they shall not
make to themselves "the likeness of anything that is in the heavens above" is
reversed for you, and that you will fulfil the highest purposes of your creation
by employing yourself in the perpetual breach of that inhibition. For my own
country in particular you must remember something like a promise that it
should be adorned with one of them. The taking of your city by the enemy
has hitherto prevented the proposition from being made & approved by our
legislature. The zeal of a true whig[10] in science must excuse the hazarding
these free thoughts, which flow from a desire of promoting the diffusion of

---

6. Benjamin Franklin (1706–90): American printer, author, inventor, revolutionary,
and politician. See note 22, Query VI, p. 86.

7. Sir Isaac Newton (1642–1727): British scientist and mathematician who formu-
lated the theories of universal gravitation, terrestrial mechanics, and color. See note
15, Query XVII, p. 128.

8. According to the Bible, Mount Sinai was the peak on which Moses received the
Ten Commandments.

9. The Ten Commandments, from which the following quotation regarding idolatry
("the likeness of anything that is in the heavens above") is taken.

10. One of the two great English political parties, dating back to the late seventeenth
century, and the one with which the American revolutionaries identified.

knowledge & of your fame, and from one who can assure you truly that he is with much sincerity & esteem Your most obedt. & most humble servt.

P.S. If you can spare as much time as to give me notice of the receipt of this, & what hope I may form of my clocks, it will oblige me. If sent to Fredericksburgh it will come safe to hand.

TO JOHN JAY[1]

Paris, Aug. 23, 1785

DEAR SIR, —I shall sometimes ask your permission to write you letters, not official but private. The present is of this kind, and is occasioned by the question proposed in yours of June 14. "whether it would be useful to us to carry all our own productions, or none?" Were we perfectly free to decide this question, I should reason as follows. We have now lands enough to employ an infinite number of people in their cultivation. Cultivators of the earth are the most valuable citizens. They are the most vigorous, the most independant, the most virtuous, & they are tied to their country & wedded to it's liberty & interests by the most lasting bonds. As long therefore as they can find employment in this line, I would not convert them into mariners, artisans or anything else. But our citizens will find employment in this line till their numbers, & of course their productions, become too great for the demand both internal & foreign. This is not the case as yet, & probably will not be for a considerable time. As soon as it is, the surplus of hands must be turned to something else. I should then perhaps wish to turn them to the sea in preference to manufactures, because comparing the characters of the two classes I find the former the most valuable citizens. I consider the class of artificers[2] as the panders of vice & the instruments by which the liberties of a country are generally overturned. However we are not free to decide this question on principles of theory only. Our people are decided in the opinion that it is necessary for us to take a share in the occupation of the ocean, & their established habits induce them to require that the sea be kept open to them, and that that line of policy be pursued which will render the use of that element as great as possible to them. I think it a duty in those entrusted with the administration of their affairs to conform themselves to the decided choice of their constituents: and that therefore we should in every instance preserve an equality of right to them in the trans-

---

1. John Jay (1745–1829) played a prominent role in early American politics, particularly in foreign affairs. He served as minister to Spain, helped negotiate the peace with Great Britain in 1782, and later worked as the Secretary of Foreign Affairs. As Secretary of Foreign Affairs, he experienced firsthand the weaknesses of the Articles of Confederation; thus, he pressed for a new government, and undertook to defend it as one of the anonymous authors of the *Federalist* (see note 4, p. 226), to which he contributed five papers. He was appointed first chief justice of the United States by George Washington and later served as governor of New York.
2. Manufacturers (as opposed to farmers).

portation of commodities, in the right of fishing, & in the other uses of the sea. But what will be the consequence? Frequent wars without a doubt. Their property will be violated on the sea, & in foreign ports, their persons will be insulted, imprisoned &c. for pretended debts, contracts, crimes, contraband, &c., &c. These insults must be resented, even if we had no feelings, yet to prevent their eternal repetition, or in other words, our commerce on the ocean & in other countries must be paid for by frequent war. The justest dispositions possible in ourselves will not secure us against it. It would be necessary that all other nations were just also. Justice indeed on our part will save us from those wars which would have been produced by a contrary disposition. But to prevent those produced by the wrongs of other nations? By putting ourselves in a condition to punish them. Weakness provokes insult & injury, while a condition to punish it often prevents it. This reasoning leads to the necessity of some naval force, that being the only weapon with which we can reach an enemy. I think it to our interest to punish the first insult; because an insult unpunished is the parent of many others. We are not at this moment in a condition to do it, but we should put ourselves into it as soon as possible. If a war with England should take place, it seems to me that the first thing necessary would be a resolution to abandon the carrying trade[3] because we cannot protect it. Foreign nations must in that case be invited to bring us what we want & to take our productions in their own bottoms. This alone could prevent the loss of those productions to us & the acquisition of them to our enemy. Our seamen might be employed in depredations on their trade. But how dreadfully we shall suffer on our coasts, if we have no force on the water, former experience has taught us. Indeed I look forward with horror to the very possible case of war with an European power, & think there is no protection against them but from the possession of some force on the sea. Our vicinity to their West India possessions & to the fisheries is a bridle which a small naval force on our part would hold in the mouths of the most powerful of these countries. I hope our land office will rid us of our debts, & that our first attention then will be to the beginning a naval force of some sort. This alone can countenance our people as carriers on the water, & I suppose them to be determined to continue such.

I wrote you two public letters on the 14th inst., since which I have received yours of July 13. I shall always be pleased to receive from you in a private way such communications as you might not chuse to put into a public letter.

---

3. Shipping.

To Charles Bellini[1]

Paris, Sept. 30, 1785

DEAR SIR, ... Behold me at length on the vaunted scene of Europe! It is not necessary for your information, that I should enter into details concerning it. But you are, perhaps, curious to know how this new scene has struck a savage of the mountains of America. Not advantageously, I assure you. I find the general fate of humanity here, most deplorable. The truth of Voltaire's[2] observation, offers itself perpetually, that every man here must be either the hammer or the anvil. It is a true picture of that country to which they say we shall pass hereafter, and where we are to see God and his angels in splendor, and crowds of the damned trampled under their feet. While the great mass of the people are thus suffering under physical and moral oppression, I have endeavored to examine more nearly the condition of the great, to appreciate the true value of the circumstances in their situation, which dazzle the bulk of spectators, and, especially, to compare it with that degree of happiness which is enjoyed in America, by every class of people. Intrigues of love occupy the younger, and those of ambition, the elder part of the great. Conjugal love having no existence among them, domestic happiness, of which that is the basis, is utterly unknown. In lieu of this, are substituted pursuits which nourish and invigorate all our bad passions, and which offer only moments of ecstacy, amidst days and months of restlessness and torment. Much, very much inferior, this, to the tranquil, permanent felicity with which domestic society in America, blesses most of its inhabitants; leaving them to follow steadily those pursuits which health and reason approve, and rendering truly delicious the intervals of those pursuits.

In science, the mass of the people is two centuries behind ours; their literati, half a dozen years before us. Books, really good, acquire just reputation in that time, and so become known to us, and communicate to us all their advances in knowledge. Is not this delay compensated, by our being placed

---

1. Charles Bellini emigrated from Italy to Virginia in 1774 and, with Jefferson's help, became professor of modern languages at the College of William and Mary in 1779.
2. François Marie Arouet de Voltaire (1694–1778): French author and philosopher. One of the most prominent figures of the European Enlightenment, he skewered French society and politics in such satirical works as his novel *Candide* (1759), in which he pokes fun at the philosopher G. W. Leibniz for arguing that this is the best of all possible worlds. Voltaire also collaborated on the ambitious *Philosophical Dictionary* (1764). See notes 18 and 24, Query VI, p. 86.

out of the reach of that swarm of nonsensical publications, which issues daily from a thousand presses, and perishes almost in issuing? With respect to what are termed polite manners, without sacrificing too much the sincerity of language, I would wish my countrymen to adopt just so much of European politeness, as to be ready to make all those little sacrifices of self, which really render European manners amiable, and relieve society from the disagreeable scenes to which rudeness often subjects it. Here, it seems that a man might pass a life without encountering a single rudeness. In the pleasures of the table they are far before us, because, with good taste they unite temperance. They do not terminate the most sociable meals by transforming themselves into brutes. I have never yet seen a man drunk in France, even among the lowest of the people. Were I to proceed to tell you how much I enjoy their architecture, sculpture, painting, music, I should want words. It is in these arts they shine. The last of them, particularly, is an enjoyment, the deprivation of which with us, cannot be calculated. I am almost ready to say, it is the only thing which from my heart I envy them, and which, in spite of all the authority of the Decalogue,[3] I do covet. But I am running on in an estimate of things infinitely better known to you than to me, and which will only serve to convince you, that I have brought with me all the prejudices of country, habit and age. But whatever I may allow to be charged to me as prejudice, in every other instance, I have one sentiment at least, founded in reality: it is that of the perfect esteem which your merit and that of Mrs. Bellini have produced, and which will for ever enable me to assure you of the sincere regard, with which I am, Dear Sir, your friend and servant,

---

3. The Ten Commandments.

TO JOHN BANISTER, JR.[1]

Paris, Oct. 15, 1785

DEAR SIR, —I should sooner have answered the paragraph in your letter, of September the 19th, respecting the best seminary for the education of youth, in Europe, but that it was necessary for me to make inquiries on the subject. The result of these has been, to consider the competition as resting between Geneva and Rome. They are equally cheap, and probably are equal in the course of education pursued. The advantage of Geneva, is, that students acquire there the habit of speaking French. The advantages of Rome, are, the acquiring a local knowledge of a spot so classical and so celebrated; the acquiring the true pronunciation of the Latin language; a just taste in the fine arts, more particularly those of painting, sculpture, architecture, and music; a familiarity with those objects and processes of agriculture, which experience has shewn best adapted to a climate like ours; and lastly, the advantage of a fine climate for health. It is probable, too, that by being boarded in a French family, the habit of speaking that language may be obtained. I do not count on any advantage to be derived in Geneva, from a familiar acquaintance with the principles of that government. The late revolution[2] has rendered it a tyrannical aristocracy, more likely to give ill, than good ideas to an American. I think the balance in favor of Rome. Pisa is sometimes spoken of, as a place of education. But it does not offer the first and third of the advantages of Rome. But why send an American youth to Europe for education? What are the objects of an useful American education? Classical knowledge, modern languages, chiefly French, Spanish and Italian; Mathematics, Natural philosophy, Natural history, Civil history, and Ethics. In Natural philosophy, I mean to include Chemistry and Agriculture, and in Natural history, to include Botany, as well as the other branches of those departments. It is true that the habit of speaking the modern languages, cannot be so well acquired in America; but every other article can be as well acquired at William and Mary college, as at any place in Europe. When college education is done with, and a young man is to prepare himself for public life, he must cast his eyes (for America) either on Law or Physic. For the former, where can he apply so ad-

---

1. John Banister, Jr. (1734–88): a Revolutionary patriot and lawyer who played an important role in drafting the Articles of Confederation.
2. The American Revolution (1775–83).

vantageously as to Mr. Wythe?[3] For the latter, he must come to Europe: the medical class of students, therefore, is the only one which need come to Europe. Let us view the disadvantages of sending a youth to Europe. To enumerate them all, would require a volume. I will select a few. If he goes to England, he learns drinking, horse racing and boxing. These are the peculiarities of English education. The following circumstances are common to education in that, and the other countries of Europe. He acquires a fondness for European luxury and dissipation, and a contempt for the simplicity of his own country; he is fascinated with the privileges of the European aristocrats, and sees, with abhorrence, the lovely equality which the poor enjoy with the rich, in his own country; he contracts a partiality for aristocracy or monarchy; he forms foreign friendships which will never be useful to him, and loses the season of life for forming in his own country, those friendships, which, of all others, are the most faithful and permanent; he is led by the strongest of all the human passions, into a spirit for female intrigue, destructive of his own and others' happiness, or a passion for whores, destructive of his health, and, in both cases, learns to consider fidelity to the marriage bed as an ungentlemanly practice, and inconsistent with happiness; he recollects the voluptuary dress and arts of the European women, and pities and despises the chaste affections and simplicity of those of his own country; he retains, through life, a fond recollection, and a hankering after those places, which were the scenes of his first pleasures and of his first connections; he returns to his own country, a foreigner, unacquainted with the practices of domestic economy, necessary to preserve him from ruin, speaking and writing his native tongue as a foreigner, and therefore unqualified to obtain those distinctions, which eloquence of the pen and tongue ensures in a free country; for I would observe to you, that what is called style in writing or speaking, is formed very early in life, while the imagination is warm, and impressions are permanent. I am of opinion, that there never was an instance of a man's writing or speaking his native tongue with elegance, who passed from fifteen to twenty years of age, out of the country where it was spoken. Thus, no instance exists of a person's writing two languages perfectly. That will always appear to be his native language, which was most familiar to him in his youth. It appears to me then, that an American coming to Europe for education, loses in his knowledge, in his morals, in his health, in his habits, and in his happiness. I had entertained only doubts on this head, before I came to Europe: what I see and hear, since I came here, proves more than I had even suspected. Cast your eye over

---

3. George Wythe (1726–1806): Jefferson's teacher before the Revolution. Wythe helped revise Virginia's laws after independence and was later appointed professor of law at William and Mary, thus becoming the first law professor in the United States.

America: who are the men of most learning, of most eloquence, most beloved by their countrymen, and most trusted and promoted by them? They are those who have been educated among them, and whose manners, morals and habits, are perfectly homogeneous with those of the country.

Did you expect by so short a question, to draw such a sermon on yourself? I dare say you did not. But the consequences of foreign education are alarming to me, as an American. I sin, therefore, through zeal, whenever I enter on the subject. You are sufficiently American to pardon me for it. Let me hear of your health, and be assured of the esteem with which I am, Dear Sir, your friend and servant,

To James Madison[1]

Fontainebleau, Oct. 28, 1785

Dear Sir, — Seven o'clock, and retired to my fireside, I have determined to enter into conversation with you. This is a village of about 15,000 inhabitants when the court is not here, and 20,000 when they are, occupying a valley through which runs a brook and on each side of it a ridge of small mountains, most of which are naked rock. The King[2] comes here, in the fall always, to hunt. His court attend him, as do also the foreign diplomatic corps; but as this is not indispensably required and my finances do not admit the expense of a continued residence here, I propose to come occasionally to attend the King's levees, returning again to Paris, distant forty miles. This being the first trip, I set out yesterday morning to take a view of the place. For this purpose I shaped my course towards the highest of the mountains in sight, to the top of which was about a league.[3]

As soon as I had got clear of the town I fell in with a poor woman walking at the same rate with myself and going the same course. Wishing to know the condition of the laboring poor I entered into conversation with her, which I began by enquiries for the path which would lead me into the mountain: and thence proceeded to enquiries into her vocation, condition and circumstances. She told me she was a day laborer at 8 sous or 4d. sterling the day: that she had two children to maintain, and to pay a rent of 30 livres for her house (which would consume the hire of 75 days), that often she could [find] no employment and of course was without bread. As we had walked together near a mile and she had so far served me as a guide, I gave her, on parting, 24 sous. She burst into tears of a gratitude which could perceive was unfeigned because she was unable to utter a word. She had probably never before received so great an aid. This little *attendrissement*,[4] with the solitude of my walk, led me into a train of reflections on that unequal division of property

---

1. James Madison (1751–1836) was Jefferson's closest political ally for over fifty years. He played a major role in helping to draft the Constitution and defended it in the *Federalist* (see note 4, p. 226). Madison succeeded Jefferson as President of the United States, and served for two terms (1809–17).
2. Louis XVI (1754–93), King of France.
3. A distance of about three miles.
4. In this context, a touching experience or emotional moment.

which occasions the numberless instances of wretchedness which I had observed in this country and is to be observed all over Europe.

The property of this country is absolutely concentred in a very few hands, having revenues of from half a million of guineas a year downwards. These employ the flower of the country as servants, some of them having as many as 200 domestics, not laboring. They employ also a great number of manufacturers and tradesmen, and lastly the class of laboring husbandmen. But after all there comes the most numerous of all classes, that is, the poor who cannot find work. I asked myself what could be the reason so many should be permitted to beg who are willing to work, in a country where there is a very considerable proportion of uncultivated lands? These lands are undisturbed only for the sake of game. It should seem then that it must be because of the enormous wealth of the proprietors which places them above attention to the increase of their revenues by permitting these lands to be labored. I am conscious that an equal division of property is impracticable, but the consequences of this enormous inequality producing so much misery to the bulk of mankind, legislators cannot invent too many devices for subdividing property, only taking care to let their subdivisions go hand in hand with the natural affections of the human mind. The descent of property of every kind therefore to all the children, or to all the brothers and sisters, or other relations in equal degree, is a politic measure and a practicable one. Another means of silently lessening the inequality of property is to exempt all from taxation below a certain point, and to tax the higher portions or property in geometrical progression as they rise. Whenever there are in any country uncultivated lands and unemployed poor, it is clear that the laws of property have been so far extended as to violate natural right. The earth is given as a common stock for man to labor and live on. If for the encouragement of industry we allow it to be appropriated, we must take care that other employment be provided to those excluded from the appropriation. If we do not, the fundamental right to labor the earth returns to the unemployed. It is too soon yet in our country to say that every man who cannot find employment, but who can find uncultivated land, shall be at liberty to cultivate it, paying a moderate rent. But it is not too soon to provide by every possible means that as few as possible shall be without a little portion of land. The small landholders are the most precious part of a state. . . . Yours affectionately.

To James Madison[1]

Paris, Jan. 30, 1787

DEAR SIR, —My last to you was of the 16th of Dec, since which I have received yours of Nov 25, & Dec 4, which afforded me, as your letters always do, a treat on matters public, individual & œconomical. I am impatient to learn your sentiments on the late troubles in the Eastern states.[2] So far as I have yet seen, they do not appear to threaten serious consequences. Those states have suffered by the stoppage of the channels of their commerce, which have not yet found other issues. This must render money scarce, and make the people uneasy. This uneasiness has produced acts absolutely unjustifiable;[3] but I hope they will provoke no severities from their governments. A consciousness of those in power that their administration of the public affairs has been honest, may perhaps produce too great a degree of indignation: and those characters wherein fear predominates over hope may apprehend too much from these instances of irregularity. They may conclude too hastily that nature has formed man insusceptible of any other government but that of force, a conclusion not founded in truth, nor experience. Societies exist under three forms sufficiently distinguishable. 1. Without government, as among our Indians. 2. Under governments wherein the will of every one has a just influence, as is the case in England in a slight degree, and in our states, in a great one. 3. Under governments of force: as is the case in all other monarchies and in most of the other republics. To have an idea of the curse of existence under these last, they must be seen. It is a government of wolves over sheep. It is a problem, not clear in my mind, that the 1st condition is not the best. But I believe it to be inconsistent with any great degree of population. The second

---

1. For biographical information on Madison, see note 1 on p. 153.
2. Shays's Rebellion in Massachusetts. At the end of 1786 and the beginning of 1787, Daniel Shays, a captain in the Revolutionary Army, led groups of farmers in western Massachusetts in a series of armed protests against the government. The rebellion culminated in a 2,000-man assault on the arsenal in Springfield. The farmers were protesting the state's post-war economic policies, which included foreclosures on their farms and imprisonment for debt. The rebellion was eventually put down and its leaders sentenced to death, though most of them, including Shays, were later pardoned by the new governor, John Hancock. Shays's Rebellion was widely considered one of the precipitating factors leading to the Constitutional Convention, which later that year would "establish justice and insure domestic tranquility."
3. The rebels tried to use force to prevent the courts from meeting.

state has a great deal of good in it. The mass of mankind under that enjoys a precious degree of liberty & happiness. It has its evils too: the principal of which is the turbulence to which it is subject. But weigh this against the oppressions of monarchy, and it becomes nothing. *Malo periculosam libertatem quam quietam servitutem.*[4] Even this evil is productive of good. It prevents the degeneracy of government, and nourishes a general attention to the public affairs. I hold it that a little rebellion now and then is a good thing, & as necessary in the political world as storms in the physical. Unsuccessful rebellions indeed generally establish the encroachments on the rights of the people which have produced them. An observation of this truth should render honest republican governors so mild in their punishment of rebellions, as not to discourage them too much. It is a medicine necessary for the sound health of government. If these transactions give me no uneasiness, I feel very differently at another piece of intelligence, to wit, the possibility that the navigation of the Mississippi may be abandoned to Spain.[5] I never had any interest Westward of the Alleghaney; & I never will have any. But I have had great opportunities of knowing the character of the people who inhabit that country. And I will venture to say that the act which abandons the navigation of the Mississippi is an act of separation between the Eastern & Western country. It is a relinquishment of five parts out of eight of the territory of the United States, an abandonment of the fairest subject for the paiment of our public debts, & the chaining those debts on our own necks *in perpetuum.*[6] I have the utmost confidence in the honest intentions of those who concur in this measure; but I lament their want of acquaintance with the character & physical advantages of the people who, right or wrong, will suppose their interests sacrificed on this occasion to the contrary interests of that part of the confederacy in possession of present power. If they declare themselves a separate people, we are incapable of a single effort to retain them. Our citizens can never be induced, either as militia or as souldiers, to go there to cut the throats of their own brothers & sons, or rather to be themselves the subjects instead of the perpetrators of the parricide. Nor would that country requite the cost of being retained against the will of it's inhabitants, could it be done. But it cannot be done. They are able already to rescue the navigation of the Mississippi out of

---

4. "I prefer a dangerous liberty to a tranquil servitude" (Rousseau, *The Social Contract*, bk. 3, ch. 4).

5. Spain was in possession of the Louisiana Territory at this time, and Congress was considering abandoning American navigation of the Mississippi and leaving it to Spain's control in exchange for a commercial treaty with them. As a southerner, Jefferson appreciated the strategic importance of this waterway more than some of the northern politicians. See note 2, p. 198 Letter to Livingston (1802).

6. For all time.

the hands of Spain, & to add New Orleans to their own territory. They will be joined by the inhabitants of Louisiana. This will bring on a war between them & Spain; and that will produce the question with us whether it will not be worth our while to become parties with them in the war, in order to reunite them with us, & thus correct our error? & were I to permit my forebodings to go one step further, I should predict that the inhabitants of the U S would force their rulers to take the affirmative of that question. I wish I may be mistaken in all these opinions. . . .

As you are now returned into Congress it will become of importance that you should form a just estimate of certain public characters: on which therefore I will give you such notes as my knolege of them has furnished me with. You will compare them with the materials you are otherwise possessed of, and decide on a view of the whole. You know the opinion I *formerly* entertained of *my friend Mr. Adams.*[7] Yourself & the governor[8] were the first who *shook* that opinion. I afterwards saw proofs which *convicted him* of a degree of *vanity*, and of a *blindness* to it, of which no germ *had appeared* in Congress. A *7-month's* intimacy with him *here* and *as* many *weeks* in *London* have given me opportunities of studying him closely. *He is vain, irritable and a bad calculator of* the force & probable effect of the motives which govern men. This is *all* the *ill* which can possibly be *said of him.* He is as disinterested as the being which made him: he is profound in his views: and accurate in his judgment *except where knowledge of the world* is necessary to form a judgment. He is so amiable, that I pronounce you will love him, if ever you become acquainted with him. He would be, as he was, a great man in *Congress.* . . .

The *Marquis de La Fayette*[9] is a most valuable *auxiliary to me.* His *zeal* is unbounded, & his *weight* with those in *power, great.* His *education* having been merely *military, commerce* was an unknown field to him. But his good sense enabling him to *comprehend* perfectly whatever is *explained to him, his agency* has been very *efficacious. He* has a great deal of *sound genius*, is well

---

7. John Adams (1735–1826): American revolutionary, diplomat, and second president of the United States. See note 1, p. 211.

8. Edmund Randolph (1753–1813): Virginia lawyer and governor of the state from 1786–88. A delegate to the Constitutional Convention, he introduced the "Virginia Plan" and served on the "committee on detail" that drew up the first draft of the Constitution. Yet he refused to sign the final document, arguing that it lacked the necessary checks and balances. He did, however, urge its ratification in 1788. Randolph was appointed attorney general of the United States in 1789, and succeeded Jefferson as secretary of state in 1793.

9. Marquis de La Fayette (1757–1834): French soldier and politician who served under George Washington during the American Revolution. A great supporter of the new American colonies, he later played important roles in the French Revolutions of 1789 and 1830 and led troops in the French war against Britain of 1792.

remarked by the *King*,[10] & rising in *popularity*. *He* has nothing against *him*, *but* the *suspicion* of *republican principles*. I think he will one day *be of* the *ministry*. His foible is, a *canine appetite for popularity and fame*; but he will get *above* this. *The Count de Vergennes*[11] is *ill*. The possibility of his *recovery*, renders it dangerous for *us to express a doubt of it*: *but* he is *in danger*. He is *a great minister* in *European affairs*, but has very *imperfect ideas* of *our institutions, and no confidence in* them. His *devotion* to the principles of *pure despotism*, renders him *unaffectionate to our governments*. But *his fear* of *England makes him value us* as a *make weight*.[12] He is *cool, reserved in political conversations, but free and familiar* on other *subjects*, and a very *attentive, agreeable person* to *do business with*. It is *impossible* to have a clearer, better *organized head*; but *age* has *chilled his heart*. Nothing should be spared, on our part, to attach this country to us. It is the only one on which we can rely for support, under every event. Its inhabitants love us more, I think, than they do any other nation on earth. This is very much the effect of the good dispositions with which the French officers returned. . . .

---

10. Louis XVI (1754–93), King of France.

11. Charles Gravier, count de Vergennes (1719–87): a French foreign minister who fashioned the alliance with the American colonists that helped them win independence from Britain. See note 6, p. 204.

12. A counterweight or counterbalance.

TO ANNE WILLING BINGHAM[1]

Paris, Feb. 7, 1787

I know, Madam, that the twelve month is not yet expired; but it will be, nearly, before this will have the honor of being put into your hands. You are then engaged to tell me, truly and honestly, whether you do not find the tranquil pleasures of America, preferable to the empty bustle of Paris. For to what does that bustle tend? At eleven o'clock, it is day, *chez madame.*[2] The curtains are drawn. Propped on bolsters and pillows, and her head scratched into a little order, the bulletins of the sick are read, and the billets[3] of the well. She writes to some of her acquaintance, and receives the visits of others. If the morning is not very thronged, she is able to get out and hobble round the cage of the Palais royal;[4] but she must hobble quickly, for the *coeffeur's*[5] turn is come; and a tremendous turn it is! Happy, if he does not make her arrive when dinner is half over! The torpitude of digestion a little passed, she flutters half an hour through the streets, by way of paying visits, and then to the spectacles. These finished, another half hour is devoted to dodging in and out of the doors of her very sincere friends, and away to supper. After supper, cards; and after cards, bed; to rise at noon the next day, and to tread, like a mill horse, the same trodden circle over again. Thus the days of life are consumed, one by one, without an object beyond the present moment; ever flying from the ennui of that, yet carrying it with us; eternally in pursuit of happiness, which keeps eternally before us. If death or bankruptcy happen to trip us out of the circle, it is matter for the buz[6] of the evening, and is completely forgotten by the next morning. In America, on the other hand, the society of your husband, the fond cares for the children, the arrangements of the house, the improvements of the grounds, fill every moment with a healthy and an useful

---

1. Anne Willing Bingham (1764–1801): renowned society leader in Philadelphia at the time when that city was the capital of the United States. Mrs. Bingham counted both George Washington and Thomas Jefferson among her acquaintances, and exchanged several letters with Jefferson.
2. At madame's house.
3. A short letter or note.
4. Originally the palace of Cardinal Richelieu (1585–1642), the Palais Royal was in Jefferson's time an amusement area with several theaters.
5. Jefferson seems to have misspelled the French word for hairdresser (*coiffeur*).
6. Gossip, the "buzz" of conversation that is forgotten by the next morning.

activity. Every exertion is encouraging, because to present amusement, it joins the promise of some future good. The intervals of leisure are filled by the society of real friends, whose affections are not thinned to cob-web, by being spread over a thousand objects. This is the picture, in the light it is presented to my mind; now let me have it in yours. If we do not concur this year, we shall the next; or if not then, in a year or two more. You see I am determined not to suppose myself mistaken. . . .

To Peter Carr[1]

DEAR PETER, —I have received your two letters of Decemb. 30 and April 18, and am very happy to find by them, as well as by letters from Mr. Wythe,[2] that you have been so fortunate as to attract his notice & good will; I am sure you will find this to have been one of the most fortunate events of your life, as I have ever been sensible it was of mine. I inclose you a sketch of the sciences to which I would wish you to apply in such order as Mr. Wythe shall advise; I mention also the books in them worth your reading, which submit to his correction. Many of these are among your father's books, which you should have brought to you. As I do not recollect those of them not in his library, you must write to me for them, making out a catalogue of such as you think you shall have occasion for in 18 months from the date of your letter, & consulting Mr. Wythe on the subject. To this sketch I will add a few particular observations.

1. Italian. I fear the learning this language will confound your French and Spanish. Being all of them degenerated dialects of the Latin, they are apt to mix in conversation. have never seen a person speaking the three languages who did not mix them. It is a delightful language, but late events having rendered the Spanish more useful, lay it aside to prosecute that.

2. Spanish. Bestow great attention on this, & endeavor to acquire an accurate knowlege of it. Our future connections with Spain & Spanish America will render that language a valuable acquisition. The antient history of a great part of America, too, is written in that language. I send you a dictionary.

3. Moral philosophy. I think it lost time to attend lectures in this branch. He who made us would have been a pitiful bungler if he had made the rules of our moral conduct a matter of science. For one man of science, there are thousands who are not. What would have become of them? Man was destined for society. His morality therefore was to be formed to this object. He was endowed with a sense of right & wrong merely relative to this. This sense is as

---

1. Peter Carr (1750–1815): nephew of Thomas Jefferson by his sister Martha Jefferson and her husband Dabney Carr. Jefferson became Peter Carr's guardian after Dabney Carr died.

2. George Wythe (1726–1806): Virginia lawyer and patriot who spoke out against the Stamp Act. Wythe taught law to both Jefferson and John Marshall. After independence from Britain, he served in the House of Burgesses and was then appointed judge and chancellor of Virginia. See note 3, p. 151, and Introduction.

much a part of his nature as the sense of hearing, seeing, feeling; it is the true foundation of morality, & not the το καλον, truth, &c. as fanciful writers have imagined. The moral sense, or conscience, is as much a part of man as his leg or arm. It is given to all human beings in a stronger or weaker degree, as force of members is given them in a greater or less degree. It may be strengthened by exercise, as may any particular limb of the body. This sense is submitted indeed in some degree to the guidance of reason; but it is a small stock which is required for this: even a less one than what we call common sense. State a moral case to a ploughman & a professor. The former will decide it as well, & often better than the latter, because he has not been led astray by artificial rules. In this branch therefore read good books because they will encourage as well as direct your feelings. The writings of Sterne[3] particularly form the best course of morality that ever was written. Besides these read the books mentioned in the enclosed paper; and above all things lose no occasion of exercising your dispositions to be grateful, to be generous, to be charitable, to be humane, to be true, just, firm, orderly, courageous &c. Consider every act of this kind as an exercise which will strengthen your moral faculties, & increase your worth.

4. Religion. Your reason is now mature enough to examine this object. In the first place divest yourself of all bias in favour of novelty & singularity of opinion. Indulge them in any other subject rather than that of religion. It is too important, & the consequences of error may be too serious. On the other hand shake off all the fears & servile prejudices under which weak minds are servilely crouched. Fix reason firmly in her seat, and call to her tribunal every fact, every opinion. Question with boldness even the existence of a god; because, if there be one, he must more approve of the homage of reason, than that of blindfolded fear. You will naturally examine first the religion of your own country. Read the bible then, as you would read Livy[4] or Tacitus.[5] The facts which are within the ordinary course of nature you will believe on the authority of the writer, as you do those of the same kind in Livy & Tacitus. The testimony of the writer weighs in their favor in one scale, and their not being against the laws of nature does not weigh against them. But those facts in the bible which contradict the laws of nature, must be examined with more care, and under a variety of faces. Here you must recur to the pretensions of

---

3. Laurence Sterne (1713–68): British author best known for his novel *Tristram Shandy*, one of Jefferson's favorite books.

4. Livy (59 BC–17 AD): Roman historian whose 142-volume *History of Rome* traced the history of Rome from its founding in 753 BC.

5. Publius Cornelius Tacitus (55–117 AD): Roman historian. His *Histories* and *Annals* traced the first century of the Roman Empire from Tiberius to Domitian.

the writer to inspiration from god. Examine upon what evidence his pretensions are founded, and whether that evidence is so strong as that its falsehood would be more improbable than a change in the laws of nature in the case he relates. For example in the book of Joshua we are told the sun stood still several hours.[6] Were we to read that fact in Livy or Tacitus we should class it with their showers of blood, speaking of statues, beasts, &c. But it is said that the writer of that book was inspired. Examine therefore candidly what evidence there is of his having been inspired. The pretension is entitled to your inquiry, because millions believe it. On the other hand you are astronomer enough to know how contrary it is to the law of nature that a body revolving on its axis as the earth does, should have stopped, should not by that sudden stoppage have prostrated animals, trees, buildings, and should after a certain time have resumed its revolution, & that without a second general prostration. Is this arrest of the earth's motion, or the evidence which affirms it, most within the law of probabilities? You will next read the new testament. It is the history of a personage called Jesus. Keep in your eye the opposite pretensions 1. of those who say he was begotten by god, born of a virgin, suspended & reversed the laws of nature at will, & ascended bodily into heaven: and 2. of those who say he was a man of illegitimate birth, of a benevolent heart, enthusiastic mind, who set out without pretensions to divinity, ended in believing them, & was punished capitally for sedition by being gibbeted according to the Roman law which punished the first commission of that offence by whipping, & the second by exile or death *in furcâ*.[7] See this law in the Digest Lib. 48. tit. 19. § 28. 3. & Lipsius Lib. 2. de cruce. cap. 2. These questions are examined in the books I have mentioned under the head of religion, & several others. They will assist you in your inquiries, but keep your reason firmly on the watch in reading them all. Do not be frightened from this inquiry by any fear of it's consequences. If it ends in a belief that there is no god, you will find incitements to virtue in the comfort & pleasantness you feel in it's exercise, and the love of others which it will procure you. If you find reason to believe there is a god, a consciousness that you are acting under his eye, & that he approves you, will be a vast additional incitement; if that there be a future state, the hope of a happy existence in that increases the appetite to deserve it; if that Jesus was also a god, you will be comforted by a belief of his aid and love. *In fine*,[8] I repeat that you must lay aside all prejudice on both sides, & neither believe nor reject anything because any other persons, or description of persons have

6. Joshua 10: 12–13.
7. Literally, "by the fork." In an ancient mode of capital punishment, a criminal was tied to the *furca* and flogged to death.
8. Finally.

rejected or believed it. Your own reason is the only oracle given you by heaven, and you are answerable not for the rightness but uprightness of the decision. I forgot to observe when speaking of the new testament that you should read all the histories of Christ, as well of those whom a council of ecclesiastics have decided for us to be Pseudo-evangelists, as those they named Evangelists. Because these Pseudo-evangelists pretended to inspiration as much as the others, and you are to judge their pretensions by your own reason, & not by the reason of those ecclesiastics. Most of these are lost. There are some however still extant, collected by Fabricius[9] which I will endeavor to get & send you.

5. Travelling. This makes men wiser, but less happy. When men of sober age travel, they gather knolege which they may apply usefully for their country, but they are subject ever after to recollections mixed with regret, their affections are weakened by being extended over more objects, & they learn new habits which cannot be gratified when they return home. Young men who travel are exposed to all these inconveniences in a higher degree, to others still more serious, and do not acquire that wisdom for which a previous foundation is requisite by repeated & just observations at home. The glare of pomp & pleasure is analogous to the motion of their blood, it absorbs all their affection & attention, they are torn from it as from the only good in this world, and return to their home as to a place of exile & condemnation. Their eyes are for ever turned back to the object they have lost, & it's recollection poisons the residue of their lives. Their first & most delicate passions are hackneyed on unworthy objects here, & they carry home only the dregs, insufficient to make themselves or anybody else happy. Add to this that a habit of idleness, an inability to apply themselves to business is acquired & renders them useless to themselves & their country. These observations are founded in experience. There is no place where your pursuit of knolege will be so little obstructed by foreign objects as in your own country, nor any wherein the virtues of the heart will be less exposed to be weakened. Be good, be learned, & be industrious, & you will not want the aid of travelling to render you precious to your country, dear to your friends, happy within yourself. repeat my advice to take a great deal of exercise, & on foot. Health is the first requisite after morality. Write to me often & be assured of the interest I take in your success, as well as of the warmth of those sentiments of attachment with which I am, dear Peter, your affectionate friend.

---

9. Johann Albert Fabricius (1668–1736): German classical scholar who held the chair in rhetoric and ethics at Hamburg.

P.S. Let me know your age in your next letter. Your cousins here are well & desire to be remembered to you.

Antient history. Herodot. Thucyd. Xenoph. hellen. Xenoph. Anab. Q. Curt. Just. Livy. Polybius. Sallust. Caesar. Suetonius. Tacitus. Aurel. Victor. Herodian. Gibbons' decline of the Roman empire. Milot histoire ancienne.

Mod. hist. English. Tacit. Germ. & Agricole — Hume to the end of H.VI. then Habington's E.IV. — St. Thomas Moor's E.5. & R.3. — Ld Bacon's H.7. — Ld. Herbert of Cherbury's H.8. — K. Edward's journal (in Burnet) Bp. of Hereford's E.6. & Mary. — Cambden's Eliz. — Wilson's Jac.I. — Ludlow (omit Clarendon as too seducing for a young republican. By and by read him) Burnet's Charles 2. Jac.2. Wim. & Mary & Anne — Ld Orrery down to George 1. & 2. — Burke's G.3. — Robertson's hist. of Scotland. American. Robertson's America. — Douglass's N. America — Hutcheson's Massachusets. Smith's N. York. — Smith's N. Jersey — Franklin's review of Pennsylvania. — Smith's, Stith's, Keith's, & Beverley's hist. of Virginia

Foreign. Mallet's Northn. Antiquities by Percy — Puffendorf's histy. of Europe & Martiniere's of Asia, Africa & America — Milot histoire Moderne. Voltaire histoire universelle — Milot hist. de France — Mariana's hist. of Spain in Span. — Robertson's Charles V. — Watson's Phil. II. & III.— Grotii Belgica. Mosheim's Ecclesiastical history.

Poetry, Homer — Milton — Ossian — Sophocles — Aeschylus — Eurip. — Metastasio — Shakesp. — Theocritus — Anacreon [. . .]

Mathematics Bezout & whatever else Mr. Madison recommends.

Astronomy Delalande &c. as Mr. Madison shall recommend.

Natural Philosophy. Musschenbroeck.

Botany. Linnaei Philosophia Botanica — Genera plantarum — Species plantarum — Gronorii flora [. . .]

Chemistry. Fourcroy.

Agriculture. Home's principles of Agriculture — Tull &c.

Anatomy. Cheselden.

Morality. The Socratic dialogues — Cicero's Philosophies — Kaim's principles of Natl. religion — Helvetius de l'esprit et de l'homme. Locke's Essay. — Lucretius — Traite d Morale & du bonheur. Religion. Locke's Conduct of the mind. — Middleton's works — Bolingbroke's philosoph. works — Hume's essays — Voltaire's works — Beattie

Politics & Law. Whatever Mr. Wythe pleases, who will be so good as to correct also all the preceding articles which are only intended as a groundwork to be finished by his pencil.

TO WILLIAM S. SMITH[1]

Paris, Nov. 13, 1787

DEAR SIR, — I am now to acknoledge the receipt of your favors of October the 4th, 8th, & 26th. In the last you apologise for your letters of introduction to Americans coming here. It is so far from needing apology on your part, that it calls for thanks on mine. I endeavor to shew civilities to all the Americans who come here, & will give me opportunities of doing it: and it is a matter of comfort to know from a good quarter what they are, & how far I may go in my attentions to them. . . . — I do not know whether it is to yourself or Mr. Adams[2] I am to give my thanks for the copy of the new constitution. I beg leave through you to place them where due. It will be yet three weeks before I shall receive them from America. There are very good articles in it: & very bad. I do not know which preponderate. What we have lately read in the history of Holland, in the chapter on the Stadtholder, would have sufficed to set me against a chief magistrate eligible for a long duration, if I had ever been disposed towards one: & what we have always read of the elections of Polish kings should have forever excluded the idea of one continuable for life. Wonderful is the effect of impudent & persevering lying. The British ministry have so long hired their gazetteers to repeat and model into every form lies about our being in anarchy, that the world has at length believed them, the English nation has believed them, the ministers themselves have come to believe them, & what is more wonderful, we have believed them ourselves. Yet where does this anarchy exist? Where did it ever exist, except in the single instance of Massachusetts?[3] And can history produce an instance of rebellion so honourably conducted? I say nothing of it's motives. They were founded in ignorance, not wickedness. God forbid we should ever be 20 years without such a rebellion. The people cannot be all, & always, well informed. The part which is wrong will be discontented in proportion to the importance of the facts they misconceive. If they remain quiet under such misconceptions it is a lethargy, the

---

1. William S. Smith (1755–1816): Revolutionary soldier who later married Abigail Amelia, the daughter of John Adams (see note 7, p. 157), and pursued a career as a politician and land speculator.

2. John Adams, Smith's father-in-law, who was at that time serving as American minister to England.

3. Shays's Rebellion (see Introduction, p. xvii and note 2, Letter to James Madison Jan. 30, 1887, p. 155).

forerunner of death to the public liberty. We have had 13. states independent 11. years. There has been one rebellion. That comes to one rebellion in a century & a half for each state. What country before ever existed a century & half without a rebellion? & what country can preserve it's liberties if their rulers are not warned from time to time that their people preserve the spirit of resistance? Let them take arms. The remedy is to set them right as to facts, pardon & pacify them. What signify a few lives lost in a century or two? The tree of liberty must be refreshed from time to time with the blood of patriots & tyrants. It is it's natural manure. Our Convention has been too much impressed by the insurrection of Massachusetts:[4] and in the spur of the moment they are setting up a kite[5] to keep the hen-yard in order. I hope in God this article will be rectified before the new constitution is accepted. — You ask me if any thing transpires here on the subject of S. America? Not a word. I know that there are combustible materials there, and that they wait the torch only. But this country probably will join the extinguishers. — The want of facts worth communicating to you has occasioned me to give a little loose to dissertation. We must be contented to amuse, when we cannot inform.

---

4. Part of the impetus for the Constitutional Convention was Shays's Rebellion.
5. Any of the various predatory birds of the hawk family.

TO JAMES MADISON[1]

Paris, Dec. 20, 1787

DEAR SIR, ...The season admitting only of operations in the Cabinet, and these being in a great measure secret, I have little to fill a letter. I will therefore make up the deficiency by adding a few words on the Constitution proposed by our Convention. I like much the general idea of framing a government which should go on of itself peaceably, without needing continual recurrence to the state legislatures. I like the organization of the government into Legislative, Judiciary & Executive. I like the power given the Legislature to levy taxes, and for that reason solely approve of the greater house being chosen by the people directly. For tho' I think a house chosen by them will be very illy qualified to legislate for the Union, for foreign nations &c. yet this evil does not weigh against the good of preserving inviolate the fundamental principle that the people are not to be taxed but by representatives chosen immediately by themselves. I am captivated by the compromise of the opposite claims of the great & little states, of the latter to equal, and the former to proportional influence. I am much pleased too with the substitution of the method of voting by persons, instead of that of voting by states: and I like the negative given to the Executive with a third of either house, though I should have liked it better had the Judiciary been associated for that purpose, or invested with a similar and separate power. There are other good things of less moment. I will now add what I do not like. First the omission of a bill of rights providing clearly & without the aid of sophisms[2] for freedom of religion, freedom of the press, protection against standing armies, restriction against monopolies, the eternal & unremitting force of the habeas corpus laws,[3] and trials by jury in all matters of fact triable by the laws of the land & not by the law of nations. To say, as Mr. Wilson[4] does that a bill of rights was not necessary because all is reserved in the case of the general government which is not

---

1. For biographical information on Madison, see note 1 on p. 153.

2. Fallacious arguments, most often used to deceive.

3. From the Latin phrase meaning "you have the body." Under these laws, a judge may order prison officials to bring a prisoner to court to determine whether he is lawfully imprisoned. Prisoners may also petition the court on their own behalf.

4. One of Pennsylvania's delegates to the Constitutional Convention, James Wilson (1742–98) vigorously defended the document, including the original omission of a bill of rights. He was appointed associate justice of the Supreme Court in 1789.

given, while in the particular ones all is given which is not reserved, might do for the audience to whom it was addressed, but is surely a gratis dictum,[5] opposed by strong inferences from the body of the instrument, as well as from the omission of the clause of our present confederation which had declared that in express terms. It was a hard conclusion to say because there has been no uniformity among the states as to the cases triable by jury, because some have been so incautious as to abandon this mode of trial, therefore the more prudent states shall be reduced to the same level of calamity. It would have been much more just & wise to have concluded the other way that as most of the states had judiciously preserved this palladium,[6] those who had wandered should be brought back to it, and to have established general right instead of general wrong. Let me add that a bill of rights is what the people are entitled to against every government on earth, general or particular, & what no just government should refuse, or rest on inferences. The second feature I dislike, and greatly dislike, is the abandonment in every instance of the necessity of rotation in office, and most particularly in the case of the President. Experience concurs with reason in concluding that the first magistrate will always be re-elected if the Constitution permits it. He is then an officer for life. This once observed, it becomes of so much consequence to certain nations to have a friend or a foe at the head of our affairs that they will interfere with money & with arms. A Galloman[7] or an Angloman[8] will be supported by the nation he befriends. If once elected, and at a second or third election out voted by one or two votes, he will pretend false votes, foul play, hold possession of the reins of government, be supported by the States voting for him, especially if they are the central ones lying in a compact body themselves & separating their opponents: and they will be aided by one nation of Europe, while the majority are aided by another. The election of a President of America some years hence will be much more interesting to certain nations of Europe than ever the election of a king of Poland was. Reflect on all the instances in history antient & modern, of elective monarchies, and say if they do not give foundation for my fears. The Roman emperors, the popes, while they were of any importance, the German emperors till they became hereditary in practice, the kings of Poland, the Deys of the Ottoman dependances.[9] It may be said that if elections are to be attended with these disorders, the seldomer they are renewed the better. But experience shews that the only way to prevent

---

5. Mere assertion.

6. A safeguard against the violation of rights or social institutions.

7. A supporter of the French.

8. A supporter of the British.

9. Military governors in Algiers, Tunis, and Tripoli.

disorder is to render them uninteresting by frequent changes. An incapacity to be elected a second time would have been the only effectual preventative. The power of removing him every fourth year by the vote of the people is a power which will not be exercised. The king of Poland is removeable every day by the Diet,[10] yet he is never removed. —Smaller objections are the Appeal in fact as well as law, and the binding all persons Legislative Executive & Judiciary by oath to maintain that constitution. I do not pretend to decide what would be the best method of procuring the establishment of the manifold good things in this constitution, and of getting rid of the bad. Whether by adopting it in hopes of future amendment, or, after it has been duly weighed & canvassed by the people, after seeing the parts they generally dislike, & those they generally approve, to say to them 'We see now what you wish. Send together your deputies again, let them frame a constitution for you omitting what you have condemned, & establishing the powers you approve. Even these will be a great addition to the energy of your government.' —At all events I hope you will not be discouraged from other trials, if the present one should fail of its full effect. —I have thus told you freely what I like & dislike: merely as a matter of curiosity, for I know your own judgment has been formed on all these points after having heard everything which could be urged on them. I own I am not a friend to a very energetic government. It is always oppressive. The late rebellion in Massachusetts[11] has given more alarm than I think it should have done. Calculate that one rebellion in 13 states in the course of 11 years, is but one for each state in a century & a half. No country should be so long without one. Nor will any degree of power in the hands of government prevent insurrections. France, with all it's despotism, and two or three hundred thousand men always in arms has had three insurrections in the three years I have been here in every one of which greater numbers were engaged than in Massachusetts & a great deal more blood was spilt. In Turkey, which Montesquieu[12] sup-poses more despotic, insurrections are the events of every day. In England, where the hand of power is lighter than here, but heavier than with us they happen every half dozen years. Compare again the ferocious depredations of their insurgents with the order, the moderation & the almost self extinguishment of ours. —After all, it is my principle that the will of the majority should always prevail. If they approve the proposed

---

10. The Polish parliament.
11. Shays's Rebellion (see Introduction, p. xvii and note 2, Letter to Madison Jan. 30, 1887 p. 155).
12. Baron de Montesquieu (1689–1755): French philosopher and political theorist. His *Spirit of the Laws* (1748) profoundly influenced Jefferson and the other founders as they worked to establish a government in the colonies. See Introduction, p. xxxi.

Convention in all it's parts, I shall concur in it chearfully, in hopes that they will amend it whenever they shall find it work wrong. I think our governments will remain virtuous for many centuries; as long as they are chiefly agricultural; and this will be as long as there shall be vacant lands in any part of America. When they get piled upon one another in large cities, as in Europe, they will become corrupt as in Europe. Above all things I hope the education of the common people will be attended to; convinced that on their good sense we may rely with the most security for the preservation of a due degree of liberty. I have tired you by this time with my disquisitions & will therefore only add assurances of the sincerity of those sentiments of esteem & attachment with which I am Dear Sir your affectionate friend & servant

P.S. The instability of our laws is really an immense evil. I think it would be well to provide in our constitutions that there shall always be a twelve-month between the ingrossing a bill[13] & passing it: that it should then be offered to it's passage without changing a word: and that if circumstances should be thought to require a speedier passage, it should take two thirds of both houses instead of a bare majority.

---

13. The writing up of a bill prior to a vote.

TO FRANCIS HOPKINSON[1]

Paris, Mar. 13, 1789

DEAR SIR, ... You say that I have been dished up to you as an antifederalist,[2] and ask me if it be just. My opinion was never worthy enough of notice to merit citing; but since you ask it I will tell it you. I am not a Federalist,[3] because I never submitted the whole system of my opinions to the creed of any party of men whatever in religion, in philosophy, in politics, or in anything else where I was capable of thinking for myself. Such an addiction is the last degradation of a free and moral agent. If I could not go to heaven but with a party, I would not go there at all. Therefore I protest to you I am not of the party of federalists. But I am much farther from that of the Antifederalists. I approved, from the first moment, of the great mass of what is in the new constitution, the consolidation of the government, the organization into Executive legislative & judiciary, the subdivision of the legislative, the happy compromise of interests between the great & little states by the different manner of voting in the different houses, the voting by persons instead of states, the qualified negative on laws given to the Executive which however I should have liked better if associated with the judiciary also as in New York, and the power of taxation. I thought at first that the latter might have been limited. A little reflection soon convinced me it ought not to be. What I disapproved from the first moment also was the want of a bill of rights to guard liberty against the legislative as well as executive branches of the government, that is to say to secure freedom in religion, freedom of the press, freedom from monopolies, freedom from unlawful imprisonment, freedom from a permanent military, and a trial by jury in all cases determinable by the laws of the land. I disapproved also the perpetual reeligibility of the President. To these points of disapprobation I adhere. My first wish was that the 9. first conventions might accept the constitution, as the means of securing to us the great mass of good it contained, and that the 4. last might reject it, as the means of obtaining

---

1. Francis Hopkinson (1737–91): prominent statesman, musician, author, and political satirist. He served as New Jersey's representative to the Continental Congress and later designed the New Jersey state seal, the seal for the University of Pennsylvania, and, in 1777, the American flag.

2. An opponent of the ratification of the U.S. Constitution. Many Antifederalists objected to the Constitution because it did not originally include a bill of rights (the Bill of Rights was incorporated into the Constitution in 1791).

3. See note 1, p. 48.

amendments.[4] But I was corrected in this wish the moment I saw the much better plan of Massachusetts[5] and which had never occurred to me. With respect to the declaration of rights I suppose the majority of the United states are of my opinion: for I apprehend all the antifederalists, and a very respectable proportion of the federalists think that such a declaration should now be annexed. The enlightened part of Europe have given us the greatest credit for inventing this instrument of security for the rights of the people, and have been not a little surprised to see us so soon give it up. With respect to the re-eligibility of the president, I find myself differing from the majority of my countrymen, for I think there are but three states out of the 11. which have desired an alteration of this. And indeed, since the thing is established, I would wish it not to be altered during the life of our great leader,[6] whose executive talents are superior to those I believe of any man in the world, and who alone by the authority of his name and the confidence reposed in his perfect integrity, is fully qualified to put the new government so under way as to secure it against the efforts of opposition. But having derived from our error all the good there was in it I hope we shall correct it the moment we can no longer have the same name at the helm. These, my dear friend, are my sentiments, by which you will see I was right in saying I am neither federalist nor antifederalist; that I am of neither party, nor yet a trimmer between parties. These my opinions wrote within a few hours after I had read the constitution, to one or two friends in America. I had not then read one single word printed on the subject. I never had an opinion in politics or religion which I was afraid to own. A costive[7] reserve on these subjects might have procured me more esteem from some people, but less from myself. My great wish is to go on in a strict but silent performance of my duty; to avoid attracting notice & to keep my name out of newspapers, because I find the pain of a little censure, even when it is unfounded, is more acute than the pleasure of much praise. The attaching circumstance of my present office is that I can do it's duties unseen by those for whom they are done. —You did not think, by so short a phrase in your letter, to have drawn on yourself such an egotistical dissertation.

---

4. If four states did not ratify, that would increase the pressure on the new government to draw up a bill of rights in order to bring them in.

5. The Massachusetts Ratifying Convention was leaning against ratification when John Hancock proposed his compromise. Instead of insisting, as the Antifederalists did, that the Constitution first be amended, or that ratification be contingent upon the acceptance of amendments, Hancock proposed that the delegates ratify the constitution and recommend amendments to be considered by the new Congress. The Massachusetts compromise became the model for subsequent states that objected to the absence of a bill of rights.

6. George Washington (1732–99): president of the Constitutional Convention and first president of the United States.

7. Stingy.

TO JAMES MADISON[1]

Paris, Mar. 15, 1789

DEAR SIR, — I wrote you last on the 12th of Jan. since which I have received yours of Octob. 17, Dec 8 & 12. That of Oct. 17. came to hand only Feb 23. How it happened to be four months on the way, I cannot tell, as I never knew by what hand it came. Looking over my letter of Jan 12th, I remark an error of the word "probable" instead of "improbable," which doubtless however you had been able to correct. Your thoughts on the subject of the Declaration of rights in the letter of Oct 17. I have weighed with great satisfaction. Some of them had not occurred to me before, but were acknoleged just in the moment they were presented to my mind. In the arguments in favor of a declaration of rights, you omit one which has great weight with me, the legal check which it puts into the hands of the judiciary. This is a body, which if rendered independent & kept strictly to their own department merits great confidence for their learning & integrity. In fact what degree of confidence would be too much for a body composed of such men as Wythe, Blair & Pendleton?[2] On characters like these the *"civium ardor prava jubentium"*[3] would make no impression. I am happy to find that on the whole you are a friend to this amendment. The Declaration of rights is like all other human blessings alloyed with some inconveniences, and not accomplishing fully it's object. But the good in this instance vastly overweighs the evil. I cannot refrain from making short answers to the objections which your letter states to have been raised. 1. That the rights in question are reserved by the manner in which the federal powers are granted. Answer. A constitutive act may certainly be so formed as to need no declaration of rights. The act itself has the force of a declaration as far as it goes; and if it goes to all material points nothing more is wanting. In the draught of a constitution which I had once a thought of proposing in Virginia, & printed afterwards, I endeavored to reach all the great objects of public liberty, and did not mean to add a declaration of rights. Probably the object was

---

1. For bibliographical information on Madison, see note 1 on p. 153.

2. See note 2, letter to Peter Carr, p. 161, for biographical information on Wythe. John Blair (1731–1800) was a noted Virginian jurist and delegate to the Federal Convention. Blair was appointed by President Washington to the Supreme Court. See note 1, letter to Edmund Pendleton, p. 141, for biographical information on Pendleton.

3. "The vehemence of citizens demanding what is wrong" (Horace, *Odes*, iii, 3). (The full sentence from which Jefferson takes this phrase is "The man who is just and firm of purpose is shaken neither by the vehemence of citizens demanding what is wrong nor by the tyrant's threatening countenance.")

imperfectly executed; but the deficiencies would have been supplied by others, in the course of discussion. But in a constitutive act which leaves some precious articles unnoticed, and raises implications against others, a declaration of rights becomes necessary by way of supplement. This is the case of our new federal constitution. This instrument forms us into one state as to certain objects, and gives us a legislative & executive body for these objects. It should therefore guard us against their abuses of power within the field submitted to them. 2. A positive declaration of some essential rights could not be obtained in the requisite latitude.[4] Answer. Half a loaf is better than no bread. If we cannot secure all our rights, let us secure what we can. 3. The limited powers of the federal government & jealousy of the subordinate governments afford a security which exists in no other instance. Answer. The first member of this seems resolvable into the first objection before stated. The jealousy of the subordinate governments is a precious reliance. But observe that those governments are only agents. They must have principles furnished them whereon to found their opposition. The declaration of rights will be the text whereby they will try all the acts of the federal government. In this view it is necessary to the federal government also; as by the same text they may try the opposition of the subordinate governments. 4. Experience proves the inefficacy of a bill of rights. True. But tho' it is not absolutely efficacious under all circumstances, it is of great potency always, and rarely inefficacious. A brace the more will often keep up the building which would have fallen with that brace the less. There is a remarkable difference between the characters of the Inconveniences which attend a Declaration of rights, & those which attend the want of it. The inconveniences of the Declaration are that it may cramp government in it's useful exertions. But the evil of this is short-lived, trivial & reparable. The inconveniences of the want of a Declaration are permanent, afflicting & irreparable. They are in constant progression from bad to worse. The executive in our governments is not the sole, it is scarcely the principal object of my jealousy. The tyranny of the legislatures is the most formidable dread at present, and will be for long years. That of the executive will come in it's turn, but it will be at a remote period. I know there are some among us who would now establish a monarchy. But they are inconsiderable in number and weight of character. The rising race are all republicans. We were educated in royalism; no wonder if some of us retain that idolatry still. Our young people are educated in republicanism, an apostasy[5] from that to royalism is unprecedented & impossible. I am much pleased with the prospect that a declaration of rights will be added; and hope it will be done in that way which will not endanger the whole frame of the government, or any essential part of it. . . .

---

4. That is, within the space of the Constitution.
5. Desertion of one's faith, principles, or party.

To James Madison[1]

Paris, Sept. 6, 1789

DEAR SIR— I sit down to write to you without knowing by what occasion I shall send my letter. I do it because a subject comes into my head which I would wish to develope a little more than is practicable in the hurry of the moment of making up general despatches.

The question Whether one generation of men has a right to bind another, seems never to have been started either on this or our side of the water. Yet it is a question of such consequences as not only to merit decision, but place also, among the fundamental principles of every government. The course of reflection in which we are immersed here on the elementary principles of society has presented this question to my mind; and that no such obligation can be transmitted I think very capable of proof. I set out on this ground which I suppose to be self evident, *"that the earth belongs in usufruct[2] to the living;"* that the dead have neither powers nor rights over it. The portion occupied by an individual ceases to be his when himself ceases to be, and reverts to the society. If the society has formed no rules for the appropriation of its lands in severalty,[3] it will be taken by the first occupants. These will generally be the wife and children of the decedent. If they have formed rules of appropriation, those rules may give it to the wife and children, or to some one of them, or to the legatee of the deceased. So they may give it to his creditor. But the child, the legatee or creditor takes it, not by any natural right, but by a law of the society of which they are members, and to which they are subject. Then no man can by natural right oblige the lands he occupied, or the persons who succeed him in that occupation, to the paiment of debts contracted by him. For if he could, he might during his own life, eat up the usufruct of the lands for several generations to come, and then the lands would belong to the dead, and not to the living, which would be reverse of our principle. What is true of every member of the society individually, is true of them all collectively, since the rights of the whole can be no more than the sum of the rights of individuals. To keep our ideas clear when applying them to a multitude, let us suppose a whole generation of men to be born on the same day, to attain mature age on

---

1. For bibliographical information on Madison, see note 1 on p. 153.

2. A term from Roman and civil law referring to an individual's right to use and enjoy all the advantages of something that belongs to another, so far as is compatible with the substance not being destroyed or impaired.

3. Exclusive ownership of lands by a single individual.

176

the same day, and to die on the same day, leaving a succeeding generation in the moment of attaining their mature age all together. Let the ripe age be supposed of 21. years, and their period of life 34. years more, that being the average term given by the bills of mortality to persons who have already attained 21. years of age. Each successive generation would, in this way, come on and go off the stage at a fixed moment, as individuals do now. Then I say the earth belongs to each of these generations during it's course, fully, and in their own right. The 2d. generation receives it clear of the debts and incumbrances of the 1st., the 3d. of the 2d. and so on. For if the 1st. could charge it with a debt, then the earth would belong to the dead and not the living generation. Then no generation can contract debts greater than may be paid during the course of it's own existence. At 21. years of age they may bind themselves and their lands for 34. years to come: at 22. for 33: at 23 for 32. and at 54 for one year only; because these are the terms of life which remain to them at those respective epochs. But a material difference must be noted between the succession of an individual and that of a whole generation. Individuals are parts only of a society, subject to the laws of a whole. These laws may appropriate the portion of land occupied by a decedent to his creditor rather than to any other, or to his child, on condition he satisfies his creditor. But when a whole generation, that is, the whole society dies, as in the case we have supposed, and another generation or society succeeds, this forms a whole, and there is no superior who can give their territory to a third society, who may have lent money to their predecessors beyond their faculty of paying.

What is true of a generation all arriving to self-government on the same day, and dying all on the same day, is true of those on a constant course of decay and renewal, with this only difference. A generation coming in and going out entire, as in the first case, would have a right in the 1st year of their self dominion to contract a debt for 33. years, in the 10th. for 24. in the 20th. for 14. in the 30th. for 4. whereas generations changing daily, by daily deaths and births, have one constant term beginning at the date of their contract, and ending when a majority of those of full age at that date shall be dead. The length of that term may be estimated from the tables of mortality, corrected by the circumstances of climate, occupation &c. peculiar to the country of the contractors. Take, for instance, the table of M. de Buffon[4] wherein he states that 23,994 deaths, and the ages at which they happened. Suppose a society in which 23,994 persons are born every year and live to the ages stated in this table. The conditions of that society will be as follows. 1st. it will consist constantly of 617,703 persons of all ages. 2dly. of those living at any one instant of time, one half will be dead in 24. years 8. months. 3dly. 10,675 will arrive

---

4. George-Louis Leclerc, Count of Buffon (1707–88): a noted French naturalist. See note 2, Query VI, p. 79.

every year at the age of 21. years complete. 4thly. it will constantly have 348,417 persons of all ages above 21. years. 5ly. and the half of those of 21. years and upwards living at any one instant of time will be dead in 18. years 8. months, or say 19. years as the nearest integral number. Then 19. years is the term beyond which neither the representatives of a nation, nor even the whole nation itself assembled, can validly extend a debt.

To render this conclusion palpable by example, suppose that Louis XIV. and XV.[5] had contracted debts in the name of the French nation to the amount of 10.000 milliards[6] of livres and that the whole had been contracted in Genoa.[7] The interest of this sum would be 500 milliards, which is said to be the whole rent-roll, or nett proceeds of the territory of France. Must the present generation of men have retired from the territory in which nature produced them, and ceded it to the Genoese creditors? No. They have the same rights over the soil on which they were produced, as the preceding generations had. They derive these rights not from their predecessors, but from nature. They then and their soil are by nature clear of the debts of their predecessors. Again suppose Louis XV. and his contemporary generation had said to the money lenders of Genoa, give us money that we may eat, drink, and be merry in our day; and on condition you will demand no interest till the end of 19. years, you shall then forever after receive an annual interest of 12.'5 per cent.* The money is lent on these conditions, is divided among the living, eaten, drank, and squandered. Would the present generation be obliged to apply the produce of the earth and of their labour to replace their dissipations? Not at all.

I suppose that the received opinion, that the public debts of one generation devolve on the next, has been suggested by our seeing habitually in private life that he who succeeds to lands is required to pay the debts of his ancestor or testator,[8] without considering that this requisition is municipal only, not moral, flowing from the will of the society which has found it convenient to appropriate the lands become vacant by the death of their occupant on the

---

*100£ at a compound interest of 6 per cent makes at the end of 19 years an ag-gregate of principal and interest of £252.14 the interest of which is a £12°°. 12". 7d. which is nearly 12". pr. cent on the first capital of £100.

---

5. Louis XIV, King of France from 1643–1715 and Louis XV, King of France from 1715–74.

6. Millions.

7. In Jefferson's day, Genoa was an independent republic in what is today northwest-ern Italy. If the previous French kings had borrowed vast sums from Genoa, the cost to the present generation of French would equal the country's net worth. Would they then have to cede the entire country to Genoa?

8. Person who makes a will.

condition of a paiment of his debts; but that between society and society, or generation and generation there is no municipal obligation, no umpire but the law of nature. We seem not to have perceived that, by the law of nature, one generation is to another as one independant nation to another.

The interest of the national debt of France being in fact but a two thousandth part of it's rent-roll, the paiment of it is practicable enough; and so becomes a question merely of honor or expediency. But with respect to future debts; would it not be wise and just for that nation to declare in the constitution they are forming that neither the legislature, nor the nation itself can validly contract more debt, than they may pay within their own age, or within the term of 19. years? And that all future contracts shall be deemed void as to what shall remain unpaid at the end of 19. years from their date? This would put the lenders, and the borrowers also, on their guard. By reducing too the faculty of borrowing within its natural limits, it would bridle the spirit of war, to which too free a course has been procured by the inattention of money lenders to this law of nature, that succeeding generations are not responsible for the preceding.

On similar ground it may be proved that no society can make a perpetual constitution, or even a perpetual law. The earth belongs always to the living generation. They may manage it then, and what proceeds from it, as they please, during their usufruct. They are masters too of their own persons, and consequently may govern them as they please. But persons and property make the sum of the objects of government. The constitution and the laws of their predecessors extinguished them, in their natural course, with those whose will gave them being. This could preserve that being till it ceased to be itself, and no longer. Every constitution, then, and every law, naturally expires at the end of 19. years. If it be enforced longer, it is an act of force and not of right.

It may be said that the succeeding generation exercising in fact the power of repeal, this leaves them as free as if the constitution or law had been expressly limited to 19. years only. In the first place, this objection admits the right, in proposing an equivalent. But the power of repeal is not an equivalent. It might be indeed if every form of government were so perfectly contrived that the will of the majority could always be obtained fairly and without impediment. But this is true of no form. The people cannot assemble themselves; their representation is unequal and vicious. Various checks are opposed to every legislative proposition. Factions get possession of the public councils. Bribery corrupts them. Personal interests lead them astray from the general interests of their constituents; and other impediments arise so as to prove to every practical man that a law of limited duration is much more manageable than one which needs a repeal.

This principle that the earth belongs to the living and not to the dead is of very extensive application and consequences in every country, and most especially in France. It enters into the resolution of the questions Whether the nation may change the descent of lands holden in tail?[9] Whether they may change the appropriation of lands given antiently to the church, to hospitals, colleges, orders of chivalry, and otherwise in perpetuity? whether they may abolish the charges and privileges attached on lands, including the whole catalogue ecclesiastical and feudal?[10] it goes to hereditary offices, authorities and jurisdictions; to hereditary orders, distinctions and appellations; to perpetual monopolies in commerce, the arts or sciences; with a long train of et ceteras: and it renders the question of reimbursement a question of generosity and not of right. In all these cases the legislature of the day could authorize such appropriations and establishments for their own time, but no longer; and the present holders, even where they or their ancestors have purchased, are in the case of bona fide purchasers of what the seller had no right to convey.

Turn this subject in your mind, my Dear Sir, and particularly as to the power of contracting debts, and develope it with that perspicuity and cogent logic which is so peculiarly yours. Your station in the councils of our country gives you an opportunity of producing it to public consideration, of forcing it into discussion. At first blush it may be rallied as a theoretical speculation; but examination will prove it to be solid and salutary. It would furnish matter for a fine preamble to our first law for appropriating the public revenue; and it will exclude, at the threshold of our new government the contagious and ruinous errors of this quarter of the globe, which have armed despots with means not sanctioned by nature for binding in chains their fellow-men. We have already given, in example one effectual check to the Dog of war, by transferring the power of letting him loose from the executive to the Legislative body, from those who are to spend to those who are to pay. I should be pleased to see this second obstacle held out by us also in the first instance. No nation can make a declaration against the validity of long-contracted debts so disinterestedly as we, since we do not owe a shilling which may not be paid with ease principal and interest, within the time of our own lives. Establish the principle also in the new law to be passed for protecting copy rights and new inventions, by securing the exclusive right for 19. instead of 14. years [ ][11] an instance the more of our taking reason for our guide instead of English precedents, the habit of which fetters us, with all the political herecies of a nation, equally remarkable for it's encitement from some errors, as long slumbering under others. I write you no news, because when an occasion occurs I shall write a separate letter for that.

---

9. The inheritance of entailable property was, by law, limited to a specific succession of heirs. (See notes 8 and 9, Query XIV, p. 111.)

10. In short, Jefferson is asking whether the present generation has the right to abolish privileges and land grants to churches and nobles that date back to the feudal era.

11. A line has faded here.

TO BENJAMIN BANNEKER[1]

Philadelphia, Aug. 30, 1791

SIR, — I thank you sincerely for your letter of the 19th instant and for the Almanac it contained. No body wishes more than I do to see such proofs as you exhibit, that nature has given to our black brethren, talents equal to those of the other colors of men, and that the appearance of a want of them is owing merely to the degraded condition of their existence, both in Africa & America. I can add with truth, that no body wishes more ardently to see a good system commenced for raising the condition both of their body & mind to what it ought to be, as fast as the imbecility of their present existence, and other circumstances which cannot be neglected, will admit. I have taken the liberty of sending your Almanac to Monsieur de Condorcet,[2] Secretary of the Academy of Sciences at Paris, and member of the Philanthropic society, because I considered it as a document to which your whole colour had a right for their justification against the doubts which have been entertained of them. I am with great esteem, Sir Your most obedt humble servt.

---

1. Benjamin Banneker (1731–1806) was the son of an Englishwoman and her husband, a liberated slave. Banneker was a talented mathematician, astronomer, and surveyor who helped survey the Federal District (now Washington, D.C.) in 1791. After that, he published an almanac, and was often pointed to as proof that blacks were not intellectually inferior to whites.
2. The Marquis de Condorcet (1743–94), Marie Jean Antoine Nicolas Caritat, was a French mathematician and philosopher best known for his work on probability and his *Sketch for a Historical Picture of the Progress of the Human Mind* (1795). See Introduction, p. xxv.

TO THE PRESIDENT OF THE UNITED STATES (GEORGE WASHINGTON)[1]

Monticello, Sept. 9, 1792

DEAR SIR, . . . I now take the liberty of proceeding to that part of your letter wherein you notice the internal dissentions which have taken place within our government,[2] & their disagreeable effect on it's movements. That such dissentions have taken place is certain, & even among those who are nearest to you in the administration. To no one have they given deeper concern than myself: to no one equal mortification at being myself a part of them. Tho' I take to myself no more than my share of the general observations of your letter, yet I am so desirous ever that you should know the whole truth, & believe no more than the truth, that I am glad to seize every occasion of developing to you whatever I do or think relative to the government; & shall therefore ask permission to be more lengthy now than the occasion particularly calls for, or could otherwise perhaps justify.

When I embarked in the government, it was with a determination to intermeddle not at all with the legislature, & as little as possible with my co-departments. The first and only instance of variance from the former part of my resolution, I was duped into by the Secretary of the Treasury and made a tool for forwarding his schemes, not then sufficiently understood by me; and of all the errors of my political life, this has occasioned me the deepest regret. It has ever been my purpose to explain this to you, when, from being actors on the scene, we shall have become uninterested spectators only. The second part of

---

1. George Washington (1732–99) was commander of the American troops during the American Revolution and the nation's first president (1789–97).

2. Principally, the split between the secretary of state, Thomas Jefferson, and the secretary of the treasury, Alexander Hamilton, over the proper scope of the federal government. The two had previously clashed over the federal assumption of state war debts, and whether speculators in government bonds should be able to reap the full profits of their investments to the detriment of the original holders, who were mostly war veterans, as well as over Hamilton's call for a federal excise tax on whiskey. On top of all this, Hamilton permanently alienated Jefferson and his supporters with his plan for a national bank. Jefferson not only questioned its constitutionality, but saw it as an instrument of corruption. Hamilton had tried to broaden ownership by selling bank shares, but a disproportionate number of shareholders were from the commercial northeast, and, to make matters worse, included at least thirty members of Congress. Jefferson charged that Hamilton was bribing members of the legislature by offering them shares of the bank.

my resolution has been religiously observed with the war department; & as to that of the Treasury, has never been farther swerved from than by the mere enunciation of my sentiments in conversation, and chiefly among those who, expressing the same sentiments, drew mine from me. If it has been supposed that I have ever intrigued among the members of the legislatures to defeat the plans of the Secretary of the Treasury, it is contrary to all truth. As I never had the desire to influence the members, so neither had I any other means than my friendships, which I valued too highly to risk by usurpations on their freedom of judgment, & the conscientious pursuit of their own sense of duty. That I have utterly, in my private conversations, disapproved of the system of the Secretary of the treasury, I acknolege & avow: and this was not merely a speculative difference. His system flowed from principles adverse to liberty, & was calculated to undermine and demolish the republic, by creating an influence of his department over the members of the legislature. I saw this influence actually produced, & it's first fruits to be the establishment of the great outlines of his project by the votes of the very persons who, having swallowed his bait were laying themselves out to profit by his plans: & that had these persons withdrawn, as those interested in a question ever should, the vote of the disinterested majority was clearly the reverse of what they made it. These were no longer the votes then of the representatives of the people, but of deserters from the rights & interests of the people: & it was impossible to consider their decisions, which had nothing in view but to enrich themselves, as the measures of the fair majority, which ought always to be respected. —If what was actually doing begat uneasiness in those who wished for virtuous government, what was further proposed was not less threatening to the friends of the Constitution. For, in a Report on the subject of manufactures (still to be acted on) it was expressly assumed that the general government has a right to exercise all powers which may be for the *general welfare*, that is to say, all the legitimate powers of government: since no government has a legitimate right to do what is not for the welfare of the governed. There was indeed a sham-limitation of the universality of this power *to cases where money is to be employed*. But about what is it that money cannot be employed? Thus the object of these plans taken together is to draw all the powers of government into the hands of the general legislature, to establish means for corrupting a sufficient corps in that legislature to divide the honest votes & preponderate,[3] by their own, the scale which suited, & to have that corps under the command of the Secretary of the Treasury for the purpose of subverting step by step the principles of the constitution, which he has so often declared to be a thing of nothing which must be changed. Such views might have justified something more than mere expressions of dissent, beyond which, nevertheless, I never went.

---

3. Exceed in weight; prevail.

— Has abstinence from the department committed to me been equally observed by him? To say nothing of other interferences equally known, in the case of the two nations with which we have the most intimate connections, France & England, my system was to give some satisfactory distinctions to the former, of little cost to us, in return for the solid advantages yielded us by them; & to have met the English with some restrictions which might induce them to abate their severities against our commerce.[4] I have always supposed this coincided with your sentiments. Yet the Secretary of the treasury, by his cabals with members of the legislature, & by high-toned declamation on other occasions, has forced down his own system, which was exactly the reverse. He undertook, of his own authority, the conferences with the ministers of those two nations, & was, on every consultation, provided with some report of a conversation with the one or the other of them, adapted to his views. These views, thus made to prevail, their execution fell of course to me; & I can safely appeal to you, who have seen all my letters & proceedings, whether I have not carried them into execution as sincerely as if they had been my own, tho' I ever considered them as inconsistent with the honor & interest of our country. That they have been inconsistent with our interest is but too fatally proved by the stab to our navigation given by the French. — So that if the question be By whose fault is it that Colo Hamilton & myself have not drawn together? the answer will depend on that to two other questions; whose principles of administration best justify, by their purity, conscientious adherence? and which of us has, notwithstanding, stepped farthest into the controul of the department of the other?

To this justification of opinions, expressed in the way of conversation, against the views of Colo Hamilton, I beg leave to add some notice of his late charges against me in Fenno's gazette;[5] for neither the stile, matter, nor venom of the pieces alluded to can leave a doubt of their author. Spelling my name & character at full length to the public, while he conceals his own under the signature of "an American" he charges me 1. With having written letters from Europe to my friends to oppose the present constitution while depending. 2. With a desire of not paying the public debt. 3. With setting up a paper to decry & slander the government. 1. The first charge is most false. No man in the U.S. I suppose, approved of every title in the constitution: no one, I believe approved more of it than I did: and more of it was certainly disproved by my accuser than by me, and of it's parts most vitally republican. Of this the few letters I wrote on the subject (not half a dozen I believe) will be a proof: & for my own satisfaction & justification, I must tax you with the reading of

---

4. English attacks on American merchant shipping. See Introduction, p. xxii.

5. A pro-Federalist (and anti-Jefferson) newspaper published by John Fenno.

them when I return to where they are. You will there see that my objection to the constitution was that it wanted a bill of rights securing freedom of religion, freedom of the press, freedom from standing armies, trial by jury, & a constant Habeas corpus act.[6] Colo Hamilton's was that it wanted a king and house of lords. The sense of America has approved my objection & added the bill of rights, not the king and lords. I also thought a longer term of service, insusceptible of renewal, would have made a President more independant. My country has thought otherwise, & I have acquiesced implicitly. He wishes the general government should have power to make laws binding the states in all cases whatsoever. Our country has thought otherwise: has he acquiesced? Notwithstanding my wish for a bill of rights, my letters strongly urged the adoption of the constitution, by nine states at least, to secure the good it contained. I at first thought that the best method of securing the bill of rights would be for four states to hold off till such a bill should be agreed to. But the moment I saw Mr. Hancock's[7] proposition to pass the constitution as it stood, and give perpetual instructions to the representatives of every state to insist on a bill of rights, I acknoleged the superiority of his plan, & advocated universal adoption. 2. The second charge is equally untrue. My whole correspondence while in France, & every word, letter, & act on the subject since my return, prove that no man is more ardently intent to see the public debt soon & sacredly paid off than I am. This exactly marks the difference between Colo Hamilton's views & mine, that I would wish the debt paid to morrow; he wishes it never to be paid, but always to be a thing where with to corrupt & manage the legislature. 3. I have never enquired what number of sons, relations & friends of Senators, representatives, printers or other useful partisans Colo Hamilton has provided for among the hundred clerks of his department, the thousand excisemen, custom-house officers, loan officers &c. &c. &c. appointed by him, or at his nod, and spread over the Union; nor could ever have imagined that the man who has the shuffling of millions backwards & forwards from paper into money & money into paper, from Europe to America, & America to Europe, the dealing out of Treasury-secrets among his friends in what time & measure he pleases, and who never slips an occasion of making friends with his means, that such an one I say would have brought forward a charge against me for having appointed the poet Freneau[8] translating clerk to

---

6. See note 3, p. 168.

7. John Hancock (1737–93): a prominent American revolutionary and politician. Though he acted as president of the Continental Congress (1775–77) and twice served as governor of Massachusetts (1780–85; 1787–93), he is perhaps now best known as the first to sign the Declaration of Independence. See note 5, p. 211.

8. Philip Freneau (1752–1832): American poet and editor of the pro-Republican newspaper the *National Gazette* (not to be confused with John Fenno's pro-Federalist *Gazette of the United States*).

my office, with a salary of 250. dollars a year. That fact stands thus. While the government was at New York I was applied to on behalf of Freneau to know if there was any place within my department to which he could be appointed. I answered there were but four clerkships, all of which I found full, and continued without any change. When we removed to Philadelphia, Mr. Pintard the translating clerk, did not chuse to remove with us. His office then became vacant. I was again applied to there for Freneau, & had no hesitation to promise the clerkship for him. I cannot recollect whether it was at the same time, or afterwards, that I was told he had a thought of setting up a newspaper there. But whether then, or afterwards, I considered it as a circumstance of some value, as it might enable me to do, what I had long wished to have done, that is, to have the material parts of the Leyden gazette[9] brought under your eye & that of the public, in order to possess yourself & them of a juster view of the affairs of Europe than could be obtained from any other public source. This I had ineffectually attempted through the press of Mr. Fenno while in New York, selecting & translating passages myself at first then having it done by Mr. Pintard the translating clerk, but they found their way too slowly into Mr. Fenno's papers. Mr. Bache[10] essayed it for me in Philadelphia, but his being a daily paper, did not circulate sufficiently in the other states. He even tried, at my request, the plan of a weekly paper of recapitulation from his daily paper, in hopes that that might go into the other states, but in this too we failed. Freneau, as translating clerk, & the printer of a periodical paper likely to circulate thro' the states (uniting in one person the parts of Pintard & Fenno) revived my hopes that the thing could at length be effected. On the establishment of his paper therefore, I furnished him with the Leyden gazettes, with an expression of my wish that he could always translate & publish the material intelligence they contained; & have continued to furnish them from time to time, as regularly as I received them. But as to any other direction or indication of my wish how his press should be conducted, what sort of intelligence he should give, what essays encourage, I can protest in the presence of heaven, that I never did by myself or any other, directly or indirectly, say a syllable, nor attempt any kind of influence. I can further protest, in the same awful presence, that I never did by myself or any other, directly or indirectly, write, dictate or procure any one sentence or sentiment to be inserted *in his, or any other gazette*, to which my name was not affixed or that of my office. — I surely need not except here a thing so foreign to the present subject as a little

---

9. A European newspaper published in Holland.

10. The grandson of founder Benjamin Franklin, Benjamin Franklin Bache (1769–98) was a journalist who founded the pro-Jeffersonian newspaper the *Philadelphia General Advertiser* (later renamed the *Aurora*).

paragraph about our Algerine captives,[11] which I put once into Fenno's paper. — Freneau's proposition to publish a paper, having been about the time that the writings of Publicola, & the discourses on Davila[12] had a good deal excited the public attention, I took for granted from Freneau's character, which had been marked as that of a good whig,[13] that he would give free place to pieces written against the aristocratical & monarchical principles these papers had inculcated. This having been in my mind, it is likely enough I may have expressed it in conversation with others; tho' I do not recollect that I did. To Freneau I think I could not, because I had still seen him but once, & that was at a public table, at breakfast, at Mrs. Elsworth's, as I passed thro' New York the last year. And I can safely declare that my expectations looked only to the chastisement of the aristocratical & monarchical writers, & not to any criticisms on the proceedings of government: Colo Hamilton can see no motive for any appointment but that of making a convenient partizan. But you Sir, who have received from me recommendations of a Rittenhouse,[14] Barlow,[15] Paine,[16] will believe that talents & science are sufficient motives with me in appointments to which they are fitted: & that Freneau, as a man of genius, might find a preference in my eye to be a translating clerk, & make good title to the little aids I could give him as the editor of a gazette, by procuring subscriptions to his paper, as I did some, before it appeared, & as I have with pleasure done for the labours of other men of genius. I hold it to be one of the distinguishing excellencies of elective over hereditary succesions, that the talents, which nature has provided in sufficient proportion, should be selected by the society for the government of their affairs, rather than that this should be transmitted through the loins of knaves & fools passing from the debauches of the table to those of the bed. Colo Hamilton, alias "Plain facts," says that Freneau's salary began before he resided in Philadelphia. I do not know what quibble he may have in reserve on the word "residence." He may mean to include under that idea the removal of his family; for I believe he removed,

---

11. In 1786, Algerian (Barbary) pirates captured two American vessels and demanded a stiff ransom for their captives. (See Introduction, pp. xvii, xxi–xxii.)

12. John Adams (see note 1, p. 211) was the author of the *Discourses on Davila* (1790–91), a work Jefferson feared strayed too far from republican principles. John Quincy Adams, writing under the pseudonym *Publicola*, defended his father against charges of "heresy."

13. See note 10, p. 144.

14. See note 1, p. 143 for biographical information on Rittenhouse.

15. Joel Barlow (1754–1812): an American poet and politician.

16. Thomas Paine (1737–1809): a British-born author of *Common Sense* (1776) and the *Rights of Man* (1791–1792). He was an ardent supporter of both the American and French Revolutions. See notes on pp. 101 and 260.

himself, before his family did, to Philadelphia. But no act of mine gave commencement to his salary before he so far took up his abode in Philadelphia as to be sufficiently in readiness for the duties of the office. As to the merits or demerits of his paper, they certainly concern me not. He & Fenno are rivals for the public favor. The one courts them by flattery, the other by censure, & I believe it will be admitted that the one has been as servile, as the other severe. But is not the dignity, & even decency of government committed, when one of it's principal ministers enlists himself as an anonymous writer or paragraphist for either the one or the other of them? — No government ought to be without censors: & where the press is free, no one ever will. If virtuous, it need not fear the fair operation of attack & defence. Nature has given to man no other means of sifting out the truth either in religion, law, or politics. I think it as honorable to the government neither to know, nor notice, it's sycophants or censors, as it would be undignified & criminal to pamper the former & persecute the latter. — So much for the past. A word now of the future.

When I came into this office, it was with a resolution to retire from it as soon as I could with decency. It pretty early appeared to me that the proper moment would be the first of those epochs at which the constitution seems to have contemplated a periodical change or renewal of the public servants. In this I was confirmed by your resolution respecting the same period; from which however I am happy in hoping you have departed. I look to that period with the longing of a wave-worn mariner, who has at length the land in view, & shall count the days & hours which still lie between me & it. In the meanwhile my main object will be to wind up the business of my office avoiding as much as possible all new enterprize. With the affairs of the legislature, as I never did intermeddle, so I certainly shall not now begin. I am more desirous to predispose everything for the repose to which I am withdrawing, than expose it to be disturbed by newspaper contests. If these however cannot be avoided altogether, yet a regard for your quiet will be a sufficient motive for my deferring it till I become merely a private citizen, when the propriety or impropriety of what I may say or do may fall on myself alone. I may then too avoid the charge of misapplying that time which now belonging to those who employ me, should be wholly devoted to their service. If my own justification, or the interests of the republic shall require it, I reserve to myself the right of then appealing to my country, subscribing my name to whatever I write, & using with freedom & truth the facts & names necessary to place the cause in it's just form before that tribunal. To a thorough disregard of the honors & emoluments[17] of office I join as great a value for the esteem of my countrymen, & conscious of having merited it by an integrity which cannot be reproached,

---

17. Payment for work done.

& by an enthusiastic devotion to their rights & liberty, I will not suffer my retirement to be clouded by the slanders of a man whose history, from the moment at which history can stoop to notice him, is a tissue of machinations against the liberty of the country which has not only received and given him bread, but heaped it's honors on his head. — Still however I repeat the hope that it will not be necessary to make such an appeal. Though little known to the people of America, I believe that, as far as I am known, it is not as an enemy to the republic, nor an intriguer against it, nor a waster of it's revenue, nor prostitutor of it to the purposes of corruption, as the American represents me; and I confide that yourself are satisfied that, as to dissensions in the newspapers, not a syllable of them has ever proceeded from me; & that no cabals or intrigues of mine have produced those in the legislature, & I hope I may promise, both to you & myself, that none will receive aliment from me during the short space I have to remain in office, which will find ample employment in closing the present business of the department. . . . In the meantime & ever I am with great and sincere affection & respect, dear Sir, your most obedient and most humble servant

To Elbridge Gerry[1]

Philadelphia, Jan. 26, 1799

MY DEAR SIR, . . . I shall make to you a profession of my political faith; in confidence that you will consider every future imputation on me of a contrary complexion, as bearing on its front the mark of falsehood & calumny.

I do then, with sincere zeal, wish an inviolable preservation of our present federal constitution, according to the true sense in which it was adopted by the States, that in which it was advocated by it's friends, & not that which it's enemies apprehended, who therefore became it's enemies; and I am opposed to the monarchising it's features by the forms of it's administration, with a view to conciliate[2] a first transition to a President & Senate for life, & from that to a hereditary tenure of these offices, & thus to worm out the elective principle. I am for preserving to the States the powers not yielded by them to the Union, & to the legislature of the Union it's constitutional share in the division of powers; and I am not for transferring all the powers of the States to the general government, & all those of that government to the Executive branch. I am for a government rigorously frugal & simple, applying all the possible savings of the public revenue to the discharge of the national debt; and not for a multiplication of officers & salaries merely to make partisans, & for increasing, by every device, the public debt, on the principle of it's being a public blessing. I am for relying, for internal defence, on our militia solely, till actual invasion, and for such a naval force only as may protect our coasts and harbors from such depredations as we have experienced; and not for a standing army in time of peace, which may overawe the public sentiment; nor for a navy, which, by it's own expenses and the eternal wars in which it will implicate us, will grind us with public burthens, & sink us under them. I am for free commerce with all nations; political connection with none; & little or no diplomatic establishment. And I am not for linking ourselves by new treaties with

---

1. Elbridge Gerry (1744–1814): Revolutionary War organizer in Massachusetts, and a delegate to the Constitutional Convention who declined to endorse the document. He was appointed emissary to France (1797), served as governor of Massachusetts (1810–11), and was later elected vice president under James Madison (1813–14). As governor, he helped redraw congressional districts to minimize the influence of the opposing Federalist party. This practice, now known as "gerrymandering," allowed for the creation of an odd-shaped electoral district in order to maximize political advantage.
2. Facilitate.

the quarrels of Europe; entering that field of slaughter to preserve their balance, or joining in the confederacy of kings to war against the principles of liberty. I am for freedom of religion, & against all maneuvres to bring about a legal ascendancy of one sect over another: for freedom of the press, & against all violations of the constitution to silence by force & not by reason the complaints or criticisms, just or unjust, of our citizens against the conduct of their agents. And I am for encouraging the progress of science in all it's branches; and not for raising a hue and cry against the sacred name of philosophy; for awing the human mind by stories of raw-head & bloody bones[3] to a distrust of its own vision, & to repose implicitly on that of others; to go backwards instead of forwards to look for improvement; to believe that government, religion, morality, & every other science were in the highest perfection in ages of the darkest ignorance, and that nothing can ever be devised more perfect than what was established by our forefathers. To these I will add, that I was a sincere well-wisher to the success of the French revolution,[4] and still wish it may end in the establishment of a free & well-ordered republic; but I have not been insensible under the atrocious depredations they have committed on our commerce.[5] The first object of my heart is my own country. In that is embarked my family, my fortune, & my own existence. I have not one farthing of interest, nor one fibre of attachment out of it, nor a single motive of preference of any one nation to another, but in proportion as they are more or less friendly to us. But though deeply feeling the injuries of France, I did not think war the surest means of redressing them. I did believe, that a mission sincerely

---

3. A bogeyman. (See note 6, p. 39.)

4. The French Revolution broke out in 1789 and went through several stages, including a Reign of Terror (1793–94) during which the revolutionaries executed thousands of people. Jefferson never wavered in his support of the French Revolution. In his mind, the American and French Revolutions were inextricably linked; to condemn the excesses of the latter would undermine the success of the former.

5. Although France had aided the United States in its war of independence, relations turned sour in 1794 when John Jay, then chief justice of the United States, negotiated what came to be known as the Jay Treaty with England. The French, who were at war with England, viewed the treaty as a sign that America had turned its back on its former ally. In retaliation against the Jay Treaty, French privateers began to attack American merchant ships in the Atlantic. Hoping to defuse the situation, President John Adams sent a delegation consisting of Charles Pinckney, John Marshall, and Elbridge Gerry to meet with the French foreign minister, Talleyrand. After waiting several weeks for a reply, the Americans met with three French agents, known only as X, Y, and Z, who demanded a cash bribe before relations could be re-established. Back home, Americans were enraged by the XYZ Affair, and pro-English Federalists attempted to pass a declaration of war. Eventually Adams succeeded in resolving the conflict and avoiding all-out war, but continued French attacks on American ships led to the Quasi-War (1798–1800) between the two countries.

disposed to preserve peace, would obtain for us a peaceable & honorable settlement & retribution; and I appeal to you to say, whether this might not have been obtained, if either of your colleagues[6] had been of the same sentiment with yourself.

These, my friend, are my principles; they are unquestionably the principles of the great body of our fellow citizens, and I know there is not one of them which is not yours also. In truth, we never differed but on one ground, the funding system; and as, from the moment of it's being adopted by the constituted authorities, I became religiously principled in the sacred discharge of it to the uttermost farthing, we are united now even on that single ground of difference.[7]

---

6. Pinckney and Marshall, Gerry's companions in the American delegation to France.

7. Jefferson is here referring to their differences over the plan, proposed by Hamilton, for the federal government to assume responsibility for the debts incurred by the states during the Revolutionary War. Since the southern states had largely repaid their debts, they were not eager to strengthen the powers of the federal government for something from which they derived no benefit. Eventually, they struck a compromise: in exchange for southern support, the capital would be moved south to what is now Washington, D.C.

To William Green Munford[1]

Monticello, June 18, 1799

DEAR SIR, — I have to acknolege the reciept of your favor of May 14 in which you mention that you have finished the 6. first books of Euclid,[2] plane trigonometry, surveying & algebra and ask whether I think a further pursuit of that branch of science would be useful to you. There are some propositions in the latter books of Euclid, & some of Archimedes,[3] which are useful, & I have no doubt you have been made acquainted with them. Trigonometry, so far as this, is most valuable to every man. There is scarcely a day in which he will not resort to it for some of the purposes of common life. The science of calculation also is indispensible as far as the extraction of the square & cube roots; algebra as far as the quadratic equation & the use of logarithms are often of value in ordinary cases: but all beyond these is but a luxury; a delicious luxury indeed; but not to be indulged in by one who is to have a profession to follow for his subsistence. In this light I view the conic sections, curves of the higher orders, perhaps even spherical trigonometry, algebraical operations beyond the 2d dimension, and fluxions.[4] There are other branches of science however worth the attention of every man. Astronomy, botany, chemistry, natural philosophy, natural history, anatomy. Not indeed to be a proficient in them; but to possess their general principles & outlines, so as that we may be able to amuse and inform ourselves further in any of them as we proceed through life & have occasion for them. Some knowledge of them is necessary for our character as well as comfort. The general elements of astronomy & of natural philosophy are best acquired at an academy where we can have the benefit of the instruments & apparatus usually provided there: but the others may well be acquired from books alone as far as our purposes require. I have indulged myself in these observations to you, because the evidence cannot be unuseful to you of a person who has often had occasion to consider which of his acquisitions in science have been really useful to him in life, and which of them have been merely a matter of luxury.

---

1. At the time of this letter, William Green Munford (1775–1825) was a young student who had struck up a correspondence with Jefferson, requesting the older man's advice on what books to read. Later, as a Virginia politician, Munford turned on his mentor and spread political gossip about him.
2. Euclid (c. 325–265 BC): Greek mathematician. See note 22, p. 115.
3. Archimedes (287–212 BC): Greek mathematician and inventor.
4. Differential calculus.

I am among those who think well of the human character generally. I consider man as formed for society, and endowed by nature with those dispositions which fit him for society. I believe also, with Condorcet,[5] as mentioned
in your letter, that his mind is perfectible to a degree of which we cannot as
yet form any conception. It is impossible for a man who takes a survey of what
is already known, not to see what an immensity in every branch of science yet
remains to be discovered, & that too of articles to which our faculties seem
adequate. In geometry & calculation we know a great deal. Yet there are some
desiderata. In anatomy great progress has been made; but much is still to be
acquired. In natural history we possess knowlege; but we want a great deal. In
chemistry we are not yet sure of the first elements. Our natural philosophy is
in a very infantine state; perhaps for great advances in it, a further progress in
chemistry is necessary. Surgery is well advanced; but prodigiously short of
what may be. The state of medecine is worse than that of total ignorance.
Could we divest ourselves of every thing we suppose we know in it, we should
start from a higher ground & with fairer prospects. From Hippocrates[6] to
Brown we have had nothing but a succession of hypothetical systems each
having it's day of vogue, like the fashions & fancies of caps & gowns, & yielding in turn to the next caprice. Yet the human frame, which is to be the subject of suffering & torture under these learned modes, does not change. We
have a few medecines, as the bark, opium, mercury, which in a few well defined diseases are of unquestionable virtue: but the residuary list of the mate-
ria medica,[7] long as it is, contains but the charlataneries of the art; and of the
diseases of doubtful form, physicians have ever had a false knowlege, worse
than ignorance. Yet surely the list of unequivocal diseases & remedies is capable
of enlargement; and it is still more certain that in the other branches of
science, great fields are yet to be explored to which our faculties are equal, &
that to an extent of which we cannot fix the limits. I join you therefore in
branding as cowardly the idea that the human mind is incapable of further advances. This is precisely the doctrine which the present despots of the earth
are inculcating, & their friends here re-echoing; & applying especially to religion & politics; 'that it is not probable that any thing better will be discovered
than what was known to our fathers.' We are to look backwards then & not
forwards for the improvement of science, & to find it amidst feudal barbarisms

---

5. The Marquis de Condorcet, Marie Jean Antoine Nicolas Caritat (1743–94): French
mathematician and philosopher. See note 2, p. 181.

6. Hippocrates (460–377 BC): Greek physician regarded as the founder of medicine.

7. The branch of medicine dealing with the preparation, dosage, and administration
of drugs.

and the fires of Spital-fields.[8] But thank heaven the American mind is already too much opened, to listen to these impostures; and while the art of printing is left to us, science can never be retrograde; what is once acquired of real knowlege can never be lost. To preserve the freedom of the human mind then & freedom of the press, every spirit should be ready to devote itself to martyrdom; for as long as we may think as we will, & speak as we think, the condition of man will proceed in improvement. The generation which is going off the stage has deserved well of mankind for the struggles it has made, & for having arrested that course of despotism which had overwhelmed the world for thousands & thousands of years. If there seems to be danger that the ground they have gained will be lost again, that danger comes from the generation your cotemporary. But that the enthusiasm which characterises youth should lift its parricide hands against freedom & science, would be such a monstrous phænomenon as I cannot place among possible things in this age & this country. Your college[9] at least has shewn itself incapable of it; and if the youth of any other place have seemed to rally under other banners it has been from delusions which they will soon dissipate. I shall be happy to hear from you from time to time, & of your progress in study, and to be useful to you in whatever is in my power; being with sincere esteem Dear Sir your friend & servt

---

8. A market area in London, rebuilt after the Great Fire of 1666.
9. College of William and Mary (founded 1693), Jefferson's *alma mater*.

TO DR. JOSEPH PRIESTLEY[1]

Washington, Mar. 21, 1801

DEAR SIR, — I learnt some time ago that you were in Philadelphia, but that it was only for a fortnight; & supposed you were gone. It was not till yesterday I received information that you were still there, had been very ill, but were on the recovery. I sincerely rejoice that you are so. Yours is one of the few lives precious to mankind, & for the continuance of which every thinking man is solicitous. Bigots may be an exception. What an effort, my dear Sir, of bigotry in Politics & Religion have we gone through! The barbarians really flattered themselves they should be able to bring back the times of Vandalism,[2] when ignorance put everything into the hands of power & priestcraft. All advances in science were proscribed as innovations. They pretended to praise and encourage education, but it was to be the education of our ancestors. We were to look backwards, not forwards, for improvement; the President[3] himself declaring, in one of his answers to addresses, that we were never to expect to go beyond them in real science. This was the real ground of all the attacks on you. Those who live by mystery & *charlatanerie*,[4] fearing you would render them useless by simplifying the Christian philosophy, — the most sublime & benevolent, but most perverted system that ever shone on man, — endeavored to crush your well-earnt & well-deserved fame. But it was the Lilliputians upon Gulliver.[5] Our countrymen have recovered from the alarm into which art & industry had thrown them; science & honesty are replaced on their high ground; and you, my dear Sir, as their great apostle, are on it's pinnacle. It is with heartfelt satisfaction that, in the first moments of my public action, I can hail you with welcome to our land, tender to you the homage of it's respect & esteem, cover you under the protection of those laws which were made for the

---

1. Dr. Joseph Priestley (1733–1804): English scientist and Unitarian minister, emigrated to America after his support of the French Revolution occasioned mob violence. Admired for his scientific contributions in the fields of chemistry and physics, his political and religious views were more controversial. Jefferson admired his work detailing the corruptions of Christianity and his Unitarianism.

2. The Vandals were a Germanic tribe that attacked the Roman Empire.

3. John Adams (for biographical information on Adams, see note 7, p. 157).

4. Quackery, imposture.

5. A reference to Jonathan Swift's *Gulliver's Travels* (1726), a satire in which the diminutive Lilliputians attempt to tie Gulliver down and kill him.

wise and good like you, and disdain the legitimacy of that libel on legislation, which under the form of a law, was for some time placed among them.

As the storm is now subsiding, and the horizon becoming serene, it is pleasant to consider the phenomenon with attention. We can no longer say there is nothing new under the sun. For this whole chapter in the history of man is new. The great extent of our Republic is new. Its sparse habitation is new. The mighty wave of public opinion which has rolled over it is new. But the most pleasing novelty is, it's so quickly subsiding over such an extent of surface to it's true level again. The order & good sense displayed in this recovery from delusion, and in the momentous crisis which lately arose, really bespeak a strength of character in our nation which augurs well for the duration of our Republic; & I am much better satisfied now of it's stability than I was before it was tried. I have been, above all things, solaced by the prospect which opened on us, in the event of a non-election of a President; in which case, the federal government would have been in the situation of a clock or watch run down. There was no idea of force, nor of any occasion for it. A convention, invited by the Republican members of Congress, with the virtual President & Vice President, would have been on the ground in 8. weeks, would have repaired the Constitution where it was defective, & wound it up again. This peaceable & legitimate resource, to which we are in the habit of implicit obedience, superseding all appeal to force, and being always within our reach, shows a precious principle of self-preservation in our composition, till a change of circumstances shall take place, which is not within prospect at any definite period.

But I have got into a long disquisition on politics, when I only meant to express my sympathy in the state of your health, and to tender you all the affections of public & private hospitality. I should be very happy indeed to see you here. I leave this about the 30th inst., to return about the twenty-fifth of April. If you do not leave Philadelphia before that, a little excursion hither would help your health. I should be much gratified with the possession of a guest I so much esteem, and should claim a right to lodge you, should you make such an excursion.

TO THE U.S. MINISTER TO FRANCE
(ROBERT LIVINGSTON)[1]

Washington, Apr. 18, 1802

DEAR SIR, ... The cession of Louisiana and the Floridas by Spain to France works most sorely on the U.S.[2] On this subject the Secretary of State[3] has written to you fully. Yet I cannot forbear recurring to it personally, so deep is the impression it makes in my mind. It compleatly reverses all the political relations of the U.S. and will form a new epoch in our political course. Of all nations of any consideration France is the one which hitherto has offered the fewest points on which we could have any conflict of right, and the most points of a communion of interests. From these causes we have ever looked to her as our *natural friend,* as one with which we never could have an occasion of difference. Her growth therefore we viewed as our own, her misfortunes ours. There is on the globe one single spot, the possessor[4] of which is our natural and habitual enemy. It is New Orleans, through which the produce of three-eighths of our territory must pass to market, and from its fertility it will ere long yield more than half of our whole produce and contain more than half our inhabitants. France placing herself in that door assumes to us the attitude of defiance. Spain might have retained it quietly for years. Her pacific dispositions, her feeble state, would induce her to increase our facilities there, so that her possession of the place would be hardly felt by us, and it would not perhaps be very long before some circumstance might arise which might make the cession of it to us the price of something of more worth to her. Not so can it ever be in the hands of France. The impetuosity of her temper, the

---

1. Robert Livingston (1746–1813) played an active role in American government from its inception, first as New York's representative to the first Continental Congress and later as chancellor of New York. He was appointed U.S. minister of France by Jefferson in 1801, and was instrumental in securing the Louisiana Purchase.

2. Louisiana was first claimed by the French in 1682 and named for King Louis XIV. In 1762, Louis XV transferred the territory to Spain, which ruled the territory until 1800. In that year, Napoleon (see note 4, p. 220) forced the Spanish to give Louisiana back to the French. This alarmed Jefferson because he saw that free navigation of the Mississippi was essential to Americans moving into the Mississippi Valley. The crisis passed when, in 1803, Napoleon offered to sell not just New Orleans, but the entire Louisiana Territory to the Americans. (See Introduction, p. xxii.)

3. James Madison. For biographical information on Madison, see note 1, p. 153.

4. France.

energy and restlessness of her character, placed in a point of eternal friction with us, and our character, which though quiet, and loving peace and the pursuit of wealth, is high-minded, despising wealth in competition with insult or injury, enterprising and energetic as any nation on earth, these circumstances render it impossible that France and the U.S. can continue long friends when they meet in so irritable a position. They as well as we must be blind if they do not see this; and we must be very improvident if we do not begin to make arrangements on that hypothesis. The day that France takes possession of N. Orleans fixes the sentence which is to restrain her forever within her low water mark. It seals the union of two nations who in conjunction can maintain exclusive possession of the ocean. From that moment we must marry ourselves to the British fleet and nation. We must turn all our attentions to a maritime force, for which our resources place us on very high grounds: and having formed and cemented together a power which may render reinforcement of her settlements here impossible to France, make the first cannon, which shall be fired in Europe the signal for tearing up any settlement she may have made, and for holding the two continents of America in sequestration for the common purposes of the united British and American nations. This is not a state of things we seek or desire. It is one which this measure, if adopted by France, forces on us, as necessarily as any other cause, by the laws of nature, brings on its necessary effect. It is not from a fear of France that we deprecate this measure proposed by her. For however greater her force is than ours compared in the abstract, it is nothing in comparison of ours when to be exerted on our soil. But it is from a sincere love of peace, and a firm persuasion that bound to France by the interests and the strong sympathies still existing in the minds of our citizens, and holding relative positions which ensure their continuance we are secure of a long course of peace. Whereas the change of friends, which will be rendered necessary if France changes that position, embarks us necessarily as a belligerent power in the first war of Europe. In that case France will have held possession of New Orleans during the interval of a peace, long or short, at the end of which it will be wrested from her. Will this short-lived possession have been an equivalent to her for the transfer of such a weight into the scale of her enemy? Will not the amalgamation of a young, thriving, nation continue to that enemy the health and force which are at present so evidently on the decline? And will a few years possession of N. Orleans add equally to the strength of France? She may say she needs Louisiana for the supply of her West Indies. She does not need it in time of peace. And in war she could not depend on them because they would be so easily intercepted. I should suppose that all these considerations might in some proper form be brought into view of the government of France. Tho' stated by us, it ought not to give offence; because we do not bring them forward as a menace, but as consequences not controulable by us, but inevitable from the course of things. We mention them not as things which we desire by any means, but as things we deprecate; and we beseech a friend to look forward and to prevent them for our common interests.

If France considers Louisiana however as indispensable for her views she might perhaps be willing to look about for arrangements which might reconcile it to our interests. If anything could do this it would be the ceding to us the island of New Orleans and the Floridas. This would certainly in a great degree remove the causes of jarring and irritation between us, and perhaps for such a length of time as might produce other means of making the measure permanently conciliatory to our interests and friendships. It would at any rate relieve us from the necessity of taking immediate measures for countervailing such an operation by arrangements in another quarter. Still we should consider N. Orleans and the Floridas as equivalent for the risk of a quarrel with France produced by her vicinage.[5] I have no doubt you have urged these considerations on every proper occasion with the government where you are. They are such as must have effect if you can find the means of producing thorough reflection on them by that government. The idea here is that the troops sent to St. Domingo, were to proceed to Louisiana after finishing their work in that island.[6] If this were the arrangement, it will give you time to return again and again to the charge, for the conquest of St. Domingo will not be a short work. It will take considerable time to wear down a great number of souldiers. Every eye in the U.S. is now fixed on this affair of Louisiana.[7] Perhaps nothing since the revolutionary war has produced more uneasy sensations through the body of the nation. Notwithstanding temporary bickerings have taken place with France, she has still a strong hold on the affections of our citizens generally. I have thought it not amiss, by way of supplement to the letters of the Secretary of State to write you this private one to impress you with the importance we affix to this transaction. I pray you to cherish Dupont.[8] He has the best dispositions for the continuance of friendship between the two nations, and perhaps you may be able to make a good use of him.

Accept assurances of my affectionate esteem and high consideration.

---

5. Proximity.

6. At the moment, Napoleon's troops were in Santo Domingo, and Jefferson feared that they would soon move to occupy Louisiana. But they became bogged down in suppressing a slave revolt.

7. The impending French occupation.

8. Pierre-Samuel Dupont de Nemours (1739–1817): an influential French philosopher and economist. See note 1, p. 229.

To Benjamin Hawkins[1]

Washington, Feb. 18, 1803

DEAR SIR, . . . Altho' you will receive, thro' the official channel of the War Office, every communication necessary to develop to you our views respecting the Indians, and to direct your conduct, yet, supposing it will be satisfactory to you, and to those with whom you are placed, to understand my personal dispositions and opinions in this particular, I shall avail myself of this private letter to state them generally. I consider the business of hunting as already become insufficient to furnish clothing and subsistence to the Indians. The promotion of agriculture, therefore, and household manufacture, are essential in their preservation, and I am disposed to aid and encourage it liberally. This will enable them to live on much smaller portions of land, and indeed will render their vast forests useless but for the range of cattle; for which purpose, also, as they become better farmers, they will be found useless, and even disadvantageous. While they are learning to do better on less land, our increasing numbers will be calling for more land, and thus a coincidence of interests will be produced between those who have lands to spare, and want other necessaries, and those who have such necessaries to spare, and want lands. This commerce, then, will be for the good of both, and those who are friends to both ought to encourage it. You are in the station peculiarly charged with this interchange, and who have it peculiarly in your power to promote among the Indians a sense of the superior value of a little land, well cultivated, over a great deal, unimproved, and to encourage them to make this estimate truly. The wisdom of the animal which amputates & abandons to the hunter the parts for which he is pursued should be theirs, with this difference, that the former sacrifices what is useful, the latter what is not. In truth, the ultimate point of rest & happiness for them is to let our settlements and theirs meet and blend together, to intermix, and become one people. Incorporating themselves with us as citizens of the U.S., this is what the natural progress of

---

1. Benjamin Hawkins (1754–1818) served for a time as U.S. senator for North Carolina and was George Washington's French interpreter during the Revolution. In 1795 he accepted the post of General Superintendent of Indian Affairs to the Creeks and all tribes south of the Ohio River. He was markedly successful in this position, introducing the Indians to agricultural practices and treating them sympathetically. The War of 1812, the British incitement of a Shawnee uprising (led by Tecumseh [1768–1813]) against American settlers and President Andrew Jackson's (1767–1845) subsequent crushing of the tribe left Hawkins bitter. He died soon thereafter.

things will of course bring on, and it will be better to promote than to retard it. Surely it will be better for them to be identified with us, and preserved in the occupation of their lands, than be exposed to the many casualties which may endanger them while a separate people. I have little doubt but that your reflections must have led you to view the various ways in which their history may terminate, and to see that this is the one most for their happiness. And we have already had an application from a settlement of Indians to become citizens of the U.S. It is possible, perhaps probable, that this idea may be so novel as that it might shock the Indians, were it even hinted to them. Of course, you will keep it for your own reflection; but, convinced of its soundness, feel it consistent with pure morality to lead them towards it, to familiarize them to the idea that it is for their interest to cede lands at times to the U S, and for us thus to procure gratifications to our citizens, from time to time, by new acquisitions of land. From no quarter is there at present so strong a pressure on this subject as from Georgia for the residue of the fork of Oconee & Ockmulgee; and indeed I believe it will be difficult to resist it. As it has been mentioned that the Creeks had at one time made up their minds to sell this, and were only checked in it by some indiscretions of an individual, I am in hopes you will be able to bring them to it again. I beseech you to use your most earnest endeavors; for it will relieve us here from a great pressure, and yourself from the unreasonable suspicions of the Georgians which you notice, that you are more attached to the interests of the Indians than of the U S, and throw cold water on their willingness to part with lands. It is so easy to excite suspicion, that none are to be wondered at; but I am in hopes it will be in your power to quash them by effecting the object.

To Wilson Cary Nicholas[1]

Monticello, Sept. 7, 1803

Dear Sir, — Your favor of the 3d was delivered me at court; but we were much disappointed at not seeing you here, Mr. Madison[2] & the Gov.[3] being here at the time. I enclose you a letter from Monroe[4] on the subject of the late treaty.[5] You will observe a hint in it, to do without delay what we are bound to do. There is reason, in the opinion of our ministers, to believe, that if the thing were to do over again, it could not be obtained, & that if we give the least opening, they will declare the treaty void. A warning amounting to that has been given to them, & an unusual kind of letter written by their minister to our Secretary of State, direct. Whatever Congress shall think it necessary to do, should be done with as little debate as possible, & particularly so far as respects the constitutional difficulty. I am aware of the force of the observations you make on the power given by the Constn to Congress, to admit new States into the Union, without restraining the subject to the territory then constituting the U S. But when I consider that the limits of the U S are precisely fixed by the treaty of 1783, that the Constitution expressly declares itself to be made for the U S, cannot help believing the intention was to permit Congress to admit into the Union new States, which should be formed out of the territory for which, & under whose authority alone, they were then acting. I do not believe it was meant that they might receive England, Ireland, Holland, &c. into it, which would be the case on your construction. When an instrument

---

1. Wilson Cary Nicolas (1761–1826): one of the leaders of Jefferson's party and his devoted follower for many years. A congressman, U.S. senator, and governor of Virginia, he worked closely with Jefferson in establishing the University of Virginia. Nicholas was a chief organizer of Madison's campaign for the presidency in 1808. A close personal friend, Jefferson cosigned a note for him, with disastrous financial consequences (see Jefferson's letter to James Madison, p. 273).

2. James Madison, then Jefferson's secretary of state. (See note 3, p. 198.)

3. John Page (1744–1808): one of Jefferson's closest friends. They were classmates at William and Mary and corresponded regularly thereafter. Page served in the Virginia militia during the Revolution and was the state's governor from 1802–05.

4. James Monroe was, with Robert Livingston, assisting in the negotiations of the Louisiana Purchase. See note 4 on p. 61, and note 1 on p. 198.

5. That is, the Louisiana Purchase, by which the United States gained not just New Orleans and the Floridas (which was all Jefferson realistically hoped for in his instructions to Robert Livingston) but the whole of the Louisiana Territory. (See note 1, Jefferson's letter to Livingston, p. 198.)

admits two constructions, the one safe, the other dangerous, the one precise, the other indefinite, I prefer that which is safe & precise. I had rather ask an enlargement of power from the nation, where it is found necessary, than to assume it by a construction which would make our powers boundless. Our peculiar security is in possession of a written Constitution. Let us not make it a blank paper by construction. I say the same as to the opinion of those who consider the grant of the treaty making power as boundless. If it is, then we have no Constitution. If it has bounds, they can be no others than the definitions of the powers which that instrument gives. It specifies & delineates the operations permitted to the federal government, and gives all the powers necessary to carry these into execution. Whatever of these enumerated objects is proper for a law, Congress may make the law; whatever is proper to be executed by way of a treaty, the President & Senate may enter into the treaty; whatever is to be done by a judicial sentence, the judges may pass the sentence. Nothing is more likely than that their enumeration of powers is defective. This is the ordinary case of all human works. Let us go on then perfecting it, by adding, by way of amendment to the Constitution, those powers which time & trial show are still wanting. But it has been taken too much for granted, that by this rigorous construction the treaty power would be reduced to nothing. I had occasion once to examine its effect on the French treaty,[6] made by the old Congress, & found that out of thirty odd articles which that contained, there were one, two, or three only which could not now be stipulated under our present Constitution. I confess, then, I think it important, in the present case, to set an example against broad construction, by appealing for new power to the people. If, however, our friends shall think differently, certainly I shall acquiesce with satisfaction; confiding, that the good sense of our country will correct the evil of construction when it shall produce ill effects.

No apologies for writing or speaking to me freely are necessary. On the contrary, nothing my friends can do is so dear to me, & proves to me their friendship so clearly, as the information they give me of their sentiments & those of others on interesting points where I am to act, and where information & warning is so essential to excite in me that due reflection which ought to precede action. I leave this about the 21st, and shall hope the District Court will give me an opportunity of seeing you.

Accept my affectionate salutations, & assurances of cordial esteem & respect.

---

6. The Treaty of Alliance between the United States and France, Feb. 6, 1778. In this treaty, France and the United States agreed to protect each other in the event of a British attack; it was this treaty that drew France into the American Revolution. (See Jefferson's *Opinion on the French Treaties*, p. 37, and Introduction.)

To Henri Gregoire[1]

Washington, Feb. 25, 1809

Sir, — I have received the favor of your letter of August 17th, and with it the volume you were so kind as to send me on the "Literature of Negroes." Be assured that no person living wishes more sincerely than I do, to see a complete refutation of the doubts I have myself entertained and expressed on the grade of understanding allotted to them by nature,[2] and to find that in this respect they are on a par with ourselves. My doubts were the result of personal observation on the limited sphere of my own State, where the opportunities for the development of their genius were not favorable, and those of exercising it still less so. I expressed them therefore with great hesitation; but whatever be their degree of talent it is no measure of their rights. Because Sir Isaac Newton[3] was superior to others in understanding, he was not therefore lord of the person or property of others. On this subject they are gaining daily in the opinions of nations, and hopeful advances are making towards their re-establishment on an equal footing with the other colors of the human family. I pray you therefore to accept my thanks for the many instances you have enabled me to observe of respectable intelligence in that race of men, which cannot fail to have effect in hastening the day of their relief; and to be assured of the sentiments of high and just esteem and consideration which I tender to yourself with all sincerity

---

1. Henri Gregoire (1750–1831), Bishop of Blois, was a supporter of the French Revolution. While a member of the Constituent Assembly, he took a strong interest in Negro emancipation and advocated racial equality for men of color in the French colonies. In 1808, he compiled *De la literature des Negres*, a copy of which he sent to Jefferson hoping to persuade him of the literary talents of the black race.

2. See Query XIV of the *Notes on Virginia*, pp. 113–17.

3. Sir Isaac Newton (1642–1727): prominent mathematician, physicist, and scientist.

TO JOHN TYLER[1]

Monticello, May 26, 1810

DEAR SIR, — Your friendly letter of the 12th has been duly received. Although I have laid it down as a law to myself, never to embarrass the President[2] with my solicitations, and have not till now broken through it, yet I have made a part of your letter the subject of one to him, and have done it with all my heart, and in the full belief that I serve him and the public in urging that appointment. We have long enough suffered under the base prostitution of law to party passions in one judge, and the imbecility of another. In the hands of one the law is nothing more than an ambiguous text, to be explained by his sophistry[3] into any meaning which may subserve his personal malice. Nor can any milk-and-water associate maintain his own dependance, and by a firm pursuance of what the law really is, extend its protection to the citizens or the public. I believe you will do it, and where you cannot induce your colleague to do what is right, you will be firm enough to hinder him from doing what is wrong, and by opposing sense to sophistry, leave the juries free to follow their own judgment.

I have long lamented with you the depreciation of law science. The opinion seems to be that Blackstone[4] is to us what the Alcoran[5] is to the Mahometans,[6] that everything which is necessary is in him, and what is not in him is not necessary. I still lend my counsel and books to such young students as will fix themselves in the neighborhood. Coke's[7] institutes and reports are their first, and Blackstone their last book, after an intermediate course of two

---

1. John Tyler (1747–1813): an early friend of Jefferson's, a Revolutionary patriot, and an ardent Republican. He opposed the ratification of the federal Constitution in 1788, served as state court judge in Virginia, and was elected governor of Virginia in 1808. He was also the father of John Tyler (1790–1862), tenth President of the United States.

2. James Madison. (For biographical information on Madison, see note 1, p. 153.)

3. Fallacious arguments most often used to deceive.

4. William Blackstone (1723–80): English jurist, whose *Commentaries on the Laws of England* dominated legal learning in England and America during the founding period. See note 8, p. 274.

5. The Koran.

6. Muslims.

7. Edward Coke (1552–1634): an English jurist who was the leading authority on the English common law. See note 16, Query XIII, p. 103, and note 14, Query XIV, p. 113.

or three years. It is nothing more than an elegant digest of what they will then have acquired from the real fountains of the law. Now men are born scholars, lawyers, doctors; in our day this was confined to poets. You wish to see me again in the legislature, but this is impossible; my mind is now so dissolved in tranquillity, that it can never again encounter a contentious assembly; the habits of thinking and speaking off-hand, after a disuse of five and twenty years, have given place to the slower process of the pen. I have indeed two great measures at heart, without which no republic can maintain itself in strength.

1. That of general education, to enable every man to judge for himself what will secure or endanger his freedom.

2. To divide every county into hundreds, of such size that all the children of each will be within reach of a central school in it.

But this division looks to many other fundamental provisions. Every hundred, besides a school, should have a justice of the peace, a constable and a captain of militia. These officers, or some others within the hundred, should be a corporation to manage all its concerns, to take care of its roads, its poor, and its police by patrols, &c., (as the select men of the Eastern townships.) Every hundred should elect one or two jurors to serve where requisite, and all other elections should be made in the hundreds separately, and the votes of all the hundreds be brought together. Our present Captaincies might be declared hundreds for the present, with a power to the courts to alter them occasionally. These little republics would be the main strength of the great one. We owe to them the vigor given to our revolution in its commencement in the Eastern States, and by them the Eastern States were enabled to repeal the embargo in opposition to the Middle, Southern and Western States, and their large and lubberly[8] division into counties which can never be assembled.[9] General orders are given out from a centre to the foreman of every hundred, as to the sergeants of an army, and the whole nation is thrown into energetic action, in the same direction in one instant and as one man, and becomes absolutely irresistible. Could I once see this I should consider it as the dawn of the salvation of the republic, and say with old Simeon, "nunc dimittas Domine."[10] But our children will be as wise as we are, and will establish in the fulness of time those things not yet ripe for establishment.

So be it, and to yourself health, happiness and long life.

---

8. Clumsy.

9. Jefferson is here praising the New England townships for their effectiveness during the Revolution and in opposing the embargo during his second administration.

10. According to the Bible, the Holy Spirit promised the aged Simeon that he would not die until he had seen the messiah. On seeing the infant Jesus in the Temple, Simeon uttered the words *nunc dimittis domine,* meaning "Now, thou dost dismiss thy servant, O Lord." (Luke 2:29–35)

To John B. Colvin[1]

Monticello, Sept. 20, 1810

SIR, . . . The question you propose, whether circumstances do not sometimes occur, which make it a duty in officers of high trust, to assume authorities beyond the law, is easy of solution in principle, but sometimes embarrassing in practice. A strict observance of the written laws is doubtless *one* of the high duties of a good citizen, but it is not *the highest.* The laws of necessity, of self-preservation, of saving our country when in danger, are of higher obligation. To lose our country by a scrupulous adherence to written law, would be to lose the law itself, with life, liberty, property and all those who are enjoying them with us; thus absurdly sacrificing the end to the means. When, in the battle of Germantown, General Washington's army was annoyed from Chew's house, he did not hesitate to plant his cannon against it, although the property of a citizen. When he besieged Yorktown, he leveled the suburbs, feeling that the laws of property must be postponed to the safety of the nation. While the army was before York, the Governor of Virginia took horses, carriages, provisions and even men by force, to enable that army to stay together till it could master the public enemy; and he was justified. A ship at sea in distress for provisions, meets another having abundance, yet refusing a supply; the law of self-preservation authorizes the distressed to take a supply by force. In all these cases, the unwritten laws of necessity, of self-preservation, and of the public safety, control the written laws of *meum* and *tuum.*[2] Further to exemplify the principle, I will state an hypothetical case. Suppose it had been made known to the Executive of the Union in the autumn of 1805, that we might have the Floridas for a reasonable sum, that that sum had not indeed been so appropriated by law, but that Congress were to meet within three weeks, and might appropriate it on the first or second day of their session. Ought he, for so great an advantage to his country, to have risked himself by transcending the law and making the purchase? The public advantage offered, in this supposed case, was indeed immense; but a reverence for law, and the probability that the

---

1. John B. Colvin (dates unknown): a Maryland editor, pamphleteer, and correspondent. A Republican, he was a strong supporter of the Jefferson administration. Among his tracts are "Republican economy; or Evidences of the superiority of the present administration, over that of John Adams," and "Republican policy; or The superiority of the principles of the present administration over those of its enemies, who call themselves Federalists; exemplified in the late cession of Louisiana."

2. *Meum* and *tuum*: mine and yours.

advantage might still be *legally* accomplished by a delay of only three weeks, were powerful reasons against hazarding the act. But suppose it foreseen that a John Randolph[3] would find means to protract the proceeding on it by Congress, until the ensuing spring, by which time new circumstances would change the mind of the other party. Ought the Executive, in that case, and with that foreknowledge, to have secured the good to his country, and to have trusted to their justice for the transgression of the law? I think he ought, and that the act would have been approved. After the affair of the Chesapeake,[4] we thought war a very possible result. Our magazines were illy provided with some necessary articles, nor had any appropriations been made for their purchase. We ventured, however, to provide them, and to place our country in safety; and stating the case to Congress, they sanctioned the act.

To proceed to the conspiracy of Burr, and particularly to General Wilkinson's situation in New Orleans.[5] In judging this case, we are bound to consider the state of the information, correct and incorrect, which he then possessed. He expected Burr and his band from above, a British fleet from below, and he knew there was a formidable conspiracy within the city. Under these circumstances, was he justifiable, 1st, in seizing notorious conspirators? On this there can be but two opinions; one, of the guilty and their accomplices; the other, that of all honest men. 2d. In sending them to the seat of government, when the written law gave them a right to trial in the territory?

---

3. John Randolph (1773–1833): ultra-orthodox Virginia Republican. At the time of this letter, Randolph was chairman of the powerful Ways and Means Committee in the House of Representatives.

4. In June of 1807 the British ship *Leopard* requested permission to board the American frigate *Chesapeake* to search for possible deserters from the British Navy. The American captain, assuming that the British simply wanted to impress some American sailors into their own navy, refused. The *Leopard* then fired on the American ship: twenty-one seamen were killed in the attack. Following the incident—often referred to as the "*Chesapeake* affair"—Jefferson closed American waters to British ships and called for an end to British impressment of American sailors. The incident was one of many that led to the War of 1812 against Britain.

5. The precise details of the Burr conspiracy remain murky. After having killed secretary of the treasury Alexander Hamilton in a duel in 1804, Aaron Burr (1756–1836)—Jefferson's vice president during his first term—fled south and became involved in a plot to detach the western territories from the United States. One of Burr's co-conspirators in the scheme was the notoriously corrupt and traitorous General James Wilkinson (1757–1825) who, among other scandals, had once been part of a plot to overthrow George Washington as commander-in-chief of the Continental Army. Wilkinson later turned against Burr and informed Jefferson of their plans. Burr escaped after his capture and, when he was apprehended, was transported to Richmond, Virginia, to stand trial on charges of treason. With Chief Justice John Marshall (see note 13, p. 213) presiding, Burr was acquitted in 1811.

The danger of their rescue, of their continuing their machinations, the tardiness and weakness of the law, apathy of the judges, active patronage of the whole tribe of lawyers, unknown disposition of the juries, an hourly expectation of the enemy, salvation of the city, and of the Union itself, which would have been convulsed to its centre, had that conspiracy succeeded; all these constituted a law of necessity and self-preservation, and rendered the *salus populi*[6] supreme over the written law. The officer who is called to act on this superior ground, does indeed risk himself on the justice of the controlling powers of the constitution, and his station makes it his duty to incur that risk. But those controlling powers, and his fellow citizens generally, are bound to judge according to the circumstances under which he acted. They are not to transfer the information of this place or moment to the time and place of his action; but to put themselves into his situation. We knew here that there never was danger of a British fleet from below, and that Burr's band was crushed before it reached the Mississippi. But General Wilkinson's information was very different, and he could act on no other.

From these examples and principles you may see what I think on the question proposed. They do not go to the case of persons charged with petty duties, where consequences are trifling, and time allowed for a legal course, nor to authorize them to take such cases out of the written law. In these, the example of overleaping the law is of greater evil than a strict adherence to its imperfect provisions. It is incumbent on those only who accept of great charges, to risk themselves on great occasions, when the safety of the nation, or some of its very high interests are at stake. An officer is bound to obey orders; yet he would be a bad one who should do it in cases for which they were not intended, and which involved the most important consequences. The line of discrimination between cases may be difficult; but the good officer is bound to draw it at his own peril, and throw himself on the justice of his country and the rectitude of his motives.

I have indulged freer views on this question, on your assurances that they are for your own eye only, and that they will not get into the hands of newswriters. I met their scurrilities without concern, while in pursuit of the great interests with which I was charged. But in my present retirement, no duty forbids my wish for quiet.

Accept the assurances of my esteem and respect.

---

6. The welfare of the people. The reference is to a well-known adage of Roman law, *salus populi suprema lex esto* ("the welfare of the people shall be the supreme law") quoted by Cicero (*De Legibus,* iii, 8).

To John Adams[1]

Monticello, June 15, 1813

DEAR SIR, ... By your kind quotation of the dates of my two letters I have been enabled to turn to them. They had compleatly evanished from my memory. The last is on the subject of religion, and by it's publication will gratify the priesthood with new occasion of repeating their Comminations[2] against me. They wish it to be believed that he can have no religion who advocates it's freedom. This was not the doctrine of Priestley,[3] and I honored him for the example of liberality he set to his order. The first letter is political. It recalls to our recollection the gloomy transactions of the times, the doctrines they witnessed, and the sensibilities they excited. It was a confidential communication of reflections on these from one friend to another, deposited in his bosom, and never meant to trouble the public mind. Whether the character of the times is justly portrayed or not, posterity will decide. But on one feature of them they can never decide, the sensations excited in free yet firm minds, by the terrorism of the day. None can concieve who did not witness them, and they were felt by one party only.[4] This letter exhibits their side of the medal. The Federalists[5] no doubt have presented the other, in their private correspondences, as well as open action. If these correspondencies should ever be laid open to the public eye, they will probably be found not models of comity[6] towards their adversaries. The readers of my letter should

---

1. John Adams (1735–1826): a Revolutionary patriot from Massachusetts, served with Jefferson on the committee that drew up the Declaration of Independence. He later served as minister to England at the same time that Jefferson was posted to France and was eventually elected second president of the United States, with Jefferson as his vice president. The two fell out over political differences, and Jefferson defeated Adams for the presidency in 1800. After Jefferson's retirement in 1808, the two were reconciled and corresponded until the end of their lives. They both died on July 4, 1826, the fiftieth anniversary of the signing of the Declaration of Independence.
2. Formal denunciations. In the Church of England, a commination is a recital of God's judgment against sinners read in churches on Ash Wednesday.
3. Dr. Joseph Priestley (1733–1804): English scientist and Unitarian minister. (See note 1, p. 196.)
4. The Republicans. (See note 2, p. 56.)
5. The opposing party, with Adams and secretary of the treasury Alexander Hamilton at its head.
6. Social harmony.

be cautioned not to confine it's view to this country alone. England and it's alarmists were equally under consideration. Still less must they consider it as looking personally towards you. You happen indeed to be quoted because you happened to express, more pithily than had been done by themselves, one of the mottos of the party. This was in your answer to the address of the young men of Philadelphia. [See selection of patriotic addresses, pa. 198.][7] One of the questions you know on which our parties took different sides, was on the improvability of the human mind, in science, in ethics, in government etc. Those who advocated reformation of institutions, pari passu[8] with the progress of science, maintained that no definite limits could be assigned to that progress. The enemies of reform, on the other hand, denied improvement, and advocated steady adherence to the principles, practices and institutions of our fathers, which they represented as the consummation of wisdom, and akme[9] of excellence, beyond which the human mind could never advance. Altho' in the passage of your answer alluded to, you expressly disclaim the wish to influence the freedom of enquiry, you predict that that will produce nothing more worthy of transmission to posterity, than the principles, institutions, and systems of education recieved from their ancestors. I do not consider this as your deliberate opinion. You possess, yourself, too much science, not to see how much is still ahead of you, unexplained and unexplored. Your own consciousness must place you as far before our ancestors, as in the rear of our posterity. I consider it as an expression lent to the prejudices of your friends; and altho' happened to cite it from you, the whole letter shews I had them only in view. In truth, my dear Sir, we were far from considering you as the author of all the measures we blamed. They were placed under the protection of your name, but we were satisfied they wanted much of your approbation. We ascribed them to their real authors, the Pickerings, the Wolcotts, the Tracys, the Sedgwicks,[10] et id genus omne,[11] with whom we supposed you in a state of Duresse. I well remember a conversation with you, in the morning of the day on which you nominated to the Senate a substitute for Pickering, in which you expressed a just impatience under 'the legacy of

7. Jefferson is here alluding to Adams' address "To the Young Men of the City of Philadelphia, the District of Southwark, and the Northern Liberties, Pennsylvania," delivered on May 7, 1798. Jefferson's bracketed note refers to the copy of Adams' A Selection of the Patriotic Addresses, to the President of the United States Together with the President's Answers (Boston, 1798) he kept in his library.

8. At an equal pace.

9. Acme, the height or peak.

10. Timothy Pickering, Oliver Wolcott, Jr., Uriah Tracy, and Theodore Sedgwick, all New England Federalists.

11. And all that sort.

Secretaries which Gen. Washington[12] had left you' and whom you seemed therefore to consider as under public protection. Many other incidents shewed how differently you would have acted with less impassioned advisers; and subsequent events have proved that your minds were not together. You would do me great injustice therefore by taking to yourself what was intended for men who were then your secret, as they are now your open enemies. Should you write on the subject, as you propose, I am sure we shall see you place yourself farther from them than from us.

As to myself, I shall take no part in any discussions. I leave others to judge of what I have done, and to give me exactly that place which they shall think I have occupied. Marshall[13] has written libels on one side; others, I suppose, will be written on the other side; and the world will sift both, and separate the truth as well as they can. I should see with reluctance the passions of that day rekindled in this, while so many of the actors are living, and all are too near the scene not to participate in sympathies with them. About facts, you and I cannot differ; because truth is our mutual guide. And if any opinions you may express should be different from mine, I shall recieve them with the liberality and indulgence which I ask for my own, and still cherish with warmth the sentiments of affectionate respect of which I can with so much truth tender you the assurance.

---

12. George Washington. (See note 1, p. 182, for more information on Washington.)

13. John Marshall (1755–1835): a Virginia Federalist, was appointed chief justice of the Supreme Court by John Adams. He wrote an admiring biography of George Washington.

TO JOHN ADAMS[1]

Monticello, Oct. 28, 1813

DEAR SIR — According to the reservation between us, of taking up one of the subjects of our correspondence at a time, turn to your letters of Aug. 16. and Sep. 2.

The passage you quote from Theognis,[2] I think has an Ethical, rather than a political object. The whole piece is a moral *exhortation*, παραίνεσις, and this passage particularly seems to be a reproof to man, who, while with his domestic animals he is curious to improve the race by employing always the finest male, pays no attention to the improvement of his own race, but intermarries with the vicious, the ugly, or the old, for considerations of wealth or ambition. It is in conformity with the principle adopted afterwards by the Pythagoreans, and expressed by Ocellus[3] in another form. Περι δε τῆς ἐκ τῶν ἀλληλων ανθρωπων γενεσως etc. — ουχ ἡδονης ἑνεκα ἡ μιξις. Which, as literally as intelligibility will admit, may be thus translated. 'Concerning the interprocreation of men, how, and of whom it shall be, in a perfect manner, and according to the laws of modesty and sanctity, conjointly, this is what I think right. First to lay it down that we do not commix for the sake of pleasure, but of the procreation of children. For the powers, the organs and desires for coition have not been given by god to man for the sake of pleasure, but for the procreation of the race. For as it were incongruous for a mortal born to partake of divine life, the immortality of the race being taken away, god fulfilled the purpose by making the generations uninterrupted and continuous. This therefore we are especially to lay down as a principle, that coition[4] is not for the sake of pleasure.' But Nature, not trusting to this moral and abstract motive, seems to have provided more securely for the perpetuation of the species by making it the effect of the *oestrum*[5] implanted in the constitution of both sexes. And not only has the commerce of love been indulged on this unhallowed impulse, but made subservient also to wealth and ambition by marriages without regard to the beauty, the healthiness, the understanding, or

---

1. For biographical information on Adams, see note 1 on p. 211.
2. Theognis (sixth century BC): Greek poet.
3. Ocellus Lucanus (fifth century BC): Greek Pythagorean philosopher.
4. Sexual intercourse.
5. A regularly recurrent state of sexual excitability during which the female of most mammals will accept the male and is capable of conceiving.

virtue of the subject from which we are to breed. The selecting the best male for a Haram[6] of well chosen females also, which Theognis seems to recommend from the example of our sheep and asses, would doubtless improve the human, as it does the brute animal, and produce a race of veritable αριστοι.[7] For experience proves that the moral and physical qualities of man, whether good or evil, are transmissible in a certain degree from father to son. But suspect that the equal rights of men will rise up against this privileged Solomon,[8] and oblige us to continue acquiescence under the Ἀμαυρωσις γενεος ἀστων[9] which Theognis complains of, and to content ourselves with the accidental *aristoi*[10] produced by the fortuitous concourse of breeders. For I agree with you that there is a natural aristocracy among men. The grounds of this are virtue and talents. Formerly bodily powers gave place among the *aristoi*. But since the invention of gunpowder has armed the weak as well as the strong with missile death, bodily strength, like beauty, good humor, politeness and other accomplishments, has become but an auxiliary ground of distinction. There is also an artificial aristocracy founded on wealth and birth, without either virtue or talents; for with these it would belong to the first class. The natural aristocracy I consider as the most precious gift of nature for the instruction, the trusts, and government of society. And indeed it would have been inconsistent in creation to have formed man for the social state, and not to have provided virtue and wisdom enough to manage the concerns of the society. May we not even say that that form of government is the best which provides the most effectually for a pure selection of these natural *aristoi* into the offices of government? The artificial aristocracy is a mischievous ingredient in government, and provision should be made to prevent it's ascendancy. On the question, What is the best provision, you and I differ; but we differ as rational friends, using the free exercise of our own reason, and mutually indulging it's errors. *You* think it best to put the Pseudo-*aristoi* into a separate chamber of legislation where they may be hindered from doing mischief by their coordinate branches, and where also they may be a protection to wealth against the Agrarian and plundering enterprises of the Majority of the people. I think that to give them power in order to prevent them from doing mischief, is arming them for it, and increasing instead of remedying the evil. For if the coordinate branches can arrest their action, so may they that of the coordinates. Mischief may be done negatively as well as positively. Of this a cabal in

---

6. Harem.

7. *Aristoi*; Aristocrats.

8. Solomon was the Biblical King of Israel; he was renowned for his wisdom.

9. "The degeneration of the race of men."

10. See note 7, above.

the Senate of the U.S. has furnished many proofs. Nor do I believe them nec-essary to protect the wealthy; because enough of these will find their way into every branch of the legislation to protect themselves. From 15. to 20. legisla-tures of our own, in action for 30. years past, have proved that no fears of an equalisation of property are to be apprehended from them.

I think the best remedy is exactly that provided by all our constitutions, to leave to the citizens the free election and separation of the *aristoi* from the pseudo-*aristoi*, of the wheat from the chaff. In general they will elect the real good and wise. In some instances, wealth may corrupt, and birth blind them; but not in sufficient degree to endanger the society.

It is probable that our difference of opinion may in some measure be pro-duced by a difference of character in those among whom we live. From what I have seen of Massachusets and Connecticut myself, and still more from what have heard, and the character given of the former by yourself, who know them so much better, there seems to be in those two states a traditionary rever-ence for certain families, which has rendered the offices of the government nearly hereditary in those families. I presume that from an early period of your history, members of these families happening to possess virtue and tal-ents, have honestly exercised them for the good of the people, and by their services have endeared their names to them.

In coupling Connecticut with you, I mean it politically only, not morally. For having made the Bible the Common law of their land they seem to have modelled their morality on the story of Jacob and Laban.[11] But altho' this hereditary succession to office with you may in some degree be founded in real family merit, yet in a much higher degree it has proceeded from your strict alliance of church and state. These families are canonised in the eyes of the people on the common principle 'you tickle me, and I will tickle you.' In Virginia we have nothing of this. Our clergy, before the revolution, having been secured against rivalship by fixed salaries, did not give themselves the trouble of acquiring influence over the people. Of wealth, there were great ac-cumulations in particular families, handed down from generation to genera-tion under the English law of entails. But the only object of ambition for the wealthy was a seat in the king's council. All their court then was paid to the crown and it's creatures; and they Philipised[12] in all collisions between the king and people. Hence they were unpopular; and that unpopularity contin-ues attached to their names. A Randolph, a Carter, or a Burwell must have great personal superiority over a common competitor to be elected by the people, even at this day.

---

11. In the Old Testament, Laban was Jacob's father-in-law, and tricked him into mar-rying his elder daughter Leah instead of Rachel. (Genesis 29–31)

12. Spoke in support of a cause under the influence of a bribe.

At the first session of our legislature after the Declaration of Independence, we passed a law abolishing entails.[13] And this was followed by one abolishing the privilege of Primogeniture,[14] and dividing the lands of intestates[15] equally among all their children, or other representatives. These laws, drawn by myself, laid the axe to the root of Pseudo-aristocracy. And had another which I prepared been adopted by the legislature, our work would have been compleat. It was a Bill for the more general diffusion of learning. This proposed to divide every county into wards of 5. or 6. miles square, like your townships; to establish in each ward a free school for reading, writing and common arithmetic; to provide for the annual selection of the best subjects from these schools who might recieve at the public expence a higher degree of education at a district school; and from these district schools to select a certain number of the most promising subjects to be compleated at an University, where all the useful sciences should be taught. Worth and genius would thus have been sought out from every condition of life, and compleatly prepared by education for defeating the competition of wealth and birth for public trusts.

My proposition had for a further object to impart to these wards those portions of self-government for which they are best qualified, by confiding to them the care of their poor, their roads, police, elections, the nomination of jurors, administration of justice in small cases, elementary exercises of militia, in short, to have made them little republics, with a Warden at the head of each, for all those concerns which, being under their eye, they would better manage than the larger republics of the county or state. A general call of ward-meetings by their Wardens on the same day thro' the state would at any time produce the genuine sense of the people on any required point, and would enable the state to act in mass, as your people have so often done, and with so much effect, by their town meetings. The law for religious freedom, which made a part of this system, having put down the aristocracy of the clergy, and restored to the citizen the freedom of the mind, and those of entails and descents nurturing an equality of condition among them, this on Education would have raised the mass of the people to the high ground of moral respectability necessary to their own safety, and to orderly government; and would have compleated the great object of qualifying them to select the veritable *aristoi*, for the trusts of government, to the exclusion of the Pseudalists:[16] and the same Theognis who has furnished the epigraphs of your two letters

---

13. The laws by which property was limited to a specific succession of heirs.
14. The right of the eldest child, usually the eldest son, to inherit the estates of both parents.
15. Individuals who have died without leaving a will.
16. Pseudalists: the pseudo-aristocracy.

assures us that 'Ουδεμιαν πω, Κυρν', αγαθοι πολιν ωλεσαν ανδρες'.[17] Altho' this law has not yet been acted on but in a small and inefficient degree, it is still considered as before the legislature, with other bills of the revised code, not yet taken up, and I have great hope that some patriotic spirit will, at a favorable moment, call it up, and make it the key-stone of the arch of our government.

With respect to Aristocracy, we should further consider that, before the establishment of the American states, nothing was known to History but the Man of the old world, crouded within limits either small or overcharged, and steeped in the vices which that situation generates. A government adapted to such men would be one thing; but a very different one that for the Man of these states. Here every one may have land to labor for himself if he chuses; or, preferring the exercise of any other industry, may exact for it such compensation as not only to afford a comfortable subsistence, but where-with to provide for a cessation from labor in old age. Every one, by his property, or by his satisfactory situation, is interested in the support of law and order. And such men may safely and advantageously reserve to themselves a wholsome controul over their public affairs, and a degree of freedom, which in the hands of the *canaille*[18] of the cities of Europe, would be instantly perverted to the demolition and destruction of every thing public and private. The history of the last 25. years of France, and of the last 40. years in America, nay of it's last 200. years, proves the truth of both parts of this observation.

But even in Europe a change has sensibly taken place in the mind of Man. Science had liberated the ideas of those who read and reflect, and the American example had kindled feelings of right in the people. An insurrection has consequently begun, of science, talents and courage against rank and birth, which have fallen into contempt. It has failed in it's first effort, because the mobs of the cities, the instrument used for it's accomplishment, debased by ignorance, poverty and vice, could not be restrained to rational action. But the world will recover from the panic of this first catastrophe. Science is progressive, and talents and enterprize on the alert. Resort may be had to the people of the country, a more governable power from their principles and subordination; and rank, and birth, and tinsel-aristocracy will finally shrink into insignificance, even there. This however we have no right to meddle with. It suffices for us, if the moral and physical condition of our own citizens qualifies them to select the able and good for the direction of their government, with a recurrence of elections at such short periods as will enable them to displace an unfaithful servant before the mischief he meditates may be irremediable.

---

17. "Good men have never harmed any city." (Curnis)
18. The rabble or mob.

I have thus stated my opinion on a point on which we differ, not with a view to controversy, for we are both too old to change opinions which are the result of a long life of inquiry and reflection; but on the suggestion of a former letter of yours, that we ought not to die before we have explained ourselves to each other. We acted in perfect harmony thro' a long and perilous contest for our liberty and independance. A constitution has been acquired which, tho neither of us think perfect, yet both consider as competent to render our fellow-citizens the happiest and the securest on whom the sun has ever shone. If we do not think exactly alike as to it's imperfections, it matters little to our country which, after devoting to it long lives of disinterested labor, we have delivered over to our successors in life, who will be able to take care of it, and of themselves.

Of the pamphlet on aristocracy which has been sent to you, or who may be it's author, I have heard nothing but thro' your letter. If the person you suspect it may be known from the quaint, mystical and hyperbolical ideas, involved in affected, new-fangled and pedantic terms, which stamp his writings.[19] Whatever it be, I hope your quiet is not to be affected at this day by the rudeness of intemperance of scribblers; but that you may continue in tranquility to live and to rejoice in the prosperity of our country until it shall be your own wish to take your seat among the *aristoi* who have gone before you. Ever and affectionately yours.

P.S. Can you assist my memory on the enquiries of my letter of Aug. 22?

---

19. John Taylor of Caroline (1753–1824): Virginia political writer and Jefferson's staunch supporter. (See note 1, p. 233.)

To J. Correa de Serra[1]

Monticello, Apr. 19, 1814

Dear Sir, — Mr. Randolph[2] first, and latterly Mr. Short,[3] have flattered me with the hope that you would pay us a visit with the returning season. I should sooner have pressed this but that my vernal visit to Bedford was approaching, and I wished to fix its precise epoch before I should write to you. I will set out now within a few days and be absent all the month of May, and shall be very happy to see you here on my return, or as soon after as may be. It will give me the greatest pleasure, and our whole family joins in the invitation. If, consulting your own convenience and comfort, you would make us as long a stay there as should permit. You know our course of life. To place our friends at their ease we show them that we are so ourselves, by pursuing the necessary vocations of the day and enjoying their company at the usual hours of society.

You will find the summer of Monticello much cooler than that of Philadelphia, equally so with that of the neighborhood of that place, and more healthy. The amusements it offers are such as you know, which, to you, would be principally books and botany. Mr. Randolph's resignation of his military commission will enable him to be an associate in your botanical rambles. Come then, my dear sir, and be one of our family as long as you can bear a separation form the science of the world.

Since Bonaparte's[4] discomfiture I wish much to see you, to converse with you on the probable effect that will have on the state of the world, of its science, its liberty, its peace and prosperity, and particularly on the situation of our literary friends in Europe. Perceiving the order of nature to be that indi-

---

1. Abbe J. Correa de Serra (1750–1823): Portuguese botanist who studied in Rome and Naples and lived for a time in Paris. He moved to the United States in order to continue his research on natural history and published several botanical papers, most notably a book entitled *Collection de libro ineditos da historia Portuguesa*.

2. Thomas Mann Randolph (1768–1828): Jefferson's son-in-law.

3. William Short (1759–1849): lawyer, diplomat, and Jefferson's valued secretary and "adoptive son."

4. Napoleon I (1769–1821): Emperor of France from 1804–1814. His massive military campaigns conquered most of continental Europe. In 1812, his winter campaign in Russia suffered a major defeat; he was captured and exiled to the island of Elba. He later escaped, regained power, and continued to rule until he was finally defeated, in the Battle of Waterloo (1815), by an alliance of European powers led by the Duke of Wellington.

vidual happiness shall be inseparable from the practice of virtue, I am willing to hope it may have ordained that the fall of the wicked shall be the rise of the good.

I can readily fulfill M. Cuvier's request for the skin and skeleton of the mink. I have procured a fine skin and can at any time get the entire subject. The difficulty will be to find a vessel which would receive so large a subject and preserve the spirits in which it would be immersed. But this shall be an article of consultation when you are with us. The cranium of the buffalo cannot be procured but from the other side of the Mississippi; there I can obtain it. But it must go thence by the way of New Orleans, which cannot well be till peace. . . .

TO THOMAS LAW[1]

Poplar Forest, June 13, 1814

DEAR SIR, — The copy of your Second Thoughts on Instinctive Impulses, with the letter accompanying it, was received just as I was setting out on a journey to this place, two or three days' distant from Monticello. I brought it with me and read it with great satisfaction, and with the more as it contained exactly my own creed on the foundation of morality in man. It is really curious that on a question so fundamental, such a variety of opinions should have prevailed among men, and those, too, of the most exemplary virtue and first order of understanding. It shows how necessary was the care of the Creator in making the moral principle so much a part of our constitution as that no errors of reasoning or of speculation might lead us astray from its observance in practice. Of all the theories on this question, the most whimsical seems to have been that of Wollaston,[2] who considers *truth* as the foundation of morality. The thief who steals your guinea does wrong only inasmuch as he acts a lie in using your guinea as if it were his own. Truth is certainly a branch of morality, and a very important one to society. But presented as its foundation, it is as if a tree taken up by the roots, had its stem reversed in the air, and one of its branches planted in the ground. Some have made the *love of God* the foundation of morality. This, too, is but a branch of our moral duties, which are generally divided into duties to God and duties to man. If we did a good act merely from the love of God and a belief that it is pleasing to Him, whence arises the morality of the Atheist? It is idle to say, as some do, that no such being exists. We have the same evidence of the fact as of most of those we act on, to-wit: their own affirmations, and their reasonings in support of them. I have observed, indeed, generally, that while in protestant countries the defections from the Platonic Christianity of the priests is to Deism,[3] in catholic

---

1. Thomas Law (1756–1834) was born in England, emigrated to America in 1793, and married a granddaughter of Martha Washington. A capitalist and economist, Law wrote a series of reports recommending the establishment of a uniform currency and devised a number of financial plans for the United States.

2. William Wollaston (1659–1724): English philosopher who wrote *The Religion of Nature Delineated* (1722).

3. The belief, based solely on reason, in a God who created the universe and then abandoned it, assuming no control over life, exerting no influence on natural phenomena, and giving no supernatural revelation.

countries they are to Atheism. Diderot, D'Alembert, D'Holbach, Condorcet,[4] are known to have been among the most virtuous of men. Their virtue, then, must have had some other foundation than the love of God.

The To καλον[5] of others is founded in a different faculty, that of taste, which is not even a branch of morality. We have indeed an innate sense of what we call beautiful, but that is exercised chiefly on subjects addressed to the fancy, whether through the eye in visible forms, as landscape, animal figure, dress, drapery, architecture, the composition of colors, &c., or to the imagination directly, as imagery, style, or measure in prose or poetry, or whatever else constitutes the domain of criticism or taste, a faculty entirely distinct from the moral one. Self-interest, or rather self-love, or *egoism*, has been more plausibly substituted as the basis of morality. But I consider our relations with others as constituting the boundaries of morality. With ourselves we stand on the ground of identity, not of relation, which last, requiring two subjects, excludes self-love confined to a single one. To ourselves, in strict language, we can owe no duties, obligation requiring also two parties. Self-love, therefore, is no part of morality. Indeed it is exactly its counterpart. It is the sole antagonist of virtue, leading us constantly by our propensities to self-gratification in violation of our moral duties to others. Accordingly, it is against this enemy that are erected the batteries of moralists and religionists, as the only obstacle to the practice of morality. Take from man his selfish propensities, and he can have nothing to seduce him from the practice of virtue. Or subdue those propensities by education, instruction or restraint, and virtue remains without a competitor. Egoism, in a broader sense, has been thus presented as the source of moral action. It has been said that we feed the hungry, clothe the naked, bind up the wounds of the man beaten by thieves, pour oil and wine into them, set him on our own beast and bring him to the inn, because we receive ourselves pleasure from these acts. So Helvetius,[6] one of the best men on earth, and the most ingenious advocate of this principle, after defining "interest" to mean not merely that which is pecuniary, but whatever may procure us pleasure or withdraw us from pain, [*de l'esprit* 2, 1,] says, [ib. 2, 2,] "the humane man is he to whom the sight of misfortune is insupportable, and who to rescue himself from this spectacle, is forced to succor the unfortunate object." This indeed is true. But it is one step short of the ultimate question. These good acts

4. All religious skeptics or atheists associated with the French Enlightenment, and contributors to Diderot's *Encyclopedia*. See note 2, p. 181.

5. The good and the beautiful.

6. Claude Adrien Helvetius (1715–71): French philosopher who subscribed to the materialistic and skeptical views of the Encyclopedists. Though his principal work *De l'espirit* (1758) was publicly burned in Paris, it was widely translated and read elsewhere.

give us pleasure, but how happens it that they give us pleasure? Because nature hath implanted in our breasts a love of others, a sense of duty to them, a moral instinct, in short, which prompts us irresistibly to feel and to succor their distresses, and protests against the language of Helvetius, [ib. 2, 5,] "what other motive than self-interest could determine a man to generous actions? It is as impossible for him to love what is good for the sake of good, as to love evil for the sake of evil." The Creator would indeed have been a bungling artist, had he intended man for a social animal, without planting in him social dispositions. It is true they are not planted in every man, because there is no rule without exceptions; but it is false reasoning which converts exceptions into the general rule. Some men are born without the organs of sight, or of hearing, or without hands. Yet it would be wrong to say that man is born without these faculties, and sight, hearing, and hands may with truth enter into the general definition of man. The want or imperfection of the moral sense in some men, like the want or imperfection of the senses of sight and hearing in others, is no proof that it is a general characteristic of the species. When it is wanting, we endeavor to supply the defect by education, by appeals to reason and calculation, by presenting to the being so unhappily conformed, other motives to do good and to eschew evil, such as the love, or the hatred, or rejection of those among whom he lives, and whose society is necessary to his happiness and even existence; demonstrations by sound calculation that honesty promotes interest in the long run; the rewards and penalties established by the laws; and ultimately the prospects of a future state of retribution for the evil as well as the good done while here. These are the correctives which are supplied by education, and which exercise the functions of the moralist, the preacher, and legislator; and they lead into a course of correct action all those whose disparity is not too profound to be eradicated. Some have argued against the existence of a moral sense, by saying that if nature had given us such a sense, impelling us to virtuous actions, and warning us against those which are vicious, then nature would also have designated, by some particular ear-marks, the two sets of actions which are, in themselves, the one virtuous and the other vicious. Whereas, we find, in fact, that the same actions are deemed virtuous in one country and vicious in another. The answer is that nature has constituted *utility* to man the standard and best of virtue. Men living in different countries, under different circumstances, different habits and regimens, may have different utilities; the same act, therefore, may be useful, and consequently virtuous in one country which is injurious and vicious in another differently circumstanced. sincerely, then, believe with you in the general existence of a moral instinct. I think it the brightest gem with which the human character is studded, and the want of it as more degrading than the most hideous of the bodily deformities. I am happy in reviewing the roll of associates in this principle which you present in your second letter, some of

which I had not before met with. To these might be added Lord Kaims,[7] one
of the ablest of our advocates, who goes so far as to say, in his *Principles of
Natural Religion*, that a man owes no duty to which he is not urged by some
impulsive feeling. This is correct, if referred to the standard of general feeling
in the given case, and not to the feeling of a single individual. Perhaps I may
misquote him, it being fifty years since I read his book.

The leisure and solitude of my situation here has led me to the indiscretion
of taxing you with a long letter on a subject whereon nothing new can be offered you. I will indulge myself no farther than to repeat the assurances of my
continued esteem and respect.

---

7. Henry Home, Lord Kames (1696–1782): Scottish moral sense philosopher. Jefferson refers to his *Essays on the Principles of Morality and Religion* (1751).

TO JOSEPH C. CABELL[1]

Monticello, Feb. 2, 1816

DEAR SIR, ... Doctor Smith, you say, asks what is the best elementary book on the principles of government? None in the world equal to the Review of Montesquieu,[2] printed at Philadelphia a few years ago. It has the advantage, too, of being equally sound and corrective of the principles of political economy; and all within the compass of a thin 8vo. Chipman's and Priestley's Principles of Government,[3] and the Federalists,[4] are excellent in many respects, but for fundamental principles not comparable to the Review. I have no objections to the printing my letter to Mr. Carr, if it will promote the interests of science; although it was not written with a view to its publication.

My letter of the 24th *ultimo*[5] conveyed to you the grounds of the two articles objected to the College bill. Your last presents one of them in a new point of view, that of the commencement of the ward schools as likely to render the law unpopular to the country. It must be a very inconsiderate and rough process of execution that would do this. My idea of the mode of carrying it into execution would be this: Declare the county *ipso facto*[6] divided into wards for the present, by the boundaries of the militia captaincies; somebody attend the ordinary muster of each company, having first desired the captain to call together a full one. There explain the object of the law to the people of the company, put to their vote whether they will have a school established, and the most central and convenient place for it; get them to meet and build

---

1. Joseph C. Cabell (1775–1856): worked closely with Jefferson in founding the University of Virginia. During his twenty-five years of public service in Virginia, Cabell advocated local government, popular education, and internal improvements, and worked to extend opportunities for general and secondary education for both sexes.

2. Comte Antoine Louis Claude Destutt de Tracy (1754–1836), a French philosopher, published a commentary and review of Montesquieu's *Spirit of the Laws* in 1811.

3. Joseph Priestley's *Essay on the First Principles of Government (1768)* and Nathaniel Chipman's *Principles of Government* (1793).

4. James Madison, John Jay, and Alexander Hamilton, writing under the collective pseudonym "Publius," defended the Constitution in a series of eighty-five pro-constitutional essays published in New York newspapers from 1787–88; these essays were later collected and published as *The Federalist* (or *The Federalist Papers*).

5. The preceding month.

6. Although "by the fact itself" is the precise meaning of this Latin expression, Jefferson seems to be using it a little loosely here to mean "in actual fact, in practice."

a log school-house; have a roll taken of the children who would attend it, and of those of them able to pay. These would probably be sufficient to support a common teacher, instructing gratis the few unable to pay. If there should be a deficiency, it would require too trifling a contribution from the county to be complained of; and especially as the whole county would participate, where necessary, in the same resource. Should the company, by its vote, decide that it would have no school, let them remain without one. The advantages of this proceeding would be that it would become the duty of the alderman[7] elected by the county, to take an active part in pressing the introduction of schools, and to look out for tutors. If, however, it is intended that the State government shall take this business into its own hands, and provide schools for every county, then by all means strike out this provision of our bill. I would never wish that it should be placed on a worse footing than the rest of the State. But if it is believed that these elementary schools will be better managed by the governor and council, the commissioners of the literary fund, or any other general authority of the government, than by the parents within each ward, it is a belief against all experience. Try the principle one step further, and amend the bill so as to commit to the governor and council the management of all our farms, our mills, and merchants' stores. No, my friend, the way to have good and safe government, is not to trust it all to one, but to divide it among the many, distributing to every one exactly the functions he is competent to. Let the national government be entrusted with the defence of the nation, and its foreign and federal relations; the State governments with the civil rights, laws, police, and administration of what concerns the State generally; the counties with the local concerns of the counties, and each ward direct the interests within itself. It is by dividing and subdividing these republics from the great national one down through all its subordinations, until it ends in the administration of every man's farm by himself; by placing under every one what his own eye may superintend, that all will be done for the best. What has destroyed liberty and the rights of man in every government which has ever existed under the sun? The generalizing and concentrating all cares and powers into one body, no matter whether of the autocrats of Russia or France, or of the aristocrats of a Venetian senate. And I do believe that if the Almighty has not decreed that man shall never be free, (and it is a blasphemy to believe it,) that the secret will be found to be in the making himself the depository of the powers respecting himself, so far as he is competent to them, and delegating only what is beyond his competence by a synthetical process, to higher and higher orders of functionaries, so as to trust fewer and fewer powers in proportion as the trustees become more and more oligarchical. The elementary republics of the wards, the county republics, the States republics, and the

7. A municipal official.

republic of the Union, would form a gradation of authorities, standing each on the basis of law, holding every one its delegated share of powers, and constituting truly a system of fundamental balances and checks for the government. Where every man is a sharer in the direction of his ward-republic, or of some of the higher ones, and feels that he is a participator in the government of affairs, not merely at an election one day in the year, but every day; when there shall not be a man in the State who will not be a member of some one of its councils, great or small, he will let the heart be torn out of his body sooner than his power be wrested from him by a Caesar or a Bonaparte.[8] How powerfully did we feel the energy of this organization in the case of embargo?[9] I felt the foundations of the government shaken under my feet by the New England townships. There was not an individual in their States whose body was not thrown with all its momentum into action; and although the whole of the other States were known to be in favor of the measure, yet the organization of this little selfish minority enabled it to overrule the Union. What would the unwieldy counties of the middle, the south, and the west do? Call a county meeting, and the drunken loungers at and about the court houses would have collected, the distances being too great for the good people and the industrious generally to attend. The character of those who really met would have been the measure of the weight they would have had in the scale of public opinion. As Cato, then, concluded every speech with the words, *"Carthago delenda est,"*[10] so do I every opinion, with the injunction, "divide the counties into wards." Begin them only for a single purpose; they will soon show for what others they are the best instruments. God bless you, and all our rulers, and give them the wisdom, as I am sure they have the will, to fortify us against the degeneracy of one government, and the concentration of all its powers in the hands of the one, the few, the well-born or the many.

---

8. Julius Caesar (100–44 BC) and Napoleon Bonaparte (1769–1821) both overthrew republics and established themselves as emperors. (See notes 8 and 4 on pp. 100 and 220, respectively.)

9. See Introduction, p. xxiii.

10. "Carthage must be destroyed." Cato is Marcus Porcius Cato (234–149 BC), or Cato the Elder, a Roman orator and writer. (See note 32, p. 117.)

TO P. S. DUPONT DE NEMOURS[1]

Poplar Forest, Apr. 24, 1816

I received, my dear friend, your letter covering the constitution for your Equinoctial[2] republics, just as I was setting out for this place. I brought it with me, and have read it with great satisfaction. I suppose it well formed for those for whom it was intended, and the excellence of every government is its adaptation to the state of those to be governed by it. For us it would not do. Distinguishing between the structure of the government and the moral principles on which you prescribe its administration, with the latter we concur cordially, with the former we should not. We of the United States, you know, are constitutionally and conscientiously democrats. We consider society as one of the natural wants with which man has been created; that he has been endowed with faculties and qualities to effect its satisfaction by concurrence of others having the same want; that when, by the exercise of these faculties, he has procured a state of society, it is one of his acquisitions which he has a right to regulate and control, jointly indeed with all those who have concurred in the procurement, whom he cannot exclude from its use or direction more than they him. We think experience has proved it safer, for the mass of individuals composing the society, to reserve to themselves personally the exercise of all rightful powers to which they are competent, and to delegate those to which they are not competent to deputies named, and removable for unfaithful conduct, by themselves immediately. Hence, with us, the people (by which is meant the mass of individuals composing the society) being competent to judge of the facts occurring in ordinary life, they have retained the functions of judges of facts, under the name of jurors; but being unqualified for the management of affairs requiring intelligence above the common level, yet competent judges of human character, they chose, for their management, representatives, some by themselves immediately, others by electors chosen by themselves. Thus our President is chosen by ourselves, directly in *practice*, for we vote for A as elector only on the condition he will vote for B, our representatives by ourselves immediately, our Senate and judges of law through

---

1. Pierre-Samuel Dupont de Nemours (1739–1817) was part of the influential circle of French thinkers, known as the *Economistes,* surrounding the economic minister Turgot (1727–81). He and Jefferson carried on an extensive correspondence. (His son, Éleuthère-Irénée, later emigrated to the United States and founded the Dupont Chemical Firm.)
2. Equatorial.

electors chosen by ourselves. And we believe that this proximate choice and power of removal is the best security which experience has sanctioned for ensuring an honest conduct in the functionaries of society. Your three or four alembications[3] have indeed a seducing appearance. We should conceive *primâ facie*,[4] that the last extract would be the pure alcohol of the substance, three or four times rectified. But in proportion as they are more and more sublimated, they are also farther and farther removed from the control of the society; and the human character, we believe, requires in general constant and immediate control, to prevent its being biased from right by the seductions of self-love. Your process produces therefore a structure of government from which the fundamental principle of ours is excluded. You first set down as zeros all individuals not having lands, which are the greater number in every society of long standing. Those holding lands are permitted to manage in person the small affairs of their commune or corporation, and to elect a deputy for the canton; in which election, too, every one's vote is to be an unit, a plurality, or a fraction, in proportion to his landed possessions. The assemblies of cantons, then, elect for the districts; those of districts for circles; and those of circles for the national assemblies. Some of these highest councils, too, are in a considerable degree self-elected, the regency partially, the judiciary entirely, and some are for life. Whenever, therefore, an *esprit de corps*,[5] or of party, gets possession of them, which experience shows to be inevitable, there are no means of breaking it up, for they will never elect but those of their own spirit. Juries are allowed in criminal cases only. I acknowledge myself strong in affection to our own form, yet both of us act and think from the same motive, we both consider the people as our children, and love them with parental affection. But you love them as infants whom you are afraid to trust without nurses; and I as adults whom I freely leave to self-government. And you are right in the case referred to you; my criticism being built on a state of society not under your contemplation. It is, in fact, like a critic on Homer by the laws of the Drama.

But when we come to the moral principles on which the government is to be administered, we come to what is proper for all conditions of society. I meet you there in all the benevolence and rectitude of your native character; and I love myself always most where I concur most with you. Liberty, truth, probity, honor, are declared to be the four cardinal principles of your society. I believe with you that morality, compassion, generosity, are innate elements of the human constitution; that there exists a right independent of force; that

---

3. Distillations.
4. On the face of it, at first sight.
5. Common spirit.

a right to property is founded in our natural wants, in the means with which we are endowed to satisfy these wants, and the right to what we acquire by those means without violating the similar rights of other sensible beings; that no one has a right to obstruct another, exercising his faculties innocently for the relief of sensibilities made a part of his nature; that justice is the fundamental law of society; that the majority, oppressing an individual, is guilty of a crime, abuses its strength, and by acting on the law of the strongest breaks up the foundations of society; that action by the citizens in person, in affairs within their reach and competence, and in all others by representatives, chosen immediately, and removable by themselves, constitutes the essence of a republic; that all governments are more or less republican in proportion as this principle enters more or less into their composition; and that a government by representation is capable of extension over a greater surface of country than one of any other form. These, my friend, are the essentials in which you and I agree; however, in our zeal for their maintenance, we may be perplexed and divaricate,[6] as to the structure of society most likely to secure them.

In the constitution of Spain, as proposed by the late Cortes,[7] there was a principle entirely new to me, and not noticed in yours, that no person, born after that day, should ever acquire the rights of citizenship until he could read and write. It is impossible sufficiently to estimate the wisdom of this provision. Of all those which have been thought of for securing fidelity in the administration of the government, constant ralliance[8] to the principles of the constitution, and progressive amendments with the progressive advances of the human mind, or changes in human affairs, it is the most effectual. Enlighten the people generally, and tyranny and oppressions of body and mind will vanish like evil spirits at the dawn of day. Although I do not, with some enthusiasts, believe that the human condition will ever advance to such a state of perfection as that there shall no longer be pain or vice in the world, yet I believe it susceptible of much improvement, and most of all, in matters of government and religion; and that the diffusion of knowledge among the people is to be the instrument by which it is to be effected. The constitution of the Cortes had defects enough; but when I saw in it this amendatory provision, I was satisfied all would come right in time, under its salutary operation. No people have more need of a similar provision than those for whom you have felt so much interest. No mortal wishes them more success than I do. But if what I have heard of the ignorance and bigotry of the mass be true, I doubt their capacity to understand and to support a free government; and fear

---

6. To separate or spread apart.
7. The Spanish Parliament.
8. Rallying.

that their emancipation from the foreign tyranny of Spain, will result in a military despotism at home. Palacios may be great; others may be great; but it is the multitude which possess force: and wisdom must yield to that. For such a condition of society, the constitution you have devised is probably the best imaginable. It is certainly calculated to elicit the best talents; although perhaps not well guarded against the egoism of its functionaries. But that egoism will be light in comparison with the pressure of a military despot, and his army of Janissaries.[9] Like Solon[10] to the Athenians, you have given to your Columbians,[11] not the best possible government, but the best they can bear. By-the-bye, I wish you had called them the Columbian republics, to distinguish them from our American republics. Theirs would be the most honorable name, and they best entitled to it; for Columbus discovered their continent, but never saw ours.

To them liberty and happiness; to you the meed of wisdom and goodness in teaching them how to attain them, with the affectionate respect and friendship of,

---

9. The elite Turkish guard; any group of highly loyal supporters.

10. Solon (d. 559 BC): Athenian lawgiver known for giving the Athenians not the best laws, but "the best they were able to receive."

11. The people of Colombia, South America.

To John Taylor[1]

Monticello, May 28, 1816

DEAR SIR, — On my return from a long journey and considerable absence from home, I found here the copy of your "Enquiry into the principles of our government," which you had been so kind as to send me; and for which I pray you to accept my thanks. The difficulties of getting new works in our situation, inland and without a single bookstore, are such as had prevented my obtaining a copy before; and letters which had accumulated during my absence, and were calling for answers, have not yet permitted me to give to the whole a thorough reading; yet certain that you and I could not think differently on the fundamentals of rightful government, I was impatient, and availed myself of the intervals of repose from the writing table, to obtain a cursory idea of the body of the work.

I see in it much matter for profound reflection; much which should confirm our adhesion, in practice, to the good principles of our constitution, and fix our attention on what is yet to be made good. The sixth section on the good moral principles of our government, I found so interesting and replete with sound principles, as to postpone my letter-writing to its thorough perusal and consideration. Besides much other good matter, it settles unanswerably the right of instructing representatives, and their duty to obey. The system of banking we have both equally and ever reprobated. I contemplate it as a blot left in all our constitutions, which, if not covered, will end in their destruction, which is already hit by the gamblers in corruption, and is sweeping away in its progress the fortunes and morals of our citizens. Funding I consider as limited, rightfully, to a redemption of the debt within the lives of a majority of the generation contracting it; every generation coming equally, by the laws of the Creator of the world, to the free possession of the earth he made for their subsistence, unincumbered by their predecessors, who, like them, were but tenants for life. You have successfully and completely pulverized Mr. Adams' system of orders, and his opening the mantle of republicanism to every

---

1. John Taylor (1753–1824): Virginia political writer and staunch supporter of Jefferson. His essays championed states' rights, localism, individualism, and agrarianism. He served in both the Virginia legislature and the U.S. Senate. After the election of 1800 he helped pass the 12th Amendment, which provided for the separate election of president and vice president. Taylor's statement of his political beliefs, *An Enquiry into the Principles and Policy of the Government of the United States,* was published in 1814.

government of laws, whether consistent or not with natural right. Indeed, it must be acknowledged, that the term *republic* is of very vague application in every language. Witness the self-styled republics of Holland, Switzerland, Genoa, Venice, Poland. Were I to assign to this term a precise and definite idea, I would say, purely and simply, it means a government by its citizens in mass, acting directly and personally, according to rules established by the majority; and that every other government is more or less republican, in proportion as it has in its composition more or less of this ingredient of the direct action of the citizens. Such a government is evidently restrained to very narrow limits of space and population. I doubt if it would be practicable beyond the extent of a New England township. The first shade from this pure element, which, like that of pure vital air, cannot sustain life of itself, would be where the powers of the government, being divided, should be exercised each by representatives chosen either *pro hac vice*,[2] or for such short terms as should render secure the duty of expressing the will of their constituents. This I should consider as the nearest approach to a pure republic, which is practicable on a large scale of country or population. And we have examples of it in some of our States constitutions, which, if not poisoned by priest-craft, would prove its excellence over all mixtures with other elements; and, with only equal doses of poison, would still be the best. Other shades of republicanism may be found in other forms of government, where the executive, judiciary and legislative functions, and the different branches of the latter, are chosen by the people more or less directly, for longer terms of years or for life, or made hereditary; or where there are mixtures of authorities, some dependent on, and others independent of the people. The further the departure from direct and constant control by the citizens, the less has the government of the ingredient of republicanism; evidently none where the authorities are hereditary, as in France, Venice, &c., or self-chosen, as in Holland; and little, where for life, in proportion as the life continues in being after the act of election.

The purest republican feature in the government of our own State, is the House of Representatives. The Senate is equally so the first year, less the second, and so on. The Executive still less, because not chosen by the people directly. The Judiciary seriously anti-republican, because for life; and the national arm wielded, as you observe, by military leaders irresponsible but to themselves. Add to this the vicious constitution of our county courts (to whom the justice, the executive administration, the taxation, police, the military appointments of the county, and nearly all our daily concerns are confided), self-appointed, self-continued, holding their authorities for life, and with an impossibility of breaking in on the perpetual succession of any faction once

---

2. For this occasion.

possessed of the bench. They are in truth, the executive, the judiciary, and the military of their respective counties, and the sum of the counties makes the State. And add, also, that one half of our brethren who fight and pay taxes, are excluded, like Helots,[3] from the rights of representation, as if society were instituted for the soil, and not for the men inhabiting it; or one half of these could dispose of the rights and the will of the other half, without their consent.

> "What constitutes a State?
> Not high-raised battlements, or labor'd mound,
>   Thick wall, or moated gate;
> Not cities proud, with spires and turrets crown'd;
>   No: men, high minded men;
>   Men, who their duties know;
> But know their rights; and knowing, dare maintain.
>   These constitute a State."[4]

In the General Government, the House of Representatives is mainly republican; the Senate scarcely so at all, as not elected by the people directly, and so long secured even against those who do elect them; the Executive more republican than the Senate, from its shorter term, its election by the people, in *practice*, (for they vote for A only on an assurance that he will vote for B,) and because, *in practice also*, a principle of rotation seems to be in a course of establishment; the judiciary independent of the nation, their coercion by impeachment being found nugatory.[5]

If, then, the control of the people over the organs of their government be the measure of its republicanism, and I confess I know no other measure, it must be agreed that our governments have much less of republicanism than ought to have been expected; in other words, that the people have less regular control over their agents, than their rights and their interests require. And this I ascribe, not to any want of republican dispositions in those who formed these constitutions, but to a submission of true principle to European authorities, to speculators on government, whose fears of the people have been inspired by the populace of their own great cities, and were unjustly entertained against the independent, the happy, and therefore orderly citizens of the United States. Much I apprehend that the golden moment is past for reforming these heresies. The functionaries of public power rarely strengthen in

---

3. The helots, a class of indentured workers in ancient Sparta, were neither slaves nor free men; they were trapped in a sort of serfdom that forced them to work but simultaneously deprived them of their rights.
4. Sir William Jones (1746–94), "An Ode in Imitation of Alcaeus."
5. Nonexistent.

their dispositions to abridge it, and an unorganized call for timely amendment is not likely to prevail against an organized opposition to it. We are always told that things are going on well; why change them? "*Chi sta bene, non si muove,*" said the Italian, "let him who stands well, stand still."[6] This is true; and I verily believe they would go on well with us under an absolute monarch, while our present character remains, of order, industry and love of peace, and restrained, as he would be, by the proper spirit of the people. But it is while it remains such, we should provide against the consequences of its deterioration. And let us rest in the hope that it will yet be done, and spare ourselves the pain of evils which may never happen.

On this view of the import of the term *republic*, instead of saying, as has been said, "that it may mean anything or nothing," we may say with truth and meaning, that governments are more or less republican as they have more or less of the element of popular election and control in their composition; and believing, as I do, that the mass of the citizens is the safest depository of their own rights, and especially, that the evils flowing from the duperies[7] of the people, are less injurious than those from the egoism of their agents, I am a friend to that composition of government which has in it the most of this ingredient. And I sincerely believe, with you, that banking establishments are more dangerous than standing armies; and that the principle of spending money to be paid by posterity, under the name of funding, is but swindling futurity on a large scale.

I salute you with constant friendship and respect.

---

6. An old Italian proverb.
7. Cons, when people are duped.

To Francis W. Gilmer[1]

Monticello, June 7, 1816

DEAR SIR — I received a few days ago from Mr. Dupont[2] the enclosed manuscript, with permission to read it, and a request, when read, to forward it to you, in expectation that you would translate it. It is well worthy of publication for the instruction of our citizens, being profound, sound, and short. Our legislators are not sufficiently apprised of the rightful limits of their power; that their true office is to declare and enforce only our natural rights and duties, and to take none of them from us. No man has a natural right to commit aggression on the equal rights of another; and this is all from which the laws ought to restrain him; every man is under the natural duty of contributing to the necessities of the society; and this is all the laws should enforce on him; and, no man having a natural right to be the judge between himself and another, it is his natural duty to submit to the umpirage of an impartial third. When the laws have declared and enforced all this, they have fulfilled their functions; and the idea is quite unfounded, that on entering into society we give up any natural right. The trial of every law by one of these texts, would lessen much the labors of our legislators, and lighten equally our municipal codes. There is a work of the first order of merit now in the press at Washington, by Destutt Tracy,[3] on the subject of political economy, which he brings into the compass of three hundred pages, octavo.[4] In a preliminary discourse on the origin of the right of property, he coincides much with the principles of the present manuscript; but is more developed, more demonstrative. He promises a future work on morals, in which I lament to see that he will adopt the principles of Hobbes,[5] or humiliation to human nature; that the sense of justice and injustice is not derived from our natural organization, but founded

---

1. Francis W. Gilmer (1790–1826): Jefferson's neighbor and acquaintance. Gilmer's grandfather, Dr. Thomas Walker, was once Jefferson's guardian. In 1824, Gilmer traveled to Europe in order to recruit professors, and buy books and equipment, for the University of Virginia.
2. Pierre-Samuel Dupont de Nemours (1739–1817): an influential French philosopher and economist. (See note 1, p. 229.)
3. Comte Antoine Louis Claude Destutt de Tracy (1754–1836): French philosopher. (See note 2, p. 226.)
4. A book composed of printer's sheets folded into eight leaves.
5. Thomas Hobbes (1588–1679): English political philosopher, author of *Leviathan* (1651).

on convention only. I lament this the more, as he is unquestionably the ablest writer living, on abstract subjects. Assuming the fact, that the earth has been created in time, and consequently the dogma of final causes, we yield, of course, to this short syllogism. Man was created for social intercourse; but social intercourse cannot be maintained without a sense of justice; then man must have been created with a sense of justice. There is an error into which most of the speculators on government have fallen, and which the well-known state of society of our Indians ought, before now, to have corrected. In their hypothesis of the origin of government, they suppose it to have commenced in the patriarchal or monarchical form. Our Indians are evidently in that state of nature which has passed the association of a single family; and not yet submitted to the authority of positive laws, or of any acknowledged magistrate. Every man, with them, is perfectly free to follow his own inclinations. But if, in doing this, he violates the rights of another, if the case be slight, he is punished by the disesteem of his society, or, as we say, by public opinion; if serious, he is tomahawked as a dangerous enemy. Their leaders conduct them by the influence of their character only; and they follow, or not, as they please, him of whose character for wisdom or war they have the highest opinion. Hence the origin of the parties among them adhering to different leaders, and governed by their advice, not by their command. The Cherokees, the only tribe I know to be contemplating the establishment of regular laws, magistrates, and government, propose a government of representatives, elected from every town. But of all things, they least think of subjecting themselves to the will of one man. This, the only instance of actual fact within our knowledge, will be then a beginning by republican, and not by patriarchal or monarchical government, as speculative writers have generally conjectured. . . .

To Samuel Kercheval[1]

Monticello, July 12, 1816

Sir, — I duly received your favor of June the 13th, with the copy of the letters on the calling a convention, on which you are pleased to ask my opinion. I have not been in the habit of mysterious reserve on any subject, nor of buttoning up my opinions within my own doublet. On the contrary, while in public service especially, I thought the public entitled to frankness, and intimately to know whom they employed. But I am now retired: I resign myself, as a passenger, with confidence to those at present at the helm, and ask but for rest, peace and good will. The question you propose, on equal representation, has become a party one, in which I wish to take no public share. Yet, if it be asked for your own satisfaction only, and not to be quoted before the public, I have no motive to withhold it, and the less from you, as it coincides with your own. At the birth of our republic, I committed that opinion to the world, in the draught of a constitution annexed to the "Notes on Virginia," in which a provision was inserted for a representation permanently equal. The infancy of the subject at that moment, and our inexperience of self-government, occasioned gross departures in that draught from genuine republican canons. In truth, the abuses of monarchy had so much filled all the space of political contemplation, that we imagined everything republican which was not monarchy. We had not yet penetrated to the mother principle, that "governments are republican only in proportion as they embody the will of their people, and execute it." Hence, our first constitutions had really no leading principles in them. But experience and reflection have but more and more confirmed me in the particular importance of the equal representation then proposed. On that point, then, I am entirely in sentiment with your letters; and only lament that a copy-right of your pamphlet prevents their appearance in the newspapers, where alone they would be generally read, and produce general effect. The present vacancy too, of other matter, would give them place in every paper, and bring the question home to every man's conscience.

But inequality of representation in both Houses of our legislature, is not the only republican heresy in this first essay[2] of our revolutionary patriots at

---

1. Samuel Kercheval, who lived in western Virginia, urged Jefferson to support a state constitutional convention to correct the malapportionment of representation in the legislature.
2. Attempt.

forming a constitution. For let it be agreed that a government is republican in proportion as every member composing it has his equal voice in the direction of its concerns (not indeed in person, which would be impracticable beyond the limits of a city, or small township, but) by representatives chosen by himself, and responsible to him at short periods, and let us bring to the test of this canon every branch of our constitution.

In the legislature, the House of Representatives is chosen by less than half the people, and not at all in proportion to those who do choose. The Senate are still more disproportionate, and for long terms of irresponsibility. In the Executive, the Governor is entirely independent of the choice of the people, and of their control; his Council equally so, and at best but a fifth wheel to a wagon. In the Judiciary, the judges of the highest courts are dependent on none but themselves. In England, where judges were named and removable at the will of an hereditary executive, from which branch most misrule was feared, and has flowed, it was a great point gained, by fixing them for life, to make them independent of that executive. But in a government founded on the public will, this principle operates in an opposite direction, and against that will. There, too, they were still removable on a concurrence of the executive and legislative branches. But we have made them independent of the nation itself. They are irremovable, but by their own body, for any depravities of conduct, and even by their own body for the imbecilities of dotage. The justices of the inferior courts are self-chosen, are for life, and perpetuate their own body in succession forever, so that a faction once possessing themselves of the bench of a county, can never be broken up, but hold their county in chains, forever indissoluble. Yet these justices are the real executive as well as judiciary, in all our minor and most ordinary concerns. They tax us at will; fill the office of sheriff, the most important of all the executive officers of the county; name nearly all our military leaders, which leaders, once named, are removable but by themselves. The juries, our judges of all fact, and of law when they choose it, are not selected by the people, nor amenable to them. They are chosen by an officer named by the court and executive. Chosen, did I say? Picked up by the sheriff from the loungings of the court yard, after everything respectable has retired from it. Where then is our republicanism to be found? Not in our constitution certainly, but merely in the spirit of our people. That would oblige even a despot to govern us republicanly. Owing to this spirit, and to nothing in the form of our constitution, all things have gone well. But this fact, so triumphantly misquoted by the enemies of reformation, is not the fruit of our constitution, but has prevailed in spite of it. Our functionaries have done well, because generally honest men. If any were not so, they feared to show it.

But it will be said, it is easier to find faults than to amend them. I do not think their amendment so difficult as is pretended. Only lay down true principles, and adhere to them inflexibly. Do not be frightened into their surrender by the alarms of the timid, or the croakings of wealth against the ascendency of the people. If experience be called for, appeal to that of our fifteen or twenty governments for forty years, and show me where the people have done half the mischief in these forty years, that a single despot would have done in a single year; or show half the riots and rebellions, the crimes and the punishments, which have taken place in any single nation, under kingly government, during the same period. The true foundation of republican government is the equal right of every citizen, in his person and property, and in their management. Try by this, as a tally, every provision of our constitution, and see if it hangs directly on the will of the people. Reduce your legislature to a convenient number for full, but orderly discussion. Let every man who fights or pays, exercise his just and equal right in their election. Submit them to approbation or rejection at short intervals. Let the executive be chosen in the same way, and for the same term, by those whose agent he is to be; and leave no screen of a council behind which to skulk from responsibility. It has been thought that the people are not competent electors of judges *learned in the law*. But I do not know that this is true, and, if doubtful, we should follow principle. In this, as in many other elections, they would be guided by reputation, which would not err oftener, perhaps, than the present mode of appointment. In one State of the Union, at least, it has long been tried, and with the most satisfactory success. The judges of Connecticut have been chosen by the people every six months, for nearly two centuries, and believe there has hardly ever been an instance of change; so powerful is the curb of incessant responsibility. If prejudice, however, derived from a monarchical institution, is still to prevail against the vital elective principle of our own, and if the existing example among ourselves of periodical election of judges by the people be still mistrusted, let us at least not adopt the evil, and reject the good, of the English precedent; let us retain amovability[3] on the concurrence of the executive and legislative branches, and nomination by the executive alone. Nomination to office is an executive function. To give it to the legislature, as we do, is a violation of the principle of the separation of powers. It swerves the members from correctness, by temptations to intrigue for office themselves, and to a corrupt barter of votes; and destroys responsibility by dividing it among a multitude. By leaving nomination in its proper place, among executive functions, the principle of the distribution of power is preserved, and responsibility weighs with its heaviest force on a single head.

The organization of our county administrations may be thought more difficult. But follow principle, and the knot unties itself. Divide the counties into

---

3. Liability to be removed or dismissed from office.

wards of such size as that every citizen can attend, when called on, and act in person. Ascribe to them the government of their wards in all things relating to themselves exclusively. A justice, chosen by themselves, in each, a constable, a military company, a patrol, a school, the care of their own poor, their own portion of the public roads, the choice of one or more jurors to serve in some court, and the delivery, within their own wards, of their own votes for all elective officers of higher sphere, will relieve the county administration of nearly all its business, will have it better done, and by making every citizen an acting member of the government, and in the offices nearest and most interesting to him, will attach him by his strongest feelings to the independence of his country, and its republican constitution. The justices thus chosen by every ward, would constitute the county court, would do its judiciary business, direct roads and bridges, levy county and poor rates, and administer all the matters of common interest to the whole country. These wards, called townships in New England, are the vital principle of their governments, and have proved themselves the wisest invention ever devised by the wit of man for the perfect exercise of self-government, and for its preservation. We should thus marshal our government into, 1, the general federal republic, for all concerns foreign and federal; 2, that of the State, for what relates to our own citizens exclusively; 3, the county republics, for the duties and concerns of the county; and 4, the ward republics, for the small, and yet numerous and interesting concerns of the neighborhood; and in government, as well as in every other business of life, it is by division and subdivision of duties alone, that all matters, great and small, can be managed to perfection. And the whole is cemented by giving to every citizen, personally, a part in the administration of the public affairs.

The sum of these amendments is, 1. General Suffrage. 2. Equal representation in the legislature. 3. An executive chosen by the people. 4. Judges elective or amovable. 5. Justices, jurors, and sheriffs elective. 6. Ward divisions. And 7. Periodical amendments of the constitution.

I have thrown out these as loose heads of amendment, for consideration and correction; and their object is to secure self-government by the republicanism of our constitution, as well as by the spirit of the people; and to nourish and perpetuate that spirit. I am not among those who fear the people. They, and not the rich, are our dependence for continued freedom. And to preserve their independence, we must not let our rulers load us with perpetual debt. We must make our election between *economy and liberty*, or *profusion and servitude*. If we run into such debts, as that we must be taxed in our meat and in our drink, in our necessaries and our comforts, in our labors and our amusements, for our callings and our creeds, as the people of England are, our people, like them, must come to labor sixteen hours in the twenty-four, give the earnings of fifteen of these to the government for their debts and daily expenses; and the sixteenth being insufficient to afford us bread, we must live, as they now do, on oatmeal and potatoes; have no time to think, no means of calling the mismanagers to account; but be glad to obtain subsistence by hiring ourselves to rivet their chains on the necks of our fellow-sufferers. Our landholders, too, like theirs, retaining indeed the title and stewardship of estates called theirs, but held really in trust for the treasury, must wander, like theirs, in foreign countries, and be contented with penury, obscurity, exile, and the glory of the nation. This example reads to us the salutary lesson, that private fortunes are destroyed by public as well as by private extravagance. And this is the tendency of all human governments. A departure from principle in one instance becomes a precedent for a second; that second for a third; and so on, till the bulk of the society is reduced to be mere automatons of misery, and to have no sensibilities left but for sinning and suffering. Then begins, indeed, the *bellum omnium in omnia*,[4] which some philosophers observing to be so general in this world, have mistaken it for the natural, instead of the abusive state of man. And the fore horse of this frightful team is public debt. Taxation follows that, and in its train wretchedness and oppression.

Some men look at constitutions with sanctimonious reverence, and deem them like the arc of the covenant,[5] too sacred to be touched. They ascribe to the men of the preceding age a wisdom more than human, and suppose what they did to be beyond amendment. I knew that age well; I belonged to it, and labored with it. It deserved well of its country. It was very like the present, but without the experience of the present; and forty years of experience in government is worth a century of book-reading; and this they would say themselves, were they to rise from the dead. I am certainly not an advocate for frequent and untried changes in laws and constitutions. I think moderate imperfections had better be borne with; because, when once known, we accommodate ourselves to them, and find practical means of correcting their ill effects. But I know also, that laws and institutions must go hand in hand with the progress of the human mind. As that becomes more developed, more enlightened, as new discoveries are made, new truths disclosed, and manners and opinions change with the change of circumstances, institutions must advance also, and keep pace with the times. We might as well require a man to wear still the coat which fitted him when a boy, as civilized society to remain ever under the regimen of their barbarous ancestors. It is this preposterous idea which has lately deluged Europe in blood. Their monarchs, instead of wisely yielding to the

---

4. *Bellum omnium in omnia:* "war of all against all," a reference to Thomas Hobbes' "war of every man against every man" (*Leviathan*, ch. 13). (See note 26 on p. 108.)
5. According to the Bible, the Ark of the Covenant was the chest in which Moses placed the Ten Commandments.

gradual change of circumstances, of favoring progressive accommodation to progressive improvement, have clung to old abuses, entrenched themselves behind steady habits, and obliged their subjects to seek through blood and violence rash and ruinous innovations, which, had they been referred to the peaceful deliberations and collected wisdom of the nation, would have been put into acceptable and salutary forms. Let us follow no such examples, nor weakly believe that one generation is not as capable as another of taking care of itself, and of ordering its own affairs. Let us, as our sister States have done, avail ourselves of our reason and experience, to correct the crude essays of our first and unexperienced, although wise, virtuous, and well-meaning councils. And lastly, let us provide in our constitution for its revision at stated periods. What these periods should be, nature herself indicates. By the European tables of mortality, of the adults living at any one moment of time, a majority will be dead in about nineteen years. At the end of that period, then, a new majority is come into place; or, in other words, a new generation. Each generation is as independent as the one preceding, as that was of all which had gone before. It has then, like them, a right to choose for itself the form of government it believes most promotive of its own happiness; consequently, to accommodate to the circumstances in which it finds itself, that received from its predecessors; and it is for the peace and good of mankind, that a solemn opportunity of doing this every nineteen or twenty years, should be provided by the constitution; so that it may be handed on, with periodical repairs, from generation to generation, to the end of time, if anything human can so long endure. It is now forty years since the constitution of Virginia was formed. The same tables inform us, that, within that period, two-thirds of the adults then living are now dead. Have then the remaining third, even if they had the wish, the right to hold in obedience to their will, and to laws heretofore made by them, the other two-thirds, who, with themselves, compose the present mass of adults? If they have not, who has? The dead? But the dead have no rights. They are nothing; and nothing cannot own something. Where there is no substance, there can be no accident. This corporeal globe, and everything upon it, belong to its present corporeal inhabitants, during their generation. They alone have a right to direct what is the concern of themselves alone, and to declare the law of that direction; and this declaration can only be made by their majority. That majority, then, has a right to depute representatives to a convention, and to make the constitution what they think will be the best for themselves. But how collect their voice? This is the real difficulty. If invited by private authority, or county or district meetings, these divisions are so large that few will attend; and their voice will be imperfectly, or falsely pronounced. Here, then, would be one of the advantages of the ward divisions I have proposed. The mayor of every ward, on a question like the present, would call his ward together, take the simple yea or nay of its members, convey these to the county court, who would hand on those of all its wards to the proper general authority; and the voice of the whole people would be thus fairly, fully, and peaceably expressed, discussed, and decided by the common reason of the society. If this avenue be shut to the call of sufferance, it will make itself heard through that of force, and we shall go on, as other nations are doing, in the endless circle of oppression, rebellion, reformation; and oppression, rebellion, reformation, again; and so on forever.

These, Sir, are my opinions of the governments we see among men, and of the principles by which alone we may prevent our own from falling into the same dreadful track. I have given them at greater length than your letter called for. But I cannot say things by halves; and I confide them to your honor, so to use them as to preserve me from the gridiron of the public papers. If you shall approve and enforce them, as you have done that of equal representation, they may do some good. If not, keep them to yourself as the effusions of withered age and useless time. shall, with not the less truth, assure you of my great respect and consideration.

To Isaac H. Tiffany[1]

Monticello, Aug. 26, 1816

SIR, — In answer to your inquiry as to the merits of Gillies' translation of the Politics of Aristotle,[2] I can only say that it has the reputation of being preferable to Ellis', the only rival translation into English. I have never seen it myself, and therefore do not speak of it from my own knowledge. But so different was the style of society then, and with those people, from what it is now and with us, that I think little edification can be obtained from their writings on the subject of government. They had just ideas of the value of personal liberty, but none at all of the structure of government best calculated to preserve it. They knew no medium between a democracy (the only pure republic, but impracticable beyond the limits of a town) and an abandonment of themselves to an aristocracy, or a tyranny independent of the people. It seems not to have occurred that where the citizens cannot meet to transact their business in person, they alone have the right to choose the agents who shall transact it; and that in this way a republican, or popular government, of the second grade of purity, may be exercised over any extent of country. The full experiment of a government democratical, but representative, was and is still reserved for us. The idea (taken, indeed, from the little specimen formerly existing in the English constitution, but now lost) has been carried by us, more or less, into all our legislative and executive departments; but it has not yet, by any of us, been pushed into all the ramifications of the system, so far as to leave no authority existing not responsible to the people; whose rights, however, to the exercise and fruits of their own industry, can never be protected against the selfishness of rulers not subject to their control at short periods. The introduction of this new principle of representative democracy has rendered useless almost everything written before on the structure of government; and, in a great measure, relieves our regret, if the political writings of Aristotle, or of any other ancient, have been lost, or are unfaithfully rendered or explained to us. My most earnest wish is to see the republican element of popular control pushed to the maximum of its practicable exercise. I shall then believe that our government may be pure and perpetual. Accept my respectful salutations.

---

1. Isaac H. Tiffany, a resident of New York, compiled a comprehensive chart of the state governments and sent it to Jefferson.

2. Aristotle (384–322 BC): Greek philosopher who wrote the *Politics* and the *Nicomachean Ethics*, among numerous other works. (See Introduction, p. xxxii.)

TO NATHANIEL BURWELL[1]

Monticello, Mar. 14, 1818

DEAR SIR, — Your letter of February 17th found me suffering under an attack of rheumatism, which has but now left me at sufficient ease to attend to the letters I have received. A plan of female education has never been a subject of systematic contemplation with me. It has occupied my attention so far only as the education of my own daughters occasionally required. Considering that they would be placed in a country situation, where little aid could be obtained from abroad, I thought it essential to give them a solid education, which might enable them, when become mothers, to educate their own daughters, and even to direct the course for sons, should their fathers be lost, or incapable, or inattentive. My surviving daughter[2] accordingly, the mother of many daughters as well as sons, has made their education the object of her life, and being a better judge of the practical part than myself, it is with her aid and that of one of her élèves[3] that I shall subjoin a catalogue of the books for such a course of reading as we have practiced.

A great obstacle to good education is the inordinate passion prevalent for novels, and the time lost in that reading which should be instructively employed. When this poison infects the mind, it destroys its tone and revolts it against wholesome reading. Reason and fact, plain and unadorned, are rejected. Nothing can engage attention unless dressed in all the figments of fancy, and nothing so bedecked comes amiss. The result is a bloated imagination, sickly judgment, and disgust towards all the real businesses of life. This mass of trash, however, is not without some distinction; some few modelling their narratives, although fictitious, on the incidents of real life, have been able to make them interesting and useful vehicles of sound morality. Such, I think, are Marmontel's new moral tales, but not his old ones, which are really immoral.[4] Such are the writings of Miss Edgeworth, and some of those of

---

1. Nathaniel Burwell (1750–1814), the son of Lewis Burwell, colonial governor of Virginia from 1750–51, was an old friend of Jefferson's family. Burwell's youngest sister Rebecca was the "Belinda" of Jefferson's college days.

2. Martha "Patsy" Jefferson Randolph. Jefferson's third daughter, Lucy Elizabeth, died as an infant in 1784; his second daughter, Maria Eppes, died in childbirth in 1804.

3. Pupils.

4. Jean François Marmontel (1723–99): French dramatist and writer who contributed to Diderot's *Encyclopedia*.

Madame Genlis.[5] For a like reason, too, much poetry should not be indulged. Some is useful for forming style and taste. Pope,[6] Dryden,[7] Thompson,[8] Shakspeare,[9] and of the French, Molière,[10] Racine,[11] the Corneilles,[12] may be read with pleasure and improvement.

The French language, become that of the general intercourse of nations, and from their extraordinary advances, now the depository of all science, is an indispensable part of education for both sexes. In the subjoined catalogue, therefore, I have placed the books of both languages indifferently, according as the one or the other offers what is best.

The ornaments too, and the amusements of life, are entitled to their portion of attention. These, for a female, are dancing, drawing, and music. The first is a healthy exercise, elegant and very attractive for young people. Every affectionate parent would be pleased to see his daughter qualified to participate with her companions, and without awkwardness at least, in the circles of festivity, of which she occasionally becomes a part. It is a necessary accomplishment, therefore, although of short use, for the French rule is wise, that no lady dances after marriage. This is founded in solid physical reasons, gestation and nursing leaving little time to a married lady when this exercise can be either safe or innocent. Drawing is thought less of in this country than in Europe. It is an innocent and engaging amusement, often useful, and a qualification not to be neglected in one who is to become a mother and an instructor. Music is invaluable where a person has an ear. Where they have not, it should not be attempted. It furnishes a delightful recreation for the hours of respite from the cares of the day, and lasts us through life. The taste of this country, too, calls for this accomplishment more strongly than for either of the others.

---

5. Maria Edgeworth (1767–1849): Irish novelist. Felicite Ducrest de St. Aubin, Madame de Genlis (1746–1830): French writer.

6. Alexander Pope (1688–1744): English author best known for his satirical epic poems *The Rape of the Lock* (1712) and *The Dunciad* (1728).

7. John Dryden (1631–1700): English poet, critical essayist, and dramatist best known for *Absalom and Achitophel* (1681) and *All for Love* (1678).

8. Though the poet James Thomson (1700–1748) is best known for his long poem, "The Seasons," he was also the coauthor of "Rule Britannia."

9. William Shakespeare (1564–1616): English playwright and poet.

10. Jean Baptiste Poquelin Molière (1622–1673): French playwright, author of the comedies *Tartuffe* (1664) and *The Misanthrope* (1666), among others.

11. Jean Racine (1639–99): French tragic dramatist who later became royal historiographer to Louis XIV. (See note 17, p. 86.)

12. Pierre Corneilles (1606–84): French playwright whose major works included *Le Cid* (c. 1637) and *Horace* (1640).

I need say nothing of household economy, in which the mothers of our country are generally skilled, and generally careful to instruct their daughters. We all know its value, and that diligence and dexterity in all its processes are inestimable treasures. The order and economy of a house are as honorable to the mistress as those of the farm to the master, and if either be neglected, ruin follows, and children destitute of the means of living.

This, Sir, is offered as a summary sketch on a subject on which I have not thought much. It probably contains nothing but what has already occurred to yourself, and claims your acceptance on no other ground than as a testimony of my respect for your wishes, and of my great esteem and respect.

TO JUDGE SPENCER ROANE[1]

Sept. 6, 1819

DEAR SIR, — I had read in the Enquirer, and with great approbation, the pieces signed Hampden,[2] and have read them again with redoubled approbation, in the copies you have been so kind as to send me. I subscribe to every tittle of them. They contain the true principles of the revolution of 1800,[3] for that was as real a revolution in the principles of our government as that of 1776 was in its form; not effected indeed by the sword, as that, but by the rational and peaceable instrument of reform, the suffrage of the people. The nation declared its will by dismissing functionaries of one principle, and electing those of another, in the two branches, executive and legislative, submitted to their election. Over the judiciary department, the constitution had deprived them of their control. That, therefore, has continued the reprobated system, and although new matter has been occasionally incorporated into the old, yet the leaven of the old mass seems to assimilate to itself the new, and after twenty years' confirmation of the federal system by the voice of the nation, declared through the medium of elections, we find the judiciary on every occasion, still driving us into consolidation.

In denying the right they usurp of exclusively explaining the constitution, I go further than you do, if understand rightly your quotation from the Federalist,[4] of an opinion that "the judiciary is the last resort in relation *to the other departments* of the government, but not in relation to the rights of the parties to the compact under which the judiciary is derived." If this opinion be sound, then indeed is our constitution a complete *felo de se*.[5] For intending to establish three departments, co-ordinate and independent, that they might check

---

1. Judge Spencer Roane (1762–1822): Virginia jurist and political writer who served for twenty-seven years on Virginia's Supreme Court of Appeals. Sometimes characterized as a "disunionist," he was a strong supporter of states' rights. He founded the *Richmond Enquirer* with his cousin Thomas Richie, and used the paper to criticize the decisions of Chief Justice John Marshall.

2. Roane's pen name.

3. Jefferson regarded his election to the presidency in 1800 as a revolution that reawakened the spirit of 1776.

4. The series of 85 pro-constitutional essays published in New York newspapers from 1787–88 by James Madison, John Jay, and Alexander Hamilton under the collective pseudonym "Publius."

5. Self-destroyer, self-killer, suicide.

and balance one another, it has given, according to this opinion, to one of them alone, the right to prescribe rules for the government of the others, and to that one too, which is unelected by, and independent of the nation. For experience has already shown that the impeachment it has provided is not even a scare-crow; that such opinions as the one you combat, sent cautiously out, as you observe also, by detachment, not belonging to the case often, but sought for out of it, as if to rally the public opinion beforehand to their views, and to indicate the line they are to walk in, have been so quietly passed over as never to have excited animadversion,[6] even in a speech of any one of the body entrusted with impeachment. The constitution, on this hypothesis, is a mere thing of wax in the hands of the judiciary, which they may twist and shape into any form they please. It should be remembered, as an axiom of eternal truth in politics, that whatever power in any government is independent, is absolute also; in theory only, at first, while the spirit of the people is up, but in practice, as fast as that relaxes. Independence can be trusted nowhere but with the people in mass. They are inherently independent of all but moral law. My construction of the constitution is very different from that you quote. It is that each department is truly independent of the others, and has an equal right to decide for itself what is the meaning of the constitution in the cases submitted to its action; and especially, where it is to act ultimately and without appeal. I will explain myself by examples, which, having occurred while I was in office, are better known to me, and the principles which governed them.

A legislature had passed the sedition law.[7] The federal courts had subjected certain individuals to its penalties of fine and imprisonment. On coming into office, I released these individuals by the power of pardon committed to executive discretion, which could never be more properly exercised than where citizens were suffering without the authority of law, or, which was equivalent, under a law unauthorized by the constitution, and therefore null. In the case of Marbury and Madison,[8] the federal judges declared that commissions, signed and sealed by the President, were valid, although not delivered. I deemed delivery essential to complete a deed, which, as long as it remains in the hands of the party, is as yet no deed, it is *in posse* only, but not *in esse*,[9] and I withheld delivery of the commissions. They cannot issue a mandamus[10] to

---

6. Strong criticism.

7. Jefferson is referring to the Alien and Sedition Acts of 1798. See Introduction, p. xx and note 1, p. 48.

8. The Supreme Court case that, in 1803, established the principle of judicial review.

9. Potential/actual.

10. A writ issued by a superior court ordering a public official or body or a lower court to perform a specified duty.

the President or legislature, or to any of their officers. When the British treaty of —— arrived, without any provision against the impressment of our seamen,[11] I determined not to ratify it. The Senate thought I should ask their advice. I thought that would be a mockery of them, when I was predetermined against following it, should they advise its ratification. The constitution had made their advice necessary to confirm a treaty, but not to reject it. This has been blamed by some; but I have never doubted its soundness. In the cases of two persons, *antenati*,[12] under exactly similar circumstances, the federal court had determined that one of them (Duane) was not a citizen; the House of Representatives nevertheless determined that the other (Smith, of South Carolina) was a citizen, and admitted him to his seat in their body. Duane was a republican, and Smith a federalist, and these decisions were made during the federal ascendancy.

These are examples of my position, that each of the three departments has equally the right to decide for itself what is its duty under the constitution, without any regard to what the others may have decided for themselves under a similar question. But you intimate a wish that my opinion should be known on this subject. No, dear Sir, I withdraw from all contest of opinion, and resign everything cheerfully to the generation now in place. They are wiser than we were, and their successors will be wiser than they, from the progressive advance of science. Tranquillity is the *summum bonum*[13] of age. I wish, therefore, to offend no man's opinion, nor to draw disquieting animadversions on my own. While duty required it, I met opposition with a firm and fearless step. But loving mankind in my individual relations with them, I pray to be permitted to depart in their peace; and like the superannuated[14] soldier, "*quadragenis stipendiis emeritis*,"[15] to hang my arms on the post. I have unwisely, I fear, embarked in an enterprise of great public concern, but not to be accomplished within my term, without their liberal and prompt support. A severe illness the last year, and another from which I am just emerged, admonish me that repetitions may be expected, against which a declining frame cannot long bear up. I am anxious, therefore, to get our University[16] so far advanced

11. During the Napoleonic Wars, the British seized naturalized Americans and forced them to serve as sailors on British ships. See note 4, letter to Colvin, p. 209, on the ships *Chesapeake* and *Leopard*.

12. Persons born before a certain time or event, especially regarding political rights, such as eligibility for citizenship.

13. The greatest good.

14. Too old to work. See note 33, p. 117.

15. Earning retirement after forty years of service (a Roman military expression).

16. The University of Virginia.

as may encourage the public to persevere to its final accomplishment. That secured, I shall sing my *nunc demittas*.[17] I hope your labors will be long continued in the spirit in which they have always been exercised, in maintenance of those principles on which I verily believe the future happiness of our country essentially depends. I salute you with affectionate and great respect.

17. A reference to Luke 2:29, in which Simeon says "*nunc dimittis servum tuum, Domine, secundum verbum tuum in pace*" ("Lord, now lettest thou thy servant depart in peace, according to thy word"). See note 10 on p. 207.

To John Holmes[1]

Monticello, April 22, 1820

I thank you, dear Sir, for the copy you have been so kind as to send me of the letter to your constituents on the Missouri question.[2] It is a perfect justification to them. I had for a long time ceased to read newspapers, or pay any attention to public affairs, confident they were in good hands, and content to be a passenger in our bark to the shore from which I am not distant. But this momentous question, like a fire bell in the night, awakened and filled me with terror. I considered it at once as the knell of the Union. It is hushed, indeed, for the moment. But this is a reprieve only, not a final sentence. A geographical line, coinciding with a marked principle, moral and political, once conceived and held up to the angry passions of men, will never be obliterated; and every new irritation will mark it deeper and deeper. I can say, with conscious truth, that there is not a man on earth who would sacrifice more than I would to relieve us from this heavy reproach, in any *practicable* way. The cession of that kind of property, for so it is misnamed, is a bagatelle[3] which would not cost me a second thought, if, in that way, a general emancipation and *expatriation* could be effected; and gradually, and with due sacrifices, I think it might be. But as it is, we have the wolf by the ears, and we can neither hold him, nor safely let him go. Justice is in one scale, and self-preservation in the other. Of one thing I am certain, that as the passage of slaves from one State to another, would not make a slave of a single human being who would not be so without it, so their diffusion over a greater surface would make them individually happier, and proportionally facilitate the accomplishment of their emancipation, by dividing the burthen on a greater number of coadjutors.[4] An abstinence too, from this act of power, would remove the jealousy excited by the undertaking of Congress to regulate the condition of the different descriptions of men composing a State. This certainly is the exclusive right of every

---

1. John Holmes (1773–1843): a representative from Massachusetts and senator from Maine after Maine separated from Massachusetts.

2. As part of the Missouri Compromise of 1820, Maine came into the Union as a free state, and Missouri a slave state. The Missouri Compromise also prohibited slavery in the Louisiana Territory north of the 36° 30′ latitude, except in Missouri. See Introduction p. xxiv and note 4, p. 258.

3. Trifle.

4. Fellow workers.

State, which nothing in the constitution has taken from them and given to the General Government. Could Congress, for example, say, that the non-freemen of Connecticut shall be freemen, or that they shall not emigrate into any other State?

I regret that I am now to die in the belief, that the useless sacrifice of themselves by the generation of 1776, to acquire self-government and happiness to their country, is to be thrown away by the unwise and unworthy passions of their sons, and that my only consolation is to be, that I live not to weep over it. If they would but dispassionately weigh the blessings they will throw away, against an abstract principle more likely to be effected by union than by scission, they would pause before they would perpetrate this act of suicide on themselves, and of treason against the hopes of the world. To yourself, as the faithful advocate of the Union, I tender the offering of my high esteem and respect.

TO JARED SPARKS[1]

Monticello, Feb. 4, 1824

DEAR SIR, — I duly received your favor of the 13th, and with it, the last number of the North American Review. This has anticipated the one I should receive in course, but have not yet received, under my subscription to the new series. The article on the African colonization of the people of color, to which you invite my attention, I have read with great consideration. It is, indeed, a fine one, and will do much good. I learn from it more, too, than I had before known, of the degree of success and promise of that colony.

In the disposition of these unfortunate people, there are two rational objects to be distinctly kept in view. First. The establishment of a colony on the coast of Africa, which may introduce among the aborigines the arts of cultivated life, and the blessings of civilization and science. By doing this, we may make to them some retribution for the long course of injuries we have been committing on their population. And considering that these blessings will descend to the "*nati natorum, et qui nascentur ab illis*,"[2] we shall in the long run have rendered them perhaps more good than evil. To fulfil this object, the colony of Sierra Leone promises well, and that of Mesurado adds to our prospect of success. Under this view, the colonization society is to be considered as a missionary society, having in view, however, objects more humane, more justifiable, and less aggressive on the peace of other nations, than the others of that appellation.

The second object, and the most interesting to us, as coming home to our physical and moral characters, to our happiness and safety, is to provide an asylum to which we can, by degrees, send the whole of that population from among us, and establish them under our patronage and protection, as a separate, free and independent people, in some country and climate friendly to human life and happiness. That any place on the coast of Africa should answer the latter purpose, I have ever deemed entirely impossible. And without

---

1. Jared Sparks (1789–1866): a Harvard-educated historian who published, among many other studies, a multivolume biography of George Washington. A Unitarian minister, editor of the *North American Review,* and Harvard professor, he later became president of Harvard.

2. *Nati natorum, et qui nascentur ab illis:* "children of the children, and those who will be born of them" (Virgil, *Aeneid* III, 98). This is a reference to the Roman people as the progeny of the Trojans.

repeating the other arguments which have been urged by others, I will appeal to figures only, which admit no controversy. I shall speak in round numbers, not absolutely accurate, yet not so wide from truth as to vary the result materially. There are in the United States a million and a half of people of color in slavery. To send off the whole of these at once, nobody conceives to be practicable for us, or expedient for them. Let us take twenty-five years for its accomplishment, within which time they will be doubled. Their estimated value as property, in the first place, (for actual property has been lawfully vested in that form, and who can lawfully take it from the possessors?) at an average of two hundred dollars each, young and old, would amount to six hundred millions of dollars, which must be paid or lost by somebody. To this, add the cost of their transportation by land and sea to Mesurado, a year's provision of food and clothing, implements of husbandry and of their trades, which will amount to three hundred millions more, making thirty-six millions of dollars a year for twenty-five years, with insurance of peace all that time, and it is impossible to look at the question a second time. I am aware that at the end of about sixteen years, a gradual detraction from this sum will commence, from the gradual diminution of breeders, and go on during the remaining nine years. Calculate this deduction, and it is still impossible to look at the enterprise a second time. I do not say this to induce an inference that the getting rid of them is forever impossible. For that is neither my opinion nor my hope. But only that it cannot be done in this way. There is, I think, a way in which it can be done; that is, by emancipating the after-born, leaving them, on due compensation, with their mothers, until their services are worth their maintenance, and then putting them to industrious occupations, until a proper age for deportation. This was the result of my reflections on the subject five and forty years ago, and I have never yet been able to conceive any other practicable plan. It was sketched in the Notes on Virginia, under the fourteenth query.[3] The estimated value of the new-born infant is so low, (say twelve dollars and fifty cents,) that it would probably be yielded by the owner gratis, and would thus reduce the six hundred millions of dollars, the first head of expense, to thirty-seven millions and a half; leaving only the expense of nourishment while with the mother, and of transportation. And from what fund are these expenses to be furnished? Why not from that of the lands which have been ceded by the very States now needing this relief? And ceded on no consideration, for the most part, but that of the general good of the whole. These cessions already constitute one fourth of the States of the Union. It may be said that these lands have been sold; are now the property of the citizens composing those States; and the money long ago received and expended. But an

---

3. See pp. 109–24.

equivalent of lands in the territories since acquired, may be appropriated to that object, or so much, at least, as may be sufficient; and the object, although more important to the slave States, is highly so to the others also, if they were serious in their arguments on the Missouri question.[4] The slave States, too, if more interested, would also contribute more by their gratuitous liberation, thus taking on themselves alone the first and heaviest item of expense.

In the plan sketched in the Notes on Virginia, no particular place of asylum was specified; because it was thought possible, that in the revolutionary state of America, then commenced, events might open to us some one within practicable distance. This has now happened. St. Domingo has become independent,[5] and with a population of that color only; and if the public papers are to be credited, their Chief offers to pay their passage, to receive them as free citizens, and to provide them employment. This leaves, then, for the general confederacy, no expense but of nurture with the mother a few years, and would call, of course, for a very moderate appropriation of the vacant lands. Suppose the whole annual increase to be of sixty thousand effective births, fifty vessels, of four hundred tons burthen each, constantly employed in that short run, would carry off the increase of every year, and the old stock would die off in the ordinary course of nature, lessening from the commencement until its final disappearance. In this way no violation of private right is proposed. Voluntary surrenders would probably come in as fast as the means to be provided for their care would be competent to it. Looking at my own State only, and I presume not to speak for the others, I verily believe that this surrender of property would not amount to more, annually, than half our present direct taxes, to be continued fully about twenty or twenty-five years, and then gradually diminishing for as many more until their final extinction; and even this half tax would not be paid in cash, but by the delivery of an object which they have never yet known or counted as part of their property; and those not possessing the object will be called on for nothing. I do not go into all the details of the burthens and benefits of this operation. And who could estimate its blessed effects? I leave this to those who will live to see their accomplishment, and to enjoy a beatitude[6] forbidden to my age. But I leave it with this admo-

---

4. A reference to the debate over the Missouri Compromise of 1820, in which Maine came into the Union as a free state and Missouri a slave state. With the exception of Missouri, slavery was forbidden above the 36° 30′ latitude in the rest of the Louisiana territory. Jefferson opposed the Missouri Compromise because he thought the dispersion of slaves to the territories would reduce the number of slaves in the southern states and thereby facilitate emancipation. See Introduction, p. xxiv and Jefferson's letter to John Holmes, p. 264.

5. Haiti, formerly the French colony of Saint Domingue, became the first black republic in the world in 1804.

6. Blessedness.

nition, to rise and be doing. A million and a half are within their control; but six millions, (which a majority of those now living will see them attain,) and one million of these fighting men, will say, "we will not go."

I am aware that this subject involves some constitutional scruples. But a liberal construction, justified by the object, may go far, and an amendment of the constitution, the whole length necessary. The separation of infants from their mothers, too, would produce some scruples of humanity. But this would be straining at a gnat, and swallowing a camel.

I am much pleased to see that you have taken up the subject of the duty on imported books. I hope a crusade will be kept up against it, until those in power shall become sensible of this stain on our legislation, and shall wipe it from their code, and from the remembrance of man, if possible.

I salute you with assurances of high respect and esteem.

TO MAJOR JOHN CARTWRIGHT[1]

Monticello, June 5, 1824

DEAR AND VENERABLE SIR, — I am much indebted for your kind letter of February the 29th, and for your valuable volume on the English constitution. I have read this with pleasure and much approbation, and think it has deduced the constitution of the English nation from its rightful root, the Anglo-Saxon.[2] It is really wonderful, that so many able and learned men should have failed in their attempts to define it with correctness. No wonder then, that Paine,[3] who thought more than he read, should have credited the great authorities who have declared, that the will of parliament is the constitution of England. So Marbois,[4] before the French revolution, observed to me, that the Almanac Royal was the constitution of France.[5] Your derivation of it from the Anglo-Saxons, seems to be made on legitimate principles. Having driven out the former inhabitants of that part of the island called England, they became aborigines as to you, and your lineal[6] ancestors. They doubtless had a constitution; and although they have not left it in a written formula, to the precise text of which you may always appeal, yet they have left fragments of their history and laws, from which it may be inferred with considerable certainty. Whatever their history and laws shew to have been practised with approbation, we may pre-

---

1. John Cartwright (1740–1824): English parliamentarian reformer who supported the American colonists in their struggle against Parliament, and argued in favor of universal suffrage, the secret ballot, and equal electoral districts in England.

2. One of the north European tribes that invaded Britain in the fifth and sixth centuries. The Normans defeated them in 1066. See note 4, p. 4.

3. Thomas Paine (1737–1809): British-born author of the revolutionary pamphlet *Common Sense* (1776). See note 11, p. 101.

4. Marquis de François Barbé-Marbois (1745–1837): French statesman and supporter of the American Revolution. Though active in the French Revolution, he was suspected of having Royalist sympathies and was subsequently exiled to French Guiana. Napoleon I later freed him and appointed him Minister of the French Treasury. Barbé-Marbois negotiated the sale of the Louisiana Territory to America (see note 4, p. 61).

5. Jefferson is here quoting Barbé-Marbois, who remarked that the official proclamations and announcements published in the almanac amounted to the French constitution. That is, as the will of Parliament is said to be the constitution of England, so the royal will was said to be the will of France. (Jefferson goes on in this letter to disagree with these top-down interpretations.)

6. Descending in a direct line from an ancestor.

sume was permitted by their constitution; whatever was not so practised, was not permitted. And although this constitution was violated and set at naught by Norman[7] force, yet force cannot change right. A perpetual claim was kept up by the nation, by their perpetual demand of a restoration of their Saxon laws; which shews they were never relinquished by the will of the nation. In the pullings and haulings for these antient rights, between the nation, and its kings of the races of Plantagenets, Tudors and Stuarts,[8] there was sometimes gain, and sometimes loss, until the final re-conquest of their rights from the Stuarts. The destitution and expulsion of this race broke the thread of pretended inheritance, extinguished all regal usurpations, and the nation re-entered into all its rights; and although in their bill of rights they specifically reclaimed some only, yet the omission of the others was no renunciation of the right to assume their exercise also, whenever occasion should occur. The new King received no rights or powers, but those expressly granted to him. It has ever appeared to me, that the difference between the whig and the tory of England[9] is, that the whig deduces his rights from the Anglo-Saxon source, and the tory from the Norman. And Hume,[10] the great apostle of toryism, says, in so many words, note AA to chapter 42, that, in the reign of the Stuarts, 'it was the people who encroached upon the sovereign, not the sovereign who attempted, as is pretended, to usurp upon the people.' This supposes the Norman usurpations to be rights in his successors. And again, C, 159, 'the commons established a principle, which is noble in itself, and seems specious, but is belied by all history and experience, *that the people are the origin of all just power.*' And where else will this degenerate son of science, this traitor to his fellow men, find the origin of *just* powers, if not in the majority of the society? Will it be in the minority? Or in an individual of that minority?

Our Revolution commenced on more favorable ground. It presented us an album on which we were free to write what we pleased. We had no occasion to search into musty records, to hunt up royal parchments, or to investigate

---

7. The Normans invaded England in 1066 and defeated the Anglo-Saxons (the "Saxons" to which Jefferson refers in the next sentence of his letter) at the Battle of Hastings.

8. The Plantagenets, Tudors, and Stewarts were the ruling houses of England, beginning in the twelfth century and extending, consecutively, through the beginning of the eighteenth.

9. The Whigs and the Tories were the two major political parties of England from the late seventeenth through the nineteenth centuries. Whigs supported the Glorious Revolution of 1689 as well as the American Revolution; Jefferson traced their political principles back to the Anglo-Saxons.

10. David Hume (1711–76): Scottish Enlightenment philosopher whose *History of England* (1754–62) was criticized by Jefferson for its sympathetic treatment of the Stuart monarch Charles I (see note 6, p. 5).

the laws and institutions of a semi-barbarous ancestry. We appealed to those of nature, and found them engraved on our hearts. Yet we did not avail ourselves of all the advantages of our position. We had never been permitted to exercise self-government. When forced to assume it, we were novices in its science. Its principles and forms had entered little into our former education. We established however some, although not all its important principles. The constitutions of most of our States assert, that all power is inherent in the people; that they may exercise it by themselves, in all cases to which they think themselves competent, (as in electing their functionaries executive and legislative, and deciding by a jury of themselves, in all judiciary cases in which any fact is involved,) or they may act by representatives, freely and equally chosen; that it is their right and duty to be at all times armed; that they are entitled to freedom of person, freedom of religion, freedom of property, and freedom of the press. In the structure of our legislatures, we think experience has proved the benefit of subjecting questions to two separate bodies of deliberants; but in constituting these, natural right has been mistaken, some making one of these bodies, and some both, the representatives of property instead of persons; whereas the double deliberation might be as well obtained without any violation of true principle, either by requiring a greater age in one of the bodies, or by electing a proper number of representatives of persons, dividing them by lots into two chambers, and renewing the division at frequent intervals, in order to break up all cabals.[11] Virginia, of which I am myself a native and resident, was not only the first of the States, but, I believe I may say, the first of the nations of the earth, which assembled its wise men peaceably together to form a fundamental constitution, to commit it to writing, and place it among their archives, where every one should be free to appeal to its text. But this act was very imperfect. The other States, as they proceeded successively to the same work, made successive improvements; and several of them, still further corrected by experience, have, by conventions, still further amended their first forms. My own State has gone on so far with its *première ébauche*;[12] but it is now proposing to call a convention for amendment. Among other improvements, I hope they will adopt the subdivision of our counties into wards. The former may be estimated at an average of twenty-four miles square; the latter should be about six miles square each, and would answer to the hundreds of your Saxon Alfred.[13] In each of these might be, 1. An elementary school.

---

11. Secret plots, conspiracies.

12. First draft.

13. The "hundred" was a unit of local administration dating back to the reign of Alfred the Great (871–899), the first Saxon King. These "hundreds" were the inspiration for Jefferson's plan to subdivide American counties into "wards."

2. A company of militia, with its officers. 3. A justice of the peace and constable. 4. Each ward should take care of their own poor. 5. Their own roads. 6. Their own police. 7. Elect within themselves one or more jurors to attend the courts of justice. And 8. Give in at their Folk-house, their votes for all functionaries reserved to their election. Each ward would thus be a small republic within itself, and every man in the State would thus become an acting member of the common government, transacting in person a great portion of its rights and duties, subordinate indeed, yet important, and entirely within his competence. The wit of man cannot devise a more solid basis for a free, durable and well administered republic.

With respect to our State and federal governments, I do not think their relations correctly understood by foreigners. They generally suppose the former subordinate to the latter. But this is not the case. They are co-ordinate departments of one simple and integral whole. To the State governments are reserved all legislation and administration, in affairs which concern their own citizens only, and to the federal government is given whatever concerns foreigners, or the citizens of other States; these functions alone being made federal. The one is the domestic, the other the foreign branch of the same government; neither having control over the other, but within its own department. There are one or two exceptions only to this partition of power. But, you may ask, if the two departments should claim each the same subject of power, where is the common umpire to decide ultimately between them? In cases of little importance or urgency, the prudence of both parties will keep them aloof from the questionable ground: but if it can neither be avoided nor compromised, a convention of the States must be called, to ascribe the doubtful power to that department which they may think best. You will perceive by these details, that we have not yet so far perfected our constitutions as to venture to make them unchangeable. But still, in their present state, we consider them not otherwise changeable than by the authority of the people, on a special election of representatives for that purpose expressly: they are until then the *lex legum*.[14]

But can they be made unchangeable? Can one generation bind another, and all others, in succession forever? I think not. The Creator has made the earth for the living, not the dead. Rights and powers can only belong to persons, not to things, not to mere matter, unendowed with will. The dead are not even things. The particles of matter which composed their bodies, make part now of the bodies of other animals, vegetables, or minerals, of a thousand forms. To what then are attached the rights and powers they held while in the form of men? A generation may bind itself as long as its majority continues in

---

14. Law of laws.

life; when that has disappeared, another majority is in place, holds all the rights and powers their predecessors once held, and may change their laws and institutions to suit themselves. Nothing then is unchangeable but the inherent and unalienable rights of man.

I was glad to find in your book a formal contradiction, at length, of the judiciary usurpation of legislative powers; for such the judges have usurped in their repeated decisions, that Christianity is a part of the common law. The proof of the contrary, which you have adduced, is incontrovertible; to wit, that the common law existed while the Anglo-Saxons were yet Pagans, at a time when they had never yet heard the name of Christ pronounced, or knew that such a character had ever existed. But it may amuse you, to shew when, and by what means, they stole this law in upon us. In a case of *quare impedit*[15] in the Year-book 34. H. 6. folio 38. (anno 1458,) a question was made, how far the ecclesiastical law was to be respected in a common law court? And Prisot, Chief Justice,[16] gives his opinion in these words, 'A tiel leis qu' ils de seint eglise ont en *ancien scripture*, covient à nous à donner credence; car ceo common ley sur quels touts manners leis sont fondés. Et auxy, Sir, nous sumus oblègés de conustre lour ley de saint eglise: et semblablement ils sont obligés de conustre nostre ley. Et, Sir, si poit apperer or à nous que l'evesque ad fait come un ordinary fera en tiel cas, adong nous devons ceo adjuger bon, ou auterment nemy,' &c. See S. C. Fitzh. Abr. Qu. imp. 89. Bro. Abr. Qu. imp. 12. Finch in his first book, c. 3. is the first afterwards who quotes this case, and mistakes it thus. 'To such laws of the church as have warrant in *holy scripture*, our law giveth credence.' And cites Prisot; mistranslating '*ancien scripture*,' into '*holy scripture*.' Whereas Prisot palpably says, 'to such laws as those of holy church have in *antient writing*, it is proper for us to give credence;' to wit, to their *antient written* laws. This was in 1613, a century and a half after the dictum of Prisot. Wingate, in 1658, erects this false translation into a maxim of the common law, copying the words of Finch, but citing Prisot. Wing. Max. 3. And Sheppard, title, 'Religion,' in 1675, copies the same mistranslation, quoting the Y. B. Finch and Wingate. Hale expresses it in these words; 'Christianity is parcel of the laws of England.' 1 Ventr. 293. 3 Keb. 607. But he quotes no authority. By these echoings and re-echoings from one to another, it had become so established in 1728, that in the case of the King vs. Woolston,

---

15. Literally, "why he impedes." Cases in *Quare impedit* are actions brought in English law to recover the right of a patron over a church or benefice.

16. Sir John Prisot, British Chief Justice of Common Pleas from 1399–1460. The question here is whether the term "*ancien scripture*" refers to the Bible or old church law. Jefferson maintained it meant the latter and argued that translating *ancien scripture* to mean the Bible constituted nothing less than a "judicial forgery" by judges from Prisot to Mansfield to make Christianity part of the common law of England.

2 Stra. 834, the court would not suffer it to be debated, whether to write against Christianity was punishable in the temporal court at common law? Wood, therefore, 409, ventures still to vary the phrase, and say, that all blasphemy and profaneness are offences by the common law; and cites 2 Stra. Then Blackstone, in 1763, IV. 59, repeats the words of Hale, that 'Christianity is part of the laws of England,' citing Ventris and Strange. And finally, Lord Mansfield,[17] with a little qualification, in Evans' case, in 1767, says, that 'the essential principles of revealed religion are part of the common law.' Thus ingulphing Bible, Testament and all into the common law, without citing any authority. And thus we find this chain of authorities hanging link by link, one upon another, and all ultimately on one and the same hook, and that a mistranslation of the words *'ancien scripture'*, used by Prisot. Finch quotes Prisot; Wingate does the same. Sheppard quotes Prisot, Finch and Wingate. Hale cites nobody. The court in Woolston's case, cite Hale. Wood cites Woolston's case. Blackstone quotes Woolston's case and Hale. And Lord Mansfield, like Hale, ventures it on his own authority. Here I might defy the best read lawyer to produce another scrip of authority for this judiciary forgery; and I might go on further to shew, how some of the Anglo-Saxon priests interpolated into the text of Alfred's laws, the 20th, 21st, 22nd and 23rd chapters of Exodus, and the 15th of the Acts of the Apostles, from the 23rd to the 29th verses. But this would lead my pen and your patience too far. What a conspiracy this, between Church and State! Sing Tantarara, rogues all, rogues all, Sing Tantarara, rogues all!

I must still add to this long and rambling letter, my acknowledgments for your good wishes to the University we are now establishing in this State.[18] There are some novelties in it. Of that of a professorship of the principles of government, you express your approbation. They will be founded in the rights of man. That of agriculture, I am sure, you will approve: and that also of Anglo-Saxon. As the histories and laws left us in that type and dialect, must be the text books of the reading of the learners, they will imbibe with the language their free principles of government. The volumes you have been so kind as to send, shall be placed in the library of the University. Having at this time in England a person sent for the purpose of selecting some Professors, a Mr. Gilmer[19] of my neighborhood, I cannot but recommend him to your patronage, counsel and guardianship, against imposition, misinformation, and

---

17. William Murray, first Earl of Mansfield (1705–93): British judge and Tory politician. See note 8, p. 274.

18. The University of Virginia.

19. Francis W. Gilmer (1790–1826): neighbor and acquaintance of Jefferson. See p. 237.

the deceptions of partial and false recommendations, in the selection of characters. He is a gentleman of great worth and correctness, my particular friend, well educated in various branches of science, and worthy of entire confidence.

Your age of eighty-four and mine of eighty-one years, insure us a speedy meeting. We may then commune at leisure, and more fully, on the good and evil, which, in the course of our long lives, we have both witnessed; and in the mean time, I pray you to accept assurances of my high veneration and esteem for your person and character.

TO HENRY LEE[1]

Monticello, May 8, 1825

DEAR SIR, . . . That George Mason[2] was the author of the bill of rights, and the constitution founded on it, the evidence of the day established fully in my mind. Of the paper you mention, purporting to be instructions to the Virginia delegation in Congress, I have no recollection.[3] If it were anything more than a project of some private hand, that is to say, had any such instructions been ever given by the convention, they would appear in the journals, which we possess entire. But with respect to our rights, and the acts of the British government contravening those rights, there was but one opinion on this side of the water. All American whigs[4] thought alike on these subjects. When forced, therefore, to resort to arms for redress, an appeal to the tribunal of the world was deemed proper for our justification. This was the object of the Declaration of Independence. Not to find out new principles, or new arguments, never before thought of, not merely to say things which had never been said before; but to place before mankind the common sense of the subject, in terms so plain and firm as to command their assent, and to justify ourselves in the independent stand we are compelled to take. Neither aiming at originality of principle or sentiment, nor yet copied from any particular and previous writing, it was intended to be an expression of the American mind, and to give to that expression the proper tone and spirit called for by the occasion. All its authority rests then on the harmonizing sentiments of the day,

---

1. Henry Lee (1787–1837): son of "Light Horse" Henry Lee—the notable American Revolutionary politician and soldier—and a Virginian. He served briefly in the U.S. Army during the War of 1812 and later wrote campaign material for John Calhoun and Andrew Jackson. Best remembered as a historian, Lee wrote books on his father and the writings of Thomas Jefferson; he was working on an epic history of Napoleon's life when he died.

2. George Mason (1725–92): American revolutionary politician known for his impassioned speeches. He was the author of the Virginia Declaration of Rights (1776) and later played a significant role in the drafting of the Constitutional Bill of Rights.

3. In his letter to Jefferson of April 29, 1825, Lee mentions "a paper, in whose writing I know not, which purports to be instructions to the Va. delegation in Congress, to present an enumeration of our grievances first to that body and then to the world." This is probably a reference to "Resolutions of the Virginia Convention Calling for Independence," May 15, 1776.

4. Jefferson here refers to the patriots who supported the American Revolution.

whether expressed in conversation, in letters, printed essays, or in the elementary books of public right, as Aristotle,[5] Cicero,[6] Locke,[7] Sidney,[8] &c. The historical documents which you mention as in your possession, ought all to be found, and I am persuaded you will find, to be corroborative of the facts and principles advanced in that Declaration. Be pleased to accept assurances of my great esteem and respect.

---

5. Aristotle (384 BC–322 BC): Greek philosopher, whose best-known political writings included the *Politics*, the *Nicomachean Ethics*, and the *Rhetoric*.

6. Cicero (first century BC): Roman statesman, philosopher, and orator. See notes 10 and 6 on pp. 83 and 210, respectively.

7. John Locke (1632–1704): British philosopher whose theories of natural rights, property, and revolution—as expounded in the *Second Treatise of Government* (published anonymously in 1689)—profoundly influenced American revolutionary thought. His other major works included *Essay Concerning Human Understanding* (1689) and the *Letters Concerning Toleration* (1689–92). See Introduction, pp. xxiv–xxv.

8. Algernon Sidney (1622–83): second son of the Earl of Leicester and nephew of the poet Phillip Sidney, Algernon Sidney supported the English Commonwealth (1649–60). He penned the *Discourses Concerning Government* in response to Robert Filmer's *Patriarcha*. Like John Locke, Sidney rejected Filmer's defense of absolute monarchy and the divine right of kings and argued that all government rests on consent. Virtue, not birth, should establish the claim to rule. Liberty is not the gift of the ruler, but comes from nature. He defended the right of revolution, arguing that those who constitute one form of government may abrogate it when it fails to serve the interests of the ruled. In 1683, Sidney was charged with plotting to assassinate King James II and beheaded. After the Glorious Revolution of 1689, he was exonerated, and the *Discourses* was published in 1698. In America, Sidney was regarded as a martyr to republican liberty, and his work was widely read. Hampden-Sydney College in Virginia is named in his honor and his words are immortalized in the motto of the Commonwealth of Massachusetts.

TO WILLIAM BRANCH GILES[1]

Monticello, Dec. 26, 1825

DEAR SIR, — I wrote you a letter yesterday, of which you will be free to make what use you please. This will contain matters not intended for the public eye. I see, as you do, and with the deepest affliction, the rapid strides with which the federal branch of our government is advancing towards the usurpation of all the rights reserved to the States, and the consolidation in itself of all powers, foreign and domestic; and that, too, by constructions which, if legitimate, leave no limits to their power. Take together the decisions of the federal court, the doctrines of the President,[2] and the misconstructions of the constitutional compact acted on by the legislature of the federal branch, and it is but too evident, that the three ruling branches of that department are in combination to strip their colleagues, the State authorities, of the powers reserved by them, and to exercise themselves all functions foreign and domestic. Under the power to regulate commerce, they assume indefinitely that also over agriculture and manufactures, and call it regulation to take the earnings of one of these branches of industry, and that too the most depressed, and put them into the pockets of the other, the most flourishing of all. Under the authority to establish post roads, they claim that of cutting down mountains for the construction of roads, of digging canals, and aided by a little sophistry on the words "general welfare," a right to do, not only the acts to effect that, which are specifically enumerated and permitted, but whatsoever they shall think, or pretend will be for the general welfare. And what is our resource for the preservation of the constitution? Reason and argument? You might as well reason and argue with the marble columns encircling them. The representatives chosen by ourselves? They are joined in the combination, some from incorrect views of government, some from corrupt ones, sufficient voting together to out-number the sound parts; and with majorities only of one, two, or three, bold enough to go forward in defiance. Are we then *to stand to our*

---

1. William Branch Giles (1762–1830): states' rights advocate from Virginia who served in Congress and the Virginia General Assembly from 1790 to 1815. He bitterly opposed Hamilton's centralizing policies and often proved more partisan in Jefferson's cause than Jefferson himself.

2. John Quincy Adams (1767–1848): son of President John Adams, and president himself from 1825–29. During his tenure as secretary of state (1817–25) he played a role in the creation of the Monroe Doctrine, which attempted to put an end to European meddling in American affairs.

arms, with the hot-headed Georgian?[3] No. That must be the last resource, not to be thought of until much longer and greater sufferings. If every infraction of a compact of so many parties is to be resisted at once, as a dissolution of it, none can ever be formed which would last one year. We must have patience and longer endurance then with our brethren while under delusion; give them time for reflection and experience of consequences; keep ourselves in a situation to profit by the chapter of accidents; and separate from our companions only when the sole alternatives left, are the dissolution of our Union with them, or submission to a government without limitation of powers. Between these two evils, when we must make a choice, there can be no hesitation. But in the meanwhile, the States should be watchful to note every material usurpation on their rights; to denounce them as they occur in the most peremptory terms; to protest against them as wrongs to which our present submission shall be considered, not as acknowledgments or precedents of right, but as a temporary yielding to the lesser evil, until their accumulation shall overweigh that of separation. I would go still further, and give to the federal member, by a regular amendment of the constitution, a right to make roads and canals of intercommunication between the States, providing sufficiently against corrupt practices in Congress, (log-rolling,[4] &c.,) by declaring that the federal proportion of each State of the moneys so employed, shall be in works within the State, or elsewhere with its consent, and with a due *salvo*[5] of jurisdiction. This is the course which I think safest and best yet.

You ask my opinion of the propriety of giving publicity to what is stated in your letter, as having passed between Mr. John Q. Adams and yourself. Of this no one can judge but yourself. It is one of those questions which belong to the forum of feeling. This alone can decide on the degree of confidence implied in the disclosure; whether under no circumstances it was to be communicated to others? It does not seem to be of that character, or at all to wear that aspect. They are historical facts which belong to the present, as well as future times. I doubt whether a single fact, known to the world, will carry as clear conviction to it, of the correctness of our knowledge of the treasonable views of the federal party of that day, as that disclosed by this, the most nefarious and

---

3. The "hot-headed Georgian" was probably George M. Troup, governor of the state at this time. He reacted to the perceived reneging of the United States on a commitment to remove Indians forcibly from Georgia by suggesting that this dissolved the compact between Georgia and the United States and left Georgia no alternative but "acquiescence or resistance."

4. Political favors exchanged to win the passage of projects advantageous to both interests.

5. An exception, a reservation.

daring attempt to dissever the Union, of which the Hartford convention was a subsequent chapter; and both of these having failed, consolidation becomes the fourth chapter of the next book of their history.[6] But this opens with a vast accession of strength from their younger recruits, who, having nothing in them of the feelings or principles of '76, now look to a single and splendid government of an aristocracy, founded on banking institutions, and moneyed incorporations under the guise and cloak of their favored branches of manufactures, commerce and navigation, riding and ruling over the plundered ploughman and beggared yeomanry. This will be to them a next best blessing to the monarchy of their first aim, and perhaps the surest stepping-stone to it.

I learn with great satisfaction that your school is thriving well, and that you have at its head a truly classical scholar. He is one of three or four whom I can hear of in the State. We were obliged the last year to receive shameful Latinists into the classical school of the University, such as we will certainly refuse as soon as we can get from better schools a sufficiency of those properly instructed to form a class. We must get rid of this Connecticut Latin, of this barbarous confusion of long and short syllables, which renders doubtful whether we are listening to a reader of Cherokee, Shawnee, Iroquois, or what. Our University has been most fortunate in the five professors procured from England. A finer selection could not have been made. Besides their being of a grade of science which has left little superior behind, the correctness of their moral character, their accommodating dispositions, and zeal for the prosperity of the institution, leave us nothing more to wish. I verily believe that as high a degree of education can now be obtained here, as in the country they left. And a finer set of youths I never saw assembled for instruction. They committed some irregularities[7] at first, until they learned the lawful length of their tether; since which it has never been transgressed in the smallest degree. A great proportion of them are severely devoted to study, and I fear not to say that within twelve or fifteen years from this time, a majority of the rulers of our State will have been educated here. They shall carry hence the correct principles of our day, and you may count assuredly that they will exhibit their

---

6. During Madison's presidency, the New England Federalists, objecting to the War of 1812 and the toll it took on their economic interests, met in Hartford, Connecticut to consider seceding from the Union. Having failed in these efforts, Jefferson now accuses them of trying to consolidate power in the national government to advance their interests.

7. University of Virginia students, taking full advantage of the school's lax disciplinary policies, rioted in October of 1825. Jefferson, then 82, was deeply disappointed in the students' inability to maintain appropriate behavior and rode in from Monticello to tell them as much. Three of the rioting students were expelled; eleven faced other disciplinary action.

country in a degree of sound respectability it has never known, either in our days, or those of our forefathers. I cannot live to see it. My joy must only be that of anticipation. But that you may see it in full fruition, is the probable consequence of the twenty years I am ahead of you in time, and is the sincere prayer of your affectionate and constant friend.

To James Madison[1]

Feb. 17, 1826

DEAR SIR, — My circular was answered by Genl. Breckenridge,[2] approving, as we had done, of the immediate appointment of Terril[3] to the chair of Law. But our four Colleagues, who were together in Richmond, concluded not to appoint until our meeting in April. In the meantime the term of the present lamented Incumbent draws near to a close. About 150. students have already entered; many of those who engaged for a 2d. year, are yet to come; and I think we may count that our dormitories will be filled. Whether there will be any overflowing for the accomodations provided in the vicinage, which are quite considerable, is not yet known. None will enter there while a dormitory remains vacant. Were the Law-chair filled it would add 50. at least to our number.

Immediately on seeing the overwhelming vote of the House of Representatives against giving us another dollar, I rode to the University and desired Mr. Brockenbrough[4] to engage in nothing new, to stop everything on hand which could be done without, and to employ all his force and funds in finishing the circular room for the books, and the anatomical theatre. These cannot be done without; and for these and all our debts we have funds enough. But I think it prudent then to clear the decks thoroughly, to see how we shall stand, and what we may accomplish further. In the meantime, there have arrived for us in different ports of the United States, ten boxes of books from Paris, seven from London, and from Germany I know not how many; in all, perhaps, about twenty-five boxes. Not one of these can be opened until the book-room is completely finished, and all the shelves ready to receive their charge directly from the boxes as they shall be opened. This cannot be till May. I hear nothing definite of the three thousand dollars duty of which we are asking the remission from Congress. In the selection of our Law Professor, we must be

---

1. For biographical information on Madison, see note 1 on p. 153.

2. James Breckinridge (1763–1846): one of the commissioners for the University of Virginia.

3. Dabney Carr Terrell: a lawyer who had studied in Europe and whom Jefferson regarded as a contender for the first University of Virginia law professorship (Terrell was not ultimately chosen for the position).

4. As first proctor of the University of Virginia, Arthur Spicer Brockenbrough oversaw construction of its main buildings.

rigorously attentive to his political principles. You will recollect that before the revolution, Coke Littleton[5] was the universal elementary book of law students, and a sounder whig[6] never wrote, nor of profounder learning in the orthodox doctrines of the British constitution, or in what were called English liberties. You remember also that our lawyers were then all whigs. But when his black-letter text,[7] and uncouth but cunning learning got out of fashion, and the honied Mansfieldism of Blackstone[8] became the student's hornbook,[9] from that moment, that profession (the nursery of our Congress) began to slide into toryism,[10] and nearly all the young brood of lawyers now are of that hue. They suppose themselves, indeed, to be whigs, because they no longer know what whigism or republicanism means. It is in our seminary that that vestal flame[11] is to be kept alive; it is thence it is to spread anew over our own and the sister States. If we are true and vigilant in our trust, within a dozen or twenty years a majority of our own legislature will be from one school, and many disciples will have carried its doctrines home with them to their several States, and will have leavened thus the whole mass. New York has taken strong ground in vindication of the constitution; South Carolina had already done the same. Although I was against our leading, I am equally against omitting to follow in the same line, and backing them firmly; and I hope that yourself or some other will mark out the track to be pursued by us.

You will have seen in the newspapers some proceedings in the legislature, which have cost me much mortification.[12] My own debts had become

---

5. Sir Thomas Littleton (c. 1422–81): English jurist who wrote on land law. Sir Edward Coke (1552–1634) wrote a commentary on Littleton's work ("Coke's Littleton") that became the standard text on property law in the eighteenth and nineteenth centuries.

6. See note 10, p. 144.

7. That is, having wide acceptance and great authority.

8. William Murray, First Earl of Mansfield (1705–93), was an English Chief Justice and Tory. Though much admired in England, he was despised by the American Revolutionaries for having supported the Declaratory Act (1766), which stated that all British laws were binding in the colonies despite the fact that the colonies were not represented in Parliament. William Blackstone (1723–80) Mansfield's contemporary, wrote the *Commentaries on the Laws of England* (1765–69), an influential history of the common law. What Jefferson objected to was Blackstone's influence in the adoption of the common law in the American colonies. The term "honied Mansfieldism" refers to Blackstone's eloquence in setting forth his Tory views.

9. Textbook.

10. See note 9, p. 261.

11. The group of celibate young women known as the vestal virgins maintained the sacred flame in the temple of Vesta, ancient Roman goddess of the hearth. The term is used here to refer to a pure republican spirit.

12. Already deeply in debt, Jefferson had signed a $20,000 promissory note for his friend Wilson Cary Nichols, which he was obliged to pay after Nicholas met with

considerable, but not beyond the effect of some lopping of property, which would have been little felt, when our friend Nicholas gave me the *coup de grace*.[13] Ever since that I have been paying twelve hundred dollars a year interest on his debt, which, with my own, was absorbing so much of my annual income, as that the maintenance of my family was making deep and rapid inroads on my capital, and had already done it. Still, sales at a fair price would leave me competently provided. Had crops and prices for several years been such as to maintain a steady competition of substantial bidders at market, all would have been safe. But the long succession of years of stunted crops, of reduced prices, the general prostration of the farming business, under levies for the support of manufactures, &c., with the calamitous fluctuations of value in our paper medium, have kept agriculture in a state of abject depression, which has peopled the western States by silently breaking up those on the Atlantic, and glutted the land market, while it drew off its bidders. In such a state of things, property has lost its character of being a resource for debts. Highland in Bedford, which, in the days of our plethory,[14] sold readily for from fifty to one hundred dollars the acre, (and such sales were many then,) would not now sell for more than from ten to twenty dollars, or one-quarter or one-fifth of its former price. Reflecting on these things, the practice occurred to me, of selling, on fair valuation, and by way of lottery, often resorted to before the Revolution to effect large sales, and still in constant usage in every State for individual as well as corporation purposes. If it is permitted in my case, my lands here alone, with the mills, &c., will pay every thing, and leave me Monticello and a farm free. If refused, I must sell everything here, perhaps considerably in Bedford, move thither with my family, where I have not even a log hut to put my head into, and whether ground for burial, will depend on the depredations which, under the form of sales, shall have been committed on my property. The question then with me was *utrum horum?*[15] But why afflict you with these details? Indeed, I cannot tell, unless pains are lessened by communication with a friend. The friendship which has subsisted between us, now half a century, and the harmony of our political principles and pursuits, have been sources of constant happiness to me through that long period. And if I remove beyond the reach of attentions to the University, or beyond the bourne of life itself, as I soon must, it is a comfort to leave that institution

---

financial ruin. He tried unsuccessfully to sell off most of his lands, and in 1826, obtained permission from the legislature to dispose of them through a lottery announced in the papers. See Introduction, p. xxiv, and note 1, p. 203.

13. A final, or fatal, blow.

14. Excess.

15. Which of these two (possibilities).

under your care, and an assurance that it will not be wanting. It has also been a great solace to me, to believe that you are engaged in vindicating to posterity the course we have pursued for preserving to them, in all their purity, the blessings of self-government, which we had assisted too in acquiring for them. If ever the earth has beheld a system of administration conducted with a single and steadfast eye to the general interest and happiness of those committed to it, one which, protected by truth, can never know reproach, it is that to which our lives have been devoted. To myself you have been a pillar of support through life. Take care of me when dead, and be assured that I shall leave with you my last affections.

To Roger C. Weightman[1]

Monticello, June 24, 1826

RESPECTED SIR, — The kind invitation I receive from you, on the part of the citizens of the city of Washington, to be present with them at their celebration on the fiftieth anniversary of American Independence, as one of the surviving signers of an instrument pregnant with our own, and the fate of the world, is most flattering to myself, and heightened by the honorable accompaniment proposed for the comfort of such a journey. It adds sensibly to the sufferings of sickness, to be deprived by it of a personal participation in the rejoicings of that day. But acquiescence is a duty, under circumstances not placed among those we are permitted to control. I should, indeed, with peculiar delight, have met and exchanged there congratulations personally with the small band, the remnant of that host of worthies, who joined with us on that day, in the bold and doubtful election we were to make for our country, between submission or the sword; and to have enjoyed with them the consolatory fact, that our fellow citizens, after half a century of experience and prosperity, continue to approve the choice we made. May it be to the world, what I believe it will be, (to some parts sooner, to others later, but finally to all,) the signal of arousing men to burst the chains under which monkish ignorance and superstition had persuaded them to bind themselves, and to assume the blessings and security of self-government. That form which we have substituted, restores the free right to the unbounded exercise of reason and freedom of opinion. All eyes are opened, or opening, to the rights of man. The general spread of the light of science has already laid open to every view the palpable truth, that the mass of mankind has not been born with saddles on their backs, nor a favored few booted and spurred, ready to ride them legitimately, by the grace of God. These are grounds of hope for others. For ourselves, let the annual return of this day forever refresh our recollections of these rights, and an undiminished devotion to them.

I will ask permission here to express the pleasure with which I should have met my ancient neighbors of the city of Washington and its vicinities, with

---

1. Roger C. Weightman (1786–1876): librarian and printer who settled in Washington, DC, and worked as a congressional printer for a short time. He served as an officer of cavalry during the War of 1812 and later became the general of the Washington, DC, militia and mayor of the district from 1824–27. Though this letter was long regarded as Jefferson's last, a later letter has recently been discovered.

whom I passed so many years of a pleasing social intercourse; an intercourse which so much relieved the anxieties of the public cares, and left impressions so deeply engraved in my affections, as never to be forgotten. With my regret that ill health forbids me the gratification of an acceptance, be pleased to receive for yourself, and those for whom you write, the assurance of my highest respect and friendly attachments.

Index

aborigines. *See* Native Americans

Adams, John, 157, 157n7, 211–19, 211n1: Alien and Sedition Acts and, 48n1; death of, 211n1, xxiv; Declaration of Independence and, xiv; *Discourses on Davila,* 187n12; as Federalist, 56n3; Jefferson's presidential defeat of, 55, xxi;

Adams, John Quincy, 269n2

African colonization, 256

African-Americans, 181, 205, 256–59: abolition of slavery and, 12; British rule and, 20; emancipation of, 120, 205n1, 258n4, xvi, xxvii; expatriation of, 120n43, 131, 254; Jefferson's heirs and, xxxv; Jefferson's plan for, xvi; laws concerning, 111, 113–15; physical and intellectual differences, 114–20, 205

agrarianism: manufacture and, 57, 132–33, 146–47, 201; attempts to domesticate Indians and, 62, 201; virtue of, 132, xvi

agriculture: commerce and, 57; government regulation of, 269; introduction of Native Americans to, 62, 201, xxiii;

Alien and Sedition Acts, 48n1, 50–1, 50n7, 251n7, xx

Alienage, laws of, 32, 32n3

aliens, 50–3

allodial land, 15

Amendments to the U.S. Constitution, 239–45: twelfth, 233n1

America, defense of Native Americans and transplanted Europeans against European criticisms, 79–88

Anglicanism, 125, xv, *see also* Church of England

Anglo-Saxon, 260, 261n7, 265: language of, 69, 72

Antifederalists: Constitution, U.S. and, 56n2, 172n2; Jefferson accused of being, xviii–xix

Archimedes, 193n4

Areopagitica (Milton), 86n20

aristocracy: as government, 150, 151, 214–19, 246, 271, xxx; natural v. artificial, 215, 217, 217n16; Republicanism and Roman, 107, xxx

Aristotle, 246, 246n2, 268, 268n5; uselessness of his political science, 246

Articles of Confederation: Jefferson on, xviii

army, standing danger to Republican governments, 190

Autobiography (Franklin), 86n22

Autobiography (Jefferson), xiii–xiv

Bache, Benjamin Franklin, 186, 186n10

Banister, John, Jr., 150–52, 150n1

banks, Jefferson's hostility toward, 233, 236

Banneker, Benjamin, 181, 181n1

Barbary powers, xxi–xxii

Barbé-Marbois, François de, 260–265, 260n4, xvi

Barlow, Joel, 187, 187n15

Bellini, Charles, 148–49, 148n1

Bible: how to read, 162–64; should not be taught in schools, 122

"Bill for Establishing Religious Freedom, A (1777)," 27–8, xv

"Bill for the More General Diffusion of Knowledge, A" xv, xxxiii

bill of rights: importance of, 168–69, 172–73, 173n4, 174–75, 185, 267, 267n2, xxi

Bingham, Anne Willing, 159–60, 159n1

blacks, *see* African-Americans

Blackstone, William, 113n14, 206n4, 265, 274, 274n8

Blair, John, 174, 174n2

Bland, Richard, 3n2

Boston Tea Party, 9–10

Boyle, Charles, Fourth Earl of Orrery, 87n28, 143n3

Breckenridge, James, 75, 273n2

Britannicus (Racine), 86n17

British America: abolition of slavery and, 12; free-trade rights and, 6–7; governance of with consent of inhabitants, 5; land holdings in, 14–15; military troops stationed in, 19; prevention of legislation by Great Britain in, 12; rejection of British rule by, 22; oppression in, 5, 8, 12–13; trial privileges in, 11; violations of rights in, 6–8

Burr, Aaron, xxi: conspiracy and, 209–10, 209n5